The New
Public Personnel
Administration

6th**EDITION**

The New Public Personnel Administration

Lloyd G. Nigro
Georgia State University

Felix A. Nigro
Emeritus, University of Georgia

J. Edward Kellough
University of Georgia

WADSWORTH
CENGAGE Learning™

Australia • Brazil • Japan • Korea • Mexico • Singapore • Spain • United Kingdom • United States

The New Public Personnel Administration, Sixth Edition
Lloyd G. Nigro, Felix A. Nigro, and J. Edward Kellough

Executive Editor: David Tatom

Development Editor: Stacey Sims

Associate Development Editor: Rebecca Green

Editorial Assistant: Eva Dickerson

Technology Project Manager: Michelle Vardeman

Marketing Manager: Janise Fry

Marketing Assistant: Teresa Jensen

Project Manager, Editorial Production: Christy Krueger

Creative Director: Rob Hugel

Art Director: Maria Epes

Print Buyer: Doreen Suruki

Permissions Editor: Audrey Pettengill

Production Service: Buuji, Inc.

Production Editor: Sara Dovre Wudali, Buuji, Inc.

Copy Editor: Robin Gold

Cover Designer: Sue Hart

Cover Image: Amy DeVoogd/ Getty Images

Compositor: Buuji, Inc.

For product information and technology assistance, contact us at
**Cengage Learning Customer & Sales Support,
1-800-354-9706**

For permission to use material from this text or product, submit all requests online at **www.cengage.com/permissions**
Further permissions questions can be e-mailed to
permissionrequest@cengage.com

Library of Congress Control Number: 2005935901

ISBN-13: 978-0-534-60239-0

ISBN-10: 0-534-60239-8

Wadsworth
20 Channel Center Street
Boston, MA 02210
USA

Cengage Learning is a leading provider of customized learning solutions with office locations around the globe, including Singapore, the United Kingdom, Australia, Mexico, Brazil, and Japan. Locate your local office at:
www.cengage.com/global

Cengage Learning products are represented in Canada by Nelson Education, Ltd.

To learn more about Wadsworth, visit
www.cengage.com/wadsworth

Purchase any of our products at your local college store or at our preferred online store **www.ichapters.com**

Printed in the United States of America
3 4 5 6 7 12 11 10 09

This edition is dedicated to Carol Nigro, Edna Nigro, and Vicki Kellough.

Contents

Chapter FIVE ISSUES IN JOB EVALUATION AND PAY   **123**

Chapter SIX PERFORMANCE APPRAISAL AND PAY FOR PERFORMANCE   **165**

Chapter SEVEN COLLECTIVE BARGAINING IN THE PUBLIC SECTOR   **199**

Chapter EIGHT PUBLIC EMPLOYEES—RIGHTS AND RESPONSIBILITIES   **233**

Preface

This edition of *The New Public Personnel Administration,* like the fifth, addresses a field of public policy and administration that has undergone a profound transformation during the past 35 years. As noted in the preface to the fifth edition, the political consensus that supported the regulatory, neutral-competence norms driving public sector merit systems for half a century in the United States has mostly evaporated—replaced by an emphasis on management, results, responsiveness, and accountability. Increasingly, civil service is defined as merely one of many elements of a governance system that is composed of a complex and dynamic network of governmental agencies, nonprofit organizations, and for-profit businesses. In 2006, public personnel is indeed "new"—so different that the generic term "human resource management" may be more descriptive of what goes on and how we think about it. Nonetheless, our focus here is on civil service, so the differences between government and the other sectors of society and the unique challenges facing those who work for governments on all levels justify continuing to call our subject "public personnel administration."

This sixth edition is intended to be an advanced undergraduate- or graduate-level introduction to the general field of *public personnel administration*. The general outlines of human resource management policies and practices of public agencies and large private businesses are similar in certain respects, but there are very real and powerful sectorial differences in context, purpose, and guiding values. Private employers function in economic markets that are significantly affected by public policies of many kinds. Public agencies operate in political environments and are significantly influenced by economic circumstances. Public personnel offers many examples of the practical implications of these differences on the policy as well as procedural levels. In other words, although this book may be of interest to students of business and nonprofit management who want to learn about how public sector personnel systems work, it is not a so-called generic human resource management text. Rather, it is about personnel policies and practices in U.S. *governments* and the issues and challenges facing those who work in these settings.

This edition has been updated regarding public policies and issues related to the political activity of public employees, law and key court rulings in such areas as affirmative action, employee rights and responsibilities, antidiscrimination law, and civil service reform. The sixth edition

- Offers an updated description of the demography of the American public service
- Sets forth a strategic human resource perspective that is linked to the role of the personnel specialist in modern public agencies
- Examines the legal framework of public personnel administration with a focus on the constitutional rights of public employees and their responsibilities to the public employer and the public interest
- Provides a focused examination of the nondiscrimination law and practice in the public service
- Closely examines several contemporary civil service reform initiatives on the state and federal levels

Discussion questions and suggested readings are provided. The questions are simply designed to encourage pre-class review of chapter content and related materials, to provoke informed discussions of relevant current events and policy questions, and to spark debate about the purposes and underlying value orientations of personnel policies and practices in government. The suggested readings are largely restricted to recently published books, but this should not obscure the fact that many excellent scholarly and professional journal articles and useful government publications are available to those seeking to build on chapter content.

We want to express our sincere thanks to those who have provided the support and encouragement needed to complete this project. Our colleagues at Georgia State University and the University of Georgia have been very helpful. In addition, our families have been loyal and patient allies, especially when things seemed to be moving forward at a very slow pace. Thanks are due also to our graduate research assistant, Jared J. Llorens, who made many critically important contributions to the updating process. We are extremely grateful for his careful and reliable work. We also want to take this opportunity to thank Robin Gold for her expert copy editing and Sara Dovre Wudali who very effectively managed the process required to bring this project to completion. In addition, we would like to express our gratitude to Eric E. Otenyo, Richard D. White, and Roseanne M. Mirabella for providing thoughtful and useful reviews of a previous version of this manuscript.

Chapter ONE

The American Public Service

For many Americans, the terms "human resources department" and "personnel office" bring to mind legions of faceless "bureaucrats" in green eyeshades keeping files and mindlessly enforcing arcane rules designed to frustrate all efforts to get real work done efficiently, if at all. In some places, this stereotype of the personnel function may be accurate, as some of us can testify on the basis of personal experiences. It is true that personnel administration in government does involve the implementation of public laws and the enforcement of regulatory policies. Human resources units are also responsible for what are to most of us unexciting day-to-day operations like payroll and benefits administration. We expect that these processes will be carried out in an efficient and timely manner and we notice if they are not.

More broadly, however, it would be a mistake to underestimate the importance of carrying out these traditional personnel functions in an efficient and timely manner. They can be in this sense important contributors to organizational performance. The public personnel administration of the early 21st century is far more than an organizational maintenance and rules-enforcement activity. Public personnel administration is rapidly coming to be seen as a key element of successful public management and strategic planning. As such, public personnel administration focuses on helping public managers on all levels to meet the challenges of attracting, retaining, motivating, and developing the large and diverse pool of highly qualified people needed to staff modern government agencies of all kinds.

Today's Americans rely on elected representatives and public administrators to directly provide or to arrange for the delivery of a wide variety of services. To mention just a few, they expect that their children will be well-educated in safe schools; that their roads and highways will be well-maintained and competently designed; that the food they eat, the water they drink, and medicines they take will be safe; that the streets of their cities will be free of violent criminals; that public health systems will anticipate and prevent epidemics; that terrorists seeking to attack American citizens and institutions will be identified and prevented from entering the country; and that their mail will reach its intended destination within two or three days. None of these services can be effectively and efficiently delivered by government (directly or indirectly) without a highly competent, dedicated, well-managed public service. The quality of American life, in other words, depends in many important ways on those who work for government—on the quality of the public service.

Public personnel policies and practices on the federal, state, and local levels can have major effects on the performance of public agencies and their employees. On the negative side, an Internal Revenue Service (IRS) that is unable to recruit and retain highly qualified accountants and lawyers is unlikely to administer a complex tax code effectively and fairly. Inadequately trained city workers who respond slowly or not at all to overflowing sewers endanger the public health, as do corrupt inspectors who fail to enforce the building code. Overworked or poorly trained police officers, air traffic controllers, transportation security personnel, and social workers are more likely to make mistakes that have disastrous consequences. Intelligence agencies that are unable to attract and retain qualified analysts and information systems experts may miss information and trends that reveal terrorist activities. Partisan and discriminatory hiring practices undermine public confidence in the objectivity and fairness of all public servants, including public managers, police, and tax collectors. On the positive side, demonstrably fair and effective personnel policies and practices can do much to support the efforts of public agencies to carry out their mandates and to build public confidence in government. As the authors of a book on civil service reform put it, "the civil service system touches everything in government. If it does not work well, neither can anything else in government" (Kettl, Ingraham, Sanders, & Horner, 1996, p. 7).

One measure of the importance of the public service in American society is statistical. Accordingly, the balance of this chapter sets forth some of the facts and figures that describe the American public service. In addition to providing a general overview, these data are relevant to many of the topics discussed in the chapters that follow, such as those

Table 1.1 Government Employees in Other Countries

Country	Government Employment as a Percentage of Total Employment*
Canada	17.5
France	21.3
Germany	12.3
Italy	15.2
Spain	15.2
United Kingdom	12.6
United States	14.6

*Producers of government services, except Australia, Canada, France, and Spain, which are general government.

Adapted from OECD Public Managerial Service, 2001 (www.oecdorg/dataoecd/27/17/1827384.xls) & (www.oecd.org/dataoecd/37/43/1849079.xls, OECD Public Management Service, 2001, © OECD 2001

on antidiscrimination law and practice, recruitment and selection, collective bargaining, and the changing American work force.

THE SIZE AND DISTRIBUTION OF THE AMERICAN PUBLIC SERVICE

The public service upon which we all depend for so many services is large, although probably not as large as many Americans assume it is. There are more than 18 million public employees in the United States, which is about 13 percent of the civilian labor force or CLF. The CLF is composed of all civilians in the noninstitutionalized population aged 16 and older who are employed, or unemployed and seeking work. In 2002, the CLF stood at about 145 million people. Of those in the public sector, more than 4 million work for the states. Almost 12 million are on the payrolls of local governments (more than half work for public school districts). The federal government currently employs around 2.7 million civilians. Is the United States overrun by public employees in comparison to other industrialized democracies? Table 1.1 shows that the United States, even with its federal system of government, does not have a public service that is overly large in comparative terms.

BULLETIN

In 2003, the March payroll for states and local governments was $54.5 billion. The states' paychecks totaled $15.1 billion, whereas those of the localities added up to $39.4 billion.

Source: U.S. Bureau of the Census. 2003 (July).

Table 1.2 Government Employment by Level—Historical

	Number of Employees (Millions)			
	1950 **(62.2)***	**1970** **(82.8)**	**1990** **(125.8)**	**2000** **(142.6)**
Federal civilian	2.117	2.881	3.105	2.899
State	1.057	2.775	4.503	4.877
Local	3.228	7.392	10.760	13.089

*Civilian labor force total (millions)

Sources: U.S. Bureau of the Census (2002) *Compendium of Public Employment: 2002.* Accessed http://www
.census.gov/prod/2004pubs/gc023x2.pdf; and U.S. Bureau of the Census (2003). *Statistical Abstract of the
United States, Employment Status of the Civilian Population: 1929 to 2002.* Accessed http://www.census.gov/
statab/hist/HS-29.pdf.

Despite a general inclination by the public to view the federal government as huge and constantly expanding, it has not been the major source of overall growth in the numbers of public employees since the end of the Second World War (1945). Although the size of the federal workforce has remained fairly stable, the states and localities have expanded greatly (see Table 1.2). In 1970, state workers numbered about 2.8 million (up from 2.2 million in 1966), and there were about 7.4 million in local governments (about one million more than in 1966). The rate of *growth* slowed considerably during the 1980s. From 1979 to 1989, state employment grew by 14.5 percent. There was some expansion on the federal and local levels; in both cases, it was less than 10 percent. Overall, the creation of jobs in the public sector lagged behind that of the private sector (the CLF grew by approximately 20 percent). Thus, in people terms, government became relatively smaller during the 1980s, and that trend continues. During the first six years of the Clinton Administration, the federal workforce dropped by roughly 250,000 or 8.4 percent.

The 18.5 million public employees in the United States are distributed across many jurisdictions. In addition to the national and 50 state governments, there are more than 3,000 counties, more than 19,000 municipalities, and more than 31,000 special purpose districts. Add in townships and school districts, and the grand total exceeds 85,000 governmental units. Primary education and law enforcement are largely local responsibilities. States administer welfare programs, construct and run prison systems, and build freeways. The federal government has exclusive control over national defense, currency, and first class mail services. These differences show up in the relative sizes of

Table 1.3 Government Employment by Level and Selected Functions

Function	Number of Employees (Thousands)		
	Federal Civilian	State	Local*
National defense	682	—	—
Postal Service	786	—	—
Education	11	2413	6712
Streets and highways	3	249	311
Police protection	157	106	791
Fire protection	—	—	311
Parks and recreation	27	40	226
Judicial and legal	62	164	248
Transit	—	33	201

*Local Employment is measured by full-time equivalent employment.

Sources: U.S. Bureau of the Census (2003). *Public Employment Data.* Accessed http://ftp2.census.gov/govs/apes/03fedfun.txt (federal), http://ftp2.census.gov/govs/apes/03stus.txt (states), http://ftp2.census.gov/govs/apes/03locus.txt (local).

governments and the occupational profiles of their workforces. Table 1.3 provides a comparative overview.

In addition to raw differences in population size, functional differences contribute to wide variations in the sizes and compositions of workforces. New York City, which operates a university system as well as its own elementary and secondary schools and delivers services typically handled by counties, has more than 400,000 full-time employees on its payroll. The cities of Los Angeles and Chicago, on the other hand, have fewer than 50,000 workers. Large populations combined with a large inventory of services, produce large work forces, so of the 5 million or so inhabitants of Cook County, Illinois, about 200,000 are county employees. Of the approximately 1.5 million full-time positions in the 50 states' systems of higher education, more than 100,000 are in California. New York has about the same number, but fewer than four thousand are to be found in South Dakota or Alaska. Table 1.4 shows the totals by functional areas for all states in 2003.

These data reveal the states' relatively heavy investments in corrections, highways, hospitals, and higher education, all of which are traditionally state responsibilities. During the past decade, the rapid expansion of state prison facilities has been a national trend, and many states have been making heavy investments in higher education. There is, however, considerable variability across states. Table 1.5 provides a comparison of four different states.

Table 1.4 State Employment by Function (2003)

Function	Full-Time Equivalent Employees	Per 10,000 Population
Total All States	4,190,667	145.5
Financial administration	168,165	5.8
Central administration	54,718	1.9
Judicial and legal	159,849	5.6
Police protection–officers	62,934	2.2
Police protection–other	41,193	1.4
Corrections	458,899	15.9
Highways	245,085	8.5
Air transportation	3,193	0.1
Water transport and terminals	4,515	0.2
Public welfare	230,449	8.0
Health	176,868	6.1
Hospitals	403,005	14.0
Social Insurance Administration	89,722	3.1
Solid waste management	1,833	0.1
Sewage	1,837	0.1
Parks and recreation	35,344	1.2
Natural resources	148,854	5.2
Water supply	671	0.0
Electric power	3,880	0.1
Transit	32,512	1.1
Elementary and secondary school–instructional	37,341	1.3
Elementary and secondary school–other	15,337	0.5
Higher education–instructional	494,058	17.2
Higher education–other	1,016,034	35.3
Other education	107,920	3.74
Libraries	573	0.0
State liquor stores	7,226	0.3
Other	202,907	7.1

Source: U.S. Bureau of the Census, *Public Employment Data.* Accessed http://ftp2.census.gov/govs/apes/03stus.txt (March, 2003).

Local governments, cities and counties, have employment profiles that are different from those of the states because they usually provide different services. Table 1.6 is an overview of local government employment throughout the country. State policies in areas such as student-teacher ratios, welfare program administration, and trans-

Table 1.5 Comparison of Selected State Employment by Function (2003)

Full-Time Equivalent Per 10,000 Population

	State			
Function	**Alaska**	**California**	**Georgia**	**Hawaii**
Overall	387.2	111.2	141.9	463.1
Financial administration	15.7	6.4	5.5	5.2
Central administration	9.7	1.2	1.4	4.3
Judicial and legal	19.0	1.2	3.0	18.3
Police protection–officers	4.0	2.3	1.4	0.0
Police protection–other	3.2	1.6	1.3	0.0
Corrections	27.6	14.4	22.8	19.4
Highways	46.5	6.2	7.1	7.1
Air transportation	0.0	0.0	0.0	8.5
Water transport and terminals	0.0	0.0	0.7	1.7
Public welfare	28.2	1.1	10.4	6.7
Health	11.7	3.4	5.4	19.7
Hospitals	3.9	11.0	9.5	32.1
Social Insurance Administration	6.9	5.5	2.6	3.5
Solid waste management	0.0	0.1	0.0	0.0
Sewage	0.0	0.0	0.0	0.0
Parks and recreations	1.3	0.9	3.5	1.8
Natural resources	35.8	4.1	5.4	9.1
Water supply	0.0	0.0	0.0	0.0
Electric power	0.0	0.0	0.0	0.0
Transit	0.0	0.0	0.0	0.0
Elementary and secondary school–instructional	33.7	0.0	0.0	174.8
Elementary and secondary school–other	17.3	0.0	0.0	46.9
Higher education–instructional	17.5	8.5	18.6	21.2
Higher education–other	57.8	31.2	35.7	47.4
Other education	6.8	1.4	3.6	1.1
Libraries	0.0	0.0	0.0	4.6
State liquor stores	0.0	0.0	0.0	0.0
Other	40.9	11.0	4.0	29.6

Source: U.S. Bureau of the Census, *Public Employment Data.* Accessed http://www.census.gov/govs/www/apesst03.html (March, 2003).

portation, as well as historical and environmental factors, will cause local government employment profiles to vary from state to state. Table 1.7 compares California, Texas, and New York as an example.

Table 1.6 Local Government Employment by Function (2003)

	Full-Time Equivalent Employees	Per 10,000 Population
Total All Locations	11,569,784	401.76
Function		
Financial administration	217,552	7.55
Other government administration	222,401	7.72
Judicial and legal	247,874	8.61
Police protection–officers	602,681	20.93
Police protection–other	187,910	6.53
Firefighters	286,693	9.96
Fire–other	24,453	0.85
Corrections	241,064	8.37
Streets and highways	300,532	10.44
Air transportation	41,141	1.43
Air transport/terminals	7,129	0.25
Public welfare	277,654	9.64
Health	253,888	8.82
Hospitals	506,915	17.60
Solid waste management	109,953	3.82
Sewerage	124,262	4.32
Parks and recreation	226,443	7.86
Housing and community development	118,107	4.10
Natural resources	37,336	1.30
Water supply	159,595	5.54
Electric power	75,205	2.61
Gas supply	10,845	0.38
Transit	200,922	6.98
Elementary and secondary school– instructional	4,446,825	154.42
Elementary and secondary school– other	1,947,927	67.64
Higher education–instructional	131,594	4.57
Higher education–other	185,917	6.46
Libraries	124,521	4.32
Other	252,445	8.77

Source: U.S. Bureau of the Census, *Public Employment Data.* Accessed http://ftp2.census.gov/govs/apes/ 03locus.txt (2004).

Table 1.7 Local Government Employment in Three Large States (2003)

Full-Time Equivalent Employees Per 10,000 Population

Function	California	State Texas	New York
Overall	404.6	454.2	493.9
Financial administration	7.1	6.5	6.7
Other government administration	7.4	6.1	7.8
Judicial and legal	14.4	8.8	6.1
Police protection—officers	17.1	19.8	36.7
Police protection—other	8.1	6.2	5.3
Firefighters	8.4	9.4	10.8
Fire—other	0.8	0.8	1.3
Corrections	9.3	11.5	13.5
Streets and highways	6.2	9.3	14.6
Air transportation	1.8	2.1	0.8
Water transport and terminals	0.6	0.4	0.1
Public welfare	18.9	1.6	25.5
Health	12.4	10.8	9.6
Hospitals	17.7	21.2	26.2
Solid waste management	2.1	2.8	7.6
Sewerage	3.8	4.1	3.3
Parks and recreation	10.4	7.4	5.8
Housing and community development	3.9	2.9	10.3
Natural resources	2.4	1.7	0.2
Water supply	6.4	6.7	3.4
Electric power	3.2	3.8	0.3
Gas supply	0.1	0.7	0.0
Transit	9.8	4.9	25.7
Elementary and secondary school—instruction	126.3	195.0	176.9
Elementary and secondary school—other	69.3	83.5	67.9
Higher education—instruction	9.5	6.6	5.4
Higher education—other	11.2	10.6	6.5
Libraries	3.8	2.9	4.7
Other	12.3	6.1	11.0

Source: U.S. Bureau of the Census, *Public Employment Data—Local Governments.* Accessed http://www .census.gov/govs/www/apesloc.html (2003).

The size and composition of the public service reflects the policy priorities of governments. Much of the recent growth in state bureaucracies is the result of federal policies designed to shift administrative responsibility for public welfare and regulatory services to the state governments. They, in turn, have sought to pass certain program mandates and costs on to local governments. The federal government is itself a good example of how political change affects the public workforce. Although his public image was that of a "bureaucrat cutter," President Reagan actually did not preside over a shrinking federal executive branch in absolute terms. Between 1980 and 1987, the number of workers in executive departments grew by some 5 percent, and the independent agencies expanded by more than 11 percent. Defense did well, expanding from 960,000 to 1,090,000, about 13.5 percent. This growth was anything but uniform across organizations. A few agencies experienced substantial increases, especially the Department of Defense, but most lost positions as the Reagan–George H.W. Bush policy priorities took hold. Although there was nondefense growth during the George H. W. Bush presidency, the Clinton administration's downsizing efforts produced an overall decline that included civilian defense employment. From 1993 to 1997, the Department of Defense "accounted for almost 64 percent of all downsizing, [but] virtually every Federal agency reduced its workforce during this 4-year period" (U.S. Office of Personnel Management, 1997, p. 4). Table 1.8 tracks the shifting fortunes of federal agencies from 1980 to 2003.

Many of those agencies that show a net increase between 1980 and 2003 actually were "downsized" during the first Clinton term, as Table 1.9 reveals. The Departments of State, Treasury, and Veterans Affairs are good examples. The end of the savings and loan crisis, of course, had produced an impressive reduction of the Federal Deposit Insurance Corporation (FDIC) staff by 1997.

Another way of tracking the evolution of the federal service is to look at employment trends in the white- and blue-collar job categories, as seen in Tables 1.10 and 1.11. Taken against the general pattern of downsizing, the long-term prospects of federal employment for blue-collar workers would seem to be dim at best because all the occupational categories shown in Table 1.11 have experienced sharp declines. These numbers reflect a vigorous federal executive policy of contracting-out for the kinds of work done by these occupations, rather than maintaining in-house capacities. Contracting-out is intended to improve efficiency and management flexibility, but it also offers political advantages, most notably "fewer bureaucrats" showing up on the payrolls. This work is being done and paid for by the federal government, but not by federal employees. White-collar occupa-

Table 1.8 Trends in Federal Civilian Employment: 1980 and 2003

Agency	1980	2003	% Change
State Department	23,497	32,448	38.1
Treasury	134,663	110,195	−18.2
Defense	960,116	664,524	−30.8
Justice	56,327	102,705	82.3
Interior	77,357	77,691	0.4
Agriculture	129,139	111,146	−13.9
Commerce	48,563	37,418	−22.9
Labor	23,400	16,228	−30.6
Health and Human Services	155,662	66,859	−57.0
Housing and Urban Development	16,964	19,557	15.3
Transportation	72,361	64,179	−11.3
Energy	21,557	15,630	−27.5
Education	7,364	4,567	−38
Veterans Administration/ Department of Veterans Affairs	228,285	230,406	0.9
Environmental Protection Agency	14,715	18,217	23.8
Equal Employment Opportunity Commission	3,515	2,589	−26.3
Federal Deposit Insurance Corporation	3,520	5,473*	55.5
National Aeronautics and Space Administration	23,714	18,954	−20.1
Office of Personnel Management	8,280	3,417	−58.7
Tennessee Valley Authority	51,714	13,379	−74.1
US Postal Service	660,014	787,818	19.4

*The Federal Deposit Insurance Corporation grew to more than 9,000 (1987) during the savings and loan crisis of the late 1980s.

Sources: U.S. Office of Personnel Management (2003). *Employment and Trends 2003.* Accessed http://www .opm.gov/feddata/html/2003/september/table2.asp; U.S. Bureaus of the Census, *Statistical Abstract of the United States: 1991* (Washington, DC, 1991), Table 529.

tions have not done as badly overall, even though a number have experienced cuts well above the average. Particularly noteworthy are a sharp drop in the number of secretaries and steep declines in several engineering categories. Supply clerical and technician workers also have not fared well in the federal scheme of things. Noteworthy and sometimes explosive growth has occurred in areas like computer specialists, management and program analysis, legal and law enforcement occupations, and support staff for automated accounting and control systems. While technological innovations—such as advanced computer hardware, new data management and analysis systems, automation, and integrated electronic communications media—often increase efficiency and may be expected to produce shifts in employment patterns,

Table 1.9 Federal Civilian Employment: 1993, 1997, and 2003

Agency	1993	1997	2003	% Change (1993–1997)	% Change (1997–2003)
Total	3,038,041	2,783,704	2,725,948	−8.4	−2.1
Legislative Branch	38,030	31,355	31,564	−17.6	0.7
Judicial Branch	28,111	30,641	34,726	9.0	13.3
US Postal Service and Postal Rate Commission	782,980	853,350	787,818	9.0	−7.7
Executive Branch	2,188,647	1,868,358	2,659,658	−14.6	42.4
Selected Executive Branch Agencies					
State Department	25,982	24,108	32,448	−7.2	34.6
Treasury	165,904	140,369	110,195	−15.4	−21.5
Defense	966,087	749,461	664,524	−22.4	−11.3
Justice	97,652	117,261	102,705	20.1	−12.4
Interior	77,313	67,865	77,691	−12.2	14.5
Agriculture	113,687	106,539	111,146	−6.3	4.3
Commerce	37,608	34,792	37,418	−7.5	7.5
Labor	17,719	15,787	16,228	−10.9	2.8
HHS	131,066	126,523	66,859	−3.5	−47.2
HUD	13,292	10,908	10,557	−17.9	−3.2
Transportation	70,086	64,179	58,668	−8.4	−8.6
Energy	20,706	17,078	15,630	−17.5	−8.5
Education	4,995	4,640	4,567	−7.1	−1.6
Veterans Affairs	260,349	243,311	230,406	−6.5	−5.3
Environmental Protection Agency	18,351	18,045	18,217	−1.7	1.0
Equal Employment Opportunity Commission	2,927	2,631	2,589	−10.1	−1.6
Federal Deposit Insurance Corporation	22,360	8,265	5,473	−63.0	−33.8
Federal Emergency Management Agency	4,554	4,888	*	7.3	—
General Services Administration	20,690	14,309	12,757	−30.8	−10.8
National Aeronautics Administration	25,191	19,844	18,954	−21.2	−4.5
National Labor Relations Board	2,132	1,992	1,931	−6.6	−3.1
Office of Personnel Management	6,861	3,603	3,417	−47.5	−5.2
Tennessee Valley Authority	19,129	14,510	13,379	−24.1	−7.8
US Information Agency	8,283	6,534	**	−21.1	—
Agency for International Development	4,218	2,783	2,368	−34.0	−14.9
Department of Homeland Security	—	—	971,952	—	—

Sources: For 1993 and 1997: U.S. Office of Personnel Management (1997), Office of Workforce Information, *Monthly Report of Federal Civilian Employment* (SF 113-a), (Washington, DC), November 20; for 2003: U.S. Office of Personnel Management (2003). *Employment and Trends* 2003. Accessed http://www.opm.gov/feddata/html/2003/september/table2.asp

*FEMA became a part of the Department of Homeland Security (DHS) in March of 2003.

**U.S. Information Agency (USIA) became a part of the State Department in October of 1999.

Table 1.10 The Twenty Largest Federal White-Collar Occupations September 1991 and September 2001

Occupation	1991	2001	Percent Change
Misc. slerk and assistant	82,859	78,224	−5.6
Miscellaneous administration and program	57,408	62,201	8.3
Computer specialist	52,893	60,817	15.0
Secretary	103,966	47,524	−54.3
Nurse	47,542	45,775	−3.7
Management and program analysis	30,973	44,780	44.6
Criminal investigating	32,067	36,209	12.9
General attorney	24,287	27,659	13.9
Contact representative	18,023	27,620	53.2
Contracting	31,818	27,112	−14.8
Social Insurance Administration	22,465	26,709	18.9
Air traffic control	26,129	24,068	−7.9
General business and industry	16,869	22,505	33.4
Medical officer	36,495	22,150	−39.3
Electronics engineering	30,202	20,352	−32.6
General engineering	21,526	18,413	−14.5
Engineering technician	25,274	17,349	−31.4
Forestry technician	18,391	16,969	−7.7
OFC automation clerical and assistance	4,540	15,470	240.7
Correctional officer	8,116	14,695	81.1

Source: U.S. Office of Personnel Management, Office of Workforce Information, *Central Personnel Data File.* Accessed http://www.opm.gov/feddata/ (September 2001).

declines in the contracting and air traffic control occupations may signal long-term threats to some agencies' ability to carry out their mandates and, therefore, to meet public expectations.

THE DEMOGRAPHICS OF THE PUBLIC SERVICE AND THE CIVILIAN LABOR FORCE

The demography of the public service is changing at an accelerating pace. In certain respects, it is becoming more representative of the increasingly diverse and pluralistic society it serves. By 2002, for example, 45 percent of federal jobs were held by women, and 30.8 percent were occupied by minorities (U.S. Office of Personnel Management, 2003). From 1990 to 2002, federal employment of minorities increased slowly but steadily, as Table 1.12 shows.

Table 1.11 The Twenty Largest Federal Blue-Collar Occupations
September 1991 and September 2001

Occupation	1991	2001	Percent Change
Maintenance mechanic	12,980	11,580	−10.8
Custodial worker	16,315	11,559	−29.2
Materials handler	23,709	11,259	−52.5
Aircraft mechanic	14,841	11,237	−24.3
Heavy mobile equipment	12,020	9,844	−18.1
Food service worker	15,701	8,979	−42.8
Electronics mechanic	13,726	6,969	−49.2
Motor vehicle operating	11,005	6,386	−42.0
Sheet metal mechanic	10,832	6,372	−41.2
Automotive mechanic	7,231	5,223	−27.8
Laboring	9,664	5,068	−47.6
Electrician	9,712	4,801	−50.6
Store Working	4,727	4,294	−9.2
Cook	4,359	3,988	−8.5
Electronic integrated systems mechanic	4,685	3,849	−17.8
Machining	7,804	3,784	−51.5
Painting	6,831	3,715	−45.6
Aircraft engine mechanic	4,989	3,619	−27.5
Pipefitting	7,906	3,321	−58.0
Engineering equipment operating	3,815	3,240	−15.1

Source: U.S. Office of Personnel Management, Office of Workforce Information, *Central Personnel Data File.*
Accessed http://www.opm.gov/feddata/ (September, 2001).

There have been corresponding increases in the proportions of women and minorities working for state and local governments over roughly the same period. In 1984, state and local workforces were 41 percent female and 24.5 percent minority. By 1995, these increased to 44.3 percent female and 28.9 percent minority (U.S. Bureau of the Census, 1997a).

Public sector recruitment, hiring, training, and career development programs are by necessity adjusting to a labor market that has experienced profound demographic changes since the 1950s. A quick scan of the American workplace shows, among other things, a growing diversity of ethnic and cultural groups, more working mothers, and a steady erosion of the traditional family background and lifestyles assumed by traditional public personnel policies and practices (see Tables 1.13 and 1.14).

Table 1.12 Federal Executive Branch Employment of Minorities and Women: 1990, 1996, and 2002 (Percentages*)

Year	Total	All**	African American	Hispanic	Asian/ Pacific Islander	American Indian/ Alaska Native	White Non-Hispanic
1990							
Men	1,223,255	12.7	6.5	3.2	2.1	0.9	44.2
Women	927,104	14.6	10.1	2.2	1.4	0.9	28.5
Total	2,150,359	27.3	16.6	5.4	3.5	1.8	72.7
1996							
Men	1,058,566	13.5	6.4	3.6	2.5	1.0	42.5
Women	831,840	15.6	10.2	2.5	1.8	1.0	28.4
Total	1,890,406	29.1	16.6	6.1	4.3	2.0	70.9
2002							
Men	1,004,612	14.1	6.4	4.0	2.6	1.0	41.4
Women	808,435	16.7	10.4	2.9	2.1	1.2	27.9
Total	1,813,047	30.7	16.9	6.9	4.8	2.2	69.3

*Percentages are based on total employment (men and women combined).

**All minorities

Sources: U.S. Office of Personnel Management (2003)). "Executive Branch Employment by Gender & Race/National Origin, September 1990–September 2002," *The Fact Book: Federal Civilian Workforce Statistics, 2003 Edition,* p. 36.

Managing diverse workforces has become a staple of many management training programs, and alternative and "family-friendly" work arrangements have become important factors in recruitment and retention strategies, as well as being significant considerations in efforts to increase productivity. The labor force participation of married women with children under the age of six has risen from 18.6 percent in 1960 to 62.7 percent in 1996 (U.S. Bureau of the Census, 1997, p. 393). The labor force also is getting older. By 2002, 22.5 percent of the CLF was in the 45 to 55 age category, up from 18.8 percent in 1980. This trend (Table 1.15) poses issues related to health and retirement benefits, as well as presenting public management with new challenges in areas such as motivation and employee development.

In 1993, the U.S. General Accounting Office noted that the growing numbers of working women and minorities "had transformed the workplace in the latter half of the 20th century. . . ." It then went on to observe,

Table 1.13 The Marital Status of Women in the CLF: 1960–2002

	Female Labor Force*				Female Participation Rate (%)**			
	Total	Single	Married	Other***	Total	Single	Married	Other
1960	23,240	5,410	12,893	4,937	37.7	58.6	31.9	41.6
1980	45,487	11,865	24,980	8,643	51.5	64.4	49.9	43.6
1996	61,857	15,842	33,618	12,397	59.3	67.1	61.2	48.1
2002	67,363	18,203	35,477	13,683	59.6	67.4	61.0	49.2

*Thousands

**Percentage of the civilian labor force.

***Widowed, divorced, separated

Source: U.S. Bureau of the Census, *Statistical Abstract of the United States 1997,* Table 630 (Washington, DC); and *Statistical Abstract of the United States 2003,* Table 596 (Washington, DC).

Table 1.14 The U.S. Civilian Labor Force and Participation Rates* with Projections: 1980 to 2010

	Civilian Labor Force (Millions)			Participation Rate (Percent)*		
	1980	2002	2010	1980	2002	2010
Total Race and Sex**	106.9	144.9	157.7	63.8	66.6	67.5
White	93.6	120.2	128.0	64.1	66.8	67.6
Male	54.5	65.3	68.2	78.2	74.8	73.8
Female	39.1	54.8	59.9	51.2	59.3	61.6
Black	10.9	16.6	20.0	61.0	64.8	67.1
Male	5.6	7.8	9.0	70.3	68.4	68.2
Female	5.3	8.8	11.1	53.1	61.8	66.2
Hispanic	6.1	17.9	20.9	64.0	69.1	69.0
Male	3.8	10.6	11.7	81.4	80.2	79.0
Female	2.3	7.3	9.2	47.4	57.6	59.4

*The participation rate represents the proportion of each group in the civilian labor force.

**Includes races not shown in the table.

Source: U.S. Bureau of the Census, *Statistical Abstract of the United States 2003,* Table 588 (Washington, DC).

The aging of the U.S. workforce is a trend that may have an equally profound impact on the world of work in the first half of the 21st century. The median age of the civilian workforce rose from 34.3 years in 1980 to 36.6 in 1990 and is expected to reach 40.6 years by 2005. The federal government's workforce is older than the civilian labor force in general—on average, about five years older in 1990. (U.S. General Accounting Office, 1993, pp. 2–3)

Table 1.15 An Aging Civilian Labor Force: 1980–2002

		Age (%)						
	CLF Total*	16–19	20–24	25–34	35–44	45–54	55–64	65+
1980	106,940	8.8	14.9	27.3	19.1	15.8	11.2	2.9
1995	132,304	5.9	10.3	25.8	27.0	19.1	9.0	2.9
2002	144,863	5.2	10.2	22.2	25.5	22.5	11.3	3.1

*Thousands

Source: U.S. Bureau of the Census, *Statistical Abstract of the United States, 2003,* Table 590 (Washington, DC).

Table 1.16 A Better-Educated Civilian Labor Force: 1970–2002

		Educational Achievement as a Percentage of the CLF			
	CLF Total*	Less than HS	HS	1–3 Years of College	4+ Years of College
1970	61,765	36.1	38.1	11.8	14.1
1980	78,010	20.6	39.8	17.6	22.0
1990	99,175	13.4	39.5	20.7	26.4
2002	122,497	10.3	30.8	27.4	31.4**

*Thousands

** It is also noteworthy that the percentage of women 25 years of age and older with 4+ years of college increased from 11.2 in 1970 to 22.8 in 2003. Likewise, for African Americans, those percentages increased from 8.3 in 1970 to 17.3 in 2003.

Sources: U.S. Bureau of the Census, *Statistical Abstract of the United States, 1997,* Table 622 (Washington, DC); *Statistical Abstract of the United States, 2003,* Table 591 (Washington, DC).

The public sector workforce is rapidly aging, and personnel systems on all levels of government will have to respond to this demographic reality (Elliot, 1995).

Although the U.S. labor force has steadily become better educated (see Table 1.16), the pace of technological innovation and change, along with an explosive growth of information and knowledge in the social and physical sciences, has forced many public employers into a highly competitive marketplace. Education, specialized knowledge, and technical expertise are at a premium.

By necessity, the public service has steadily become increasingly professionalized, better educated, and more highly trained. The "professional state," a system of government in which experts working in a wide variety of specialized fields are key actors in the process of making as well as implementing public policies, is a reflection of the cen-

Table 1.17 Union Membership and Representation in 2004:
Private and Public Sectors*

Sector	% Union Members	% Represented by Unions**
Private	7.9	8.6
Agricultural	2.2	2.9
Nonagricultural	8.0	8.7
Public	36.4	40.7
Federal	29.9	35.0
State	30.7	34.3
Local	41.3	45.8

*In 1983, about 20 percent of U.S. wage and salary workers belonged to unions; by 2004, that percentage had fallen to 12.5.

**For purposes of collective bargaining/covered by negotiated contracts.

Source: U.S. Bureau of Labor Statistics (2005). Accessed http://www.bls.gov/news.release/pdf/union2/pdf

tral role government plays in American society (Mosher, 1968). On all levels of government, many functions require people with highly developed professional skills and training. The federal government alone employed more than 400,000 professionals in 2000. The list of occupational specialties and professional skills needed by the public sector is very long and it is growing. One indicator of this trend is the steady escalation of the average General Schedule Grade of federal workers in that system. In 1972, the average pay grade was 7.96; by 2002, it was 9.75. In 2002, for example, 41 percent of federal employees held a bachelor's or a higher degree (U.S. Office of Personnel Management, 2003). The Bureau of Labor Statistics projects that the overall employment of persons with professional specialties in the United States will increase by more than 25 percent between 1996 and 2006. Executive, administrative, and managerial employment is projected to grow by 17 percent during the same period (U.S. Bureau of Labor Statistics, 1998b). If public employers are to compete successfully with the private sector for the highly qualified professionals and specialists they need, they will have to develop effective recruitment strategies, design efficient

BULLETIN

Some of the Fastest Growing Occupations in the United States: Projected Growth 2002–2012

Medical Assistants   +59%
Network Systems and Data Communications
    Analysts   +57%
Physician Assistants +49%
Social and Human Services Assistants
             +49%

Source: U.S. Bureau of Labor Statistics. Accessed http://www.bls.gov/news.release/ecopro.t04.htm

and flexible selection processes, and be able to offer attractive pay and benefits. Heavy investments in employee development and training will be needed if the public sector workforce is to maintain the currency of its knowledge, skills, and abilities.

The last set of numbers related to the American public service we will review here deal with the growth of unions in public employment. As Table 1.17 shows, public employees are much more likely to belong to unions and to be represented by unions than are their private sector counterparts. The federal government and many states and localities bargain collectively with their nonmanagement employees, and labor relations have become an important specialty within the general field of personnel administration or human resources management.

CONCLUSION

In this chapter, we have taken a very brief look at some data that should help orient you to the American public service. One very important fact to remember is that demographic, technological, and other trends in the social and economic environment of government have powerful effects on the size, composition, and administrative organization of the public service. Contemporary public personnel policies, practices, issues, and problems are reflections of these trends, some of which have deep roots in the political, economic, and social history of the United States. It is, therefore, difficult to understand the public service of today without an understanding of its historical context, and Chapter 2 provides a brief historical overview, starting with the founding of the United States.

DISCUSSION QUESTIONS

1. Is 14.6 percent of the CLF working for U.S. governments too many, too few, about right? How can we answer this question?
2. From a human resources point of view, what demographic and other trends should be monitored closely by public employers? Why?

References

Elliot, Robert H. (1995). "Human Resource Management's Role in the Future Aging of the Workforce." *Review of Public Personnel Administration,* Vol. 15, No. 2 (Spring), pp. 5–17.

Kettl, Donald F., Patricia W. Ingraham, Ronald P. Sanders, and Constance Horner (1996). *Civil Service Reform: Building a Government That Works* (Washington, DC: Brookings Institution Press).

Mosher, Frederick C. (1968). *Democracy and the Public Service* (New York: Oxford University Press).

U.S. Bureau of the Census (1997). *Statistical Abstract of the United States: 1997* (Washington, DC), Table 508.

————. (2003). *Statistical Abstract of the United States, Employment Status of the Civilian Population: 1929 to 2002.* Accessed http://www.census.gov/statab/hist/HS-29.pdf (July).

U.S. Bureau of Labor Statistics (1998a). "Employment by Major Occupational Group, 1986, 1996, and Projected 2006," *Employment Projections.* Accessed http://bls.gov/news.release/ecopro.table3.htm. Data source: *Monthly Labor Review* (November 1997).

U.S. General Accounting Office (1993). *Federal Personnel: Employment Policy Challenges Created by an Aging Workforce* (Washington, DC: GAO, GAO/GDD-93–138, September).

U.S. Office of Personnel Management (1997). "The Statistical Story of Federal Downsizing," (Washington, DC: Office of Personnel Management, Employment Service, WRO 97–102, August).

————. (2003). *Demographic Profile of the Federal Workforce—2002 Edition.* Accessed http://www.opm.gov/feddata/demograp/demograp.asp

Chapter TWO

Public Personnel Administration: An Historical Overview

Although public personnel administration did not emerge as a specialized field of study or practice in the United States until the early 20th century, governments have been recruiting, hiring and firing, training, paying, and managing public employees since the founding of the republic. In these terms, of course, the organizational functions now associated with public personnel administration have been around for many thousands of years. This chapter traces the development of public personnel practices in the United States. Like Chapter 1, this chapter is intended to provide a general background and introduction to the chapter-length discussions of current trends, issues, and challenges that follow.

THE ERA OF POLITICAL RESPONSIVENESS: PATRONAGE AND SPOILS

For roughly the first one hundred years of its existence (1790–1890), the public service on all levels of government in the United States was political or partisan in the sense that public employees were expected to actively work for and in many cases financially support candidates for elective office on all levels of government. There was no separation between partisan politics and administration in practice. Government jobs and contracts traditionally were awarded to those who faithfully served the winning party, its candidates, and its policy agenda. Hence the saying, "to the victor goes the spoils."

Normative arguments for patronage or spoils approaches to public employment rely heavily on the idea that democratic governance requires a civil service that is highly responsive to public opinion and electoral mandates. In addition to providing a strong incentive to work for the party, spoils systems virtually guarantee responsiveness to legislators and elected executives, because those hired are at once loyal and fully aware that they may be dismissed for partisan reasons. In theory, hiring and firing on the basis of political loyalty and active support for the party or candidate allows the personnel system to ensure that "bureaucrats" will be responsive to the will of elected officials and, through them, to public opinion.

Presidents, as well as governors and mayors throughout the country, have used patronage to build powerful and very effective political coalitions. Some students of American history argue that presidential control of the federal patronage greatly strengthened that office's position in the Constitutional system of separated powers (Fish, 1904). President Abraham Lincoln freely and often personally dispensed federal jobs in an effort to build loyalty to and support for the Union cause during the Civil War (1861–1865). In fact, the White House was often overrun by job seekers during his tenure; he is reported to have remarked, "The spoils system might in the course of time become far more dangerous to the Republic than the rebellion itself" (Van Riper, 1958, p. 44).

The spoils system that Lincoln adeptly used and privately feared bore little resemblance to that used by presidents in earlier days. In general, the policy of the first six presidents (1789–1829) was to make appointments to federal offices on the basis of what President Washington had described as "fitness of character." In those days, fitness of character meant that the person was of good character, was able to do the work involved, *and* was in conformity with the political views and policy objectives of the chief executive and his associates. Normally, *all three standards* had to be satisfied, and typically, individuals who met those standards were drawn from the country's economic and social elite. That pattern persisted even when political party control of the presidency changed. By the time of Washington's second term, political parties had begun to emerge. Washington and Adams were of the Federalist party, which stood for, among other things, strength in the national government. The third president, Thomas Jefferson, led a separate party known today as the Democratic-Republicans. That group, which had evolved from earlier anti-Federalist organizations, favored more authority resting with the states rather than the national (that is, the federal) government. When Jefferson began his first term, he inherited a government staffed almost entirely by Federalists. In response, he removed some people on partisan grounds to make room for his supporters, but the people he and Presidents James Madison, James Monroe, and John Quincy Adams appointed generally conformed to the standard of fitness of character that had been established earlier (Caldwell, 1944; Van Riper, 1958, pp. 22–27).

Indeed, the reliance upon the American upper class to fill positions in the national government was so complete during this early time that Fredrick Mosher has referred to the period as one of a "Government By Gentlemen" (Mosher, 1968; see also White, 1948, 1951, 1954). American society was very stratified, and as Van Riper states, "The government of our early days was a government led by the well-educated, the well-born, the prosperous, and their adherents" (Van Riper, 1958, pp. 17–18). The early presidents were looking for men who had backgrounds like theirs, who shared their commitment to the U.S. Constitution, and who believed that governance was a responsibility or obligation of their social class. Thus, during this rather brief period, the federal service was very exclusive. Considering the requirement for political loyalty, it can hardly be said that the first six presidents implemented a merit system in the modern sense of that term, but the national government did have a "good reputation for integrity and capacity." However, the situation was very different at the state and local levels. By 1829, the practice of handing out jobs simply on partisan grounds had entrenched itself in large states like New York and Pennsylvania.

The United States of 1829 was in the midst of a profound social, political, and economic transformation. The old socioeconomic and political order established during colonial times was being washed away by an emerging industrial and market system in which people believed that wealth, power, and position should be and could be *achieved* rather than *inherited*. All that was needed was equality of opportunity and the ambition, intelligence, and hard work needed to take advantage of it. Democracy and an expanding franchise were giving rise to larger and better-organized political parties. The country was expanding westward, urbanizing, and industrializing (Miller, 1972). Swelled by large numbers of immigrants, the population, especially in the cities, was growing rapidly.

Within this context, President Andrew Jackson first assumed office and, in doing so, stated views on the work of government and the distribution of government jobs. Of course, Jackson was from the newly formed Democratic party. He rejected the elitist views of his predecessors in favor of a much more egalitarian approach to public service. Jackson is often called the father of the *spoils system* because he argued that the public service should be opened to all segments of society and that there was no need for long tenure in office since the duties of most federal jobs were simple and did not require experience. Accordingly, he reasoned, rotation in office was the best policy. In the new era of democratic politics, Jackson's position was popular, responding as it did to "widespread resentment at the monopolizing of public office by representatives of the upper classes." Indeed, some families "had maintained themselves from father to son in the civil service" (Van Riper, 1958, pp. 27, 33).

Given what happened during the second half of the 19th century, Jackson could hardly be called a practitioner or advocate of *unmitigated* spoils. His appointments to top-level federal positions mirrored earlier attention to ability and competence. The available pool of qualified persons was still relatively small, and most of them came from upper-class backgrounds (Mosher, 1968, p. 62). Nonetheless, his egalitarian rhetoric did much to open the gates for spoils on the national level, and those who followed him in office were far more inclined to sweep out incumbents and to replace them with party loyalists. Their objective was a practical one: to win elections by strengthening the party machinery from the grassroots up. By 1861, when Lincoln assumed the presidency, the spoils system had developed to the point that it "had an adhesive grip upon the political machinery of the United States" (Van Riper, 1958, p. 42). The same could be said of civil service in the states and cities, especially the large cities where the "machines" prospered and the "bosses" ruled (Freedman, 1994). For example, the goals of New York City's notorious Tammany machine during the 1880s were as follows: "To nominate candidates for public office, get out the vote, and win elections. Once in power, the organization enjoyed a patronage feast" (Riordon, 1963, p. xii).

George Washington Plunkitt was a Tammany district leader or ward boss who happily explained his political "philosophy" to William Riordon of the *New York Evening Post* in a series of interviews conducted around the turn of the century. Plunkitt colorfully described the logic underpinning the spoils system:

> What is representative government anyhow? Is it all a fake that this is a government of the people, by the people, and for the people? If it isn't a fake, then why isn't the people's voice obeyed and Tammany men put in all the offices? . . . We stood as we have always stood, for rewardin' the men that won the victory. . . . First, this great and glorious country was built up by political parties; second, parties can't

hold together if their workers don't get the offices when they win; third, if the parties go to pieces, the government they built up must go to pieces. . . . (Riordon, 1963, pp. 12–13)

CIVIL SERVICE REFORM I: NEUTRAL COMPETENCE IN GOVERNMENT

In the United States, the patronage system that Plunkitt advocated had become synonymous with high levels of graft and corruption. The system was targeted for reform by proponents of the progressive movement of the late nineteenth and early twentieth centuries. That movement had many political objectives, but at the top of their agenda was the destruction of the party machines that ran the nation's major cities. In the reformers' eyes, these machines fostered rampant corruption, institutionalized administrative inefficiency and waste, and ignored the legitimate interests of electoral minorities while taxing them heavily. Advocates of the reform agenda included members of the banking and commercial sector, middle- and upper-income groups, and the growing numbers of university-trained professionals. Advocates of civil service reform wanted a stable infrastructure for their commercial activities and to "take the reins of power away from the lower classes and the Irish bosses." Thus, economic and political self-interest helped to motivate the reform movement, but "the major force propelling civil service reform was moral outrage at the greedy excesses of the spoilsmen" (Freedman, 1994, p. 17).

By advancing "neutral competence" as *the* core value of public service, the civil service reformers sought to undermine a critical element of the machine's base of electoral power and administrative control—the patronage. Men like Plunkitt, of course, had reason to be alarmed (Schiesl, 1977). The reformers were trying to fundamentally alter the political landscape, and as time passed, they were increasingly successful in limiting the scope of patronage in public employment.

Plunkitt certainly would have agreed with U.S. Supreme Court Justice Lewis F. Powell's *dissenting* opinion in *Elrod v. Burns* (1976). In this decision, a majority of the Supreme Court ruled that removals of "non-policymaking" employees solely for reasons of their affiliation with a political party violated their First Amendment rights. Powell, however, disagreed, saying that it was naive to think that political activities were motivated by "some academic interest in 'democracy' or other public service impulse." He stated, "For the most part, as every politician knows, the hope of some reward generates a major portion of the local political activity supporting parties."

Powell concluded, "History and long prevailing practice across the country support the view that patronage hiring practices make a sufficiently substantial contribution to the practical functioning of our democratic system to support their relatively modest intrusion on First Amendment rights." Plunkitt would have seen nothing wrong with his logic, but Justice Powell was in the minority, and *Elrod v. Burns* was the first of several Court decisions that eventually limited constitutionally acceptable patronage to situations where the hiring authority could show that being a member of a particular political party was an essential qualification for performing the duties associated with the job. Through these decisions, most notably *Branti v. Finkel* (1980) and *Rutan v. Republican Party of Illinois* (1990) the Court provided a constitutional underpinning for the merit principle (Daniel, 1992).

IMPLEMENTING NEUTRAL COMPETENCE WITH MERIT SYSTEMS

American democracy and egalitarianism have historically supported the ideal that people should get and keep government jobs on the basis of their relative ability and performance. Likewise, the belief that rewards such as job status and income should be *achieved* by the individual enjoys widespread popular support. Disinterested, nonpartisan administration of the law is also highly valued. With regard to the personnel function, these norms are the foundation of the *merit principle*. Basing the administration of personnel systems on the merit principle was high on the agenda of the early civil service reformers.

In application, the merit principle dictates that appointments, promotions, and other personnel actions should be made exclusively on the basis of relative ability and job performance. This idea has usually meant the administration of competitive examinations to measure qualifications. Scores on these "objective" tests are then used to rank applicants. For other personnel actions such as pay raises, reduction-in-force, and dismissals, the assumption has also been that the employee's "merit" could be determined through performance appraisals and that he or

> **BULLETIN**
>
> Justice Brennan delivered the opinion of the Court in *Rutan:* "To the victor belong only those spoils that may be constitutionally obtained . . . the *First Amendment* forbids government officials to discharge or threaten to discharge public employees solely for not being supporters of the political party in power, unless party affiliation is an appropriate requirement for the position involved. Today we are asked to decide the constitutionality of several related political patronage practices [or] whether promotion, transfer, recall, and hiring decisions involving low-level public employees may be constitutionally based on party affiliation and support. We hold that they may not."

she should be treated accordingly. Government personnel systems based on these values and assumptions are called *merit systems*. In O. Glenn Stahl's words, "In its broadest sense a merit system in modern government means *a personnel system in which comparative merit or achievement governs each individual's selection and progress in the service and in which the conditions and rewards of performance contribute to competency and continuity of the service*" (Stahl, 1962, p. 28).

On the federal level, after several unsuccessful initiatives, legislation establishing the foundation for a rudimentary merit system was passed by Congress in 1883. The Pendleton Act was passed over a year after President Garfield was shot down by "a disappointed office seeker." A more immediate and less sentimental reason for its passage was the incumbent Republicans' fear that the next president would be a Democrat who would remove all Republican officeholders. The law called for a merit system based on three interrelated concepts: (1) open competitive examinations as the basis for selection, (2) political neutrality by employees, and (3) relative security of tenure, which meant that employees would be removed only for reasons having to do with malfeasance in office; they were not to be removed for political reasons. The victory for reformers, while a watershed in the history of the U.S. Civil Service, was not overwhelming in its impact at the time. Initially, it covered only about 10 percent of the positions in the executive branch. Provisions within the law allowed for expansion of its coverage by presidential order, however, and by 1952 well over 90 percent of the federal workforce was included within the merit system.

The administrative machinery set up to carry out the Pendleton Act was a bipartisan Civil Service Commission (CSC) rather than an executive-controlled agency. This meant that the CSC would enjoy considerable independence from the president in its policy making and day-to-day administrative activities. However, the CSC was far from autonomous because the three commissioners were appointed by the president, subject to Senate confirmation, and he or she could remove them. The president also had to approve civil service rules and regulations recommended by the CSC before they could be implemented. Another key provision was presidential authority to place additional positions under the classified civil service or merit system and to remove positions from such coverage. As state and local

---

BULLETIN

In Section 12, the Pendleton Act requires, "That no person shall, in any room or building occupied in the discharge of official duties by any officer or employee of the United States mentioned in this act . . . solicit in any manner whatever, or receive any contribution of money or any other thing of value for any political purpose whatever."

Source: 22 Stat. 27 (1883)

governments adopted merit systems, they tended to follow the federal example and created commissions or boards to administer them.

The first merit systems were poorly funded and struggled to survive (many did not). Besides being limited in coverage, they were narrowly gauged; basically, they gave routine tests to applicants, kept employee records, and did little else. Commissions were staffed largely by clerks, and those clerks took care of the departments' personnel chores.

The first state to adopt civil service legislation applying the merit principle was New York in 1883, followed by Massachusetts in 1884. The limited success of the reform movement on the state level is revealed by the fact that no new state laws reforming civil service were approved during the next 20 years. Albany, New York, was the first municipality to establish a merit system (1884). During the 1890s, Milwaukee, Philadelphia, New Orleans, and Seattle were among the cities approving charter amendments that established civil service regulations. The first county to do so, in 1895, was Cook County, Illinois. As the machines and reform parties struggled for control of the nation's cities and counties, it was not unusual for merit systems to come and go, depending on the outcomes of elections. Often, commissions established under reform administrations became fronts for spoils when the machines gained the upper hand (Aronson, 1973, p. 38). In Chicago, for example,

> Jobs have been the lifeblood of the Cook County Democratic Organization since . . . the early 1930s. . . . In the heyday of the machine during the Daley years (1955–1976) all patronage jobs were personally controlled by Richard J. Daley [and] . . . were allocated to ward and township committeemen in proportion to the individual committeeman's influence and the number of votes his ward delivered for machine candidates. (Freedman, 1994, p. 39)

Although the number of civil service systems at least nominally based on the merit principle continued to expand between 1900 and 1930, the scope of their activities remained quite limited. At best, "merit" was making sure that public employees were appointed through competitive entrance examinations, prohibited from engaging in partisan politics, and compensated on the basis of "equal-pay-for-equal-work." In practice, little if any attention was paid to potential connections between personnel practices and organizational productivity and effectiveness. During this period, the scientific management approach and principles of administration movement did influence thinking about efficiency in government (Merrill, 1960). Their influence on personnel administration, however, was minimal. For the most part, administrators of merit systems concentrated on "keeping the rascals out" by severely constraining line management's role in personnel matters.

POSITIVE PERSONNEL ADMINISTRATION

The explosive growth of the federal government during the Depression (1930–1940) and World War II (1941–1945) quickly outpaced the CSC's capacity to handle day-to-day personnel operations. In 1916, there were about 400,000 federal employees; by 1940, that number had risen to one million, and by 1945, it stood at more than 3.5 million. In 1935, *total* state and local employment was less than 3 million. As President Franklin D. Roosevelt (FDR) dramatically expanded the size of the classified civil service to encompass the New Deal agencies, it became clear that much of the Commission's work would have to be decentralized to the agency level. It had become a serious bottleneck. This practical reality, in combination with a recognition that skilled personnel administration might help agencies function more efficiently, led to FDR's 1938 Executive Order 7916 requiring the various departments to set up professionally staffed personnel offices.

Historically, Roosevelt's order signaled the arrival of "modern" personnel administration (U.S. Library of Congress, 1976, pp. 258–260). In this case, *modern* meant expanding departmental-level personnel units and improving the efficiency of services they provided, such as position classification, the administration of applicant testing, and records-keeping. It also meant that the CSC's responsibilities would shift toward policy formulation, research and development, and program evaluation. Because these mandates required that the CSC and departmental personnel offices develop expertise across a wide variety of topics, college graduates began to replace the clerks. Personnel administration gradually became more professionalized and specialized.

The concept of personnel administration as a tool or arm of management began to take hold, not only in the federal government but also in some states and localities. World War II greatly increased the pressure on departmental personnel shops to be responsive and supportive. By the end of the war, the perception of personnel administration as a routine activity with limited technical content and little relation to managerial needs had been largely abandoned by its leading practitioners, as well as by students of public administration. Thus, by the end of the 1940s, Simon, Smithburg, and Thompson (1950) were prepared to state in their widely read textbook that personnel specialists deal with matters "that are of the greatest long range importance to the organization" (p. 312).

The definition of personnel administration's role continued to evolve as efficiency and productivity assumed greater importance. Between 1945 and 1960, the field became somewhat more people-oriented and less fixated on the enforcement of rules and regulations. Essentially, two related criticisms of the pre-war approach to personnel administration were heard. First, increasingly professionalized and formalized personnel operations, although efficient in their own terms, frequently worked to frustrate line officials who were interested in accomplishing departmental or organizational goals. Personnel offices typically acquired reputations with line managers as centers of "bureaucratization," where rules and procedures were all-important. Second, personnel specialists tended to assume a highly legalistic definition of their responsibilities while neglecting the implications of a growing body of information on social-psychological factors related to performance and productivity in organizations.

This kind of criticism was probably inevitable, given the increasingly technical nature of the personnel function and the formation of personnel offices staffed by specialists. Those in staff roles normally will exert considerable control because they monopolize the expertise needed to administer often-complex policies and procedures. In the public sector, personnel specialists commonly have the legal as well as organizational authority to enforce and adjudicate the rules that managers must follow. Nevertheless, as part of a trend that would culminate on the federal level in the 1978 Civil Service Reform Act, appeals for "flexibility" and a "management-orientation" were often heard during the late 1950s.

As to the second criticism, personnel specialists did not seem at all "people-minded." They concentrated on day-to-day tasks, applying technical skills but showing little interest in developing a broad-gauged approach to the development and management of the organization's human resources. The human relations approach to organizational management was having some limited influence in the private sector before World War II, but this was not the case in the public sector (Roethlisberger & Dickson, 1939). This situation began to change after the war as an "accent-on-people" orientation gained followers. Advocates believed that the insights of human relations could be applied to the personnel function in the following specific ways:

- Attending to social and psychological factors in productivity such as supervisory leadership, incentives, and the design of jobs and work settings.
- Focusing attention on the behavioral as well as technical skills and conditions people need to develop their potential and to

function effectively in the workplace. This includes enhancing job satisfaction and commitment to organizational goals through psychologically rewarding work settings, supportive management styles, and opportunities for career development and training.

- Recognizing the importance of effective supervision on the social and psychological levels. Supervisors are usually the first point at which employees relate to the organization, so it is essential that supervisors be prepared to deal with a broad range of interpersonal and group processes that may affect morale and productivity. Personnel specialists, therefore, should be able to provide this kind of support through training programs and other programs designed to help supervisors be effective in human as well as technical terms.

- Increasing the knowledge base of personnel administration. In other words, at least some personnel specialists should be conducting research into the social and psychological effects of personnel policies and practices. Applied research of this kind is vitally necessary if personnel administration is to be firmly grounded in an understanding of the human side of organizations.

- Requiring personnel workers themselves to have sufficiently broad backgrounds of training and experience to understand human behavior. The value of the personnel specialist, therefore, should not be judged only by command over techniques such as position classification and testing; they should also be schooled in human relations theory and its practical applications.

By 1960, on the federal level and in a growing number of state and local jurisdictions, some progress could be reported in making personnel systems more professional, better related to management needs, and more attuned to a "human resources management" point of view. The concept of public personnel, as set forth in textbooks, journals, and the recommendations of professional societies and commissions, firmly supported all of these values in addition to the merit principle. However, just how much progress had been made toward realizing them in practice was a matter of opinion. For many governments, patronage was still the dominant and accepted way of doing business. In 1940, the Congress had amended the 1935 Social Security Act (SSA) to require merit-based personnel systems in state agencies administering SSA funds, and this method of "forcing" merit was extended to the broad array of federal grants-in-aid to states and localities that developed during the 1960s and 1970s. Similarly, in most states, prohibitions against partisan activity covered only agencies administering federal funds (as required by the 1940 amendments to the Hatch Act). Finally, even the most nonpartisan merit systems tended to be inward-looking and unresponsive to many of management's concerns.

During the 1960s and 1970s, however, the range of core issues associated with pubic personnel administration was expanded significantly. This development helped further underscore the central importance of personnel procedures and processes for public management generally. The rise of unions and collective bargaining, the expansion of public employee rights under the Constitution, and the emergence of substantial equal employment opportunity programs and affirmative action all had a significant impact on personnel policy and management in the public sector. Each of these issues is reviewed briefly in the following sections.

COLLECTIVE BARGAINING IN GOVERNMENT

The "state of the art" set forth in the personnel texts of the 1950s would be rendered obsolete (or at least very incomplete) by changes that took place during the next 10 years. One such change was the rapid spread of collective bargaining in the public sector—a process by which employer and employee representatives negotiate a contract governing specified terms and conditions of employment. Before 1960, most merit system administrators thought of collective bargaining as something peculiar to the private sector that had no place in government. By experience, they had little or no familiarity with collective bargaining or appreciation of its institutional significance as a system of internal governance in private businesses. They saw it to be a real menace to the merit principle and believed that the unstated goal of most union leaders was to wipe out civil service laws and regulations and to replace them with agreements negotiated under the threat of strikes and other disruptions of public services.

For many personnel administrators, public employee unionization and collective bargaining were in the same category as spoils: something to be vigorously resisted on the legal, legislative, and organizational levels. By 1968, however, the federal courts had firmly established that the First Amendment protected the right of public employees to form and join unions. The courts had also ruled that public workers have no constitutional right to collective bargaining or to strike against their employers. More importantly, however, they identified no constitutional reason why public employers could not bargain collectively. Thus, the choice was essentially political, and state legislatures could enact laws requiring localities to engage in collective bargaining, proscribing collective bargaining, or anything in between. It was also possible for the state to say nothing and, in so doing, to make collective bargaining a local option. State legislatures, in addition, could decide if the state should bargain collectively with all or some of its workers. In many states, organized employees were politically effective (and unions warmly received by workers who saw their pay and benefits falling behind those of the private sector), and collective bargaining was to dramatically change the landscape of personnel administration over the next 20 years.

In 1959, Wisconsin was the only state to have passed legislation requiring *municipal* employers to bargain collectively with unionized workers. None of the states bargained with its employees. In the federal service, there was no law or executive order providing for collective bargaining or any government-wide labor relations policy. In stark contrast, most nonagricultural workers in the private sector had been guaranteed the right to bargain collectively by the 1935 National Labor Relations Act (NLRA, also known as the Wagner Act). President Roosevelt had supported the NLRA while expressing strong opposition to any form of collective bargaining in the federal government.

The present situation is very different. By 1985, 40 states and the District of Columbia had statutes or executive orders setting up frameworks for collective bargaining with some or all of their employees. In the federal government, a limited form of collective bargaining began in 1962 and is now a statutory requirement of the Civil Service Reform Act of 1978 (postal workers have been bargaining collectively since 1970). In fact, as noted in Chapter 1, while the proportion of nonagricultural private sector workers belonging to unions and covered by negotiated contracts had declined to around 9 percent in 2003, in the public sector it had grown to more than 40 percent.

Currently, about half of all state and local government full-time workers are members of employee organizations of one kind or another. The percentage of organized employees is even higher in such functions as education, highways, public welfare, hospitals, police, fire, and sanitation services. Collective bargaining is no longer a novelty in the public sector. In many jurisdictions, it has become a normal and accepted aspect of personnel administration.

One highly visible result has been the emergence of a new specialty within the field: labor relations and collective bargaining. It has also become commonplace to find offices of labor relations either within personnel departments or as separate units. A more complete discussion of the role of unions and collective bargaining in the public sector is provided in Chapter 7 of this book.

EXPANDING THE CONSTITUTIONAL RIGHTS OF PUBLIC EMPLOYEES

Since the 1950s, the federal courts have significantly strengthened the individual public employee's constitutional position in the employment relationship. As late as the mid-1950s, this relationship was dominated by the employer, who was free to impose many conditions on workers that they had to accept to keep their jobs. Historically, the courts had ruled that employees did not have *any* rights in the job that were based on the Constitution. Thus, in fixing the terms of employment, the public employer could and often did deny workers civil and political rights universally enjoyed by those in the private sector.

For example, the due process clauses of the Fifth and Fourteenth amendments prohibiting government from denying individuals life, liberty, or property without due process of law were held not to apply to public employees facing termination because government employment could not be considered an employee's property, employees had no liberty interest connected to employment decisions, and public employment policies certainly did not involve the denial of life. Likewise, freedom of speech was restricted because public employment was seen as a privilege rather than a right. Decades earlier in a case involving freedom of expression, Justice Holmes had famously announced, "The petitioner may have a constitutional right to talk politics, but he has no constitutional right to be a policeman" (*McAuliffe v. Mayor of New Bedford,* 1892). Freedom of association was also severely restricted in that the Court had upheld prohibitions on numerous forms of political participation by public employees set forth in the Hatch Act of 1939. As a result, the scope of judicial review of personnel actions taken by managers was very limited through the first half of the 20th century. As one observer wrote in 1955, "From the assertion that there exists no constitutional right *to* public employment, it is also inferred that there can be no constitutional right *in* public employment. The progression is that, since there are no fundamental claims in employment, employment is maintained by the state as a privilege" (Dotson, 1955, p. 87).

Beginning in the late 1950s, under the leadership of the Warren Court, the federal judiciary issued a series of decisions that eroded and eventually ended the "doctrine of privilege" in association with public employment. In its place, the federal courts erected a doctrine that sought to protect the substantial constitutional interests of public employees. In the context of a termination or dismissal, the court applied the following standard: "whenever there is a substantial interest, other than employment by the state, involved in the discharge of a public employee, he can be removed neither on arbitrary grounds nor without a procedure calculated to determine whether legitimate grounds exist" (Rosenbloom, 1971, p. 421). The courts, therefore, have narrowed management's discretion by extending certain constitutional protections and guarantees to public employees on all levels of government. Chapter 8 provides an extended discussion of the status of these and related topics including restrictions on the political activities of public employees.

FROM EXCLUSIVE TO INCLUSIVE PERSONNEL POLICIES AND PRACTICES

Traditional definitions of merit in public employment appeared to leave no room for hiring and other personnel actions based on anything other than the individual's qualifications and job performance. There has been, however, a long and well-known history of discrimination directed against minorities and women both the private and the public sectors. In government, patronage systems did much to *exclude* minorities in many jurisdictions, and in practice, the merit principle often applied only to white males.

The roots of this kind of discrimination run deep in the American public service. President Woodrow Wilson, a strong advocate of civil service reform as a part of the progressive agenda, ordered African Americans removed from all but menial jobs in the federal service in an effort to maintain the southern base of the Democratic party. Like ethnic and racial minorities, women have also historically been confined to lower-grade jobs. Traditionally, their opportunities were restricted largely to clerical, secretarial, and service positions (so-called women's work according to the then dominant stereotype).

Until the civil rights movement of the 1960s, the failure of public personnel systems to ensure genuine equality of opportunity or equal employment opportunity (EEO) went virtually unchallenged. Social norms, unequal educational opportunities, the exclusion of minorities from the political process, and intentional discrimination by personnel administrators played major roles in the exclusion of minorities and women from all but the lowest levels of the public service. A passive approach to the administration of merit systems also reinforced the pattern. Typically, those running merit systems argued that the very low representation of minority groups in the public service and their concentration in the lowest ranking jobs was not a violation of the merit principle. They reasoned that so long as there was no *overt* discrimination to be found, the absence of minorities was unfortunate but no fault of the merit system.

While noting that many cases of overt discrimination could be documented, the U.S. Commission on Civil Rights concluded in a 1969 report that "static" and arbitrary civil service procedures did much to exclude minority groups. It cited as examples the use of unvalidated tests, rigid educational requirements, and automatic disqualification for an arrest record. The Commission also stressed that most merit system agencies made no positive effort to recruit minorities by regularly visiting black colleges and universities (U.S. Commission on Civil Rights, 1969).

At the time this report was issued, the civil rights movement was having a major impact on public policy. Several lower court decisions, based on the Fourteenth Amendment and the Civil Rights Acts of 1866 and 1871, made it clear that the federal judiciary was inclined to void discriminatory practices and to impose affirmative action programs if public employers did not do so voluntarily. The Civil Rights Act of 1964, originally applicable only to the private sector, was amended in 1972 to cover the public sector as well. Presidents Johnson, Nixon, and Carter authored affirmative action programs, and federal rules and regulations requiring EEO and affirmative action remedies of private contractors and governments receiving federal funds were set forth during this period. In general, the 1960s and 1970s were marked by a growing *inclusiveness* of public personnel policies and practices.

The federal courts have also interpreted the prohibitions in the Civil Rights Act of 1964 to include sex discrimination. They have clearly established that, to be upheld, decisions restricting certain job classifications only to men or women must have a rational basis, or an occupationally valid reason. Affirmative action programs now typically include women in their recruitment, hiring, and career development initiatives. As a result, women are now being hired to fill many kinds of positions previously argued to be too strenuous or otherwise unsuitable for them (such as police and fire services). Intentional as well as "socially traditional" forms of discrimination against women, including sexual harassment, are illegal under Title VII of the Civil Rights Act, and the Equal Employment Opportunity Commission (EEOC) is empowered to investigate complaints by women against their employers.

EEO protections also apply to discrimination based on age or disability. The Age Discrimination in Employment Act of 1967, as amended in 1978, prohibits public as well as private employers from discriminating against persons on the basis of age. Employers must be able to show that age is a legitimate employment qualification, and the courts now require reasonable evidence that a certain entrance or retirement age is disqualifying. In other words, employers may not favor younger workers simply for reasons of age unrelated to ability to do the job in question.

Disabled persons are protected by the Rehabilitation Act of 1973 and the Americans with Disabilities Act of 1990 (ADA). The Rehabilitation Act applies to the federal government and state, local, or private agencies that receive federal funds. It requires that these agencies have written affirmative action programs for the disabled, and reasonable accommodation must be made by the employer to facilitate the employment of disabled persons (this now includes people who are HIV-positive or have active AIDS). The ADA expanded coverage to nearly public and private employers. Chapter 9 provides a detailed review of the status of antidiscrimination law and its application to the public service.

CIVIL SERVICE REFORM II: EFFECTIVE AND RESPONSIVE GOVERNMENT ADMINISTRATION

By the time Jimmy Carter assumed the presidency in 1976, pressure was building for further reform of the federal civil service. As we have seen, the 19th and early 20th century civil service reform movement sought to replace spoils with merit systems and to limit line management's control over many aspects of personnel administration. This, however, is not what the term "civil service reform" meant in 1976. It referred instead to efforts to better align personnel practices with the day-to-day needs of public managers, to improve the performance of public employees, and to make the "bureaucracy" more responsive to executive leadership.

An important feature of Civil Service Reform II was its emphasis on improving the control chief executives and public managers had over the personnel function. Proponents of reform argued that merit systems have functioned far too independently since their creation and have seemed intent on imposing restrictive and cumbersome controls over line management's discretion in personnel matters. They disagreed with the assumption that elected chief executives and line managers must be kept at arm's length because they cannot be relied upon to protect the merit principle.

According to this line of reasoning, the old reform movement created a separation between general management and personnel administration despite the fact that personnel, like budgeting and finance, is an integral part of the management function in any public agency. Although it may have kept the rascals out, critics argued that this approach seriously compromised management's capacity to effectively use human resources. If governments were to satisfy public demands and overcome the difficulties created by the fiscal stress of the 1970s and 1980s, the split between executive management and the personnel function had to be eliminated. There was, reformers argued, no necessary contradiction between the merit *principle* and a management-oriented personnel system. Accordingly, a number of changes were proposed.

These changes included abolishing the traditional independent civil service commission and replacing it with an office of personnel management or a department of human resources headed by a director appointed by and directly accountable to the chief executive. This structural change allows the chief executive to establish direct policy control over the personnel function and, through the department of human resources, to use it in support of *organizational* efforts. Advocates of reform reasoned that this arrangement does not necessarily threaten the merit principle if the executive is made legally responsible for protecting that principle and, equally important, is held strictly accountable for violations. In addition, independent boards or commissions established to hear employee appeals and empowered to conduct investigations of personnel practices would ensure fairness and prevent political abuses. Critics pointed out that this executive-oriented model, in practice, might easily lead to partisan manipulations of personnel systems if no effective independent regulatory agency existed.

The U.S. Civil Service Reform Act of 1978 (CSRA) followed this model by abolishing the Civil Service Commission and establishing in its place the Office of Personnel Management whose director reports to the president, and the Merit Systems Protection Board (MSPB), which is responsible for the "watchdog" function. In state and local governments, civil service commissions with personnel policymaking, appellate, and administrative responsibilities continued to operate in many jurisdictions. In a growing number, however, the commissions were either abolished or limited to advisory, appellate, and investigatory roles. The personnel director reports directly to the governor in over half of the states.

Another feature of the reform initiatives of the 1970s was an effort to require central personnel agencies and the personnel offices in line departments to eliminate the numerous unnecessary rules and regulations they used to closely control managers' discretion in personnel matters. To make the personnel function a partner in building the effectiveness of public agencies, it was argued that procedures had to be streamlined and simplified. Along these lines, in testimony before the Congress in 1978, then CSC Chairman Alan K. Campbell suggested that the CSRA was needed to reduce "the accumulation of laws, regulations, and policies which have grown up over the last 95 years." He included the following in a long list of problems then confronting the federal civil service:

- Supervisors, employees, political leaders, and others were confused about what they could and could not do without violating essential merit principles.
- Excessive centralization of personnel authorities took many types of day-to-day personnel decisions out of the hands of line managers who nonetheless were held responsible for accomplishment in major program areas. Managers had to go through extensive paperwork justifications to obtain Civil Service Commission approval of relatively minor decisions.
- Over-centralized and restrictive systems for examining and selecting employees made it hard for managers to hire expeditiously the best-qualified people and to meet their equal employment opportunity goals and timetables.
- Managers faced a confusing array of regulations and procedures standing in their way when they sought to reward good work performance, to discipline employees, or to remove employees whose performance was clearly inadequate and could not be improved.
- A jumble of laws, regulations, and special provisions affecting executive positions made it very difficult for department and bureau heads to utilize their staffs effectively. (Campbell, 1978)

According to Campbell and other supporters of the CSRA, problems such as these could be solved only if the personnel system shifted from a *regulatory* to a *service* orientation. In these terms, the proper role of the central personnel agency was to provide general policy guidance and technical assistance to line departments in such areas as EEO, selection, performance appraisal, and training. Within the limits set by law and negotiated contracts, control of the details of the personnel function and authority to tailor practices to specific conditions were to be left to the departments. Finally, a central agency like the U.S. Office of Personnel Management (OPM) should conduct research and development programs, exercise quality control through periodic evaluations of departmental policies and practices, and provide leadership across the spectrum of human resources challenges facing the government.

Campbell also suggested that separate personnel systems were needed for high-level executives and senior career administrators. The success of specific programs, as well as the entire federal establishment, depended heavily on the loyalty, expertise, and energy of this group. Traditional civil service systems, however, did not make any special provisions to assure strong executive leadership and effective use of administrative talent. Procedural flexibility, appropriate incentives, and well-planned career development systems for executives were needed.

Such was the rationale for senior executive services (SES), such as that established in the federal government by the CSRA and now found in some 20 states. In an SES, rank is in the person, not in the job or position. This arrangement means that pay, for example, is determined by characteristics of the individual employee rather than characteristics of the tasks associated with the job or position. Supposedly, this structure will facilitate mobility across agency lines and promote the emergence of a highly professional cadre of experienced senior administrators. The system also usually allows some discretion in setting the entrance salaries of executives, and they typically use some form of merit pay and bonuses instead of automatic step and inflation increases. Federal SES members are untenured and may be returned to lower level positions if their performance is less than satisfactory—a further element of flexibility for agency management.

A central item on the reform agenda during this time was giving management the capacity to reward good performers and to discipline and remove poor performers who did not improve the quality of their work. This meant that sound, valid, and credible performance appraisal systems had to be developed and competently administered in conjunction with *merit pay* plans. Under the previous personnel systems, few incentives to carefully measure performance existed, and complex, drawn-out, appeals procedures often discouraged supervisors' efforts to remove unsatisfactory employees. Merit pay plans were very helpful in getting legislative approval of civil service reform packages on the federal and state levels, but they proved to be very difficult to implement and evaluations of their effects on performance were discouraging. Interestingly, however, that reality did not significantly dampen enthusiasm for the concept.

President Carter had very little time to implement the CSRA along lines he had intended and, with Ronald Reagan's election, Alan K. Campbell was replaced as Director of OPM in 1980. His successor was a conservative Republican who believed the federal bureaucracy was dominated by "liberals." On the federal level, and in many of the states and localities struggling to deal with new political and fiscal realities, civil service reform (and even the idea of civil service as an important and valuable part of American government) lost much of its momentum (Ban, 1984, pp. 54–55).

By the mid-1980s, reform along the lines advocated by authors of the CSRA was stalled, at least on the federal level. One student of the CSRA concluded, "One can question whether the newly created organizational structures have succeeded in improving either the protection of the rights of individuals or the clarity and efficiency of the personnel function" (Ban, 1984, p. 58). By the end of the decade, concerns about the capacity of the civil service to function in an effective and responsive manner on all levels of government were continuing to be expressed.

In its 1989 report, the National Commission on the Public Service (also known as the Volcker Commission) observed that the United States' need for a highly competent and trustworthy public service was steadily growing, not diminishing. On both counts, however, the Commission saw a serious deterioration taking place. Its recommendations for changes in federal personnel policies and practices were intended to address what some called the "quiet crisis" of the civil service. The Commission's central message was clearly stated— the U.S. needed to build a national consensus on the importance of a truly excellent public service:

> In essence, we call for a renewed sense of commitment by all Americans to the highest traditions of the public service—to a public service responsive to the political will of the people and also protective of our constitutional values; to a public service able to cope with complexity; to a public service attractive to the young and talented from all parts of our society and also capable of earning the respect of all our citizens. (National Commission on the Public Service, 1989, p. 1)

Although the Commission's elevated vision of the values that should be embodied by the American public service were as old as the republic, translating that vision (or elements of it) into specific policies and administrative means enjoying broad public support had always been difficult. In part, this problem could be attributed to deeply entrenched public suspicions about "big government" and "bureaucrats." Between 1965 and 1989, the fragile base of public support enjoyed by the public service on all levels of government had been greatly eroded by a continuous barrage of partisan attacks, unsatisfied expectations, scandals such as Watergate, fiscal stress, and outright neglect by those in positions of political leadership. In this context, it is difficult to know the extent to which problems are grounded in operational realities as opposed to public perceptions consistent with anti-bureaucratic rhetoric.

Although much attention was focused on the federal civil service at this time, many state and local government systems were criticized as well. By the end of the 1980s, fears of existing or impending shortages of needed human resources and of a declining morale in many areas of the public service were accumulating. In many instances, the public sector was finding it increasingly difficult to recruit and retain people with the skills and abilities needed to meet the complex technical and social challenges confronting governments. Civil service reforms calculated to improve productivity, agency effectiveness, and responsiveness to political leadership had produced at best mixed results. Public indifference, partisan attacks, and increasingly noncompetitive rates of pay and fringe benefits lowered morale and dampened enthusiasm for careers in government (Goodsell, 2004).

In response to these concerns, the National Commission on the Public Service urged the George H. W. Bush administration to pursue 15 goals related to personnel policies and human resources management. Each of these goals addressed specific issues, but the Commission's general purpose was to focus attention on three basic problem areas: the higher civil service, recruitment and retention, and performance and productivity.

THE HIGHER CIVIL SERVICE

Here, the Commission called for a renewed commitment to building and maintaining a high-quality senior federal service. Like the authors of the 1978 CSRA, the Commission recognized that a competent personnel system on this level is essential because these are the people who are responsible for the administration of federal agencies and for the coordinated policy direction of the federal establishment. The higher civil service provides much of the day-to-day expertise and leadership necessary for successful governance. Public confidence and trust in government depends heavily on the extent to which those at the top of the civil service are seen to be competent, responsive, and consistently honest and fair. The Commission's evaluation of the condition of the higher civil service, along with those of other knowledgeable observers, had to be considered alarming:

> Unfortunately, there is growing evidence that the supply of talented managers, political and career, in government is dwindling. Among

presidential appointees . . . turnover rates have become a serious problem. . . . Among career senior executives . . . over half say that if a suitable job outside government became available, they would take it. . . . Today, sadly, fewer than half the government's most senior and most successful executives are willing to recommend a career in public life to their children. (National Commission on the Public Service, 1989, p. 12)

RECRUITMENT AND RETENTION OF QUALIFIED PERSONNEL

The Commission also added its voice to those warning of serious weaknesses in government's ability to attract "the best and the brightest" to public service careers. Recruiting talented people with needed technical and professional skills had become difficult in an increasingly competitive labor market. Similarly, turnover and early retirements were undermining the foundation of experience and skill federal agencies needed to function effectively.

The national government's ability to offer competitive pay and benefits had steadily deteriorated during the 1980s, and one report on the situation stated, "According to recent studies, federal pay and benefits trail the private sector by an estimated 7 to 24 percent for comparable jobs, with the gap growing larger every year" (Levine & Kleeman, 1986, p. 6). On the executive level, the gaps were even more striking. For responsibilities comparable with those of federal Level II Executives, private executives made about eight times the pay. In specific "shortage" occupations such as accountants and computer specialists, federal pay was as much as 45 percent behind that in the private sector.

PERFORMANCE AND PRODUCTIVITY

The third area of concern addressed by the Commission was the ability of the federal personnel management system to promote and sustain a "culture of performance." The Commission recog-

---

BULLETIN

From *The Report of the National Performance Review:*

> Year after year, layer after layer, the rules have piled up. The [MSPB] reports there are now 850 pages of federal personnel law . . . 1,300 pages of OPM regulations on how to implement those laws and another 10,000 pages of guidelines. . . . Costs to the taxpayer for this personnel quagmire are enormous. In total, 54,000 people work in federal personnel positions. We spend billions of dollars for these staff to classify each employee within a highly complex system of some 459 job series, 15 grades and 10 steps. . . .

Source: *From Red Tape to Results: Creating a Government That Works Better & Costs Less* (Washington, DC: U.S. Government Printing Office, 1993), pp. 20–21.

nized that the American public had every right to expect that civil servants would work hard to deliver programs in an efficient, timely, and responsive manner. However, simply demanding high levels of performance was not enough. The personnel system had to be supportive. As the Commission's report stated,

> The commitment to performance cannot long survive, however, unless the government provides adequate pay, recognition for jobs done well, accessible training, and decent working conditions. Quality service must be recognized, rewarded, and constantly reinforced. It is not enough to exhort the work force to do better— government must provide tangible signals that performance matters. (National Commission on the Public Service, 1989, p. 34)

Although "pay-for-performance" systems in various forms had been a very popular idea on all levels of government in the United States for some time, efforts to implement them successfully had proven to be far more of a challenge than most reformers had anticipated. Funding of merit pay and bonus plans was often so inadequate that the intended connections between performance and compensation often were not achieved, especially in the minds of public employees, many of whom became openly skeptical and suspicious of management's motives. Likewise, efforts to develop performance appraisal systems that truly discriminated among levels of performance and enjoyed broadly based support in the workforce had been largely unsuccessful (National Research Council, 1991). In 1989, the U.S. General Accounting Office (GAO) reported that its preliminary examination of the federal government's merit pay structure, known as the Performance Management and Recognition System (PMRS), revealed widespread unhappiness with the system. Because the PMRS had been designed to overcome weaknesses of the agency merit pay plans initially established under the CSRA, the GAO concluded that its apparent failure to remedy the situation after some four years was reason for concern, and it concluded, "The lack of an effective program for motivating employees at these levels [GS 13–15] could seriously impede creation of what the [Volcker] Commission called 'a culture of performance' in government" (U.S. General Accounting Office, 1989, p. 3).

The Volcker Commission's report set the stage for renewed reform efforts across a broad front of organizational and personnel-related functions. On the federal level, this process began in earnest with the Clinton-Gore "reinvention" and "re-engineering" initiatives, which emphasized decentralization, deregulation, simplification, cooperative labor relations, *and* downsizing the federal workforce. These reforms reflected a broader shift away from traditional bureaucratic forms of organization in both the public and private sectors. In the words of a 1995 GAO report,

> The necessity to improve performance in the face of steady or declining resources led some organizations . . . to make radical changes in the way they manage people. . . . .in place of centralized, rule-based systems, they are creating decentralized, flatter, more flexible arrangements. And in place of highly detailed rules to manage their employees, they are relying increasingly on a well-defined mission, a clearly articulated vision, and a coherent organizational culture to form the foundation for the key business systems and processes they use to ensure the successful outcome of their operations. Recognizing that people are central to any organization's success, these organizations give their managers greater prerogatives to manage and their employees greater opportunities to participate in the decisions that affect them and their work. (U.S. General Accounting Office, 1995a, p. 3)

The GAO report reflected the conventional wisdom of the reinventing government movement and identified several interrelated principles common to presumably more effective government organizations, including several that directly apply to the personnel function:

- Holding managers accountable for achieving results, rather than rigidly making them do things "by the book."
- Integrating personnel functions into the organization's planning and policy-making activities on all levels by decentralizing and deregulating them.
- Treating employee development and training as an investment required to keep up with changing citizen needs, to meet new skills requirements, and to build overall organizational capacities.
- Valuing people as assets to be developed and encouraged, as opposed to costs that should be minimized. (U.S. General Accounting Office, 1995b, pp. 5–6)

The National Commission on the State and Local Public Service (NCSLPS) also issued a widely read report in 1993 that identified what it considered to be important reform needs on the state and local levels. The reports of the National Performance Review or NPR and the NCSLPS shared the general reinvention orientation described earlier by the GAO, and both recommended extensive decentralization of the personnel function, delegation of hiring and other authorities to the agency level, and streamlining of personnel processes such as recruitment, hiring, position classification, and appeals (Thompson, 1994). Highlights of the NPR recommendations included the following:

- OPM should abolish its central registers of applicants and authorize federal agencies to set up their own recruitment and examining programs.
- Agencies should be given greater flexibility in classifying and paying employees.
- Agencies should be allowed to establish their own performance management programs for improvement of performance on the individual and organizational levels.
- Agencies should establish procedures for resolving disputes that serve as alternatives to established systems in the EEO and labor relations areas, and OPM should eliminate its regulations covering agency grievance systems, so they can tailor their approaches to various situations.
- Creative, flexible, and responsive hiring systems should be created and the standard application forms (most notably Standard Form 171) should be abolished [which was done in late 1994].
- Unnecessary red tape should be done away with and the entire personnel system simplified, in part by phasing out the entire Federal Personnel Manual [which was done in late 1993]. (U.S. General Accounting Office, 1995b)

Both reports recommended changes that should increase the authority of chief executives over personnel policy through control of top-level appointments and organizational structures. There were some significant differences, however. In Frank Thompson and Beryl Radin's words: "The most fundamental difference between the Winter and Gore reports involves their orientation toward downsizing. The Gore report sees reinvention as a vehicle for reducing the number of federal employees [see Chapter 1] and saving money, whereas the Winter report offers no such prescription for state and local governments" (Thompson & Radin, 1997, p. 15).

On one level, Civil Service Reform II focused attention on efforts to improve the competence and productivity of civil servants. It also urged changes in personnel policies, forms of administrative organization, and day-to-day practices intended to improve the likelihood that public employees will be highly responsive to the policy goals and directives of elected officials and, through them, to the public interest. Once the great engine of accountability and responsiveness, the patronage had steadily declined in scale and importance and, in an era requiring technical competence and increasing professionalization of the public workforce, no widely accepted functional equivalent had emerged. The highly protective and semi-autonomous personnel systems that emerged from Civil Service Reform I now were closely linked in the minds of the nation's political leaders with an incompetent and unresponsive public bureaucracy (Barzelay, 1992). The challenge was to "invent" public personnel systems that supported the merit principle in practice, allowed elected executives to establish firm policy control over the bureaucracy, and did both in a manner consistent with achieving high levels of agency performance and productivity.

By the late 1990s, key elements of the civil service reform agenda included the following (Kellough & Nigro, 2005; Walters, 2002):

- Integrating human resources policy making and administration into the executive leadership and management functions of government
- Structural decentralization and delegations of many human resource functions to line organizations
- Broad grants of discretion to agencies and departments in such areas as recruitment, selection, hiring, and promotions
- Streamlined and simplified job classification and pay systems
- Streamlined reduction-in-force, grievance, and appeals processes
- Performance management systems using a variety of merit pay systems intended to reward individuals and groups
- Lowering labor costs and achieving other efficiencies through contracting-out or privatization
- Moving toward "at will" employment relationships under which public employees do not enjoy the job tenure protections afforded those holding classified positions in traditional merit systems

By the early 21st century, public personnel management systems were being asked to engage a wide variety of challenges. In 2001, Hays and Kearney published the findings of a national survey of personnel professionals asking what they expected to be the most important changes in human resource management (HRM) over the next decade. The respondents placed many elements of Civil Service Reform II on their lists of anticipated changes. Hays and Kearney concluded,

> Public personnel administration remains in a state of flux and turbulence. Change has become a constant in the practice of HRM as reform proceeds apace across virtually every conceivable front. Even the most lethargic, rule-bound personnel office must contend with the forces of change emanating from reinvention advocates and the

increasing number of other elected, appointed, and career officials who understand the need to improve operations ranging from selection to compensation. (Hays & Kearney, 2001, 595)

Many of the deregulating and decentralizing civil service reforms implemented on all levels of government during the previous decade are in place, but, as one observer noted, concerns about accountability and responsiveness were surfacing as politicians found that they had "far fewer levers available to . . . control the civil service" and deregulation and decentralization reduced their "capacity as leaders to exert as much control over policy implementation as they might have had in the past" (Peters, 2001, p. 138). The core mandate had not changed in a fundamental sense: public personnel systems are still asked to establish and sustain a civil service that is reliably responsive to public policies and executive leadership (Kettl, Ingraham, Sanders, & Horner, 1996; Hays, 1996).

CONCLUSION

In this chapter, we have provided a very general overview of the history of public personnel policies and practices in the United States since its founding. While this history is intrinsically interesting, it is most important here as the background or context needed to understand the conditions, issues, and challenges *now* confronting students and practitioners of public personnel administration.

American public personnel administration has always confronted a dynamic and changing social, political, economic, and technological environment. If anything, the pace of change in all of these areas will accelerate during the next decade. The potential for challenging intersections between trends will likely increase, as will the demands on personnel specialists to contribute to solving the management and policy problems these intersections generate (Hays, 1997). One such area is the changing demography of the American workforce outlined in Chapter 1 (Naff & Kellough, 2003). In addition, the search for effective responses to growing pressures to improve the "family friendliness" of public agencies will continue. Effectively managing an increasingly diverse workforce will almost certainly become a major human resources training and development concern (Pomerleau, 1994). Increasingly, the labor pool from which public agencies will draw their personnel will be composed of women, ethnic and racial minorities, and immigrants. Currently, these groups make up about half of the workforce; however, during the next 10 years, it is estimated that they will contribute more than 80 percent of the net additions. As pointed out in Chapter 1, along with the rest of the U.S. population, the public service will be gradually "aging," and this trend will bring with it a variety of challenges in the areas of health care, retirement programs, age discrimination, and job design (Elliott, 1995). As the skills demanded by jobs in the public sector continue to increase, heavy investments in employee training and education and executive development will be required.

Public as well as private employers also will continue to face a host of social, legal, and organizational challenges flowing from larger social problems such as violence, inadequate education and training, and poverty. Health problems in the work place, such as drug addiction and alcoholism (substance abuse), and AIDS, will continue to demand sustained attention. Implementing laws and public policies intended to prevent discrimination against minority groups, disabled persons, and women will be an ongoing responsibility of public personnel specialists, as well as line managers.

Emerging areas of concern include the direction and pace of technological change and the growing popularity of privatization as the answer to public demands for lower taxes, fewer bureaucrats, and better public services. The pace of change and innovation in communications, data processing, and other computer-related technologies, for example, has required and will continue to require large investments in employee training and development programs because skills become obsolete very quickly. New technologies, such as desktop computers and local area networks built around servers, have the potential to profoundly change skills needs of public agencies. The knowledge (intellectual technology) required by virtually all organizational roles, from those who operate and maintain increasingly complicated machinery to white-collar professionals of all kinds, is constantly expanding as well. Attracting, retaining, and sustaining the high-skill or knowledge-based work force of the 21st century will be a major challenge for public employers (Shareef, 1994).

Finally, questions about how best to operate public personnel systems in an environment where many services traditionally provided by public employees have been shifted to private sector contractors will need to be answered. Contracting out services such as garbage collection, public transportation, security, prisons, and water and sewer systems, and social programs has become a very popular way to try to cut or control costs on all levels of government. However, the impacts of extensive "privatization" on long-term cost-efficiency, government performance, and citizens' quality of life have not been systematically evaluated.

DISCUSSION QUESTIONS

1. Can we really trust public managers to conduct agency personnel matters according to the merit principle without close supervision and enforcement by an outside agency, such as a civil service commission?

2. Is patronage necessary to ensure that the bureaucracy will be responsive to the elected leadership and, if some is needed, how much?

3. Can the merit principle be protected if public employee unions are allowed to negotiate personnel policies and procedures with management?

REFERENCES

Aronson, Albert H. (1973). "Personnel Administration: The State and Local Picture." *Civil Service Journal,* Vol. 13, No. 3 (January–March), pp. 37–42.

Ban, Carolyn (1984). "Implementing Civil Service Reform: Structure and Strategy," in Patricia W. Ingraham and Carolyn Ban (Eds.), *Legislating Bureaucratic Change: The Civil Service Reform Act of 1978* (Albany: State University of New York Press), pp. 42–62.

Barzelay, Michael (1992). *Breaking Through Bureaucracy: A New Vision for Managing in Government* (Berkeley: University of California Press).

Branti v. Finkel (1980). 445 U.S. 507.

Caldwell, Lynton K. (1944). *The Administrative Theories of Hamilton and Jefferson* (Chicago: University of Chicago Press).

Campbell, Alan K. (1978). "Testimony on Civil Service Reform and Organization." *Civil Service Reform, Hearings of the U.S. House Committee on Post Office and Civil Service* (Washington, DC: U.S. Government Printing Office).

Daniel, Christopher (1992). "Constitutionalizing Merit? Practical Implications of Elrod, Branti, and Rutan." *Review of Public Personnel Administration,* Vol. 12, No. 2 (January–April), pp. 26–34.

Dotson, Arch (1955). "The Emerging Doctrine of Privilege in Public Employment." *Public Administration Review,* Vol. 15, No. 2 (Spring), pp. 77–88.

Elliott, Robert H. (Ed.). (1995). "Symposium on Human Resource Management and the Aging of the Workforce." *Review of Public Personnel Administration,* Vol. 15, No. 2 (Spring), pp. 5–83.

Elrod v. Burns (1976). 427 U.S. 347.

Freedman, Anne (1994). *Patronage: An American Tradition* (Chicago: Nelson-Hall).

Fish, Carl R. (1904). *The Civil Service and the Patronage* (Cambridge, MA: Harvard University Press).

Goodsell, Charles (2004). *The Case for Bureaucracy: A Public Administration Polemic,* 3rd edition, (Washington, DC: CQ Press).

Hayes, Steven (1996). "'The State of the Discipline' in Public Personnel Administration." *Public Administration Quarterly,* Vol. 20, No. 3 (Fall), pp. 285–304.

———. (1997). "Reinventing the Personnel Function: Lessons Learned from a Hope-Filled Beginning in One State." *American Review of Public Administration,* Vol. 27, No. 4 (December), pp. 324–342.

Hays, Steven, and Richard Kearney (2001). "Anticipated Changes in Human Resource Management: Views from the Field." *Public Administration Review,* Vol. 61, No. 5 (September/October), pp. 585–597.

Kellough, J. Edward, and Lloyd G. Nigro (2005). "Radical Civil Service Reform: Ideology, Politics, and Policy," in Stephen E. Condrey (Ed.), *Handbook of Human Resource Management in Government,* 2nd ed. (San Francisco: Jossey-Bass), pp. 58–75.

Kettl, Donald F., Patricia W. Ingraham, Ronald P. Sanders, and Constance Horner (1996). *Civil Service Reform: Building a Government that Works* (Washington, DC: Brookings Institution Press).

Levine, Charles H., and Rosslyn S. Kleeman (1986). *The Quiet Crisis of the Civil Service: The Federal Personnel System at the Crossroads* (Washington, DC: National Academy of Public Administration.

McAuliffe v. Mayor of New Bedford (1892). 155 Mass. 216, 29 N. E. 517.

Merrill, Harwood F. (1960). *Classics in Management* (New York: American Management Association).

Miller, Douglas T. (Ed.). (1972). *The Nature of Jacksonian Democracy* (New York: Wiley).

Mosher, Frederick C. (1968). *Democracy and the Public Service* (New York: Oxford University Press).

Naff, Katherine C., and J. Edward Kellough (2003). "Ensuring Employment Equity: Are Federal Diversity Programs Making a Difference?" *International Journal of Public Administration*, Vol. 26, No. 12 (October).

National Commission on the Public Service (1989). *Leadership for America: Rebuilding the Public Service* (Washington, DC: National Commission on the Public Service).

National Research Council (1991). *Pay for Performance: Evaluating Performance Appraisal and Merit Pay* (Washington, DC: National Academy Press).

Peters, B. Guy (2001). *The Future of Governing,* 2nd ed., revised (Lawrence: University Press of Kansas).

Pomerleau, Raymond (1994). "A Desideratum for Managing the Diverse Workforce" *Review of Public Personnel Administration,* Vol. 14, No. 1 (Winter), pp. 85–100.

Riordon, William L. (1963). *Plunkitt of Tammany Hall* (New York: Dutton).

Roethlisberger, Fritz J., and William J. Dickson (1939). *Management and the Worker* (Cambridge, MA: Harvard University Press).

Rosenbloom, David H. (1971). "Some Political Implications of the Drift Toward a Liberation of Federal Employees." *Public Administration Review,* Vol. 31, No. 4 (July–August), pp. 420–426.

Rutan v. Republican Party of Illinois (1990). 497 U.S. 62.

Schiesl, Martin J. (1977). *The Politics of Efficiency* (Berkeley: University of California Press).

Shareef, Reginald (1994). "Skill-Based Pay in the Public Sector: An Innovative Idea." *Review of Public Personnel Administration,* Vol. 14, No. 3 (Summer), pp. 60–74.

Simon, Herbert A., Donald W. Smithburg, and Victor A. Thompson (1950). *Public Administration* (New York: Knopf).

Stahl, O. Glenn (1962). *Public Personnel Administration,* 5th ed. (New York: Harper & Row).

Thompson, Frank J. (Ed.). (1994). "The Winter Commission Report: Is Deregulation the Answer for Public Personnel Management?" *Review of Public Personnel Administration,* Vol. 14, No. 2 (Spring), pp. 5–76.

Thompson, Frank J., and Beryl A. Radin (1997). "Reinventing Public Personnel Management: the Winter and Gore Initiatives," in

Carolyn Ban and Norma M. Riccucci (Eds.), *Public Personnel Management: Current Concerns, Future Challenges* (New York: Longman), pp. 3–20.

U.S. Commission on Civil Rights (1969). *For All the People . . . By All the People: A Report on Equal Opportunity in State and Local Government Employment* (Washington, DC: U.S. Government Printing Office).

U.S. General Accounting Office (1989). *Pay for Performance: Interim Report on the Performance Management and Recognition System* (Washington DC: GAO), May.

———. (1995a). *Transforming the Civil Service: Building the Workforce of the Future* (Washington, DC: GAO/GGD-96–35), December.

———. (1995b). *Federal Personnel Management: Views on Selected NPR Human Resource Recommendations* (Washington, DC: GAO/GGD-95–221BR), September.

U.S. Library of Congress (1976). *History of Civil Service Merit Systems of the United States and Selected Foreign Countries* (Washington, DC: U.S. Government Printing Office), December 31.

Van Riper, Paul P. (1958). *History of the United States Civil Service* (New York: Harper & Row).

Walters, Jonathan (2002). *Life After Civil Service Reform: The Texas, Georgia, and Florida Experiences* (White Plains, NY: IBM).

White, Leonard D. (1948). *The Federalists* (New York: Macmillan).

———. (1951). *The Jeffersonians* (New York: Macmillan).

———. (1954). *The Jacksonians* (New York: Macmillan).

SUGGESTED READINGS

Pfiffner, James P., and Douglas A. Brook (Eds.). (2000) *The Future of Merit.* (Washington, DC: Woodrow Wilson Center Press).

Perry, James L. (1996). *Handbook of Public Administration,* 2nd ed. (San Francisco: Jossey-Bass).

Van Riper, Paul P. (1958). *History of the United States Civil Service* (New York: Harper & Row).

Chapter THREE

Human Resources and Organizational Performance

Public personnel administration in the United States has undergone a pronounced shift in emphasis (Hays, 1989, 2004). _Compliance_ or enforcement of merit system laws and regulations was a central theme of Civil Service Reform I, but enhancing organizational performance and responsiveness has been at the top of Civil Service Reform II's agenda (Jorgensen, Fairless, & Patton, 1996; Moynihan, 2004). This agenda often is set forth in a strategic human resources management (SHRM) framework that advances a greatly expanded role for human resource specialists in the strategic planning and policy implementation processes of public agencies.

The SHRM approach argues that human resources should be fully represented in the policy-making and management group that defines an organization's mission and sets its goals and objectives through a strategic planning process. Strategic planning is a rational analysis process that involves all levels of organizational activity in a systematic evaluation of the existing state of an organization and trends in its external environment given its mission. Strategic planning is designed to establish goals and objectives for the future, to identify the means and resources to be used in achieving them, and to set the criteria that will be used to evaluate outcomes or results (Bryson, 1996). An example of how SHRM is becoming integrated into the strategic planning and implementation methods of public agencies is the impact of the 1993 Government Performance and Results Act (GPRA) on federal personnel and human capital policies.

Intended to improve the efficiency of all federal executive branch agencies, GPRA instructs them to develop "customer focused" strategic plans, to establish concrete missions and goals, to develop mission-driven budgets and management systems, and to measure results to justify appropriations and authorizations. In general terms, GPRA's purpose is to improve public confidence in government's efficiency and effectiveness, force improvements in federal program management, and to improve the quality of the information Congress uses to allocate resources. Since fiscal year 1999, with their budget requests to the Office of Management and Budget (OMB) and to the Congress agencies have been required to submit strategic plans for program activities and annual performance plans covering those activities as set forth in their budgets. After the completion of a fiscal year, the agencies must submit a performance report that covers goal accomplishments relating to the measures defined in their strategic and performance plans.

In recognition of the critical role played by human resources in agency performance, the U.S. Office of Personnel Management established *human capital standards* designed to guide agency human resource policies and practices (U.S. Office of Personnel Management, 2005a):

- The *strategic alignment standard* requires that federal agencies have a human capital strategy that is carefully aligned or coordinated with their missions, goals, and objectives. Human capital strategies should be fully integrated into agency strategic plans, performance plans, and budgets.
- The *workforce planning and deployment standard* requires agencies to be citizen-centered, results-focused, and effective users of e-Government and "competitive sourcing" or contracting out alternatives.
- The *leadership and knowledge management standard* requires agency leadership to implement systems needed to effectively manage people, to ensure continuity of effective leadership, and to establish learning or developmental environments that sustain continuous improvement in performance on all levels.
- The *results-oriented performance culture standard* requires agency leadership to establish human capital policies designed to build a diverse, results-oriented, high-performance workforce. Agencies are required to implement performance management systems that reliably discriminate between high and

low performance and reliably connect performance on the individual, team, and unit levels to organizational goals and objectives.

- The *talent standard* requires agencies to take those steps needed to close any gaps between existing workforce skills, knowledge, and competencies and those required to achieve their goals and to meet performance standards. In other words, they are expected to implement human resource development plans and programs that address existing and anticipated needs.

- The *accountability standard* requires that federal agencies demonstrate that their human capital decisions and practices are informed by results-oriented planning and accountability systems.

A good example of an application of the Office of Personnel Management (OPM) standards in the context of an agency's strategic plan is the Environmental Protection Agency's (EPA) human capital strategy. In the *Human Capital* section of its *2003–2008 Strategic Plan,* the EPA states,

> Protecting human health and the environment requires a diverse, highly skilled, and motivated workforce that seeks creative solutions to environmental problems and is committed to achieving excellence.
>
> . . . Our updated human capital strategy will help us integrate workforce planning, employee development, and targeted recruitment with our ongoing strategic planning and resource management processes. (U.S. Environmental Planning Agency, 2003, p. 146)

EPA's human capital strategy is designed to meet the OPM standards through initiatives that fall into several categories.

The first of these categories is *strategic workforce planning and deployment.* The EPA has identified some 20 occupational categories with unique skills and competencies to help it align mission-critical work with the skills of its workforce. Its workforce planning system is intended to "enable line managers to make decisions on deploying employees with mission-critical skills and competencies both programmatically and geographically to fulfill EPA's mission" (p. 148). The EPA's plan goes beyond numbers of employees and their skills to include opportunities to increase efficiency by outsourcing (contracting out) as well as internal improvements in organizational technologies and management systems. The EPA reports ongoing experiments or innovations in human capital management that include the following:

- An *assignments, not positions program* that offers voluntary rotations where employees are encouraged to "swap jobs and learn about technical programs outside their immediate areas of expertise (p. 148)."
- A *senior executive service mobility program* designed to match talents with organizational needs and to strengthen leadership skills and familiarity with programs throughout the EPA.
- A *PeoplePlus* information system that improves access to personnel data for career planning and human resource management purposes. This system allows employee access to their personnel records for purposes of updating information on emergency contacts and other business-related information, an *E-Development* resource that allows web-based access to training information and training opportunities, and a *manager's desktop* that gives supervisors and managers access to workforce information to facilitate organizational decision-making.
- *E-Government* activities undertaken by the EPA include consolidated electronic payroll systems, integrated personnel records information systems, and *Recruitment One-Stop* that incorporates automated resume assessment and routing tools and allows real time information on the status of job applications (p. 149).

The second category is *managing leadership and knowledge*. The EPA is building human resource systems intended to retain essential leadership and knowledge capabilities as managers and employees with mission-critical skills retire or otherwise leave the agency. In this area, the EPA is using several approaches:

- It uses a *workforce development strategy* that includes a variety of programs focused on the EPA's core competencies and required executive core qualifications. These programs include classroom training, mentoring, coaching, and rotational assignments.
- The EPA also has a *candidate development program* intended to prepare managers for promotion to Senior Executive Service (SES)—positions as high-level executives become eligible for retirement.
- Its *performance management system* is also designed to promote workforce development by providing "regular performance feedback to employees and helps them understand how their work aligns with the Agency's mission" (p. 150).

■ The Agency is also using a "360-degree feedback program that enables employees and peers to provide feedback on managers' performance" (p. 150)

The third category is *developing a performance culture*. EPA's efforts to build a results-oriented workforce and organizational culture that values performance include a redesigned performance management system (PERFORMS), diversity initiatives, and fostering collaborative relationships with employee unions.

> PERFORMS stresses clear and timely communication about performance expectations and outcomes across all levels of the agency. It separates cash awards from performance ratings "so that feedback and rewards occur not just at appraisal time, but throughout the year to highlight and reinforce excellence in a timely manner" (p. 151). A mix of monetary and non-monetary incentives is available to motivate and recognize high performance on the individual, team, and organizational levels.
>
> EPA's diversity initiatives include education programs for employees on diversity issues, promoting ongoing dialogue about a broad range of diversity issues, and targeted recruitment to identify well-qualified candidates for critical positions.
>
> In the area of labor relations, EPA seeks to foster "collaborative relationships between Agency managers, unions, and employees to improve working conditions, career development, and employee morale" (p. 151). It has established a *Workforce Solutions Staff* that provides employees with a range of services for preventing and resolving workplace conflicts that includes informal mediation, and alternative dispute resolution (ADR). The *workforce solutions staff* helps employees to resolve disputes before they result in formal grievances and complaints, and a database has been created to track the status of labor-management relations with regard to agreements, decisions, and disputes. (p. 151)

The fourth is *recruiting and retaining talent*. The EPA has responded to the increasing pace of retirements and competitive labor market with a human capital strategy that emphasizes recruitment and retention of highly qualified people who will be ready and able to fill existing or anticipated gaps in mission-critical skills and competencies.

> The agency is using special hiring authorities, incentives, and internship and fellowship programs to attract and retain researchers and scientists. It is evaluating a pilot program under which it would be able "to offer the competitive salaries needed to attract and retain world-class scientists and researchers." (p. 152).
>
> EPA's recruitment and retention strategy also calls for extensive use of flexible organizational structures, collaborative work systems and

multiskilled teams, and family-friendly work environments. In addition, EPA is exploring phased retirement for those in critical hard-to-fill positions, voluntary separation incentives, and early retirement authority: "These tools provide more flexibility than do those offered under current regulations, and they may aid in reshaping the workforce when an organization's mix is no longer optimal for carrying out the Agency's mission" (p. 152).

Finally, EPA has established a *human resources management accountability program* intended to ensure that its human capital strategies and policies are understood and implemented on all levels. In accord with OPM's human capital standard in this area, this program is designed to collect and analyze data needed to determine if human capital goals and objectives are being accomplished. The program is designed to allow data-based evaluations of (1) organizational compliance with merit principles, (2) human resource's contributions to organizational effectiveness, (3) the extent to which human resources management is achieving its goals and objectives, and (4) strengths and weaknesses of human resource programs (p. 153).

GPRA, OPM's human capital standards, and EPA's strategic plan combine to illustrate how SHRM involves a dramatic shift to a management-centered concept of personnel administration within the framework of Civil Service Reform II. The federal government may be the most comprehensive example, but many state and local governments are re-orienting their personnel systems toward SHRM and outcomes-oriented evaluation criteria (Condrey, 2002; Hays, 2004). In the balance of this chapter, we will discuss a variety of ways public personnel can make positive contributions to managerial and organizational performance. Two broad areas of organizational activity in the human capital area will be examined: (1) attracting human resources that are required to meet current and anticipated organizational needs; and (2) motivating, developing, and retaining a workforce that possesses the required knowledge, skills, and abilities (KSAs). As the OPM standards and the EPA's human capital plan suggest, success in both areas is essential.

Three strategies for obtaining reliable access to human resources are *competition, cooperation,* and *incorporation* (Yuchtman & Seashore, 1967). Each of these strategies is a response to the interface between an organization's human capital requirements and the kind of labor markets it faces. Often, the overall human capital strategy of a public agency will contain a more or less complex mix of competition, cooperation, and incorporation.

THE COMPETITIVE STRATEGY

Competitive approaches stress acquiring human resources by doing better than other organizations in the relevant labor markets. Several areas of organizational performance are involved. First, as an employer, the organization must be able to offer attractive pay and benefits, as well as a psychologically supportive and physically safe working environment. Second, it is important to maintain the organization's prestige as a place to work. Positions in high-prestige agencies often attract qualified people who could make the same or more money in less prominent jobs. Third, the organization should have the internal flexibility needed to make timely adjustments to conditions in the labor market. The capacity to align recruitment processes, hiring procedures, compensation plans, and job designs with the *available* pool of human resources is a great advantage. For public employers, these are more often than not very difficult objectives to meet.

Competitive strategies do not mesh easily with the dominant values and practices of the traditional regulation-oriented merit systems. The current wave of change and innovation (Civil Service Reform II) illustrated by the OPM standards and the EPA human capital strategy has increased agency flexibility in areas such as position classification and selection, and it has strengthened line management's hand in pay administration in some states and localities as well as the federal government (Barrett & Greene, 2005). This discretion is far from unlimited.

In the public sector, important political and legal considerations set limits on the degree to which competitive advantage can be the sole rationale driving personnel policies and practices. Equal employment opportunity policies, classification systems, and legislatively mandated pay and compensation systems, for example, may require recruitment, selection, and hiring procedures that limit management's flexibility and, hence, its capacity to act quickly and conclusively in situations where private corporations and nonprofit agencies are competing for the same people.

Public personnel systems are expected to pursue multiple and, at times, conflicting goals. Unlike their private counterparts, public employers routinely are subject to constant scrutiny by an audience made up of many groups intensely interested in one or more phases of personnel administration from recruitment to retirement. These stakeholders, including, to name just a few, veterans, minorities, private contractors, and public employee unions, may resist policies intended to increase competitiveness because they see them as threatening other values such as pay equity, equal opportunity, political neutrality, and the "free market."

For broad public interest and more narrow partisan reasons, legislators and elected executives are seldom eager to relinquish control over key aspects of personnel policy (Wechsler, 1994). For example, the process leading to the creation of the U.S. Department of Homeland Security (DHS) included a major conflict in the U.S. Senate between the George W. Bush administration and interests representing public employee unions. The Bush administration argued that the new department required a level of human resource flexibility not possible under the federal labor relations statute, and eventually it succeeded in having DHS workers exempted from its coverage (Moynihan, 2005; Woodard, 2005). It is highly unlikely that the competitive strategies used by public employers can ever be as narrowly bottom line oriented as those of many businesses. This is not to imply that public employers cannot compete effectively with the private sector for human resources under any conditions. It does mean, as the EPA's human capital strategy suggests, that they have to be very persistent, as well as creative (U.S. General Accounting Office, 2002).

Pay, benefits, working conditions, and career opportunities are key elements of a public agency's competitive position. In the long term, the attractiveness of the pay and benefits offered by public employers will vary in relation to economic conditions. A slow or recessionary economy usually makes it easier to attract and retain high-quality employees because jobs are hard find. During periods of expansion, when profits are high and good jobs are plentiful, public sector recruitment suffers and highly mobile employees are more likely to leave (turnover) for better paying jobs in the private sector.

Historically, legislatively set pay schedules and benefits have tended to adjust slowly and often inadequately to changes in the labor market, but blanket statements about governments' competitiveness are difficult to make. On one hand, for some categories of scientists, professionals, and technicians, comparatively low salaries have made the public sector an unattractive place to work. On the other, for many jobs, public employers consistently have been able to offer prevailing rates of pay and relatively good benefits (such as health insurance, retirement plans, and job security).

Public employers mainly rely on legislative appropriations and executive support for the money needed to compete, but widespread public opposition to increasing taxes to fund pay raises means that politicians' backing often is not forthcoming. Governments, in other words, have been told to substantially increase the productivity of public employees, rather than asking for larger budgets to cover growing citizen demand for services. In turn, heavy pressure has been put on public personnel systems to use available funds and employees to maximum effect, rather than depending on general increases to keep pace.

Pay increases and enhanced benefit plans traditionally have been implemented across-the-board without much attention being paid to whether or not they were needed to maintain or build an agency's ability to compete effectively for specific categories of employees. At best, in competitive terms, they have been blunt instruments. For example, for some skills, an across-the-board increase will not be sufficient to keep the agency competitive in a particular location or region, but in another place the salary or wage actually will be higher than required. The same situation can apply to benefits. Reductions in personnel budgets, wage and salary freezes, and other cutbacks typically have been insensitive to competitiveness issues. Increasingly, public employers have turned to reforms such as locality pay, pension portability, and pay-for-performance plans in an effort to create the flexibility needed support a competitive approach to recruitment and retention.

Government's ability to attract and retain qualified personnel has been impaired by fiscal stress, but another important factor may be the low status or prestige of public employment in the United States. Attitudes about government work and beliefs about career opportunities are significant contributors to the competitiveness of the public sector. The problems created by negative attitudes toward the public service are not restricted to the impact on those considering where to work; relations with influential actors in the organization's environment are affected as well. A vicious circle develops. Politicians, civic leaders, corporate executives, clientele groups, and voters may be hostile or at best noncommittal about the talent, commitment, and responsiveness of civil servants. Financial resources and political support are withheld, and the competitiveness of public employers is further reduced. In the long run, the quality of the public service actually declines, attitudes about it become more negative, and levels of support drop even more. One of the elements of Civil Service Reform II, therefore, has been an effort to improve the public's image of the competence, integrity, and responsiveness of the civil service.

Along these lines, Alan K. Campbell, the first director of OPM, stated that one of the purposes of the Civil Service Reform Act (CSRA) was to improve the reputation of the federal civil service. More recently, the *Report of the National Performance Review* (1993) asserted, "Today's crisis is [that] people simply feel that government doesn't work" and "the central issue we face is not *what* government does, but *how* it works" (p. 2). In the section on cutting red tape and decentralizing personnel policy, the *Report* said,

> To create an effective federal government, we must reform virtually the entire personnel system: recruiting, hiring, classification, promotion, pay, and reward systems. We must make it easier for federal managers to hire the workers they need, to reward those who do good work, and to fire those who do not. (NPR, p. 22)

The NPR argued that adaptiveness and flexibility are often keys to competitive success. Accepting the Volcker Commission's conclusion, "The complexity of the hiring process often drives all but the most dedicated away," the NPR recommended that all departments and agencies be given "authority to conduct their own recruiting and examining for all positions, and abolish all central registers and standard application forms" (pp. 22–23). The reasoning was that to be competitive, federal agencies such as the EPA must be able to respond to the conditions they face in an effective and timely manner, and deregulation and decentralization make it much easier for agencies to do so. They now are able to seek and secure delegation agreements with OPM that permit extensive authority related to staffing functions (U.S. Office of Personnel Management, 2005b).

Even if they are able to offer competitive pay and benefits, and have a reasonably good public image, public agencies may have difficulty locating and attracting enough candidates having skills and other qualities that are in high demand. Supply may not meet demand and, although it normally will adjust to demand over time, in the relatively short term, there may be serious shortfalls in specific skills categories. This kind of situation is caused by a number of factors, including limited capacities of sources such as universities and technical schools, long training or apprenticeship periods, policies of regulatory or licensing bodies, demographic trends, and social biases for and against certain kinds of work.

Eventually, the labor market probably will respond, but matching supply to demand may take several years or more and, as school teachers, aerospace engineers, and other working in fields requiring extensive education and experience can testify, maintaining such a balance is not easy. In contrast, the unskilled and semiskilled component of the labor market responds rather quickly because these workers do not need a great deal of education, training, or experience. As we have already noted, however, the public sector is becoming increasingly professionalized, and its skill requirements are constantly rising. Consequently, a passive approach that fails to monitor organizational needs and to anticipate labor market conditions leaves the public employer open to a performance-threatening situation: the chronic inability to recruit and retain persons for certain key high-skill positions.

One way to improve the match between agency needs and available workers is to make adjustments in internal task structures and technologies. Here, personnel specialists are in a position to make important contributions to human resources planning capacities of public agencies (Ospina, 1992). It is often possible to redesign jobs and to restructure relationships among jobs in ways that improve an organization's capacity to make better use of those human resources available to it. Sometimes, positions can be simplified or broken down into several less complex sets of tasks, whereas others can be enlarged or "enriched" to take better advantage of employees' abilities and potential. Para-professionals may be used to reduce the numbers of highly trained, expensive, and scarce professionals such as doctors, registered nurses, lawyers, and engineers that an agency might need. With paraprofessional support, professional personnel may be used differently and more efficiently. Mechanized, automated, or computerized systems can be installed to replace or supplement human resources in ways that reduce labor costs, lower or redistribute skills requirements, and increase overall productivity. Minimum position requirements and job progression may be altered to accommodate post-entry upgrading and retraining; similarly, on-the-job training or educational opportunities can be provided to make it possible to fill positions through promotions and transfers.

Public personnel systems have long had the reputation of being unimaginative human resources planners, of legalistic rigidity in their approaches to job design and position classification, and of an inclination to assume that the labor market will respond readily to staffing needs. To the extent to which this reputation is deserved, it signals a serious competitive disability, an organizational weakness that is most evident when human resources are limited or a sellers' market exists. There is, of course, no reason why public employers must be internally inflexible or passive in the face of stiff competition and an other-than-perfect balance between supply and demand in the labor market.

ADMINISTRATIVE DESIGNS AND HUMAN CAPITAL

As described in Chapter 2, traditional merit systems on all levels of government relied on administrative arrangements that stress micromanagement of the personnel function by a central authority and standardization of practices across governmental units or departments.

Centralization of policy, rule-making, and decision-making authority had its roots in two main goals of Civil Service Reform I: limiting management's influence over personnel matters and establishing neutral competence as the normative core of public personnel practices. Although these administrative arrangements may have been somewhat effective in keeping the rascals out and seeing to it that the merit principle was insulated from the threat posed by managerial discretion, they were notoriously rigid and insensitive to changing environmental conditions and organizational mandates.

Complex and changeful environments often place the stability-oriented administrative designs of traditional merit systems at a competitive disadvantage. Today's approaches to managing relationships between organizations and their environments emphasize strategic planning processes that recognize and address the full range of human capital issues. In other words, from a competitive standpoint, an administrative structure for human resources management should be a strategic response to a specific set of organizational and environmental conditions. Organizations dealing with dynamic, diverse, and highly competitive conditions tend to rely heavily on decentralized decision making within broad policy guidelines, and they stress managerial flexibility and discretion on the operational levels. One structural option is to have a central personnel office for overall policy-making, evaluation, and audit purposes, but to delegate day-to-day personnel operations to agency offices having extensive authority to develop policies and methods best suited to handling the competitive challenges presented by local conditions. Another is to decentralize authority for human resource policy making and management to the department or agency level within a statutory framework that establishes general principles to be followed (Light, 2003).

THE COOPERATIVE STRATEGY

Like competition, cooperation is a strategy designed to maintain organizational access to essential human resources. Basically, cooperation involves entering into mutually beneficial agreements with other organizations and resource-controlling actors in the environment. These arrangements may be bilateral or multilateral, and more or less formal, but in any case, they involve commitments intended to reduce levels of uncertainty and risk faced by all of those involved. Unlike competition, which usually results in winners and losers, cooperative strategies focus on building or negotiating relationships that benefit *all* of the participants. We will focus here on three common forms of cooperation directly related to public personnel policy and administration. These are intergovernmental joint ventures, contracts with businesses and not-for-profit suppliers of goods and services, and negotiated labor agreements with public employee unions.

JOINT VENTURES

Public agencies may be able to address certain human resources problems by agreeing to pool or share their personnel, as well as other organizational capacities under specified conditions. In addition to increasing organizational effectiveness by allowing these agencies to increase their quantitative and qualitative ability to handle problems, such as natural disasters, these negotiated arrangements may also lower the personnel costs of each participant. Multigovernment cooperative recruitment, testing, and placement services are feasible. Other types of intergovernmental cooperation include joint ventures to provide training for law enforcement personnel and agreements whereby police and fire departments use one another's personnel under specified conditions. In the training field, it has been possible for some state and local workers to attend federal training sessions that deal with problems or policy issues requiring intergovernmental action, such as those offered by the Federal Bureau of Investigation, the U.S. Internal Revenue Service, and the Federal Executive Institute (FEI). User-funded statewide or multistate regional training centers for police and fire fighters provide services well beyond the individual capacities of the employers who send their personnel to these centers for basic or advanced training.

Direct sharing of personnel is possible under agreements negotiated between jurisdictions on the same or different levels of government. Cities may agree to share police and fire personnel under emergency, disaster, or other special conditions. Costs are shared and the participating jurisdictions usually retain recall rights, but emphasis is placed on recognizing interdependency and dealing with it through mutual support rather than on very expensive, perhaps futile, efforts to become self-sufficient. Within governmental units, interagency joint ventures are also feasible, an interesting example being the cross-training of workers in two or more organizations (for example, police and fire departments) so that they are able to back each other up and, if need be, move from one job to another in response to shifting work loads.

Governments also contract with each other for services in functional areas such as law enforcement, fire protection, sanitation, streets and roads, and administration. Under these intergovernmental contracts, one government undertakes to provide services to another for a fee. For example, counties often sell police services to incorporated municipalities. Other services commonly contracted for by municipalities are water supply, sewage treatment, tax collections, and libraries.

Intergovernmental contracting is used by smaller jurisdictions because it is usually less expensive than building an in-house capacity to deliver a full range of services. It gives the user immediate access to established personnel systems, equipment, and skills of the supplier. Intergovernmental contracting appears to reduce operating costs to smaller communities, mainly because of the economies of scale enjoyed by large suppliers. The contract allows the provider to sell unused or underutilized capacity, and to generate a profit that can be used to support and expand operations. Thus, in economic terms, the intergovernmental contract becomes a winning proposition for both parties.

CONTRACTING WITH PRIVATE CORPORATIONS AND NONPROFITS

Privatization is currently a popular option for the public sector, and governments on all levels are scrutinizing their operations to determine which might be more productively handled by outside contractors. Although contracting out for goods and services is far from unusual in the United States, as noted in Chapter 2, fiscal stress and changing philosophies of government have generated considerable interest in and agitation for extending its scope to services ordinarily provided by public employees. Thus, parks and recreation, building inspection and maintenance, sanitation, fire and police services, prisons, and even general administration are among the many functions now considered reasonable possibilities for contracting out.

Although competition among rival profit-oriented contractors is supposed to lower costs to the taxpayer, contracting creates a cooperative relationship between supplier and consumer because they agree to help each other through an exchange. The same may be said for contractual arrangements with non-profit organizations to deliver social and health services, such as child care, shelters, and medical clinics. An interesting cooperative approach to developing the large numbers of military officers needed during wartime, and cold war, is the Reserve Officer Training Corps (ROTC) through which the Department of Defense taps into the capacities of civilian universities and colleges while providing funding to these institutions. In organization theorist James D. Thompson's words, contracting involves the negotiation of "an agreement for the exchange of performances in the future" (Thompson, 1967, pp. 34–36). Contracting, of course, is not cost-free in human resources terms; it is an alternative to the direct delivery of services, not a device for eliminating administrative oversight responsibilities, and contracts must be negotiated and administered by people with expertise in these areas.

From a human resources management point of view, contracting out is potentially attractive for several reasons. First, under certain conditions, primarily the existence of active and genuine competition among alternative suppliers, it can lower the per-unit cost of public services. Second, contracting out increases administrative flexibility. Rather than build expensive in-house capabilities involving long-term investments or sunk costs, public agencies can rent the human and other resources of the contractor. This advantage is particularly important when public agencies are asked to carry out programs or to assume responsibilities requiring skills and technologies not readily available on an in-house basis, or when an activity is of a temporary nature. State departments of transportation (DOTs) provide a good illustration of this point. DOTs contract out the actual construction of new highways to private businesses, which hire the needed personnel and provide the necessary equipment. When the highway is finished, the DOT and contractor part company unless they have negotiated another contract for maintenance services. The DOTs themselves focus on continuing activities such as project design and specifications, contract negotiation and administration, and fiscal management. Another interesting (and controversial) example is the federal government's use of private contractors to operate its nuclear weapons production facilities.

With contracting, programs can be terminated, re-oriented, or downsized without the need to go through the demoralizing, costly, and protracted reductions-in-force (RIF) procedures that are typical of merit systems. The contractor takes on these risks and uncertainties. Also, in situations where private enterprises or not-for-profits are able to offer compensation packages superior to those available to public employers, it may be possible to use contracting to tap "expensive" human resources by avoiding personnel ceilings, inadequate wage and salary scales, and cumbersome staffing procedures. Finally, by shifting responsibility for day-to-day management to the contractor, governments may improve their ability to reduce or at least to slow the growth of administrative overhead costs; it may also be possible to escape having to add supervisory personnel as new programs are acquired or existing ones expanded.

The third category of reasons for contracting out is political factors. As the U.S. Department of Defense (DOD) amply illustrates, an extensive web of contractual relationships provides the foundation for a powerful political coalition. Private corporations and labor unions often come to rely heavily on the money and jobs they get through government contracts; they develop a vested interest in the political and budgetary health of public agencies such as the DOD. From an agency point of view, the active support of concerned (self-interested) contractors and other clientele groups is vitally important when budgets have to be defended against proposed cuts and when efforts are being made to expand or add new programs.

A related symbolic value of contracting is to deflect criticism that governments are overgrown, inefficient, and encroaching on the proper domain of private enterprise. Public attention is easily drawn to the size of the civil service, so significant expansion is more than likely to produce attacks from those fearing tax increases, "creeping socialism," or "big government." In very practical terms, although contracting does not necessarily mean smaller budgets or even higher productivity in the long run, it is a way of acquiring the use of facilities and human resources without the political risks associated with having to request more money for more bureaucrats.

NEGOTIATED LABOR AGREEMENTS

Although public attention is usually drawn to the adversarial side of labor-management relations, particularly strikes and other job actions in the public sector, collective bargaining is a process intended to provide a framework for long-term cooperation between employers and unions (see Chapter 7). A negotiated labor contract is a legally binding document detailing the terms and conditions under which management and the employee organization or union will jointly administer key elements of the personnel system. This contract also specifies how each side will supply the other with some of the inputs needed to operate effectively, and it sets up mechanisms for resolving disputes between the parties that arise in the process of administering the contract.

Management typically agrees to pay clearly stipulated wages and salaries, to provide fringe benefits such as health care and pensions plans, and to maintain safe working conditions. Management may also reduce uncertainty for the union by agreeing to various forms of so-called union security (for example, dues checkoff and an agency or union shop). The union, on the other hand agrees to deliver human resources and to participate in the good faith administration and enforcement of the rules of the workplace as set forth in the contract. Finally, and this is critical from an organizational point of view, the union agrees to follow contractually established appeals procedures for resolving conflicts between management and workers. In effect, the union and the employer become partners in an effort to minimize the possibility that the workplace will be disrupted or productivity reduced by unresolved conflicts.

Collective bargaining is way of identifying, formulating, and implementing cooperative solutions to problems presented by the interdependence of management and labor organizations (Walton & McKersie, 1965, p. 3). Where employee organizations or unions are forces in their environments, public employers must be equipped to deal with them effectively; in most cases, this means being able to work out mutually beneficial relationships. So-called win-lose con-frontations resulting in job actions, strikes, court sanctions, firings, and the like are almost inevitably very costly to both sides. Therefore, considerable attention is now paid to the development of effective labor relations programs in government. Labor relations offices have been created by many jurisdictions to provide the expertise necessary to organize and carry out negotiations and to assist line management in the administration of contracts.

THE INCORPORATION STRATEGY

Competition and cooperation strategies will work if an organization's environment can reliably generate the needed human resources. If an agency faces an economy or labor market that is unpredictable or is chronically incapable of supplying appropriately trained and educated people in sufficient numbers, creating an *internal* source may be the more appropriate strategy. What this approach does is reduce or elim-inate uncertainty by expanding or restructuring the organization to establish direct administrative control over the supplier.

In a country like the United States, with its vast system of edu-cation and training, public as well as private employers find it possible to obtain many of the skills and other human capabilities they need from sources outside the organization. Most also need to supplement or complement external sources with internal training and develop-ment programs that often fall under the personnel or human resources department. Even highly educated and trained recruits are likely to need on-the-job-training (OJT) in specific techniques and organiza-tional practices. On a more basic skills level, it is now commonplace to hear complaints from managers in both sectors about the system of public education's failure to reliably graduate students who are able to read, write, and compute at levels required by today's increasingly complex organizational processes and technologies.

In some cases, the response has been to establish classes within organizations where employees receive education and training in the basic skills they need. On a much more advanced level, the employer or government may have to create its own system of higher education because no functional equivalent exists outside the organization. For example, because there is little or no capacity to train qualified career military officers outside of government in the United States, the military academies were established to perform that function, starting with West Point in the early 19th century. This is an incorporation, or build-your-own-capacity, strategy. Police and fire training academies are another example of the incorporation strategy in practice.

On the federal level, good illustrations of the incorporation strategy may be found in the field of civilian training and development. The FEI, an OPM facility, offers broad-gauged administrative training for high-ranking executives. Established in 1968, the FEI was designed to fill what was seen to be a serious gap in the federal system for developing senior career executives. It caps an extensive training and career development systems that gives the federal government a valuable internal complement to external suppliers. Because the system is financed, staffed, and administered by OPM and the federal agencies, the content and methods of training can be closely controlled and designed to meet specific needs. These internal resources reduce uncertainty by improving the probability that federal agencies will have reliable access to a steady stream of qualified managers and executives (U.S. Office of Personnel Management, 2005c).

During the past 50 years, government in the United States has grown in response to public demands for new and expanded services. Where governmental effectiveness is crucial and a capacity to perform services such as police, fire, air traffic control, national defense, and public health is essential, long-term investments in an internal capacity to train and develop the required human resources may be justified. Incorporation initiatives are seldom without controversy because they are, in effect, extensions of government. Although the issue of *what* services government will or should provide is always on the political agenda of a democracy, but as an organizational function, public personnel administration is more directly concerned with *how* effectively and efficiently to acquire and use the human resources needed to deliver public services. Seen in this context, incorporation is simply one of several approaches available to public policy makers.

MANAGING WORK FORCE PERFORMANCE

At least potentially, human resources specialists are in a position to help create working conditions and to design incentives or performance management systems that encourage workers to make the many technical and behavioral contributions that public agencies need to be effective. Personnel policies and practices should promote the following:

- Low absenteeism, or regular attendance and participation in organizational tasks and activities by members, by creating working conditions that lead to high levels of job satisfaction.
- Low turnover of high-skill and other difficult to replace employees by establishing material and nonmaterial rewards that induce people and their valuable skills, knowledge, and experience to stay with the organization.
- Reliably good performance by workers of the technical and social requirements of their positions or jobs.
- A workforce that is consistently willing to carry out more than formal job or position requirements by actively cooperating with others, by helping to advance the organization's interests, by developing innovative ways to solve problems, and by working to keep skills current and to acquire new abilities. (Katz & Kahn, 1978, p. 403)

Achieving and sustaining these behavioral patterns is difficult, and this effort requires the design and administration of mutually beneficial *transactions* or exchanges between an organization and its workers.

HUMAN RESOURCES AND THE INDUCEMENTS-CONTRIBUTIONS TRANSACTION

The term "inducements-contributions transaction" is used to describe an ongoing exchange of values between all organizations and their members (Simon, 1965, pp. 110–122). The terms "inducement" and "incentive" often are used interchangeably in this context. In organization theorist William G. Scott's words, the term "'incentive' is applicable to any inducement, material or nonmaterial, which impels, encourages, or forces a person to perform a task to accomplish a goal" (Scott, 1967, pp. 284–285). A major question facing management, therefore, is which incentives available to the organization will influence employees to make those contributions it needs to perform effectively and efficiently.

From a management point of view, creating a successful set of transactions with employees requires an understanding of what inducements will meet their needs and expectations. Research on the connections between technological, social, and psychological factors in the workplace and such contributions-related variables as morale, job satisfaction, and productivity has generated a very complicated and incomplete picture.

Simplistic and overgeneralized assumptions about human nature and how it relates to organizational needs have been largely discredited, but they have not been replaced by any broadly accepted and empirically confirmed alternatives. The near term will not bring anything resembling a set of principles that tells public managers how to design and run a universally effective system of organizational inducements or incentives. This does not mean that progress has not been made. Today's public managers are as a group far more likely to be sensitive to the social and psychological dimensions of motivation than earlier generations that relied almost exclusively on formal command systems and economic incentives.

Another problem has to do with the assumptions about the human resources management function that are associated with bureaucracies. Modern ideas about motivation in organizations stress gearing incentives to specific conditions and to the social-psychological traits of small groups and individuals. However, bureaucracies are designed to handle people in large groups or categories and to deal with them in largely depersonalized and formalized ways. Centralization and standardization, hallmarks of the "Weberian Bureaucracy," have been typical of the approaches taken to managing incentives by public personnel systems, which function largely in bureaucratic settings (Bendix, 1962, pp. 423–431). In practice, line managers and supervisors have had little control over the design and day-to-day administration of incentives plans. Not surprisingly, much of the current argument for management-centered personnel systems hinges on the proposition that meaningful increases in productivity will come only when supervisors have the capacity to *manage* performance by tailoring incentives and their administration to the conditions and people they must deal with.

Extrinsic and Intrinsic Incentives

It is traditional to divide the list of incentives potentially available to organizations into two general categories: extrinsic and intrinsic. Extrinsic incentives are material and psychological rewards that are external to the job itself. Pay, working conditions, and fringe benefits are examples of *material* extrinsic rewards. Promotions, professional honors, and commendations are *nonmaterial* extrinsic rewards that may function as incentives. Most organizations rely primarily on material extrinsic inducements.

Intrinsic incentives, on the other hand, are the psychological rewards to the individual that flow from doing the work itself. Persons, in other words, are *intrinsically* motivated if they do something because they derive feelings of competence, personal worth, self-determination, solidarity with co-workers, or simple happiness. Here, the available evidence strongly suggests much of the effort people put into their jobs is related to how interesting, challenging, and personally meaningful they are. Varied activities, influence over how work is done, autonomy, or self-direction are also important needs for many employees (Vasu, Stewart, & Garson, 1990, pp. 47–56). People differ in the degree to which they have these needs, but the overall pattern is for job satisfaction to be higher for jobs that offer these kinds of intrinsic rewards.

Job content, operating technologies, and working relationships are at least potentially sources of important organizational inducements. Public managers and personnel specialists should pay close attention to the social-psychological implications of how jobs are designed and interrelated, and the impact of supervisory styles and group dynamics on employee attitudes and behavior. In both cases, it may be possible to create conditions under which people are more likely to be more productive and committed than they would be if management limited its attention and efforts to external material and nonmaterial incentives.

MEMBERSHIP-BASED AND INDIVIDUALIZED INCENTIVES

Extrinsic as well as intrinsic incentives may be divided into two types, depending on how they are administered. Under one approach, the organizational choice is to tie incentives to membership in functional units, job classifications, hierarchical levels, or some other grouping of employees. Satisfactory performance means that employees may keep their membership in the group and, in turn, will receive the same rewards as all other members. For purposes of connecting inducements to contributions, or rewards to performance, organizational attention is focused on identifying those who have met a standard of *acceptable* performance. Historically in the public sector, for example, those with "satisfactory" annual performance ratings would receive the same percentage pay raises.

In contrast, another way of structuring inducements-contributions transactions is to tie rewards *directly* to an individual worker's job performance or output. Rewards such as pay increases, bonuses, promotions, and honors are allocated on the basis of differences in productivity among individuals. For example, each person in a work group or job category (such as a secretarial pool or nursing staff) is paid according to his or her scores on certain measures of performance. Membership-based systems are still the dominant type in the public sector, but currently there is widespread sentiment to the effect that at best they encourage mediocre performance while offering no positive incentive to do work that is above average or superior in quantity and quality.

Membership-based inducements have not been found to be particularly successful devices for promoting above-average performance by *individuals*. However, employers may be able to achieve high levels of *overall* productivity by setting high standards for achieving and maintaining membership in a work group, organization, or job category. There is also evidence to suggest that under certain conditions "gainsharing" or group-based performance rewards can raise productivity and increase job satisfaction (Miami-Dade County, 2005). Since organizations are seldom merely collections of competing individuals, relying instead on high-quality performance by interdependent groups, membership-based inducements may be the most appropriate (Gilbert & Nelson, 1989; Siegel, 1994).

Nonetheless, overlaying membership-based with individualized incentives now has a great deal of support in the public sector. Although most of the attention has been focused on "pay-for-performance" or "merit pay" systems, other individualized inducements are available (See Chapter 6), including time off, educational opportunities or sabbaticals, payment for unused sick leave, honors and commendations, and cash awards for cost-saving suggestions. In the merit pay area, there has been renewed interest in using within-grade salary increases as rewards for better-than-average to superior performance instead of the common practice of giving these increases to workers who achieve "satisfactory" ratings. The federal government, many localities, and about half the states are using some form of merit pay, pay-for-performance, or bonus system, although evidence suggests that the impact of these systems is quite limited (Selden, Ingraham, & Jocobson, 2001, pp. 604–605; U.S. General Accounting Office, 2003).

STRUCTURING THE RELATIONSHIP BETWEEN INDUCEMENTS AND CONTRIBUTIONS

Despite the saying, "a happy employee is a productive employee," there is little evidence to suggest that simply meeting the material, social, and psychological needs of people will somehow make them work harder or be more productive. Actually, a large body of research on job satisfaction does not support the idea that job satisfaction *causes* greater effort or better performance. There is, in fact, no logical reason why it should. As Scott and Mitchell (1976) put it:

> There is no reason to believe that liking the job will prompt one to higher levels of effort. People are attracted to jobs for various reasons (the work conditions, the friendships, the supervision, and so on). They may find that all of these things can be obtained without extra effort, and indeed, this is the case in many organizations. It is true that some rewards may be lost such as a bonus or a promotion, but in many cases these incentives are not of utmost importance. The other incentives are typically not related to effort, and it should not be surprising, therefore, that overall job satisfaction is only slightly related to output. (p. 159)

From an organizational point of view, the problem is to identify and manage inducements in a manner designed to motivate contributions that lead to desired levels of organizational performance (U.S. General Accounting Office, 2003).

EXPECTANCY THEORY

One approach to solving this problem is offered by the expectancy theory of motivation. According to this theory, the level of *effort* people will put into a behavior or task is related to three factors. The first is *expectancy,* or the extent to which a person believes that a certain behavior or outcome is possible; for example, getting to work on time or finishing a project. The second is *instrumentality,* or the degree to which the behavior in question is seen to be likely to result in a specific outcome for the individual, such as getting a pay raise or promotion. The third is *valence,* which is the relative value or importance attributed to that outcome by a person. Using always coming to work on time as the example, expectancy theory predicts that the level of effort made to get to work on time will depend on (1) whether or not a person really believes it is possible to do this, given the circumstances they face; (2) the degree to which the person is convinced that the inducement offered by the organization, such as a pay raise, will actually happen if he or she always gets to work on time; and (3) the relative value placed on the inducement itself (Gortner, Mahler, & Nicholson, 1997, pp. 281–285). The theory is based on an assumption that the relationship between these variables is multiplicative, which indicates that all three must be present at relatively high levels for motivation to be high.

Expectancy theory posits that people have needs that they want to satisfy, that they are able rationally to calculate expectancies and instrumentalities, and will behave accordingly. Management, in turn, must know what rewards are valued by workers and be able to set up conditions wherein: (1) the workers have a high level of expectancy, that is, they believe that if they make an effort, they will be able to perform well, (2) the connections between job performance and rewards established by the organization are clear and highly predictable in their administration, and (3) the rewards offered are valued by employees. Continuing with the coming to work on time illustration, if a public employer's productivity is suffering because many of its employees habitually arrive a few minutes after the start of the work day, expectancy theory suggests the following course of action will work better than punishment-centered responses that might depress morale and encourage various forms of evasion. Initially, management should have as its goal the implementation of a system of positive incentives that promises to increase workers' efforts to be at work on time. One factor it must consider is the extent to which they believe it is possible to get to work on time routinely (expectancy). There may be reasons why people often are late that the organization may be able to address, such as inadequate public transportation or a lack of affordable child care facilities. Once expectancy is high, management is in a position to take the next step, which is an incentive plan that connects attractive outcomes to the behavior it wants, coming to work on time. In addition to offering rewards that are valued by workers (valence), the plan must be administered in a consistent and highly predictable manner by supervisors (instrumentality).

Expectancy theory does have some practical limitations. It asks management to acquire a great deal of information about individuals, their attitudes, and circumstances. It also proceeds on the assumption that everybody engages in rational, quasi-economic calculations before choosing a particular course of action, and "critics suggest that expectancy theory defers too much to the nineteenth century ideal of the economic man . . . [but] employees cannot be as knowledgeable about outcomes as the model assumes" (Stewart & Garson, 1983, p. 33). Nevertheless, expectancy theory does offer guidelines for thinking about structuring and managing relationships between inducements and contributions.

First, expectancy theory stresses the importance of clearly communicating to employees the linkages between job performance and rewards. Second, it reminds policy makers and supervisors that personnel systems must be administered in a manner that firmly establishes these linkages in the eyes of employees. Third, it tells management that it must make an effort to understand, at least in general terms, the importance different groups and types of employees place on specific material and nonmaterial rewards. Information of this kind is necessary if an inducements strategy is to be reasonably well aligned with the values and needs of employees. Fourth, expectancy theory highlights the roles of perceived and objective ability in employee effort and performance. Perceptually, ability is a factor in expectancy; that is, does the person believe he or she has the ability to perform? Objectively, ability sets limits because no amount of effort will yield performance if ability actually does not exist or cannot be developed, as many aspiring professional athletes have discovered. Equally important factors in ability are the technical and other resources the organization makes available to its workforce. No matter how much effort they make, framing carpenters wielding hand saws are not likely to be as productive as those using power saws.

It is possible to improve the objective ability of an organization's human resource base in addition to increasing the effort it exerts. Personnel-related actions of this kind include investments in recruitment programs, upgrading selection and promotion standards, making available training and other employee development opportunities, and designing jobs and career paths to take better advantage of workers' interests and abilities. Investments in technological aids (such as computers, word processors, communications equipment, and automated machinery) and related training often raise productivity on the individual as well as organizational levels.

Fifth, expectancy theory illuminates the significance of perceived as well as actual equity and fairness in the allocation of rewards. If employees believe that rewards are not actually given on the basis on accurate and unbiased measures of performance, this perception may seriously cripple any incentives plan. Supervisors, who are in large measure responsible for its administration, must be trusted to implement the plan competently and impartially. Operationally, perceived equity also depends on clearly defined performance objectives and standards, and on the existence of broadly accepted and trusted performance evaluation procedures and instruments.

STRATEGIC HUMAN RESOURCES MANAGEMENT AND THE PERSONNEL SPECIALIST

The human resource management perspective requires above all that personnel specialists assume an organizational and performance-driven point of view. Increasingly, they are being asked to have the analytic skills and information management needs to formulate and implement human capital strategies that reach well beyond their organization's formal boundaries. Personnel specialists can make important contributions in four areas of activity that will better utilize human resources. Personnel specialists should be prepared to

- Help in the design, administration, and evaluation of incentives plans that reflect current knowledge about human motivation and behavior in organizations.
- Play an important role in the design of systems to attract, select, and place employees who are most likely to respond favorably to the range of inducements an organization is able to offer.
- Take the lead in developing ways of monitoring employee perceptions and attitudes. Management needs accurate and timely information about how workers feel about their jobs, supervisors, coworkers, working conditions, and personnel policies and practices.
- Play an important analytic or evaluation role by conducting rigorous evaluations of the human resources management programs of the organization, including those related to incentives, employee training and development, and performance evaluation. Well-done evaluations are needed to provide a solid foundation for initiatives designed to improve performance.

Steven Hays (1989) found that "the central theme of much of the relevant literature is that the personnel office must become more closely integrated with line management" (p. 114). In the current environment, personnel specialists need to have the expertise and, equally important, the organizational perspective needed to actively support public managers' efforts to enhance performance and productivity on all levels.

The contemporary emphasis on managerial capacity and achieving organizational goals and objectives does not mean that other values should be set aside or ignored. For public personnel, actively contributing to policies and practices that promote organizational performance is a major objective, but it is not and cannot be the *only* one. Other values are important. As Buchanan and Millstone (1979) observe, "numerous structural embodiments of democratic morality" may be found in any personnel system, and any of "these structural instruments for the protection of individual rights is capable of disrupting or slowing program operations, in the interest of securing *priority* attention for the 'equal protection' or 'procedural due process' rights of individual citizens" (pp. 273–274). In other words, the values underpinning the operations of public personnel systems encompass far more than using people as instruments of organizational efficiency and goal accomplishment. Protecting the dignity of individuals, assuring their legal and constitutional rights, and creating a fair and equitable employment relationship also are important values to be realized (See Chapters 2, 9 and 10).

DISCUSSION QUESTIONS

1. Why would people want to work for the public sector if they can make more money working for a private business?
2. What could public employers do to make working for government more attractive to college graduates?
3. Would you prefer to work for an employer who offers group-based or gainsharing performance incentives or one who has an individualized incentives plan? Why?
4. What could public employers do to better anticipate and plan for labor market conditions?
5. In what functional and program areas could local governments develop cooperative agreements to share personnel, training facilities, and other resources?

REFERENCES

Barrett, Katherine, and Richard Greene (Eds.). (2005). "Grading the States: A Report Card on Government Performance." *Governing* (February), pp. 24–95.

Bendix, Rinehard (1962). *Max Weber: An Intellectual Portrait* (New York: Anchor Books).

Bryson, John M. (1996). *Strategic Planning for Public and Nonprofit Organizations* (San Francisco: Jossey-Bass).

Buchanan, Bruce, and Jeff Millstone (1979). "Public Organizations: A Value-Conflict View." *International Journal of Public Administration,* Vol. 1, No. 3, pp. 261–305.

Condrey, Stephen E. (2002). "Reinventing State Civil Service Systems: The Georgia Experience." *Review of Public Personnel Administration,* Vol. 22, No. 2 (Summer), pp. 114–124.

Gilbert, G. Ronald, and Ardel E. Nelson (1989). "The Pacer Share Demonstration Project: Implications for Organizational Management and Performance Evaluation." *Public Personnel Management,* Vol. 18, No. 2 (Summer), pp. 209–225.

Gortner, Harold F., Julianne Mahler, and Jeanne Bell Nicholson (1997). *Organization Theory: A Public Perspective,* 2nd ed. (New York: Harcourt Brace).

Hays, Steven (1989). "Environmental Change and the Personnel Function: A Review of the Research." *Public Personnel Management,* Vol. 18, No. 2 (Summer), pp. 110–126.

———. (2004). "Trends and Best Practices in State and Local Human Resource Management: Lessons to Be Learned?" *Review of Public Personnel Administration,* Vol. 24, No. 3 (September), pp. 256–275.

Jorgensen, Lorna, Kelli Fairless, and David W. Patton (1996). "Underground Merit Systems and the Balance Between Service and Compliance." *Review of Public Personnel Administration,* Vol. 16, No. 2 (Spring), pp. 5–20.

Katz, Daniel, and Robert Kahn (1978). *The Social Psychology of Organizations,* 2nd ed. (New York: Wiley).

Light, Paul C. (2003). House Congressional Testimony on Civil Service and National Security. Committee on House Government Reform, Subcommittee on National Security, Veterans Affairs, and International Relations, Washington, DC (April 6).

Miami-Dade County (2005). "Performance Improvement: Gainsharing." Accessed http://www.miamidade.gov/opi/gainsharing.asp (May).

Moynihan, Donald P. (2004). "Protection Versus Flexibility: The Civil Service Reform Act, Competing Administrative Doctrines, and the Roots of Contemporary Public Management Debate." *Journal of Policy History,* Vol. 16, No. 1 (January), pp. 1–33.

Moynihan, Donald P. (2005). "Homeland Security and the U.S. Public Management Policy Agenda." *Governance,* Vol. 18, No. 2 (April), pp. 171–196.

Ospina, Sonia (1992). "When Managers Don't Plan: Consequences of Nonstrategic Public Personnel Management." *Review of Public Personnel Administration,* Vol. 12, No. 2 (January–April), pp. 52–67.

Report of the National Performance Review (1993). "Creating a Government that Works Better & Costs Less" (Washington, DC: U.S. Government Printing Office).

Scott, William G. (1967). *Organization Theory: A Behavioral Analysis for Management* (Homewood, IL: Richard D. Irwin).

Scott, William G., and T. R. Mitchell (1976). *Organization Theory: A Structural and Behavioral Analysis* (Homewood, IL: Richard D. Irwin).

Selden, Sally Coleman, Patricia W. Ingraham, and Willow Jacobson (2001). "Human Resource Practices in State Government: Findings from a National Survey." *Public Administration Review*, Vol. 61, No. 5 (September–October), pp. 598–607.

Siegel, Gilbert B. (1994). "Three Federal Demonstration Projects: Using Monetary Performance Awards." *Public Personnel Management*, Vol. 23, No. 1 (Spring), pp. 153–164.

Simon, Herbert A. (1965). *Administrative Behavior*, 2nd ed. (New York: Free Press).

Stewart, Debra W., and G. David Garson (1983). *Organizational Behavior and Public Management* (New York: Marcell Dekker).

Thompson, James D. (1967). *Organizations in Action* (New York: McGraw-Hill).

U.S. Environmental Protection Agency (2003). "2003–2008 Strategic Plan: Directions for the Future." Washington, DC: U.S. Environmental Protection Agency (September 30).

U.S. General Accounting Office (2002). *Human Capital: Effective Use of Flexibilities Can Assist Agencies in Managing Their Workforces*, GAO-03-2, Washington, DC (December 6).

U.S. General Accounting Office (2003). *Results-Oriented Cultures: Creating a Clear Linkage Between Individual Performance and Organizational Success*, GAO-03-488, Washington, DC (March 14).

U.S. Office of Personnel Management (2005a). "Human Capital Standards." Washington, DC: U.S. Office of Personnel Management. Accessed http://apps.opm.gov/humancapital/standards/index.cfm

———. (2005b). "Human Resource Flexibilities." Washington, DC: U.S. Office of Personnel Management. Accessed http://www.opm.gov/account/omsoe/hr-flex/index.htm

——— (2005c). "Federal Executive Institute & Management Development Centers." Washington, DC: U.S. Office of Personnel Management. Accessed http://www.leadership.opm.gov/fei.cfm

Vasu, Michael L., Debra W. Stewart, and G. David Garson (1990). *Organizational Behavior and Public Management*, 2nd ed. (New York: Marcel Dekker).

Walton, Richard E., and Robert B. McKersie (1965). *A Behavioral Theory of Labor Negotiations* (New York: McGraw-Hill).

Wechsler, Barton (1994). "Reinventing Florida's Civil Service System: The Failure of Reform." *Review of Public Personnel Administration,* Vol. 14, No. 2 (Spring), pp. 64–76.

Woodward, Colleen A. (2005). "Merit by Any Other Name—Reframing the Civil Service First Principle." *Public Administration Review,* Vol. 65, No. 1 (January/February), pp. 109–115.

Yuchtman, Ephraim, and Stanley Seashore (1967). "A System Resource Approach to Organizational Effectiveness." *American Sociological Review,* Vol. 32, No. 2 (December), pp. 891–903.

SUGGESTED READINGS

Barnard, Chester I. (1938). *The Functions of the Executive* (Cambridge, MA: Harvard University Press).

Donahue, John D. (1989). *The Privatization Decision: Public Ends, Private Means* (New York: Basic Books).

Lawler, Edward E. III (1994). *Motivation in Work Organizations* (San Francisco: Jossey-Bass).

Perry, James L. (1996). *Handbook of Public Administration,* 2nd ed. (San Francisco: Jossey-Bass).

Vroom, Victor H. (1964). *Work and Motivation* (New York: Wiley).

Walton, Mary (1986). *The Deming Method* (New York: Praeger).

Peters, Guy, and Jon Pierre (Eds.). (2003). *Handbook of Public Administration* (Thousand Oaks, CA: Sage).

Chapter FOUR

Recruitment and Selection

To be effective, an agency's human resources program must be able to identify, recruit, and acquire people who are well qualified at entry, responsive to available incentives, and able to develop new skills and abilities. Success in acquiring and retaining needed human resources depends on many factors, some of which may be beyond the control of public managers. Inadequate pay and benefits, deteriorating working conditions, and public antipathy have done much to make jobs in the public service unattractive to many of today's potential applicants, particularly those with skills that are in high demand. Many of the best and brightest products of U.S. higher education look to the private sector for jobs that pay well and offer high-prestige careers, so the public sector starts out with a competitive disadvantage. An expansive economy, where jobs are plentiful in the private sector, makes recruiting more difficult. But these are not the only reasons why public employers may have difficulty attracting qualified personnel.

Historically, personnel managers within traditional merit systems have not invested heavily in aggressive recruitment efforts unless forced to do so by outside agencies, such as the federal courts. Managers often have settled for a passive (announce-and-wait) approach to filling vacancies and new positions. Rules and processes designed in large measure to prevent patronage hiring and discrimination have been notoriously complicated and cumbersome. Highly qualified job applicants are driven away by these systems' complexity and slowness, or they simply never apply. Public managers, in turn, are frustrated by their inability to acquire the human resources they need in a timely and efficient manner.

A major task now confronting public personnel is to develop recruitment and selection techniques and processes that: (1) take a management point of view by actively supporting efforts to acquire, develop, and retain the human resources needed by government, and (2) are in conformance with the merit principle and meet the standards set by existing equal employment opportunity (EEO) and antidiscrimination law and policy. On the federal level, for example, the 1978 Civil Service Reform Act (CSRA) requires that recruitment "should be from qualified individuals from appropriate sources in an endeavor to achieve a work force from all segments of society, and selection and advancement should be determined solely on the basis of relative ability, knowledge, and skills, after fair and open competition which assures that all receive equal opportunity."

As the CSRA's language implies, although recruitment and selection are conceptually discrete steps, they are in practice inseparable. Recruitment for public sector employment generally refers to efforts to encourage people to apply for available positions. Selection refers to the decision to hire, on the basis of demonstrated merit, a particular individual or individuals. As the Volcker Commission noted, complicated and slow selection procedures undermine recruitment efforts because potential candidates "see getting government jobs as an exercise in frustration." On the other side of the coin, ineffective recruitment may leave the employer in the position of having to select from a list of eligibles that does not have enough qualified applicants on it. Important positions may remain open for a long time. Weak recruitment programs often produce candidate pools that underrepresent women and minorities, an outcome that makes it very difficult to achieve affirmative action goals or, in a larger sense, to convince these groups that EEO is really a serious concern for the employer.

In its guidance to state agencies, the State of Georgia's central personnel agency, known as the Georgia State Merit System, identifies the following as important considerations in the formulation of an effective recruitment program:

- The program should permit employers to identify recruitment sources, such as universities and trade schools, that are the most likely to provide enough applicants with the needed skills and abilities.
- It should be funded and staffed at the levels required to carry out an active recruitment effort.
- In addition to meeting short-term or immediate needs, the program should be designed to meet long-term needs by acquiring entry-level personnel who will later be able to advance and fill more responsible positions.

- Recruitment must be seen as the initial step in the selection process and, therefore, it must "ensure compliance with existing federal and state laws and guidelines concerning fairness, equal opportunity, and . . . minimize potential adverse impact on legally protected groups."
- The program should meet the public's expectation that all phases of the hiring process will be "fair" in the sense that merit and EEO are the core values guiding that process. (Georgia Merit System, 1997, pp. 1–2)

RECRUITMENT: FINDING AND ATTRACTING QUALIFIED APPLICANTS

In many countries, government workers traditionally have been accorded high social status and prestige. Highly qualified candidates are more often than not willing to accept lower pay than they could get in the private sector because of the status and authority that comes with public service careers. Public attitudes and social values thus allow government to pick and choose from candidate pools that offer the most talented and best educated people the society has to offer. With rare exceptions, this has not been the case in the United States, and public employers on all levels have had to struggle to overcome a general inclination to value careers in the private sector over those in the public service. Recent thinking about recruitment in the U.S. public sector has stressed three approaches to overcoming, or at least compensating for, government's problems in this area. The first involves taking advantage of government's potential to compete successfully for minorities and women. The second concentrates on reducing public employers' dependence on outside sources by continuously upgrading the skills of existing employees to meet changing or new requirements. This approach involves commitments to substantial investments in training and other human resources development (HRD) programs (Hudson Institute, 1988, pp. 38–41). The third consists of initiatives designed to improve the image of the public service as an employer and to make the public sector an effective economic competitor across certain critical segments of the labor market, particularly the technical and professional occupations (National Academy of Public Administration, 1987).

In all cases, a recruitment plan should

- Clearly define who is responsible for the implementation of its components and set goals and timetables for completion of each of these components.

- Include procedures for ongoing evaluation and revision of the plan in light of the results achieved, including the performance of the workforce.
- Specify the kinds of job and job vacancy information that will be made available internally to existing workers, as well as to the general public.
- Assure that accurate information will be readily accessible to all interested parties through a variety of media, such as publications, postings, radio and television, and the Internet.
- Identify and establish reliable contacts with productive referral sources, including promotions and transfers, current employees, schools and colleges, employment agencies, and executive search companies.
- Target and establish contact with applicants who are the most likely to have needed qualifications and skills.
- Clearly set forth the policies and procedures to be used in recruitment efforts designed to improve diversity. (Georgia Merit System, 1997, p. 4)

RECRUITMENT OF WOMEN AND MINORITIES

Although its record is certainly far from perfect, the public sector has been a leader in the process of breaking down barriers to the employment and promotion of women and minorities. To the degree that public employment is associated with equality of opportunity and career mobility for minorities and women, government has an advantage in the competition with private businesses (Hudson Institute, 1988). An example of minority-oriented recruitment is provided by OPM's Hispanic Employment Initiatives, which include helping to implement Executive Order 12900, the White House Initiative on Educational Excellence for Hispanic Americans. In addition to issuing guidance on recruiting strategies for Hispanic students, OPM works with federal agencies to identify job opportunities and institutions that offer training and education opportunities that prepare Hispanic students to qualify for those jobs. Other OPM initiatives in this area are the following:

- Providing employment information to students, faculty, and the Hispanic community by sponsoring Employment Information (Touch Screen) Computer kiosks and placing them in Hispanic-serving institutions.
- Expanding the Presidential Management Fellowship Program (PMF) recruitment program to include visiting more institutions graduating significant numbers of Hispanics.

- Providing assistance in coordinating placements with federal agencies of Hispanic students under the National Internship Program of the Hispanic Association of Colleges and Universities (HACU). HACU interns are college students with grade point averages of 3.0 or better who work in federal agencies for 10 weeks over the summer.
- Using the flexibilities available under the federal Student Employment Program (this program is described later) to bring Hispanic students into federal occupations where there are shortages of qualified applicants, as well as all other occupations.
- Developing mentoring programs to encourage and support young Hispanics' educational development and career progress.
- Encouraging participation of Hispanics in agency career development programs, including intergovernmental rotational assignments for senior executives, management, and professional/technical occupations. (U.S. Office of Personnel Management, 1997)

The Hudson Institute also recommended that public employers develop recruitment programs geared to the changing demographics of the labor force and, more broadly, the growing diversity of U.S. society. The rapidly growing proportion of women in the workforce creates an opportunity *if* innovations such flexible work schedules, extended leave policies, and child care benefits are pursued aggressively. The Institute's comments regarding the federal government are equally relevant to the recruitment programs of the states and localities.

> Few employers have been able to satisfy the desires of two-earner families for more time away from work to care for children and aging family members. Organizations that are able to offer more flexible work schedules . . . are more likely to have their pick of the available candidates for hard-to-fill jobs. . . . [E]very agency should be seeking to find cost-effective ways to assist parents in providing high-quality child care. The Federal government should not allow itself to lag behind other employers . . . if it wishes to hire and keep large numbers of mothers (and fathers) during the 1990s. (Hudson Institute, 1988, p. 39)

INVESTMENTS IN CONTINUOUS TRAINING AND EDUCATION

Rapid social and technological change places great pressure on organizations to maintain workforces that have the skills, knowledge, and abilities needed to handle new responsibilities and job tasks. It is no longer safe to assume that a high school or college education, once completed, will equip workers with the basic knowledge and skills they need to handle their jobs until they retire. Historically, this has been the assumption, and when government needed personnel with new or different skills, it recruited them from outside sources. Retraining or re-educating existing staff to fill positions that may not actually exist for several years has been a seldom-exercised option because it has been virtually impossible to generate political support for these kinds of investments.

In the long term, however, one way to reduce the pressure on external recruitment is, in effect, to create conditions under which an *internal recruitment* dimension is added to the mix. This may be done by anticipating human resources needs and by systematically upgrading and changing the skills profiles of those who already work for public agencies. This approach applies particularly to situations where certain skills are already in short supply or are likely to be in the foreseeable future. Skills upgrading programs like tuition reimbursement for job-related education and training, sabbaticals to pursue advanced degrees, and specialized training opportunities may be used in the fields where they are most needed and by agencies that will benefit most in recruitment and retention. Education and training of this kind also could be designed to help employees work their way up a career ladder from, for example, paraprofessional to professional positions. Another goal might be to improve the basic skills of those who would otherwise not be qualified for lower level jobs.

Along these lines, OPM developed a series of initiatives designed to strengthen federal human resources development efforts that covered the following: (1) probationary period training for new employees, (2) basic skills and literacy training, (3) continuing technical/professional education and training, (4) retraining for occupational changes, (5) participation in professional associations, and (6) academic degree training. OPM also supports training and development programs for supervisors and managers, and it helps federal agencies to assess their needs in these areas (U.S. Office of Personnel Management, 1992).

RECRUITING COLLEGE GRADUATES

In the coming years, the number of public sector jobs requiring college degrees will continue to increase as it has for some time, and the number of people graduating with bachelor's and master's degrees may not be sufficient to meet the demand, especially in areas requiring technical skills. Although the shortage is expected to be particularly acute on the federal level, state and local governments may also have problems recruiting the college graduates they need to fill these positions. Even under the best of conditions, the competition for talent will be intense, and public employers commonly face several self-imposed obstacles.

First, in comparison with large corporations and firms, public employers do not have a track record of investing heavily in campus recruitment. In 1989, an OPM study of college recruitment efforts concluded that most federal agencies showed a lack of commitment to campus recruitment and, when the federal government did recruit on campus, its presence was too limited and sporadic to effectively promote federal jobs. When asked about federal recruitment efforts in 1990, college students told the General Accounting Office (GAO) that they were not getting enough information about job opportunities and how to apply for them. They also got the *feeling* that jobs were unavailable and that the agencies did not value students as potential employees. College placement offices, typically well stocked with recruiting literature from businesses, seldom had up-to-date materials on jobs and careers in federal agencies. The image of the public sector did not help because students were not disposed to approach agencies directly because they believed that contacting the government was a frustrating and lengthy process.

In an effort to solve these kinds of problems, OPM launched several recruitment initiatives intended to help federal agencies. In the early 1980s, OPM had maintained regional information centers where information on positions available within each region was made available. At these centers, job postings were simply printed and placed on bulletin boards. Information on jobs in regions other than the one where the posting was made was not available. Effectiveness was limited because job seekers were required to visit the center during normal business hours to view the job postings. Later, OPM began a new initiative known as *Career America,* through which a collection of sophisticated brochures describing career opportunities and highlighting attractive features of federal service were made available to federal agencies at relatively low cost. The agencies, in turn, made the brochures available to the public. Eventually, OPM also provided federal agencies with a service called the *Career America Connection,* which was "a nationwide automated telephone system that provided quick, easy-to-use, current Federal Employment information 24 hours a day, 7 days a week" (U.S. Office of Personnel Management, 1997b, p. 1).

In the late 1980s, OPM began to draw upon computer technology. The first effort was the initiation of an electronic Federal Job Opportunities Board. This system enabled people with computers and

modems to dial into an electronic list of job vacancies available nationwide. Applicants were still required to obtain and complete paper
applications that they then would send via the postal service to a processing center. Still, this was a significant advancement in that it provided an improved means of making information about federal job
opportunities available to the general public—or at least those members of the public that had computer access.

By the 1990s, as technology began to improve, OPM set up
computerized job information kiosks in federal buildings nationwide.
At these kiosks, job seekers, who perhaps had no computer of their
own, could view and print announcements for jobs they found interesting. Later, as Internet technology was refined and the use of personal computers became increasingly common, OPM began to make
job information available via the World Wide Web. The first step in
this direction was the launching of a federal job-search website called
USAJobs in 1996 (www.usajobs.opm.gov). The website provided
nationwide vacancy information that was available to anyone with an
Internet connection. Once the website was up and running, OPM terminated the direct dial-in system for obtaining job information and all
computer kiosks in federal facilities were removed by 2001. Vacancy
information via the automated telephone system was maintained so
that there would be access for individuals without computer resources
and the visually impaired, but the number of phone lines used was radically reduced (Llorens & Kellough, forthcoming).

THE FEDERAL RECRUITMENT ONE-STOP INITIATIVE

In August 2003, OPM significantly updated and revised the USAJobs
website to provide one central location from which job seekers could
find information on federal employment opportunities and federal
agencies could find potential employees. In recognition of this objective, the concept underlying the revised site was labeled "Recruitment
One-Stop." The technological advancements incorporated into
Recruitment One-Stop have made it possible for those looking for
jobs to actually apply for positions and complete preliminary examinations entirely online. In addition, job seekers are able to build as many
as five web-based resumes and store them on the USAJobs website
and recruiters from federal agencies can review applicant qualifications
(Llorens & Kellough, forthcoming).

OPM invested heavily in advertising the new website through
paid advertising, traditional job fairs, and a variety of other means.
More than 14.5 million unique hits were registered on the website and

job seekers created more than 185,000 resume profiles between its launch date of August 4, 2003, and November 2, 2003. The website provides an array of application tips and tools and can be displayed in Spanish as well as English. Overall, OPM hopes this website will prove to be an effective mechanism for getting the word out about federal job opportunities, will streamline the application and examination process, and will, as a result, significantly reduce the time it takes for agencies to locate and hire exceptional candidates. Ultimately, it is envisioned that the USAJobs website will become the central location for information about federal job opportunities. Federal agencies are currently authorized to develop and operate their own websites to provide information on available jobs, but they are also required to post job announcements on the USAJobs website. OPM's objective is to have all agencies direct job seekers from the agency sites to the USAJobs website to make the process of finding a federal job simpler and or less confusing. Whether that goal will be achieved is uncertain at this point, however, because it would require that agencies possess the technology necessary to integrate their sites with the USAJobs site.

At this point, there is no requirement that agencies possess automated recruitment capabilities or that the technology they possess be consistent with that of OPM. Furthermore, there are no standards for which software packages agencies may purchase if they choose to do so. As a result, the Recruitment One-Stop project is facing a situation in which some agencies do not have any system in place to accept automated applications and those that do are not necessarily capable of being integrated with the new USAJobs system. At present, many agencies still require applicants to either mail, fax, or e-mail their applications into a servicing personnel office, even after they have already built a resume on USAJobs. If the system becomes integrated in this manner, applicants could simply apply online and their applications would be electronically sent to agency personnel offices through OPM. Most large agencies have either taken this step, or are in the process of doing so. Legislation mandating the integration of software systems may be necessary, however, to ensure the participation of all agencies in the Recruitment One-Stop initiative (Llorens & Kellough, forthcoming).

CAMPUS VISITS AND PRESENTATIONS

Although innovations such as the USAJobs website and Recruitment One-Stop are important new developments in employee recruitment, direct contact between employers and potential employees remains an important recruitment strategy for certain types of positions and recruitment pools. The GAO found in 1990, for example, that college students favor personal contacts with employer representatives over other recruitment methods, and campus interviews and presentations to classes or student groups are given high marks for effectiveness because they make face-to-face meetings with knowledgeable employees possible. Brochures such as the Career America portfolio and electronic media did attract interest, but were judged not to be substitutes for personal contacts. Recruiting videos, for example, were not considered particularly effective, in part, because many students believed they did not provide an accurate description of work and careers in government agencies. Impersonal pre-recorded telephone messages and computer information systems also did not please college students. Along similar lines, career fairs where public employers set up booths on university campuses and collect resumes are not likely to attract top candidates, most of whom don't go to job fairs or wait to be processed through OPM registers. They are "courted by the private sector and skimmed off like cream" declared the GAO (U.S. General Accounting Office, 1990b, p. 19). The GAO suggested that college placement centers have a federal employment contact person so that information could be channeled and questions answered quickly and accurately, and many federal agencies now provide the names, addresses, and numbers of contact persons for positions they are currently seeking to fill.

STUDENT HIRING PROGRAMS

Another way of helping people become familiar with job and career opportunities in the public service is to hire students on a part-time basis. Here, an example is provided by OPM's *Student Educational Employment Program*. This program, established in 1994, offers federal employment opportunities to students in accredited high schools, technical and vocational training centers, and two- or four-year colleges and universities. It has two components, the Student Temporary Employment Program (STEP) and the Student Career Experience Program (SCEP). Under STEP, students' work does not have to be directly related to their academic programs and career goals. The SCEP, however, is intended to provide work experience that is directly related to academic and career interests, and students "may be non-competitively converted to *term, career* or *career-conditional* appointments following completion of their academic and work experience requirements" (U.S. Office of Personnel Management, 1997d, p. 1). According to OPM,

In Fiscal Year 1996, there were 34,578 participants in the Student Educational Employment Program. The Temporary Employment Component had 26,045 (75 percent) participants; the Career Experience component had 8,533 (25 percent) participants. The number of female participants [was] 19,852 (57 percent of program participants). There were 16,540 minorities . . . [and] Blacks had the largest representation with 10,002 students (29 percent . . .). There were 1,058 *career* or *career-conditional* conversions from the Career Experience component in FY 96. (U.S. Office of Personnel Management, 1997e, p. 1)

Internships like the Presidential Management Fellowship Program also may be effective recruiting devices. Formerly known as the Presidential Management Internship Program, and established in 1977, the PMF is designed to attract highly qualified graduate students. Students are nominated by their schools and undergo a competitive selection process. Once they graduate, those selected are given the opportunity for challenging assignments including rotational responsibilities, mentoring, and attendance in development seminars. Those who successfully complete the program are eligible for conversion to permanent positions. Examples of this kind of approach are also found at the state level. For example, *The Illinois Commission on the Future of the Public Service* recommended in 1991 that the state expand all its internship and cooperative education programs because they "provide the greatest potential for increasing the pool of undergraduate and graduate students interested in public service" (Illinois Commission on the Future of the Public Service, 1991, p. 32). Currently, the Illinois Department of Natural Resources offers internships to college and graduate students in natural resources management, conservation law enforcement, environmental education, and other areas. The department's programs "allow students to obtain practical experience and meet hands-on training requirements necessary to earn

BULLETIN

"The State of Illinois maintains a commitment to the continuing improvement of public service for its citizens. The success of this commitment depends upon an available talent pool of bright, highly motivated individuals who are prepared to assume important government positions. Recognizing that college and graduate students represent a significant reservoir of potent government talent, the Governor's Office has, since 1977, sponsored two internship programs. . . ." A third, the 1998 Vito Marzullo Internship Program, has the following purposes:

1. Helping to meet the public sector's future need for competent administrators.
2. Encouraging talented college graduates to consider careers in state government.
3. To help students complement their academic expertise with vocational training within their fields.
4. Achieve affirmative action goals.

Source: State of Illinois, Office of the Governor, 1998.

their degrees" (Illinois Department of Natural Resources, 1998, p. 1). Another Illinois initiative is the Prescott E. Bloom Internships in Government Program. In one, college juniors, seniors, and graduate students "work in the Governor's Office and in various agencies under the Governor's jurisdiction learning, first hand, the operations of Illinois State Government." In another, college graduates spend a year assigned on a rotational basis to various departments in the governor's office and to an executive branch agency (Office of the Governor, State of Illinois, 1997).

CHANGING THE IMAGE OF PUBLIC EMPLOYMENT

The image of what it is like to work in government compounds already-negative feelings about pay and benefits in the public sector. Many potential job applicants see government as an environment where it is next to impossible to get anything done, as offering careers where they are unlikely to be able to fully use their talents, as a place infested with specialists in red tape, and where dreary working conditions prevail. Fueled by political rhetoric, media depictions, and the long-standing American tendency to ascribe all manner of evils to the bureaucracy, this image of the public service is a serious liability.

To the degree that these perceptions are factually inaccurate, public employers need to come up with strategies for countering and changing them. Public information and education programs designed to describe the challenges, rewards, and opportunities associated with public service and careers in particular agencies may be productive, particularly if recruiters are prepared to follow up in terms relevant to potential applicants. Systematically building direct contacts with the public service through internship and co-op programs also should be helpful. More broadly, as the Volcker Commission noted, the nation's political leadership must be willing to describe the public service and its functions in positive terms *and* to back its words with supportive policies and needed resources.

ADMINISTRATION OF RECRUITMENT PROGRAMS

On all levels of government, complaints about procedural rigidities, overcentralized and unresponsive personnel offices, and a widespread lack of organizational attention to recruitment are commonplace. Studies of the recruitment process reveal that relatively successful programs share certain characteristics.

First, and probably most important, top-level management must actively support and participate in the planning, implementation, and evaluation phases of agency recruitment programs. Second, recruitment activity should be decentralized in the sense that line managers are directly involved and have been delegated considerable authority to plan and carry out recruiting initiatives and, under some conditions, to offer jobs to highly qualified candidates without waiting for the approval of a central personnel agency. Third, line managers must work closely with personnel specialists in the design and implementation of recruitment strategies keyed to specific agency needs and labor market conditions. Fourth, those actually doing the recruitment in the field should have the necessary resources and technical support, be well trained and fully informed about agency needs and opportunities, and possess the authority required to make commitments on behalf of the employer. Fifth, appropriate media and technologies should be available to support all phases of the recruitment and selection process.

SELECTION: METHODS, ISSUES, AND PROBLEMS

A hallmark of the first civil service reform movement was its focus on the methods used to select people for public service jobs and to determine who should be promoted. Its intensive concentration on both initial selection and promotion was a direct result of the movement's effort to eliminate patronage or spoils as an organizing principle of public personnel administration. Thus, traditional merit systems emphasize political neutrality and objectivity at every stage of the selection process. To achieve this goal, the selection process had to be designed *and* controlled by personnel specialists housed in central personnel agencies or independent commissions. Centralized oversight and control were seen as essential to ensure the realization of merit principles.

Conventional civil service selection procedures stress measuring a candidate's ability to perform a specific job. To make this determination, one or more tests or examinations are used to evaluate the qualifications of job applicants. Once these tests are scored, the scores are used to rank those who apply. Typically a cut or pass point is determined that separates those who are qualified and those who do not possess minimum qualifications. Those with scores above the pass point are ranked according to their scores on a list of eligibles. Selection rules generally require that employees be chosen from among those with the highest scores. The "rule of three," which requires selection from among those with the top three scores, dates from the time of the Grant Administration, was incorporated into the Pendleton Act, and remains in relatively common use today.

Technically, all measurements of capacity or qualifications are considered tests, and they do not necessarily involve taking a written (pencil-and-paper) examination. For example, some tests measure physical abilities and others are conducted orally. Tests can also be assembled in the sense that people come together in one location for the examination, whereas others are "unassembled," meaning that they are administered on an individual basis or perhaps they consist simply of a review of an applicant's dossier. The mix of tests and examinations used will vary, depending on the skills, knowledge, and abilities required. The tests applied by public employers usually will involve some combination of the following:

- Assessments of minimum qualifications requirements
- Evaluations of training, education, and experience
- Written tests of knowledge and analytic skills
- Job performance tests and simulations
- Oral examinations by individual examiners or boards
- Background checks or investigations
- Medical and physical examinations

In civil service selection, the goal is to determine if an applicant has the knowledge, skills, abilities, and other traits deemed necessary or important to successful performance in a particular job. The content of most selection tests is supposed to be based on the results of careful job analysis (U.S. Office of Personnel Management, 1979). Although most civil service tests in the United States are geared to the requirements of particular positions, some are intended to assess the likelihood that an applicant will have a successful career in a variety of occupations or administrative roles. These types of tests are most often used for entry-level professional positions, and the questions "do not require applicants to possess knowledge or experience that can only be acquired on the job" (U.S. Merit Systems Protection Board, 1990). They emphasize general traits such as verbal skills and reasoning abilities that are believed to be closely linked to performance.

TEST VALIDITY

From a technical standpoint, the purpose of selection tests is to provide the employer with a reasonably accurate prediction of how applicants are likely to perform in specific jobs. In other words, the problem is to construct tests that are *valid*. As Norma Riccucci stresses, "Test validation continues to be relied on to conceptualize and operationalize merit . . ." (Riccucci, 1991, p. 80). A valid test measures only what is it intended to measure (such as knowledge of labor law or accounting principles). Tests must also be *reliable* or consistent in their results. All other things being equal (controlling for other potential sources of variation), if a person takes the test twice (or a hundred times), and it is reliable, the scores should be roughly the same. If the scores are significantly different, the test is unreliable and as a result, of undeterminable validity.

The validation methods generally accepted by specialists in testing are (1) criterion-related validity, (2) construct validity, and (3) content validity. These three validation strategies correspond to those used in social science measurement generally and were described by the American Psychological Association as early as 1966 in its *Standards for Educational and Psychological Tests and Manuals*. The term "test" includes all examination methods described earlier including oral examinations, written tests, physical ability tests, and evaluations of training and experience.

Criterion-related validity requires that test scores be correlated with a criterion accepted as a reasonable indicator of job ability. Typically under this approach, actual job performance is the criterion used, and criterion validity is established in two ways. In the first approach, known as *predictive validity*, test scores of those hired are correlated with subsequent performance measures for the same individuals. Assuming that these performance ratings are accurate (and this is not an insignificant assumption as we will see later), a valid test is one that produces scores that are positively correlated with performance. In other words, test scores of job applicants accurately predict subsequent performance. A major limitation of this approach, however, is that those who do not pass the test (or receive a passing score but are not hired) are given no opportunity to perform. No organization is likely to ignore test scores when hiring workers to validate the test. To deal with that limitation, a second approach to criterion-related validity, known as *concurrent validity*, was developed. This approach involves administering a proposed new test to incumbent employees and comparing their scores concurrently to their performance ratings. Again, test scores should be positively associated with performance ratings if the test is valid. Critics argue that the concurrent validation technique promotes the creation of selection tests that overemphasize the characteristics of incumbent workers, not the actual requirements of positions.

Construct validity, the second general approach to establishing test validity, requires that tests be designed to measure certain general traits or constructs, such as intelligence or creativity, that are presumed or demonstrated to be associated with satisfactory job performance. When the test accurately measures the construct at issue, and the construct is in fact associated positively with job performance, the test is said to have construct validity. Of course, these connections can sometimes be tenuous. For example, questions can often be raised about the extent to which a test is a valid measure of a given psychological construct, and, as was the case with criterion-related validity, the entire assessment is only as good as the measure of job performance used. A test for a legal position could provide a good example. Assuming a certain logical frame of mind that incorporated a facility for legal reasoning was shown to be positively associated with job performance, a test would have construct validity to the extent that it accurately measured that type of mental capacity. Construct validity often relies on constructs that are hard to define, such as intelligence, so convincing empirical evidence of associations between scores on measures of constructs and elements of job performance is often hard to find, and as a result, this approach to validity is controversial and usually is thought to be of limited utility.

Content validity, the third conceptualization of measurement validity, is established when the content of a test closely matches the content of a job. Examples are written job knowledge tests that ask about knowledge actually required on the job and performance tests in which the actual duties are carried out, as in typing, driving, or welding tests. A content validity approach is attractive to employers because it is conceptually simple and it avoids problems associated with strategies that depend on measures of employee performance. As a result, this is the most commonly used approach to assessing examination validity. However, questions may be asked about how scores are interpreted in hiring decisions and the extent to which job analysis accurately reflect conditions faced by those holding the positions in question (Riccucci, 1991, pp. 81–83).

VALIDITY AND EQUAL EMPLOYMENT OPPORTUNITY

In principle, selection tests should discriminate among job applicants *only* on the basis of their relative ability to perform the work in question. In *Griggs v. Duke Power Company* (1971), the U.S. Supreme Court ruled that if a selection test had an adverse or disparate impact with regard to race, color, religion, or national origin, *and its validity had not been established,* its use constituted unlawful discrimination under Title VII of the Civil Rights Act of 1964. Of course, the Equal

Employment Opportunity Act of 1972 extended Title VII coverage to "governments," "governmental agencies," and "political subdivisions" making the principles articulated in *Griggs* applicable to the public sector. In practical terms, this meant that if a selection test was challenged on EEO grounds and could not be validated, it had to be discarded by the employer and replaced with one that could be validated using an accepted methodology.

During the late 1960s and early 1970s, the Equal Employment Opportunity Commission, the U.S. Department of Labor, and Civil Service Commission each issued guidelines on selection procedures. Their guidelines concerning how to demonstrate the job-relatedness of selection methods were not the same, and efforts to get uniform guidelines failed. The principal issue was a disagreement between the EEOC and the Civil Rights Commission on the one hand and the Civil Service Commission, Labor, and Justice on the other. In late 1976, the latter agencies agreed on and adopted what were called the Federal Executive Agency or FEA Guidelines, but the Civil Rights Commission and the EEOC were opposed, and the EEOC retained the guidelines it had adopted in 1970 (Equal Employment Opportunity Commission, 1970; Federal Register, 1977). The EEOC guidelines were the most difficult to satisfy.

The following were the principal points of disagreement:

1. The EEOC guidelines did not offer a concrete definition of *adverse impact* but indicated that its existence would be determined by comparing the rates at which different applicant groups pass a particular selection procedure. The FEA guidelines, on the hand, did set forth a definition of sorts: a "substantially different selection rate . . . which works to the disadvantage of members of a racial, sex, or ethnic group." A rule-of-thumb for determining if selection rates were substantially different was provided. This so-called 80 percent rule stated that if the selection rate for a group was within $4/5$ of the rate for the group with the highest rate, the enforcement agency will generally not consider adverse impact to exist.

2. The EEOC guidelines required validation of every component of the selection process used to fill a position. In practice, this meant making investigations of adverse impact for all examination components even when the examination as a whole did not have an adverse impact. In contrast, the FEA guidelines stated that adverse impact was to be determined for the overall selection process for each job cate-

gory. If no overall adverse impact was found, there was no obligation to validate the various selection components. If it was, then each component would have to be analyzed, and any having adverse impact would have to be validated if the employer wanted to continue using them.

3. Whereas the EEOC expressed a preference for criterion-related validity, the FEA pointed out, "Generally accepted principles of the psychological profession do not recognize such preference, but contemplate the use of criterion-related, content, or construct validity strategies as appropriate." In addition to other problems discussed earlier, criterion-related validity studies are often difficult to conduct because small jurisdictions do not test or hire enough people in single job classifications to give a statistical sample large enough for meaningful analysis comparing test scores and performance measures. In large jurisdictions, the sample is usually big enough only in a few classifications.

4. The EEOC required that an employer, while in the process of validating a selection procedure, be able to show that an alternative procedure with less adverse impact does not exist. The main objection to this standard was that it could mean an endless "cosmic" search for alternatives with less adverse impact. The FEA guidelines stated that in the course of a validity study, the employer should try to find and use procedures that have as little adverse impact as possible. Once a good faith effort had been made and the chosen procedure had been shown to be valid, the employer did not have to search further for alternatives.

5. Finally, the EEOC guidelines required that tests be validated for each minority group to ensure that differential validity did not exist. Differential validity is a situation in which a test has significantly different validity coefficients for different race, sex, or ethnic groups. Clearly, to use a test that routinely overestimates or underestimates job performance for one group or another would be unfair. The FEA guidelines were less demanding because they simply recommended that data be compiled separately for all groups to determine test fairness.

After extensive negotiations, agreement on *Uniform Guidelines for Employee Selection Procedures* finally was reached in 1978 (Federal

Register, 1979). In general, they followed the FEA guidelines closely. The *Uniform Guidelines* are not regulations, but they have had a major impact because the Supreme Court has said that as the administrative interpretations of the enforcing agencies they are entitled to "great deference." Nonetheless, when legal disputes arise, the courts make the final determinations about test validity requirements and whether or not an employer has met them.

Apart from the question of costs to employers, the *Uniform Guidelines* have been criticized as technically unsound in some respects, unclear in many others, and requiring excessive record keeping. Nevertheless, efforts to change them have met strong political opposition. In any case, the reality is that against a long history of relatively little pressure for test validation, public personnel agencies were suddenly placed in the position of having to validate a wide variety of selection tests for EEO reasons. Meeting the full requirements of the *Uniform Guidelines* is now and will continue to be a challenge to public employers. The technical, organizational, and political barriers to fully realizing this aspect of the merit principle are formidable. However distant the ideal, test validation is now fully established as an important objective for public personnel systems and is necessary for each of the selection criteria outlined in the following sections.

MINIMUM QUALIFICATIONS

The reason for imposing minimum qualifications such as extent and type of education, training, physical abilities, and experience is to screen out applicants who are realistically not likely to be able to carry out the tasks and responsibilities associated with a position. Examples would be requiring applicants for legal positions to have a degree from an accredited school of law, requiring firefighters to be able to lift and carry a certain weight, and asking that applicants for senior administrative positions have prior experience in equivalent or related positions. Residency in the employing state or locality may also be required.

The key standard for minimum qualifications is that they are actually *essential* to job performance and do not arbitrarily deny persons who might be able to do the job a chance to compete. Until recently, little attention was paid to establishing the validity of minimum qualifications, and the personnel technicians' best judgment sufficed. For predicting applicants' relative ability to perform, minimum qualifications such as requiring a high school diploma of janitors, truck drivers, and machine operators are at best questionable. As a practical matter, public employers must now be prepared to offer convincing evidence of validity, because the courts are routinely striking down minimum qualifications that cannot be shown to be logically related to the demands of a particular job. Currently, the trend is to remove minimum requirements that cannot be validated and to add flexibility by allowing for substitution of education for experience up to a certain point (and vice versa), and by including the catchall phrase, "or any equivalent combination of training and experience."

Some minimum qualifications may be imposed as a matter of law and social policy. Residence, age, and citizenship status requirements, though not necessarily related to job performance, may serve wider political, social, or economic purposes. It is not unusual for police departments to require that their officers reside in the city or county where they work to build effective community relations. National child labor laws were passed to protect children from exploitation by employers, and even the most talented 13 year old is not eligible for a computer programmer position in a local government. In 1978, the Supreme Court ruled that New York State could make U.S. citizenship a requirement for police positions, on grounds that policy making is the exclusive responsibility of citizens *and* the exercise of discretion by police officers is a form of policy making (*Foley v. Connelie*, 1978). These types of requirements are fixed by federal, state, or local laws, so the personnel agency has no discretion in their application beyond determining whether or not to argue for changes in the law.

PREVIOUS TRAINING AND EXPERIENCE

Evaluations of training and experience may be used in combination with written or oral examinations to generate a more complete evaluation of applicants' knowledge, skills, and abilities (KSAs). In other cases, written and oral examinations may not be practical, and the evaluation of training and experience as reflected in an applicant's resume constitutes the entire examination. This, as noted earlier, would be an example of an *unassembled examination* because candidates do not gather in one place to sit for a written test.

In some cases, suitable written tests may not exist or may be redundant because the applicants have already passed examinations for licenses or degrees needed to practice their profession (for example, law, medicine, engineering, social work). Experience has shown that many highly qualified persons will not apply for government jobs if they have to take a written test, believing that their academic degrees, professional credentials and licenses, and experience should be enough to demonstrate their competence. Unassembled examinations are often used in the federal service, in some cases for entry-level professional positions, and some use is made of them in state and local governments. Evaluation of training and experience, plus an oral examination, is a combination commonly found on all levels of government.

The evaluation of training and experience is based on a more or less thorough understanding of the KSAs required by a position. Applicants are ranked by trained examiners according to the extent to which they have these KSAs, a process that is inevitably judgmental. Many personnel experts believe that the most effective way of minimizing the subjective content of the evaluation process is to use the job element method. Job elements are KSAs determined through job analysis to be significant requirements for successful performance. Using this method, candidates are ranked using various types of evidence determined to be acceptable for showing relative competence in the different job elements. For example, ratings of the job element "Knowledge of the Theory of Electronics" are based on such evidence as "verified experience in mathematical analysis requiring electronic theory *or* outstanding record in advanced theory courses *or* score of 85–100 on theory test" (Maslow, 1968).

WRITTEN TESTS

Written tests are extensively used in the public sector to measure job knowledge or skills. Personnel agencies may construct tests or purchase them from consulting or other organizations such as the International Personnel Management Association. Small jurisdictions typically do not have the expertise or financial resources needed to develop and validate their own written tests. Multiple-choice tests are most commonly used. Essay-type examinations are rare, primarily because they are difficult to construct, take a long time to grade, and are open to the interpretations and biases of the readers. Despite problems associated with validity and adverse impact, written tests are likely to continue as the dominant way of rating applicants for a large variety of civil service positions. For personnel departments and agencies, they are administratively convenient and provide a quantitative and seemingly objective basis for ranking candidates. This does not mean that they are equally popular with agency management and job applicants, however.

Commenting on OPM's then new written tests for entry-level professional positions (Administrative Careers with America or ACWA), the Merit Systems Protection Board (MSPB) concluded in 1990 that these tests had the potential to be an efficient and inexpensive way of making selections when an agency hired a large number of employees from among a large number of applicants. By 1994, however, the GAO had concluded that this was not the case because "agencies said they have generally found alternative hiring methods better meet their needs" (U.S. General Accounting Office, 1994, p. 3). According to the GAO,

> Agency hiring officials said they prefer other hiring methods to ACWA for several reasons. They believe that using ACWA certificates is more time-consuming than using other hiring methods. Agencies receive ACWA certificates from OPM soon after they are requested, but the agencies may need/take several weeks to (1) contact the candidates; (2) receive and review their resumes; (3) interview them; and (4) verify past employment, education, and experience. Although these steps are required when agencies use other hiring methods, they can often be completed earlier in the process. (pp. 3–4)

The GAO noted other problems with the ACWA as a recruitment-selection device, including the following:

- Applicants who had lost interest in federal employment failed to respond to agencies' inquiries or to decline consideration for jobs, further slowing the process.
- Under the conditions imposed by the rule of three and veterans' preference, agencies were having difficulty meeting affirmative actions goals for women through ACWA certificates.
- Most of the applicants found their experience with the ACWA frustrating, and the GAO's survey revealed that 85 percent of the respondents were dissatisfied with some aspect of the process.
- More than half of the respondents to the GAO survey thought their chances of getting a federal job were outstanding or good after getting their scores because they had not been given much information about hiring patterns which should have revealed that a minute percentage of those with passing scores are hired; over a two-year period, 300,000 exams were given, there were more than 182,000 passing scores, and 3,228 applicants were hired. (U.S. General Accounting Office, 1994, pp. 4–5)

A clear indication of the extent to which federal agencies preferred alternatives to ACWA hiring is provided by Table 4.1. Under the Outstanding Scholar Program, federal agencies could hire candidates with a 3.50 or better grade point average or who graduated in the top 10 percent of their class. Those individuals were not required to take

Table 4.1 Hires into Occupations Covered by ACWA: Fiscal Years 1991 and 1992

Type of Appointment	Number of Appointments
ACWA	2,797
Outstanding Scholar and Other Direct Hire	8,905
Veterans Readjustment	1,194
Temporary	3,733
Excepted	5,574
Internal Placements	15,002

Source: U.S. General Accounting Office, 1994.

the ACWA test. Under Veterans Readjustment Appointments, agencies are able to hire eligible veterans noncompetitively. Temporary employees may be hired for up to four years without OPM approval, with appointments being renewed annually. The GAO noted that agencies often fill permanent positions with temporary employees in order to speed up the hiring process, escape limits on permanent employment levels, and to "hire a selected employee who could not be reached on an OPM certificate" (U.S. General Accounting Office, 1994, p. 6). Additional flexibility is available through excepted appointments under Schedules A, B, and C, which can include positions in the ACWA occupations. Finally, positions may be filled through reassignments, transfers, reinstatements, and promotions into ACWA occupations without taking or passing the ACWA (U.S. General Accounting Office, 1994, pp. 6–7). Given the experience with the ACWA process and standing registers of eligibles, OPM decided to make them an optional screening method for agencies, and "candidates now apply for a specific job, either directly through the agency or at OPM" (Ban, 1997, 197–198).

PERFORMANCE TESTS

Simply stated, a performance test asks the applicant to perform essential tasks related to job performance; the test simulates major facets of the job. Theoretically, all kinds of KSAs could be tested using performance tests, but they are most likely to be used to evaluate skills such as typing speed and accuracy, operating vehicles and machinery, and doing computational tasks. Simulating complex jobs and situations is technically difficult and expensive. As computer technologies and software become more sophisticated, it is probable that more complex mixes of KSAs will be evaluated using performance tests, such as those now being used in simulators to test pilots' responses to a range of situations they will (or might) face in real life.

In comparison with the other kinds of tests, performance tests yield very direct measures of how candidates perform on a series of job elements. Accordingly, these tests have high face validity. From the perspective of the test taker, they are concrete and, if clearly job-related, likely to be seen as fair and objective. For these reasons, many jurisdictions are switching to performance tests when this is feasible in technical as well as budgetary terms. A major limitation is cost because often expensive equipment must be acquired and maintained, and related personnel costs may be high.

ORAL EXAMINATIONS

The terms "oral examination" and "interview" are sometimes used synonymously, but an "interview" typically refers to the meeting that a hiring official has with persons who have already passed qualifying tests or examinations and are certified as eligible for appointment. We use the term "oral examination" to refer to a question-and-answer session conducted orally to measure basic qualifications. The weight or influence assigned to the results of an oral exam will vary with the importance given to an employee's ability to communicate ideas verbally and interact effectively with others. Such abilities often carry heavy weight in managerial positions, but they are likely to have relatively less impact on overall examination scores for technical or manual jobs. Oral examinations are used most extensively for higher-level managerial and administrative positions, but it is not unusual for them to be a part of test batteries for entry-level professional positions as well.

The results of oral examinations are inherently liable to distortions flowing from examiner bias and/or poor structuring of the examination's content and process. To deal with these problems, oral examinations must be "well planned in terms of the behaviors and responses to be observed, the evaluation standards to be applied, and the procedures for conducting the process" (U.S. Office of Personnel Management, 1979a). To ensure comparability and consistency, examiners should record their observations according to a standardized format. Training of those conducting the examination is very important because their expertise is the foundation for confidence in the validity of the ratings. The inclusion of women and minority group members on examination panels minimizes the possibility that discrimination will occur. It may also increase the probability that women and minorities will have confidence in the fairness of the process.

The Group Oral Performance Test

The individual examination is the most common form of oral, but another type is the group oral performance test. In the group oral, candidates are assembled in small groups, and a topic is assigned for discussion. Civil service examiners evaluate how the candidates *perform* during the discussion, particularly how they interact with the other members of the group. Advocates of the group oral argue that it shows how well the candidates "think on their feet" and, because the examiners only listen, they have more time for careful observation.

As critics point out, however, the group oral is staged, and the participants may not behave as they would in a normal administrative situation. The attention of examiners may be frequently disrupted, so they may really have *less* time to size up each person than they would in a panel interview. Furthermore, the examiners may end up rating each participant by how the group performed rather than the actual requirements of the position in question. In other words, the group oral raises significant validity and reliability concerns. As a way of compensating for these liabilities, some jurisdictions use both individual examinations and a group oral and then take the average of the candidates' scores on both.

Background Investigations

Background investigations are used for a variety of purposes. For most civil service jobs, they are routine reference checks done through mail and telephone inquiries. For some categories of positions, investigators employed by the central personnel agency will visit and interview former employers and others who have direct knowledge of an applicant's educational preparation, work experience, abilities, and personal qualities. On the state and local levels, the most intensive and comprehensive background checks are done for law enforcement positions. For federal jobs where access to sensitive or secret information is involved, the FBI conducts detailed and comprehensive loyalty and security checks. Recently, OPM contracted-out its background check function to a private corporation established by former employees. Faced with limited resources and time, public employers do not conduct thorough background investigations for most positions. The relative neglect of this phase of the selection process is regrettable because those who have worked with or supervised candidates on previous jobs often can supply far more information about them than can be obtained in an interview.

THE PROBATIONARY PERIOD

Although technically not a test or examination, the probationary period is the last stage in the screening process; no matter how much effort is put into making pre-employment tests valid, they may not screen out some applicants who actually lack the ability, motivation, or work habits needed to perform satisfactorily in particular jobs. The probationary period (usually six months to a year) gives supervisors the chance to evaluate new employees' situations and to approve for permanent status only those who have done satisfactory work. Probationary employees usually do not have appeal rights, nor, as will be explained in Chapter 8, do they have property rights in their jobs. As a result, they may be dismissed more easily than when they achieve permanent status.

All-too-often, management does not act as if the probationary period were an important part of the selection process. In practice, only a tiny percentage of appointees—in many cases less than 1 percent—is removed during or at the end of the probationary period. This has traditionally been the situation, despite such schemes to prod supervisors as requiring the appointing officer to certify in writing that the employee's services have been satisfactory, in the absence of which certification all salary payments are suspended. Needless to say, the practice of routinely moving probationary employees to permanent status without careful performance evaluations undermines the selection process.

A CLOSER LOOK AT LISTS OF ELIGIBLES AND RELATED ISSUES

As noted earlier, for every position or category of positions, applicants are evaluated and ranked according to their scores on one or more tests. Background checks and medical examinations are used only after an initial offer of employment is made. Each test is weighted in accordance with the civil service agency's determination of the relative importance of the qualifications it is intended to measure. For example, mathematical skills may be very important to an accounting position, but relatively unimportant in the case of a file clerk or secretary. Minimum qualifications are not weighted since the applicant must meet them to receive further consideration. The same rule applies to background checks and medical examinations. Tests are sequenced, with minimum qualifications coming as the first hurdle. If the applicant satisfies the minimum qualifications, he or she then undergoes one or more of the following: an evaluation of training and experience, a written test, or a performance test. If they are used, oral examinations come next, followed by a background investigation. This sequencing is economical in the sense that it places the most expensive and time consuming tests at the end of the process where the fewest number of candidates need to be considered. It would make little sense, for example, to administer physical agility tests to everybody who applies for a firefighter position before determining if they meet a minimum requirement such as a high school degree.

As we have seen, the list of names of individuals who have passed the examination is referred to as a *list of eligibles*. Applicants are ranked on this list in order of their composite examination scores. Traditionally, when hiring officials in agencies that have openings to fill, they request the civil service agency to certify names of eligibles from these lists in the order specified in the civil service law and regulations. There are two basic kinds of hiring procedures using lists of eligibles: register hiring and case examining. Register hiring is a process using standing lists of eligibles rank-ordered by scores. These inventories of candidates are created to fill openings as they arise. Case examining "involves recruiting, examining applicant submissions, and producing a certificate of eligibles for specific individual vacancies rather than using a register of candidates that has already been established" (U.S. Merit Systems Protection Board, 1995, p. vii). Case examining is currently the most common competitive hiring method used by the federal government.

Until recently, the rule of three (the three highest-ranking eligibles) was by far the most common system for ensuring that selection would be from among those at the top of a list of eligibles. Historically, this rule emerged as a device for protecting the merit system while giving some discretion to appointing officers. The assumption was that the examination scores would reflect real differences in ability to do the work and that three was a reasonable number of names to certify for each opening. In practice,

BULLETIN

A vacancy announcement from the City of San Jose, California: Senior Analyst for Research and Development in the Office of the Chief of the Police Department. Open to City of San Jose Employees Only. MINIMUM QUALIFICATIONS: Any combination of training and experience equivalent to completion of a Baccalaureate Degree from an accredited college or university in accounting, business, public administration, or any related field leading to a bachelor's degree, and 4 years of increasingly responsible experience in general management/administrative analytical work in the areas of personnel, budget, fiscal and/or organizational methods analyses, including general staff analytical work. Possession of a valid driver's license is required.

veterans preference, which results in extra points and serves as a tie-breaker when applicants have the same score, tends to bias the system in favor of veterans when the rule of three is used. Advocates of the rule of three argued that certifying more names, or the entire list of those *passing* the examination, would increase the risk that line managers would use the opportunity to make appointments on a partisan basis. Some jurisdictions were so concerned about political contamination that they adopted a rule of one, and a few state and local governments still operate on that basis. As questions about validity have increased, EEO concerns have mounted, and pressures for flexibility have grown, public employers have increasingly moved in the opposite direction. Some states, for example, have modified the rule by allowing the three highest test *scores* to be certified, a practice that often results in more that three candidates being certified because ties are commonplace. In 1995, the MSPB issued a report on the rule of three in which it concluded that a growing body of evidence supported the following conclusions:

- The rule of three does not represent the best way to foster merit-based hiring.
- The interaction between the rule of three and current approaches to veterans preference often produce results that are not in the best interests of managers or job candidates, including those with veterans preference (U.S. Merit Systems Protection Board, 1995, pp. ix–x).

The MSPB recommended that the rule of three be replaced by "a requirement that selecting officials shall select from an adequate number of well-qualified candidates who are referred to them by the appropriate OPM or delegated examining office" (p. x). In addition, the report suggested that federal agencies go to a category rating system (such as the "quality" and "eligible" categories used in a U.S. Department of Agriculture demonstration project) rather than numerical ratings.

THE UNEASY RELATIONSHIP BETWEEN COMPETITIVENESS, VALIDITY, AND EEO: FROM PACE TO ADMINISTRATIVE CAREERS WITH AMERICA

Presumably, for those who believe in the merit principle, the best of all possible worlds would be one in which public employers have highly competitive recruitment processes using valid selection tests that produce no adverse impact whatsoever. Unfortunately, as the federal government experience with efforts to implement a screening examination for entry-level professionals and administrators illustrates, such ideal outcomes are difficult to achieve.

A chronic complaint about traditional merit system recruitment, examination, and selection processes is that they are slow—so slow that many highly qualified applicants become frustrated and accept offers elsewhere. For entry-level administrative and professional positions in the federal service, lengthy delays were often the result of centralized control over the ranking and certification of applicants for positions publicized by agencies. The rationale for this procedure was that it was the most reliable way to ensure that quality candidates were referred to the agencies for selection through an equitable process and, thus, to protect merit from potential abuses on the agency level. Until 1982, OPM used a nationwide written examination to rank applicants for entry-level professional and administrative career (PAC) positions. Thousands of college graduates sat for this exam every year. In 1981, the Professional and Administrative Career Examination (PACE) was derailed by a class-action suit challenging its validity. During 1981, a consent decree was negotiated that required OPM to stop using PACE and to replace it with job-specific written tests that did not have an adverse impact on minorities.

Before the consent decree, OPM had gone to great lengths to establish the validity of PACE. The first step had been to identify the abilities important for successful performance in PACE jobs and to decide how they would be measured. Twenty-seven PACE occupations accounting for about 70 percent of PACE hires during the early 1970s were chosen for intensive analysis. Senior-level supervisors in these occupations prepared lists of the duties of the jobs in these 27 occupations, assessed the relative importance of these duties, and rated the required KSAs according to their importance to successful job performance.

The OPM analysts matched the KSAs and other traits identified in the 27 PACE occupations with those found in earlier tests, and they wrote examination questions similar to those in the earlier tests. After PACE was administered, OPM made criterion-related validity studies that revealed a positive relationship between test scores and job performance scores of persons already in PACE positions, such as social security claims examiners (an example of concurrent validity research).

The general abilities found necessary for successful job performance in PACE jobs included the following:

1. Verbal skills, meaning the ability to understand and interpret complex technical reading materials and to communicate effectively orally and in writing

2. Judgment, or the capacity to make decisions or to take actions in the absence of complete information and to solve problems by inferring missing facts or events to arrive at the most logical conclusion

3. Induction, relating to the ability to discover underlying relations or principles in specific data by formation and testing of hypotheses

4. Deduction, meaning skill at discovering implications of facts and logically applying general principles to specific situations

5. Numbers-related abilities, such as performing arithmetic operations and solving quantitative problems when a specific approach or formula is not specified.

PACE did have a disparate or adverse impact on African Americans and Hispanics. Data compiled by OPM on the April 1978 administration of PACE showed that 8.5 percent of whites taking the test received "unaugmented scores" (not including veterans preference points) of 90 or higher, but the percentages of African Americans and Hispanics who took the test and got such scores were 0.3 and 1.5 percent respectively. In practice, very few appointments were made of persons earning scores of less than 90. Other administrations of PACE produced similar results.

Those who brought the class action suit challenging PACE's validity argued that the five constructs upon which the test was based were far too general in nature to measure the ability to succeed in all 118 occupations covered. Critics also questioned the technical soundness of OPM's validity research. For better or worse, the courts did not have the opportunity to rule on PACE's validity. Instead, two weeks before Ronald Reagan assumed office as president, the Carter administration entered into a consent decree to settle the suit (*Luevano v. Campbell*).

Opponents of "preferential hiring" interpreted Carter's action as a politically motivated response to minority group pressures. The Reagan administration strongly opposed the decree and was able to negotiate modifications, including elimination of a requirement that the government continue affirmative action efforts until African-Americans and Hispanics were at least 20 percent of all employees at the GS-5 and higher grade levels in the job categories covered by PACE. As OPM Director Donald Devine later said, the Reagan administration had wanted to withdraw from the terms of the decree but had regretfully concluded that the matter was in the "hands of the

court, beyond the power of the government unilaterally to bar"
(Valdes, nd).

The main terms of the modified decree (*Luevano v. Devine*) were
as follows:

1. OPM was to phase out PACE as a selection test by 1985
2. Applicants for PACE occupations were to be selected
   using alternative examination procedures based on the
   requirements of the particular occupation.
3. If the alternative procedures had adverse impact, their
   validity had to be established.
4. Federal agencies were to make "all practicable efforts" to
   eliminate adverse impact from the interim use of PACE or
   from alternative procedures through recruiting and other
   special programs.
5. The D.C. District Court was to retain jurisdiction for five
   years after the implementation of an alternative examining
   procedure for each occupation.

On May 11, 1982, OPM announced that PACE was being abolished
and replaced by a new Schedule B appointment authority. Schedule B
applies to positions where it is not practical to hold competitive examinations. Under Schedule B authority, agencies are allowed to hire
people for entry-level professional and administrative positions without competitive examinations if they can show there are no qualified
internal candidates. Those selected in this manner are placed in the
excepted (noncompetitive) service. Until 1987, employees selected in
this manner were required to compete for competitive positions to
advance to the GS-9 level. If they were selected for a GS-9 position,
they were converted to the competitive service. In 1987, however,
President Reagan issued Executive Order 12596, which authorized
noncompetitive conversions of Schedule B appointments based on
"proven performance."

The Reagan administration offered several explanations for ending PACE and turning to Schedule B appointments. First, it argued
there were no alternative written tests and other merit selection procedures available. Second, reductions in federal hiring rates were
expected to result in substantially fewer appointments from outside
the service. Third, the cost of developing validated competitive examinations consistent with the decree would be prohibitive. In fact, at the
time, OPM showed little interest in a serious effort to develop alternative selection procedures. In fact, as late as 1987, OPM had devel-

oped only 16 tests which, by its own estimate, covered no more than 60 percent of the positions involved.

Whatever the motivations of those concerned, the use of Schedule B appointments did much to decentralize hiring for professional and administrative positions in the federal government. Under Schedule B, agencies develop and use their own recruitment and selection procedures. Federal line agencies, long frustrated with centralized and slow-moving hiring processes that undermined their recruitment efforts, were generally pleased with the Schedule B authority for PAC positions.

However, interests concerned about protecting the merit principle, maintaining overall quality control over agency hiring practices, and ensuring that potential applicants could access the system from outside were less than enthusiastic. OPM's monitoring and evaluation efforts were minimal, and it was very difficult for agencies to get approval to fill entry-level PAC positions from outside the government. College placement offices were given very little information about job opportunities for specific entry-level positions in the excepted service and the delays and frustrations involved in attempting to locate and be considered for positions caused many well-qualified candidates to pursue other options. The GAO and MSPB were critical, calling for more effective OPM oversight and guidance.

In early 1987, a suit brought by the National Treasury Employees Union (NTEU) signaled the end of OPM's glacial movement toward alternative selection procedures. The D.C. District Court ruled that OPM had inappropriately abolished the PACE while alternative examinations were unavailable. The judge also ruled that OPM had not made a convincing case about the prohibitive costs connected with developing and validating alternative tests. The original order gave OPM only six months to produce a competitive examination, and it ordered OPM to stop using Schedule B authority to fill PACE positions. Although a stay was granted, the need to implement a legally as well as technically viable alternative was obvious.

In 1988, OPM set forth a two-pronged strategy for replacing PACE. First, it proposed expansion of direct hire programs such as the Outstanding Scholars Program described earlier. Second, it announced the development of the ACWA examinations covering six occupational categories: (1) health and environment, (2) writing and information, (3) business and program management, (4) human resources and administration, (5) examining and adjudicating, and (6) investigation and inspection. A seventh category included some 16 occupations having specific educational or experience requirements (such as economist, international relations, and museum curator).

Applicants for positions in this seventh category were to be rated on the basis of their training and experience. All applicants for ACWA positions were also required to answer a series of questions intended to provide information traditionally sought through interviews: self-discipline, leadership qualities, and problem-solving skills. This component of the ACWA was called the Individual Achievement Record (IAR), had a multiple-choice format, and was machine scored.

Veterans preference points were added to the total ACWA score and the candidate placed on a standing list of eligibles. The new examinations were first given in June 1990, and OPM revoked Schedule B authority, effective July 1, 1990. The less than satisfactory experience with ACWA as a way of improving the competitiveness of federal recruitment and selection processes since that date is described earlier in this chapter. By the late 1990s, it had been effectively supplanted by a variety of decentralized recruitment and selection procedures driven largely by agency needs and priorities.

Initially, however, OPM's strategy was to balance agency-level demands for flexible, streamlined, recruitment and selection against pressures for central oversight and control. Although federal agencies applauded the idea that they should be given direct-hire authority for students with high grade point averages, this proposal was controversial because of concerns about validity, EEO, and the potential impact on workforce quality. The new examinations, though generally well received, raised questions about their capacity to improve recruitment success because, as the GAO observed, OPM's application procedure was potentially slow-moving and, as a result, potentially frustrating to agencies as well as applicants. The GAO's most recent evaluation of the ACWA suggests that it has indeed been slow moving and frustrating (U.S. General Accounting Office, 1994).

The GAO had noted earlier that the ACWA program might "also create difficulties for agencies, especially those with active recruiting programs" because

> The ACWA program effectively breaks the link between recruiting and hiring. Unless a student interested in an ACWA occupation can be employed through the Outstanding Scholar provision, there is no guarantee that agencies can hire the candidates they meet and interview on college campuses. (U.S. General Accounting Office, 1990a, p. 22)

In 1990, the GAO noted that although the "ACWA is aimed at supporting the goal of merit-based non-discriminatory hiring," (U.S. General Accounting Office, 1990a, p. 22), its impact on federal agencies' ability to compete in the labor market is uncertain. By 1994,

OPM was prepared to say, "Statistics for fiscal years 1991 and 1992 tend to support the belief that ACWA is less effective in helping agencies meet affirmative action goals for females. . . . However, the percentage of minorities hired through ACWA was similar to that of minorities hired through other methods" (U.S. Office of Personnel Management, 1994, p. 13). After almost 20 years of turbulence and controversy in the area of recruitment and selection, the federal personnel system is still struggling to devise an approach that satisfies demands for flexibility and competitiveness, supports efforts to increase the representation of women and minorities in administrative and professional jobs, and can be shown to be valid in all of its important phases.

CONCLUSION

During the past 25 years, many public personnel systems have implemented extensive delegations of authority to agencies in the areas of recruitment, testing, and hiring in an effort to remove procedural barriers to effective and efficient management. Indeed, the delegation of examination authority to line agencies has now become a norm and is part of a broader effort to decentralize the public personnel management process. This move away from the regulatory or compliance-centered personnel systems toward a "deregulated" and management-centered *human resources* approach responds to strong political pressures for reform, public dissatisfaction with government's performance, and a new definition of public management's role that stresses flexibility and accountability for results or outcomes. The danger in decentralization, however, is that inadequate oversight may be provided to ensure the protection of core merit system principles related to examination validity and equity. Centralized control of the examination process was designed to help ensure those values, but as it had been implemented in the past, it was presumed to cause significant delays in the selection process. Decentralization has been touted as a means of enhancing efficiency. As Carolyn Ban, Dean of the Graduate School of Public and International Affairs at the University of Pittsburgh, notes, however, within this new and decentralized environment, "we will always have to struggle to find the proper balance between the need for control to prevent abuses and the need to give managers enough discretion to do their jobs well" (Ban, 1997, p. 201). Rather than making the job of the personnel specialist easier, the current reforms require an ongoing effort to simultaneously advance the values of responsiveness, merit, equal employment opportunity, and performance. Within this context, the most recent developments in the area of electronic recruitment and examination are becoming increasing important. They may make it possible to maximize efficiency while ensuring adequate levels of centralized oversight and control. Experience with systems such as the federal government's Recruitment One-Stop initiative and other similar experiments will undoubtedly help to shape the future of public sector recruitment and selection.

DISCUSSION QUESTIONS

1. As a college or university student, what steps would you like to see taken to improve the recruitment efforts of public employers on the local, state, and federal levels?

2. Is using grade point averages (GPA) or class standing to make direct hires under the federal Outstanding Scholar Program a good way of ensuring that agencies will be hiring highly qualified applicants?

3. With extensive delegations and deregulation of the recruitment, testing, and hiring processes, will it be possible to protect the merit principle and equal employment opportunity?

4. How can public agencies do a better job of preparing their employees to fill more responsible positions and to be promoted?

5. What could be done to ensure that supervisors will carefully evaluate new employees during their probationary periods?

6. What is your image of the public sector as a place to work in comparison with the private and non-profit sectors?

REFERENCES

American Psychological Association (1966). *Standards for Educational and Psychological Tests and Manuals* (Washington, DC: American Psychological Association).

Ban, Carolyn (1997). "Hiring in the Public Sector: 'Expediency Management' or Structural Reform?" in Carolyn Ban and Norma M. Riccucci (Eds.), *Public Personnel Management: Current Concerns, Future Challenges* (New York: Longman), pp. 189–203.

Equal Employment Opportunity Commission (1970). "Guidelines for Employee Selection Procedures." *Federal Register,* Vol. 35, No. 149 (August 1).

Federal Register (1977). "Questions and Answers on the Federal Executive Agency Guidelines on Employee Selection Procedures," Part VI, Vol. 42, No. 14 (January 21).

——— (1979). "Adoption of Questions and Answers to Clarify and Provide a Common Interpretation of the Uniform Guidelines for Employee Selection Procedures," Vol. 44, No. 43 (March 2).

Foley v. Connelie (1978). 435 U.S. 291.

Georgia Merit System (1997). *Guidelines for Model Human Resource Procedures and Standards—Recruitment and Job Posting.* (Atlanta, GA). Accessed wysinyg://581http://www.gms.state.ga.us//model pro/recruit.htm (June 1999).

Hudson Institute (1988). *Civil Service 2000* (Washington, DC), June.

Illinois Commission on the Future of the Public Service (1991). *Excellence in Public Service: Illinois' Challenge for the '90s* (Chicago: Chicago Community Trust/Government Assistance Project), January.

Illinois Department of Natural Resources (1998). *DNR Internship Programs* (Springfield, IL). Accessed, June 1999 http://dnr.il.us/events/intpro.utm (June).

Llorens, Jared J., and J. Edward Kellough, *Public Personnel Management,* forthcoming.

Maslow, Albert P. (1968). "Evaluating Training and Experience," in J. J. Donovan, *Recruitment and Selection in the Public Service* (Washington, DC: International Personnel Management Association).

National Academy of Public Administration (1987). *Statement Concerning Professional Career Entry into the Federal Service* (Washington, DC), April.

Office of the Governor, State of Illinois (1997). *1998 Michael Curry and Vito Marzullo Internship Programs* (Springfield, IL: Office of the Governor), November 15.

Riccucci, Norma M. (1991). "Merit, Equity, and Test Validity." *Administration and Society,* Vol. 23, No. 1 (May), pp. 74–93.

U.S. General Accounting Office (1990a). *Federal Recruiting and Hiring: Making Government Jobs Attractive to Prospective Employees* (Washington, DC), August.

———. (1990). *Letter to The Honorable David Pryor, Chairman, Subcommittee on Federal Services, Post Office and Civil Service Committee on Governmental Affairs* (Washington, DC), September 27.

———. (1994). *Federal Hiring: Testing for Entry-Level Administrative Positions Fall Short of Expectations* (Washington, DC), March.

U.S. Merit Systems Protection Board (1990). Attracting and Selecting Quality Applicants for Federal Employment (Washington, DC: MSPB), April.

———. (1995). "The Rule of Three in Federal Hiring: Boon or Bane?" (Washington, DC: MSPB), December.

U.S. Office of Personnel Management (1979). *Job Analysis for Selection: An Overview* (Washington, DC), August.

———. (1992). *OPM HRD Policy Initiatives* (Washington, DC), June.

———. (1997a). *Hispanic Employment Initiative* (Washington, DC). Accessed http://www.opm.gov/pressrel/html/9point.htm (September).

——— (1997b). *Career America Connection Teleservice Center and Recruiting Messages* (Washington, DC). Accessed http://opm .gov/employ/html/cac.htm (October).

——— (1997c). *Federal Employment Information Touch Screen Computer Kiosks* (Washington, DC). Accessed April 2004, http:// www.gov.employ/html/feic.htm (October).

——— (1997d). *Student Educational Employment Program* (Washington, DC). Accessed http://www.opm.gov/employ/ students/intro.htm (December).

——— (1997e). *Student Educational Employment Program: Program Highlights From 1996* (Washington, DC). Accessed http://www .opm.gov/ employ/ students/studrpt.htm (June 1999).

Valdes, William C. (nd). *The Selection of College Graduates for the Federal Civil Service: The Problem of the "PACE" Examination and the Consent Decree* (Washington, DC: National Academy of Public Administration).

SUGGESTED READINGS

Gatewood, Robert D., and Hubert S. Feild (1998). *Human Resource Selection,* 4th ed. (Fort Worth, TX: Dryden Press).

Hays, Steven W. (1998). "Staffing the Bureaucracy: Employee Recruitment and Selection," in Condrey, Stephen E. (Ed.), *Handbook of Human Resource Management in Government* (San Francisco: Jossey-Bass), pp. 298–321.

Hays, Steven, and Jessica E. Sowa (2005). "Staffing the Bureaucracy: Employee Recruitment and Selection." in Stephen E. Condrey (Ed.), *Handbook of Human Resource Management in Government* (San Francisco: Jossey-Bass), pp. 97–124.

Kilpatrick, Franklin P., Milton C. Cummings, and M. Kent Jennings (1964). *The Image of the Federal Service* (Washington, DC: Brookings Institution).

Chapter FIVE

Issues in Job Evaluation and Pay

In all organizations where work is performed, it is typically structured in such a way that discrete and interrelated sets of tasks are collected into identifiable jobs. Positions are then established to perform the work associated with those jobs. To enhance efficiency and equity in a variety of core personnel functions such as recruitment, examination, selection, performance management, and compensation, it is useful, and many would say imperative, that we understand the content of jobs and that we evaluate and group jobs that are similar in their associated tasks and responsibilities together into categories or classes. This approach to organizing work is built on an American tradition known as "rank in job" rather than an alternative concept rooted in European custom and known as "rank in person." Under a rank-in-job system, the characteristics of the job rather than characteristics of the person holding the job determine rank. The assignment of jobs into categories facilitates other personnel tasks such as such as recruitment, examination, and selection; simplifies the development of broadly based employee performance appraisal processes; and helps ensure that a measure of equity is achieved in the development of pay systems. As a result, the design, application, and maintenance of job evaluation systems is considered a major responsibility of human resource specialists, especially in government merit systems where emphasis is placed on achieving equity in selection procedures and pay administration. In this chapter, we will focus on (1) the methods and processes associated with job analysis and evaluation, (2) job pricing and the construction of employee pay systems, and (3) issues and trends in public sector pay policies.

JOB ANALYSIS AND EVALUATION

To understand and ultimately describe the content of jobs, an analysis of the required tasks and the knowledge, skills, and abilities (KSAs) associated with them is necessary. It is only after that analysis is completed that job descriptions can be written and jobs can be evaluated and categorized.[1] If previously written, formal job descriptions exist, they can usually provide valuable information for job analysis. However, unless job descriptions are maintained regularly, they quickly become outdated and inaccurate. Jobs change over time as technology, organizational structure, and demands placed on jobs change. As a result, old job descriptions may be of only limited usefulness. In addition, if a job is new, there is likely to be no job description that reflects its content. It is important, therefore, to have other sources of information.

One of the best additional sources is the incumbent employee, assuming such a person is in place. One could argue that current employees should be able to provide an excellent source of information regarding the jobs they perform. After all, they should be better positioned than anyone else to know what it is that they do. The analyst can ask employees about the content of their jobs by administering a survey consisting of a job analysis questionnaire designed to provide information about the variety of tasks associated with specific jobs; the amount of time spent on each task in a typical day, week, or month; and the types of KSAs needed to perform the job satisfactorily. The survey is an efficient way to collect a substantial amount of information, but responses can sometimes be ambiguous and may lack sufficient detail. Consequently, it is sometimes useful to ask employees about their jobs in direct personal interviews. These interviews, conducted by trained personnel specialists, allow for follow-up questions and a probing of responses that are unclear. The drawback here is that

---

[1] In this text we use the terms "job analysis," "job description," and "job evaluation." In other discussions of these subjects one may encounter the terms "position analysis," "position description," and "position evaluation" to refer to the same concepts. Although there is a conceptual distinction between jobs and positions, there is a lack of consistent usage of those terms in the field. We believe the usage presented here is the most common and technically correct.

job analysis interviews are time consuming and, as a result, comparatively expensive. Frequently, it is most useful to rely upon the administration of job analysis questionnaires and to supplement the information obtained in that manner with a few selected interviews designed to provide information to augment and confirm survey data. Employees have an interest in portraying their jobs in the most favorable way possible. It may also be occasionally true that they will understate their job responsibilities, and for entirely new jobs, there may be no current employees. For these reasons, it will become necessary again to look in other places to fully understand how jobs operate or how they should operate.

The third common source of information about job content is the supervisor who has responsibility to oversee work performed in the jobs under analysis. The supervisor should be able to determine the accuracy of information provided by employees and provide his or her own assessment of how a new job should be conducted. It can be useful, therefore, to ask supervisors to review completed employee questionnaires or to complete those questionnaires independently. Direct interviews with supervisors can also be useful. It may well be the case, however, that a supervisor will not fully understand the content of the jobs performed by subordinates. As a result, there can be both advantages and limitations to using supervisors as a source of job analysis data.

If further information is deemed necessary, a job or desk audit may be conducted. These terms refer to a process by which trained specialists directly observe work being performed. Clearly, this can be the most time-intensive and costly approach to collecting job information, but it can also yield detailed knowledge of job content and the context within which work is completed. An example would be to have a personnel examiner accompany municipal road maintenance workers or police officers through their daily routines. Through this process, the examiner may be able to gain insight into the job and its requirements that is not obtainable by other means. Of course, one must be concerned that the sample of work performed on a given day may not be typical of what is usually accomplished. Any particular day, for example, could be unusually light or heavy in the workload performed in many jobs.

Because all the sources of job content information have their limitations, the wisest course of action may be to use as many of the various approaches outlined here as possible given the time and other resources one has available for job analysis. Multiple sources may balance or supplement each other. If a consensus regarding job content emerges from data colleted using a variety of techniques, one may have increased confidence that an accurate understanding of the job can be developed.

After job content data are collected, the analyst's next step is to summarize those data in a written job description. The job description will typically present a list of the major tasks associated with the job, a summary of the KSAs needed to perform those tasks effectively, and a statement of the educational or experience requirements for the job. Once the description is written, supervisors or employees may be asked to review it to be certain that it is accurate and complete. When it is finalized, it then becomes the basis for job evaluation requiring that jobs either be directly compared with one another or that they be compared with evaluation standards associated with various job groups or classes.

Four specific techniques of job analysis are used in both the public and private sectors (Persson, 1987). These methods are distinguished on two dimensions. The first is whether jobs are evaluated by comparing them with each other or by comparing them with an independent standard. The second dimension is whether they are evaluated as a whole or by examining and comparing compensable characteristics or factors that make up the jobs such as knowledge required, working conditions, or responsibilities. Whole-job approaches rely on an entirely qualitative assessment, whereas the factor-based approaches generate numerical scores that represent the relative value of jobs. These two dimensions and the four techniques they produce are illustrated in Table 5.1.

Consider first the whole-job method in which jobs are compared to each other. This technique, known as "ranking," is perhaps the simplest of all of the approaches. It requires only that a personnel specialist read job descriptions and place them in rank order from the most important to the least. The ranking rests entirely on the unstructured judgment of the analyst. Interpretations are tied to the contents of the job description, and the results will indicate whether one job is more valuable than another, but there is no indication of how much difference in value there is between jobs. For small organizations with only a very few jobs, this approach may be satisfactory. Certainly, it can be better than not having a system, but for larger organizations, the amount of judgment exercised could lead to unsatisfactory results. In addition, the subjectivity involved here may be difficult to defend because there are no specified evaluative criteria to guide the analyst (Persson, 1987).

The second whole-job approach, known as "grade description" or "job classification," provides a modest improvement over the ranking technique. In this approach, jobs are compared with evaluation

Table 5.1 Job Evaluation Techniques

	Method	
Basis for Comparison	**Whole Job**	**Factor-Based**
Jobs Compared with Each Other	Ranking	Factor Comparison
Jobs Compared with Standards	Grade Description/Job Classification	Factor/Point

Source: Adapted from Persson (1987) p. 4.

standards. Those standards are written descriptions of job categories or grades that form the basis for pay within the organization. Implementation of this approach requires the analyst to simply compare job descriptions with the descriptions of pay grades and to place or classify a job into the grade that best matches the job's duties and responsibilities. This job evaluation technique has been widely used in public sector organizations for a long time. It is often referred to as job classification because it is based directly on the classification of jobs into predetermined grades or pay categories.[2] Its simplicity is its greatest strength and appeal. It requires, however, that an a priori determination be made regarding how many pay grades should exist within a given organization. That poses an interesting question. How many grades should there be? Because pay grades reflect different levels of work, the obvious answer is there should be a number equal to the number of meaningfully different levels of work. Determination of that number, however, requires a detailed knowledge of the content of an organization's jobs and a sense of how the jobs may be compared with one another, before formal comparisons associated with this job evaluation technique are made.

In an effort to develop more systematic approaches to job evaluation that structure the exercise of subjective judgment by the personnel analyst, the factor-based methods were created. The factor-comparison approach was first developed and is perhaps the most difficult technique to explain. It begins with the identification of "benchmark" jobs that are determined to be appropriately compensated. Next, job factors or characteristics that justify compensation are identified. As noted earlier, these factors may include knowledge

---

[2] Of course, sometimes the term "position classification," rather than "job classification," is used to describe this technique. Also, reflecting the lack of consensus about the use of language in this field (see Note 1 earlier), it is common for many observers and practitioners to refer to "job evaluation" in general as "position classification."

required, responsibility exercised, working conditions, or similar characteristics. It is important to remember that there is no one set of job factors that must always be used. In the third step, a determination is made of how much of the pay of each benchmark job is attributable to each of the selected factors. For example, if a job paid $16.00 per hour, and the amount of knowledge required was significant enough that it was believed to account for half of the value of the job, then $8.00 of the hourly rate could be attributed to the knowledge factor. Once these determinations are made, other jobs can be compared with the benchmark jobs factor by factor so that an estimate of the total dollar value of each job can be determined. Each job evaluated in this manner becomes, in effect, an additional benchmark. The dollar values determined through this process are then considered "point" values that indicate the relative worth of each job. The dollar sign and even the decimal point can be removed, and the resulting number provides a quantitative indication of a job's relative value. The actual amount paid for each job is, as is always the case, determined through a separate process that involves an examination of pay rates in the relevant labor market. The advantage of the factor-comparison approach is that it structures the exercise of judgment regarding the value of jobs. Subjective determinations are made at identifiable points in the process, such as in the selection of benchmark jobs, in the selection of job factors, and in the comparison of factors across jobs. If disputes arise regarding the outcome, each of these separate decision points can be reassessed. The disadvantage is that the system is more complicated than the more elementary whole-job approaches.

The final approach to job evaluation is the factor/point technique. This approach requires that jobs be broken down into compensable factors for purposes of evaluation, and that the presence of those factors be compared with predetermined standards. The process begins with the selection and definition of compensable factors. As before, a variety of factors, including knowledge required, responsibilities, or working conditions could be used. Next, the factors are weighted to determine the relative influence each should have in determining the value of a job. This can be accomplished most easily by determining the percentage of total job value that can be ascribed to each factor if it is present at its highest level in a given job. These percentages, which must sum to 100, can be equated to point totals reflecting the maximum value awarded for each factor. The numerical scale can then be shifted to sum to any point total desired as long as the percentages attributed to each job factor remain the same. Each of these decisions rests on the judgment of those who are developing the system.

The next step is to identify and define specific levels of each factor. For example, it may be determined that there are three meaningfully different levels of knowledge that will allow the jobs in an organization to be distinguished from one another. A narrative description of each level must then be written and a proportion of the points available for that factor assigned to each level. If knowledge at its fullest level is equal to 500 points (perhaps on a 1,000 point scale), and if there are only three meaningful levels of knowledge, then we might determine that the lowest level is equal to 150 points and the middle level is assigned 300 points. Once this procedure is finished for each factor, the resulting narrative description of the factors, their levels, and the assigned point values for each level becomes the standard (known in the job evaluation field as the Primary Standard) against which jobs are evaluated. That process simply involves reading a job description that has been written to specifically speak to each factor and determining which level of each factor is present in that job. The job will receive the number of points associated with those factor levels, and the sum of those points across all factors will produce a total point value for the job. After all jobs are evaluated in this fashion, the point totals indicate their relative values.

Job Pricing

Each of the four job evaluation methods discussed earlier will produce a rank ordering of jobs from those most highly valued to those determined to be of less value. Once this is accomplished, that information can be used to develop a pay structure that will set compensation levels for each job reflecting its relative value and will, as a result, ensure pay equity internal to the organization. In addition, however, it is vitally important that compensation levels also reflect the labor market so the resulting compensation system will provide equitable pay relative to that market—a concept known as external equity. In most cases, the concepts of internal and external equity must be balanced against one another. In small organizations with only a few jobs, a rudimentary labor market analysis will suffice, and pay can be assigned in accordance with the results of that analysis, but for large organizations, more careful market analysis is needed. That process usually involves identifying key or benchmark jobs and a survey of employers in the relevant market designed to determine the range of pay they offer for those or very similar jobs. If a point-based system was used for job evaluation, that is, factor comparison or the factor/point technique was used, then salary survey data can be used to determine the functional relationship between job point values and pay levels that best characterizes the job market. That relationship may be calculated mathematically using techniques such as regression analysis. Once that relationship is known, pay levels for all jobs can be set.

In large organizations, job point totals should be clustered into groups or pay grades that, as we indicated earlier, reflect the different levels of work in the organization. This grouping of similar jobs together for pay purposes helps to simplify and streamline the resulting compensation structure. Within each pay grade, a minimum and maximum salary is established so that the resulting structure may look similar to that presented in Figure 5.1. The range in each grade can be divided into step increases that are either awarded annually or bi-annually as an incentive for staying in an organization, or are awarded on the basis of performance (a process reviewed in Chapter 6). It is important when establishing such structures that the number of pay grades accurately reflects the number of meaningfully different levels of work in the organization. That determination rests on subjective reasoning, but with a given range within each grade, a positive slope dictated by the labor market, and an overall minimum and maximum pay level for the structure as a whole, each additional pay grade added to the structure will further the extent to which pay levels overlap among the grades. As you can see from Figure 5.1, some overlap is inevitable, unless there is an extraordinarily high and unrealistic slope, but excessive overlap will undermine the purpose for having distinct pay grades.

JOB EVALUATION IN THE FEDERAL SERVICE

Throughout the 19th century, the federal government, at best, organized its employees into only a handful of broadly defined pay classes. By the 1920s, however, that system had become unworkable and an effort to bring greater order and equity to the federal pay system resulted in passage of the Classification Act of 1923. That act first established very broad occupational categories called "services." These included the Professional and Scientific Service; the Subprofessional Service; the Clerical, Administrative and Fiscal Service; the Custodial Service; and the Clerical-Mechanical Service. Each service was then subdivided into a number of grades or levels of work and descriptions of the kinds of work falling into each grade were developed. Individual jobs were allocated to the grades based on an assessment of their content. Thus, this earliest attempt at systematic job evaluation rested on the grade description or job classification technique. To aid in the allo-

Figure 5.1

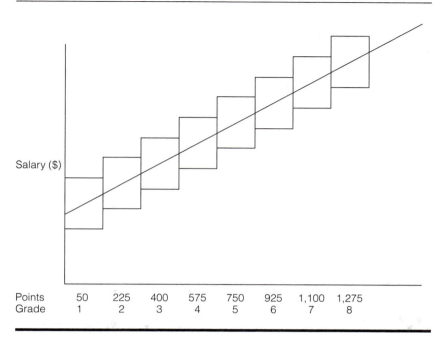

Points	50	225	400	575	750	925	1,100	1,275
Grade	1	2	3	4	5	6	7	8

cation of jobs to pay grades, job classes were established within the grades and class specifications were written to serve as guides for personnel specialists responsible for job evaluation (Van Riper, 1958, pp. 298–299). The 1923 Act was an important first step, but it applied to only approximately 10 percent of the federal service; jobs outside of Washington, D.C., and blue-collar jobs not of a custodial nature were exempt. The act reinforced the concept of rank-in-job, and it set the stage for eventual expansion of the job evaluation to all federal positions (Van Riper, 1958, pp. 299).

The next major overhaul of federal pay and job evaluation processes came with the Classification Act of 1949. This law consolidated the occupational series of the 1923 Act into the General Schedule (GS) system for white-collar employees (which consisted of 18 grades) and a Crafts, Protective, and Custodial Schedule for blue-collar workers. The job evaluation system used was still based on a grade description technique. The 1949 law required, for example, that the criteria used to assign positions to classes and grades (classification standards) consider the following:

- The nature and variety of work performed in carrying out a position's responsibilities
- The amount and kind of supervision provided to the person occupying the position
- The nature of guidelines available for performing the work
- The level of originality or independent decision making required
- The importance and scope of decisions, commitments, and conclusions reached by the position's incumbent
- The number and kinds of positions over which the position in question exercises supervisory authority
- The technical skills, experience, and other qualifications required to successfully carry out the position's responsibilities (National Academy of Public Administration, 1991, p. B4)

Narrative job descriptions were developed to serve as the basis for evaluation and typically included four kinds of information:

- An *introduction* in which the primary purpose of the position and its relationship to the organization are described.
- A *statement of major duties and responsibilities,* which covers the important, regular, and recurring duties and responsibilities of the position. For supervisors, this included a description of the kind and degree of supervision exercised (authority to plan work, assign and review work, and evaluate performance).
- A *description of the controls over the position,* which is a statement of how the work is assigned, the kind of supervision and guidance received, and the kind of review given to work in progress or upon completion.
- A *statement of special qualification requirements* that sets forth knowledge, skills, education, certification, or licenses required if they are not apparent from reading the rest of the position description.

Responsibility for developing classification standards was assigned by the 1949 act to the government's central personnel agency, the U.S. Civil Service Commission (CSC). The Civil Service Reform Act of 1978 shifted those duties to the U.S. Office of Personnel Management (OPM). Provisions of the 1949 Classification Act, along with those of other civil service laws are codified in Title V of the U.S. Code, which now requires OPM to define federal GS occupations, establish official job titles, and describe various levels of work. Although postal workers and recently the civilian employees of the Defense Department and workers within the new Department of Homeland Security are in separate personnel systems outside of Title V, the GS system still comprises an extremely large number of federal civilian employees. To carry out its responsibility regarding job evaluation, OPM "approves and issues position classification standards that must be used by agencies to determine the title, series, and grade of positions covered by Title 5" (U.S. Office of Personnel Management, 1997, p. 4).

Standards defined by OPM cover each job class within the GS system, and classes are assigned to pay grades on the basis of the duties, responsibilities, and qualifications considered necessary for each grade level. In addition, jobs within the federal GS are clustered into 22 *occupational groups,* each of which is further subdivided into *job series* or subgroups that include all jobs at various skill levels in a particular kind of work. For example, the *Personnel Management and Industrial Relations Group* has almost 20 series, including the *Personnel Management Series,* the *Personnel Staffing Series,* and the *Contractor Industrial Relations Series.* All jobs or positions in a series are related to each other by their difficulty, complexity, and skills requirements. Based on this information, they are assigned to a class using existing standards. The intended result is equal pay for work of substantially equal difficulty and responsibility, no matter the occupational group.

Beginning in 1975, the federal government began to supplement its reliance on the grade description or job classification technique with a factor/point method applied to nonsupervisory jobs and known as the Factor Evaluation System (FES). The FES uses nine job factors common to most non-supervisory positions in GS occupations, and point values are assigned to each job. As in other factor/point systems, the total number of points determines a job's grade. The FES factors can be describes as follows:

- *Factor 1:* The knowledge required by the position. This factor addresses the kind of knowledge and skills required and how they are used in doing the work.
- *Factor 2:* Supervisory controls over the position, including how work is assigned, the employee's responsibility for carrying out the work, and how the work is reviewed or evaluated.
- *Factor 3:* Guidelines available for doing the work and the judgment needed to apply these guidelines or to develop new guidance.

- *Factor 4:* The complexity of the work involved, including the difficulty in identifying what needs to done, the difficulty level of the work, and the level of originality or creativity required.
- *Factor 5:* The scope and effect of the work, which includes the impact or importance of the work product.
- *Factor 6:* The personal contacts that occur on the job, including the conditions or settings in which such contacts are made.
- *Factor 7:* The purposes or reasons for personal contacts.
- *Factor 8:* Physical demands of jobs, which may vary widely in the nature, frequency, and intensity of activity.
- *Factor 9:* The nature of the work environment, job hazards, and the safety precautions required to perform the work safely.

FES job descriptions are required to cover all the information needed to assign points in all nine factor areas, which may not be the case for more narrative job descriptions used in the whole-job grade description or job classification approach. As a result, FES position descriptions tend to be very detailed and contain the information needed to classify positions using either narrative job classification or FES standards. According to the OPM, "many federal agencies have decided to prepare all position descriptions following the FES factor format" (U.S. Office of Personnel Management, 1997, p. 17).

JOB EVALUATION AND CLASSIFICATION ISSUES

The primary contribution of job evaluation and classification systems in the public sector was to bring relative order out of a chaos of misleading job titles, grossly inequitable pay for the same kind and level of work, and recruitment and selection processes largely uninformed by a detailed understanding of job content and its relationship to organizational functions and human resource needs. Adoption of job evaluation and accompanying compensation plans, beginning as early as the 1920s, was an important stage in the development of merit systems because it curbed the widespread practice of manipulating pay rates for partisan or personal reasons. The grade description or job classification approach in particular gained wide professional support as a reform that applied scientific management's emphasis on job analysis and efficiency to the technical problems of public administration (Merrill, 1960). Reform candidates for elective office were supportive because job classification conveyed their commitment to "rational and businesslike" approaches to government. Nevertheless, job classification and its practitioners have a long history of being at the center of ongoing battles between supporters of traditional merit systems and those in favor of a management-centered model. The former argue that classification is fundamental to achieving and maintaining neutral competence. The latter are fond of describing it as a major example of the "triumph of technique over purpose" (Sayre, 1991).

According to the National Academy of Public Administration (NAPA), the design and administration of job evaluation systems should promote the accomplishment of two objectives. First, they should support efforts to treat job applicants and employees in an equitable and impartial manner. Second, they should be designed to promote effective and efficient agency performance. The first objective reflects the values of the first civil service reform movement and its stress on regulating and policing the personnel-related actions of managers. It was, in turn, assumed that only a politically neutral and technically competent civil service could be efficient and effective. The second of NAPA's objectives for job evaluation is related to the contemporary focus on human resources management. In NAPA's words, job evaluation systems "must be brought more into the mainstream of essential processes in an organization's management structure. These should be as important as an agency's budget, information or accounting systems; in fact, they should have the ability to interface with these and other administrative systems to enhance the management process" (National Academy of Public Administration, 1991, p. 14).

Frequently, however, job evaluation systems in government have come under attack from critics who argue that they are incapable of achieving either of NAPA's objectives. Regarding fairness and equity, the accuracy and objectivity of job analysis and classification actions have always been suspect because none of the systems in use comes close to completely eliminating professional or managerial judgment and discretion. As we have seen, job evaluation systems, including those based on quantitative approaches like the FES, inevitably rest on subjective processes. In many cases, it is very hard to draw absolutely clear lines between jobs regarding levels of difficulty and responsibility. Classification analysts, in other words, are doing more than plugging numbers into formulas; they are often required to exercise considerable discretion and judgment, and OPM recognizes this reality in its instructions:

OPM prepares classification standards on the assumption that the people using them are either personnel specialists or managers trained in how to classify positions and knowledgeable about the occupations and organizations concerned. Regardless of the specific format of the standard, you must consider and apply it as a *guide* to grade level decisions. You should not use grade level criteria mechanically to match or "force fit" a position to specific elements, factors, situations, or duties. You must always use sound classification judgment to determine the extent to which an individual job fits the *intent* of the standard. (U.S. Office of Personnel Management, 1997, p. 34)

Classification audits conducted by central personnel agencies may be expected to find that a certain percentage of job evaluation decisions made on the agency level are wrong because of factual inaccuracies and misinterpretations of classification standards (U.S. Office of Personnel Management, 1981). Errors of this type are unfortunately unavoidable, but OPM suggests they may be minimized by regular "desk audits" of jobs and better training of those doing the evaluation.

The more significant challenge to the fairness of the job evaluation process and the equity of its outcomes comes from the possibility that its discretionary nature will allow personal and organizational biases to play significant roles. Most importantly, those with a stake in a classification action are in a position to try to influence the analyst's decision. Many so-called overgrading errors may be traced to pressures from line managers who for one reason or another wanted higher salaries for *their* subordinates. More broadly, however, elected executives, line managers, and personnel specialists may become involved in a struggle for control over the job evaluation and classification process, and analysts are in a position to act as organizational politicians who are more responsive to powerful organizational actors than they are to merit principles or the formal rules of job evaluation (Shafritz, 1973).

Another reason to question the objectivity of job evaluation in government is the well-documented phenomenon called "grade creep," which refers to an unplanned rise in the *average* grade of all employees in a jurisdiction or agency. Periodically, legislative oversight committees or executive budget offices will "discover" that average grades have risen and, with them, personnel budgets. In short order, there will be calls for adjustments and downgrades, politicians will complain about "overpaid and under-worked bureaucrats," taxpayers will become irate over the increase in the government's expenditures for wages and salaries, and employee organizations will mobilize to oppose downgrading of positions.

Some of the inflation in average grade level is the result of intentional over-grading. Often, the motive is to keep a valuable employee who has received an outside offer, to compensate for inflation that has eroded purchasing power, or to reward exceptional performance. Over time, the cumulative effect may be a breakdown of internal pay equities, the emergence of highly visible biases in the grade structures of agencies, and a widespread perception among workers that the administration of the system is neither objective nor fair.

Inflated job descriptions do occur, job evaluations are sometimes manipulated, and some public employees do receive salaries that are out of line with their job responsibilities and qualifications. If enough of this goes on long enough, it can lead to significantly higher average grades throughout the government or in certain agencies. However, the reasons for grade creep are usually far more complicated than simple greed and favoritism. Much of it is associated with the changing nature of the public workforce. Governments on all levels are employing growing numbers of professional, administrative, and technical employees needed to carry out new and often complex programs. There is no reason to assume, therefore, that the largest numbers of public employees will be in the lowest grades. To the contrary, the largest numbers frequently are toward the middle of the grade structure. In 2003, for examples, fully 65 percent of GS positions were in grades 9–15, with 40 percent in grades 9–12 (U.S. Office of Personnel Management, 2005a, p. 29). Often, however, public employers fail to acknowledge this reality in their formal classification plans and workforce projections. It is worth noting that the average federal GS grade rose from 7.39 in 1964 to 9.82 in 2003 (U.S. Office of Personnel Management, 2005a, p. 26).

Another rather predictable cause of grade creep is the direct connection between classes and pay ranges. A great deal of over-grading happens because jobs are in relatively narrow classes or grades with pay levels that cannot be changed without legislation. Legislative bodies and elected executives are notoriously reluctant to raise pay scales and pressure will build up over time to place positions in higher grades to prevent turnover of valuable employees and to reward superior performance. From an organizational performance point of view, grade creep, while informal and extralegal, may be a functional response to the rigidity of the formal system. Over time, however, the job evaluation process and related procedures may become a facade behind which operates an opportunistic and highly inequitable approach to compensation that has little if any connection to organizational performance.

Contracts negotiated with employee organizations or unions (see Chapter 7) can also affect job evaluation processes. In most governments, setting job evaluation standards and the classification of individual positions are management prerogatives and are not negotiable. Traditionally, unions have concentrated on improving pay and fringe benefits, but this does not mean that they have always been content to leave job evaluation completely to management. In some places, they have succeeded in making evaluation standards subject to negotiation, and disputes over their interpretation may be subject to binding arbitration.

Most public managers are strongly opposed to making job evaluation plans a negotiable matter. They argue that management's effectiveness will be undermined if it cannot establish a job evaluation system that fits organizational needs. To analysts specializing in job evaluation, bargaining in these areas is anathema because they consider the process of evaluating and ranking jobs a technical field requiring substantial training, experience, and professional judgment. For the most part, this point of view has held sway on all levels of government, but there are exceptions. One of these is the U.S. Postal Service where job evaluation is subject to negotiation under terms of the Postal Reorganization Act of 1970.

When public employers bargain collectively with unions representing several bargaining units, they often find it hard to maintain a unified job evaluation and pay plan. This problem develops when there are several bargaining units; no single union is likely to win the representation in all the units, and thus, the employer must bargain with a number of different unions. In each unit, the union will concentrate on doing all it can to improve pay and benefits for its members. Improvements negotiated for one unit may create inequities for employees doing the same kind and level of work in other units. As a result of unit-by-unit bargaining, separate job evaluation and pay plans eventually are created for each unit; the grading and pay may be equitable *within* each unit, but not *between* units.

With varying degrees of success, public sector job evaluation systems have concentrated on achieving fairness and equity and, in so doing, have tended to neglect the organizational performance concerns of managers. During the past half-century, U.S. public administrators have consistently complained that existing classification structures and processes are barriers to effectiveness and efficiency. In its review of studies and articles published between 1941 and 1991, NAPA found that the following problems were most often cited:

1. Classification standards are complex and hard for nonspecialists to understand, much less use on day-to-day basis. In practical terms, this means that managers and supervisors play little, if any role, in the classification process, which is the province of analysts who have little interest in management's human resource problems.

2. Central personnel agencies do not provide needed leadership and they are notoriously resistant to change, especially to changes that reduce their control over classification standards and procedures.

3. Public managers experience the process as burdensome and unintelligible, and they see little reward in supporting an effort to accurately describe and classify positions.

4. Supervisors learn to pressure analysts to over-grade positions, and they do not use the system as a human resources management tool.

5. The rank-in-position approach is rigid and inflexible. It does not accommodate specific agency needs, and classification standards often neglect employees' impact on the job and important differences in levels of performance.

6. Classification plans and position descriptions are typically at least several years out-of-date (it is not unusual to find systems that have not been revised for decades), which makes it difficult to recruit for new occupations, to clearly define and anticipate human resource needs, and to meet staffing requirements in rapidly changing technical fields (National Academy of Public Administration, 1991, pp. 17–18).

Overall, NAPA's study revealed that federal personnel directors, classifiers, administrative officials, and managers favored several important reforms, including the following: (1) authorizing significant delegations of classification authority to line managers, (2) broad-banding, or consolidation of existing grades into three or four grades with wide pay ranges, and (3) allowing skills-based pay differentials. In fact, these kinds of changes are found in the systems used by federal agencies excluded from the statute covering classification (Title V) and in several OPM-sponsored demonstration projects that tested alternative approaches to one or more aspects of personnel administration. According to NAPA, high levels of satisfaction with these innovative or different classification systems was found to be linked to these agencies' ability "to pay salaries more in keeping with the marketplace than is possible for agencies covered by Title 5" (p. 33).

In addition to issues associated with pay, NAPA found that the federal agencies conducting demonstration projects cited at least three human resources management problems as reasons for reforming the job evaluation or classification system. First, overly complex job evaluation standards with too many narrow occupations and grades purportedly undermined management's efforts to recruit highly qualified personnel, to effectively assign work, and to sustain high levels of *organizational* performance. Second, it was taking far too long to have job evaluated; it often took months to complete the staffing process and to fill a vacant position. Third, inflexible job evaluation structures tended to force outstanding performers out of their primary areas of expertise and into higher graded supervisory jobs where they could make higher salaries (pp. 33–34).

The current emphasis on flexibility and responsiveness has focused attention on three reform models potentially available to public employers. First, the dominant rank-in-job model could be replaced by a rank-in-the-person system for part or all of the civil service. Second, authority over the design of grading systems could be shifted to the agency level and the idea of a governmentwide system discarded in favor of multiple systems tailored to fit the specific situations and needs of agencies (a policy of planned fragmentation). Third, existing governmentwide systems could be retained but modified to allow more agency-level discretion under general policies set forth by central personnel agencies.

THE RANK-IN-PERSON SYSTEM

In many countries, personnel systems are structured around the "rank-in-the-person" concept, and civil servants' educational backgrounds, technical and administrative qualifications, special abilities, and relevant experiences (not the characteristics of a particular job) determine their pay and organizational status. Nevertheless, as we have noted, the rank-in-job approach dominates the public service on all levels of government in the United States. Rank-in-person systems have been generally restricted to the foreign service, military services, and agencies such as the Department of Veterans Affairs, Federal Bureau of Investigation, and the Central Intelligence Agency. On the local level, police departments typically use a rank-in-person system or some variant that combines it with the job-based model.

The U.S. Department of State's Foreign Service offers a good example of a U.S. version of the rank-in-person approach (U.S. Department of State, 2005). Currently, the Foreign Service numbers about 14,500 personnel, which includes the Senior Foreign Service, Foreign Service officers and staff, and ambassadors. Work within the service is career-oriented with everybody starting at the same point and progressing through as many as three stages: junior officer, career officer, and senior Foreign Service officer. Upon entry, employees are referred to as junior officers and they are in a probationary status. In contrast to a position-based approach, functional or technical specializations are not expected on the first step of the career ladder. Junior officers, therefore, enter into the career line without a specific functional designation or specialty. On entering, they receive basic orientation at the National Foreign Affairs Training Center and as many as seven months in training (mostly language skills) before their first overseas assignment, which can run from two to four years.

Within the service, emphasis is placed on general skills and the potential to continuously develop and to make successful progress through the various stages of the career line. All junior officers are reviewed for tenure and commissioning as career Foreign Service officers (FSOs) by the Commissioning and Tenure Board about 36 months after entry. The only standard used for tenuring and commissioning is "a candidate's demonstrated potential to serve effectively as an FSO over a normal career span." The Board evaluates candidates in five areas: intellectual skills, interpersonal skills, leadership, managerial skills, and substantive knowledge. Because Foreign Service careers stress broadly gauged functional expertise and flexibility, employees *are* assigned a functional specialty or track at the time they are offered tenure, and they are expected to spend most of their career working in that specialty area. Presently, there are five tracks:

- Officers in the *management track* coordinate the support operations of U.S. embassies and consulates around the world. Their duties are diverse, including hiring foreign nationals, managing financial operations, and purchasing equipment and material.

- Those in the *consular track* have two primary functions. They issue visas to foreign country nationals who want to enter the United States, and they provide special services to American citizens overseas.

- If they are assigned to the *economic track,* FSOs develop assessments of commercial and economic issues ranging from fishing rights to environmental impacts of economic development. FSOs also establish professional contacts to obtain information on local economic conditions and their implications for American trade and investment policies.

- FSOs in the *political track* assess foreign support for U.S. policies and establish contacts with a wide range of local groups and organizations to determine their positions on domestic and foreign policies in certain countries.

■ FSOs in the *public diplomacy track* manage cultural and information programs, explain U.S. history and values to foreign audiences, describe and represent U.S. foreign policy and oversee exchange programs intended to build linkages with citizens and leaders of other nations.

After they receive tenure, FSOs acquire further functional, specialized, expertise during their first several assignments. As their careers develop, they will serve in out-of-track positions, and the Department of State encourages them to acquire skills in more than one functional area so that they can achieve the knowledge and experience needed to serve effectively in a variety of roles. Because continuous development and regular promotion are required to stay in the service, simply having performed adequately at one level is not enough. Having broad policy and management skills as well as specialized expertise is important, because promotions are competitive and, for each grade, there is a time limit before which candidates must be promoted to the next grade. Those who are not promoted must leave the service. Recommendations for promotion are determined by a selection board, which reviews the files and performance evaluations of all FSOs in each grade who are eligible for promotion. After this review, the board issues a list of officers recommended for promotion, based on merit. The top of the FSOs' career line is the Senior Foreign Service, a relatively small group of officers (about 1,000) who formulate, organize, coordinate, and implement U.S. foreign policy. These are the most responsible and sensitive positions in the service, and entry into this level of responsibility and authority is highly competitive.

Arguments in favor of replacing rank-in-job systems with those based on the rank-in-person concept stress the flexibility, adaptability, and "fit" with decentralized personnel management structures of the later approach. In 1991, for example, the U.S. Merit Systems Protection Board favorably evaluated the modified rank-in-person system used by the Department of Veterans Affairs (VA). The statute under which the VA operates (Title 38) establishes "a methodology in which the qualifications of each *person* are evaluated against agency-established qualification standards, and a grade (rank) is assigned to the person based on his or her individual qualifications regardless of the position held." Another difference from the Title V model is the use of groups of VA employees (standards boards) in the same or related occupations to recommend the grade to which a person should be assigned. The VA's approach is not a pure rank-in-person system because the job held often determines an incumbent's ability to qualify for a higher grade, and "the highest three registered nurse grades and the highest two grades for physicians are assigned exclusively on the basis of the position held" (U.S. Merit Systems Protection Board, 1991, pp. 17–18).

Given its study of the VA's personnel system, the MSPB concluded that it offered a potential alternative for some agencies and occupations operating under Title V. Specifically, the MSPB report noted that the VA's managers believed the method used to set employee grades was easier and more equitable. In its recommendations, the MSPB suggested that those concerned with reforming the Title V system consider the use of peer panels as a part of the grade- and pay-setting process because they increase flexibility and are more likely to reflect an understanding of the actual work environment. The MSPB also cited the VA's extensive delegations of personnel authority to line managers as providing a model that the rest of the federal service should consider (pp. 45–48).

In recent years, there has been strong support for applying the rank-in-person concept to high-level professional and executive employees. In the federal government, the Senior Executive Service (SES) is a limited example, and several states have established versions of the SES under which top managers are assigned a rank and pay grade. In the United States, however, possibilities of adopting the rank-in-person principle for middle- and lower-level jobs appear small. A primary objection to such reforms is that they would lead to a revisitation of the chaos and pay inequities that prevailed before job evaluation plans were adopted.

Also, rank-in-person classification schemes as implemented in other countries have been rejected by U.S. lawmakers as an anti-democratic way of staffing civil services that could lead to the creation of powerful administrative elites. In U.S. merit systems, relative ability to perform the work assigned to a specific position is supposed to be the main standard, and it is argued that this is a democratic approach to staffing that can only work in the context of a well-designed and administered rank-in-job system. Rank-in-person systems, on the other hand, tend to emphasize the general educational backgrounds and social skills of those seeking to pursue careers that lead to high-level posts in the civil service, and this almost always restricts access to members of social and economic elites, particularly those who have attended certain universities. These career lines, in practice, are "closed" to others with different social and educational backgrounds. Under such conditions, the hierarchies of civil service bureaucracies mirror the larger class structures of societies, with representatives of the upper class at the top. Although there may be ways of "democratizing" access to and progress through rank-in-the-person career systems, Americans have traditionally been suspicious of them in most areas of civilian bureaucracy.

FRAGMENTATION

Fragmentation is a policy option supported by those who believe that a single classification system or concept simply cannot effectively address the human resources management needs and human capital strategies of all public agencies under all conditions. In the federal service, numerous complete and partial agency exclusions from Title V, demonstration projects, and ongoing modifications of traditional classification practices are pointed to by some observers as evidence of the need to adapt these systems to fit specific agency circumstances (National Academy of Public Administration, 1991, p. D-3). Although not a formal policy, fragmentation is taking place at an accelerating pace. In 2004, of about 1,750,000 full-time federal civilian employees, around 500,000 were not in the General Schedule (U.S. Office of Personnel Management, 2004). This trend was extended with the development of independent personnel systems for the Departments of Defense and Homeland Security.

REFORMING EXISTING SYSTEMS

In practice, efforts to deal with the problems posed by conventional job evaluation and classification systems on all levels of government in the United States have concentrated on (1) increasing their flexibility, (2) making it easier for supervisors to understand and use them, and (3) connecting them in supportive ways to the human resources management efforts of agencies. With the exception of senior executive services and a limited number of agencies, rank-in-the-person models have not taken hold, and fragmentation has not yet become the model of choice for most jurisdictions.

Probably the most significant reform trends have been decentralization of classification authorities to the agency and sub-agency levels and the restructuring of classification plans through *broadbanding*. A central theme of almost all reform proposals has been the need to make job evaluation systems flexible and responsive to managerial and organizational conditions and needs. One element of flexibility recently supported by many public managers is the elimination of numerous narrow classes in favor of a relatively small number of occupational categories and grade levels. Narrowly defined and numerous classes or grades often work to greatly limit management's discretion to adjust job tasks and rates of pay without having positions reclassified by personnel specialists. Broadbanded pay grade structures make it much easier for managers to design and interrelate positions around work processes. They also facilitate recruitment on the basis of occupations and career planning, make moving people from job to job in the organization much less complicated, and support efforts to administer pay in ways intended to meaningfully reward performance and recognize differences in skills and abilities.

The popularity of broadbanding with public managers is illustrated by the frequency with which it appears as a central theme in demonstration projects designed to test new and innovative approaches to personnel management in the federal government. These demonstration projects, authorized by Title VI of the Civil Service Reform Act of 1978 (CSRA) and approved by OPM, have more often than not included a broadbanding component. The first experiment of this kind was the Navy's *China Lake Demonstration Project,* which was approved for implementation by OPM in 1980 and extended indefinitely (made permanent) through legislation in 1994. A key feature of this project was a simplified job evaluation and pay grade system that consolidated the GS grades into a few broader pay bands. Under the China Lake reforms, managers were allowed increased control over classification, pay, and other personnel matters (Nigro & Clayton, 1984). OPM conducted a series of evaluations of this project over a decade, concluding that it was successful in improving personnel management in the covered research and development laboratories. Specifically, simplified and delegated classification procedures dramatically reduced the time needed to complete classification actions, and conflicts between personnel specialists and managers were reduced. According to the OPM evaluation,

> Recruitment, retention, and reduced turnover of high performers and increased turnover of low performers have all improved. Perceived supervisory authority over classification, pay, and hiring increased, as did employee satisfaction with pay and performance management . . . (U.S. Office of Personnel Management, 1998, p. 2)

It must be noted, however, that there were several reforms besides broadbanding at China Lake, including a new performance appraisal process, a pay-for-performance system, and pay levels higher than those at the control locations, so it is impossible to know which of these changes were responsible for any perceived improvements. Nevertheless, as the OPM commentary on the China Lake demonstration suggests, broadbanding often has been seen as a useful way of expanding the authority of line managers. Empowering managers to use the classification process as a human resources management tool is supposed to lower the overall cost of administering the job evaluation and classification plan by simplifying and speeding up the process. It may also relieve central personnel departments of large inventories of routine classification actions that must be handled before personnel specialists can respond to the organization's human resources development and management needs. Of course, efforts must be made to ensure that principles of fairness and equity are followed, and that, as always, requires some measure of centralized oversight.

ISSUES REGARDING PAY IN THE PUBLIC SERVICE

Issues related to public employees' pay often spark public interest and political controversy. As we have seen, many aspects of pay setting and plan administration are quite technical. Here, we will concentrate on broad policy issues, managerial concerns, and efforts to improve the effectiveness of *pay systems* in the public sector. It should be remembered also, that pay is only one part of the compensation packages used by public employers. These packages include benefits such as health care and pension plans that may be equivalent to 25 percent or more of an employee's pay, so the discussion of pay that follows should be understood in this context.

Policy issues and political debates related to civil servants' wages and salaries can attract intense public interest. Taxpayers may be outraged when they learn about what appear to be excessive pay rates and overly generous benefits, especially if they are less than happy about government's performance. Local media, of course, are ever alert to scandals involving overpaid and underworked public servants. The public's overall impression is that public employees, at worst, are well paid and that they have very secure jobs.

Public sector pay is in important respects a *political outcome*. Most public employees are paid with legislatively appropriated funds that come from tax revenues. At least a large proportion of their total compensation will come from these sources. Even during times when revenues are growing, there are many competing claims on these financial resources, including personnel budgets. Policy makers with limited options must focus on personnel-related costs when expenditures have to be cut or growth curtailed. Pay rates and other compensation policies often become issues as politicians and interest groups maneuver for public support and votes.

In addition, pay is often a major issue in collective bargaining where such negotiations are permitted. Union negotiators demand more, and management typically counters that fiscal conditions and demands on existing resources require smaller increases or, perhaps, reductions. Public employees vote and join organizations that support candidates for elective office and lobby legislative bodies for better benefits and higher pay. Supporting pay raises is often politically hazardous. Making long-term, and ultimately far more expensive, commitments to pension plans and other benefits may be much easier. Legislatively mandated improvements in pension plans (which may be "pay-as-you-go") and other financial commitments to employee compensation packages worry experts in public finance and others who ask where the money needed to meet these future obligations will come from (Kearney, 2003).

As noted in Chapter 3, public employers may be confronted by serious recruitment, retention, and motivation problems stemming at least in part from a chronic inability to offer truly competitive pay. In some cases, the response has been to create several pay plans within the same government to address special problems on a case-by-case basis. Often, this approach is resisted by those who believe in preserving the standardization and internal equity that are hallmarks of traditional merit systems' classification and pay plans.

In a 1986 report on the status of the federal civil service done for NAPA, Charles Levine and Rosslyn Kleeman noted "increasing support for proposals that would have the effect of 'splintering' the civil service into several separate pay schedules and formulas" (Levine & Kleeman, 1986, p. 30). Continued fragmentation poses the threat of a system so complex that it cannot be managed in "an accountable fashion," and pay disparities between occupations and agencies will frustrate all efforts to maintain fairness and equity. Finally, in Levine and Kleeman's judgment, it threatens the very idea of *a* federal civil service and, in effect, replaces it with *several* services. Since 1986, the "splintering" of the federal system has continued and by 2004, there were literally dozens of agency pay plans and salary rates (U.S. Office of Personnel Management, 2005a).

In the United States, the prevailing norm is that governments should have pay rates that are comparable with those in the private sector for similar jobs in similar labor markets; that is, they should offer a "prevailing rate." This is a change from earlier times when it was generally assumed that public servants, particularly white-collar workers, should expect to make less than their private sector counterparts. The convention at the time was that since public employees enjoyed far greater job security and superior benefits, they should expect smaller paychecks. The payment of prevailing wages (in specific labor markets) for blue-collar workers, however, does have a long history, going back to 1862 in the federal service. During the early part of the Civil War (1861–1865), when the federal side was struggling to build a navy capable of cutting off the Confederacy's maritime commerce with Europe, Congress passed a law directing the Navy Department to offer prevailing rates of pay in the shipyards. Today, many state and local governments also use the prevailing rate standard for setting blue-collar pay.

In applying the principle of prevailing or comparable rates, public employers are trying to use information generated by the interplay of supply and demand in a labor market. Prevailing rate surveys are done to establish pay rates for *benchmark jobs,* or jobs that are comparable across organizations and employment sectors. These jobs are then placed into a salary grade structure based on the average competitive rates of pay. After reviewing this structure, management places all remaining jobs in it on the basis of their value in relation to the benchmark jobs.

In theory, a prevailing rate or market pricing evaluation approach allows public employers to construct pay scales that allow them to acquire and retain needed human resources without paying more than they need to. Although the methods used to conduct and interpret prevailing rate surveys may be complex, the logic underpinning them is straightforward: identify and pay the going market price for a particular combination of knowledge, skills, and abilities (KSAs).

Although the desirability of offering prevailing rates as a matter of public policy enjoys widespread support, there are issues to be confronted. For example, prevailing rates are presumably the product of an open and competitive labor market. They may have the effect, however, of perpetuating long-standing inequities and patterns of economic discrimination embedded in society, such as those that have resulted in lower prevailing rates of pay for women. Later in this chapter, we will discuss comparable worth, which is designed to establish pay equity for women.

Another highly relevant set of issues is centered on the degree to which the methods used to conduct prevailing rate surveys are influenced by the efforts of "stakeholders" to skew their outcomes. For example, should the survey be restricted to a metropolitan area, a state, a region, or the nation? Should other governments and charitable organizations be included? Nurses in public hospitals have historically suffered because these institutions routinely surveyed each other, thereby keeping pay at "Florence Nightingale" levels for years. Should fringe benefits and intangibles be factored into the equation? If so, relatively generous pension plans (deferred compensation) may be used to justify keeping wages down. What criteria should be used to establish comparability between organizations? Is working in a small police department the same as working for a large metropolitan department? How should positions with no functional equivalents in the private sector be handled? Public managers, executives, legislators, employee organizations, and taxpayers' associations are among the groups actively seeking to have these crucial decisions made in their favor. The politics of prevailing rates is quite intense and very relevant to the seemingly objective numbers produced by surveys of prevailing rates.

In addition, establishing what the prevailing rate for a particular job is does not assure that it will be offered in the labor market or actually paid. For public employers, the political climate inevitably has a major impact on how information about prevailing rates is used (or not used) by legislative bodies and chief executives. This reality often has translated into a general reluctance to spend the money necessary to achieve and sustain prevailing rates for many public sector jobs, especially those on the higher levels of the civil service. States and localities may be forced to choose between achieving comparability and adequately funding a variety of important programs with strong, aggressive constituencies. When authorizing changes in base pay, legislators tend to be more generous with those in the lower ranks. These lower-paid workers are more numerous, and they are more likely to be able to exert strong political pressure. Managerial and executive personnel, on the other hand, usually do not have much clout in the electoral process. In the face of relatively high pay on the top levels of the non-elected bureaucracy, legislators and the voting public are more likely to be responsive to the plight of the underdog. Finally, the wages of nonmanagerial personnel may be set through collective bargaining in many jurisdictions whereas managers do not have unions representing their interests.

In the federal government, congressional pay historically has placed a ceiling on executive branch pay because legislators have resisted paying civil servants more than they make. In general, legislators' paychecks increase slowly (incrementally) because of the political firestorms ignited by large adjustments; the federal government is no exception to this rule. This slowly rising cap on federal pay, in combination with regular presidential refusals to recommend systemwide increases that could achieve comparability, has at times led to a debilitating gap between federal and private sector pay for certain hard-to-recruit occupational categories and higher grades.

Governments on all levels have experienced *salary compression* problems. Salary compression is the result of policies such as caps on top salaries and problems such as grade creep. The net effect of compression is to flatten the organization's pay structure, gradually closing the gap between the highest and lowest paying positions. Over time, therefore, salary compression frustrates efforts to establish meaningful differences in pay on the basis of job responsibilities and qualifications. It is impossible to offer prevailing rates, and this situation makes it very difficult to recruit and retain highly qualified administrative and technical personnel who can command higher pay for the work they are doing from other governments or private enterprises.

RECENT DEVELOPMENTS IN THE FEDERAL SERVICE

By the 1980s, in addition to a general erosion of comparability caused by presidential reluctance to recommend pay increases that kept pace with the private sector, federal competitiveness in specific labor markets or locations was undermined by Washington's reliance on *national averages* to determine prevailing rates. Private sector pay rates varied considerably across localities, regions, and labor markets. In San Francisco, for example, the 1988 Bureau of Labor Statistics Survey showed that a secretary in the private sector was paid 60 percent more than one doing the same kind of work in Scranton, Pennsylvania, but federal pay was the same in both cities. In some places, the federal government paid more than the private sector, but the private sector paid more than the federal government in about 90 percent of the cases. In many metropolitan statistical areas (MSAs), the private sector enjoyed competitive pay advantages running well over 20 percent (U.S. General Accounting Office, 1990, pp. 5–17).

Before 1990, the only way the federal government could vary GS pay by locality for certain occupations was by offering special rates. OPM had to approve agency requests for special rates based on recruitment or retention problems "caused by higher private sector pay or other reasons." The agencies making these requests had to certify that they had the funds needed to pay the higher rates within their existing budgets. By 1990, about 13 percent of the GS (190,000 employees) was on special rates, and severe problems in a number of agencies such as the FBI and IRS (agents resisted transfers to places like New York City, where they could not afford a reasonable standard of living) were highlighting the need for a general reform of the system (Shoop, 1990).

THE FEDERAL EMPLOYEES PAY COMPARABILITY ACT OF 1990

During the past 15 years, federal white-collar pay policies have become more management-centered and flexible. In large measure, the logic driving the system has shifted from equity and consistency to enhanced competitiveness and responsiveness to management's human resources needs. After considering several alternatives, the Congress passed and President Bush signed the Federal Employees Pay Comparability Act (FEPCA) in late 1990. Like most such reforms, this legislation represented a compromise between those who favored comprehensive reform and actions designed to quickly reach comparability and those preferring incremental adjustments and close attention to budgetary consequences. The president retained across-the-board authority to alter pay recommendations and the executive branch was given greater discretion in matters of pay administration. A nine-member (three neutral experts and six representatives of employee organizations) Federal Salary Council was created to advise the president on locality pay matters. The act set forth four guiding principles for setting pay under the GS: (1) There should be equal pay for substantially equal work within each local pay area; (2) within local pay areas, pay distinctions were to be maintained on the basis of work *and* performance distinctions; (3) federal pay should be comparable with *nonfederal,* rather than only private sector, rates for the same levels of work; and (4) "any existing pay disparities between federal and non-federal employees should be completely eliminated."

The FEPCA's main provisions were expressly designed to allow greater flexibility by the following:

- Setting up criteria and procedures under which pay disparities could be reduced by adding locality-based comparability adjustments to systemwide increases the GS's base pay schedule.
- Providing for special pay authorities to help agencies fill critical *positions* that had remained vacant because of an inability to compete successfully in the labor market.
- Authorizing establishment of special *occupational* pay systems needed to achieve comparability.
- Approving delegations of a wide variety of case-by-case (non-base) pay decisions to the agency management level, thereby providing legislative support for one-time bonuses or variable pay for performance arrangements geared to agency needs and conditions.

Another significant feature was a new Bureau of Labor Statistics (BLS) survey including nonfederal jobs in state, local, and nonprofit agencies. A principal criticism of the methods used by OPM and the BLS for determining white-collar comparability rates had been their failure to include jobs in state and local governments and in nonprofit organizations. The FEPCA responded to these concerns by specifying that the president prepare a report comparing pay under the General Schedule with that of *nonfederal workers* for the same levels of work within each pay locality. In the Federal Salary Reform Act of 1962, the Congress had excluded comparisons with jobs in state and local governments because it was convinced at the time that salary data from this segment of the workforce (then about six million) would be outweighed by private enterprise data. State and local employment has more than doubled by 1990, so this logic was no longer valid, particularly because certain kinds of jobs not included in the previous survey are numerous on these levels of government (for example, nurses, police officers, fire fighters, and social workers). In an example of the politics of prevailing rate surveys because pay is often lower in small state and local governments, unions representing federal employees have strongly objected to including them in prevailing rate surveys. The management point of view, of course, is that they should be included.

The impact of the 1990 legislation on federal pay has been significant. There is now considerable diversity in pay plans, although the majority of full-time workers are still covered by the GS. By 2004, about 18 percent of all full-time federal employees were not under either the white-collar GS or the blue-collar wage system. In addition, the locality pay provisions of the act have meaningfully improved the federal government's capacity to compete in high cost-of-living areas. It has also allowed far greater flexibility regarding occupational groups and senior level positions. The FEPCA "requires not only an annual GS pay adjustment, but a second adjustment that varies by geographic locality." In addition to the GS, locality pay adjustments were extended to several other pay plans, including Scientific and Professional, Senior Level, Senior Foreign Service, and the SES. Special geographic pay adjustments were also authorized for law enforcement officers in several large metropolitan areas.

FEDERAL BLUE-COLLAR PAY

Before 1968, there was no comprehensive policy for setting the pay of trade and craft employees. In some local areas, federal agencies paid different rates for the same occupations. This situation was corrected in 1968 when the U.S. Civil Service Commission implemented a Coordinated Federal Wage System (CFWS). This system provided for a common set of policies and operating procedures covering "grade structures, occupational standards, survey coverage, labor organization participation, and other matters." In 1972, Congress enacted the principal features of the CFWS into law (Title V, U.S. Code). The number of federal employees in the CFWS has steadily declined over recent years; in 2004, it was about 184,000 or 10.5 percent. For the most part, this decline has been caused by federal competitive sourcing or contracting out of blue-collar work to private businesses.

Under the 1972 law, OPM sets uniform national job-grading standards and criteria to be followed by agencies as they define wage areas, design wage surveys, and set up wage schedules. Although agencies do not formally negotiate blue-collar wages, the Federal Wage System (FWS) does allow for considerable union influence in all phases of the process. Local wage surveys are done by lead agencies, that is, those with large numbers of blue-collar jobs in the area, frequently the Department of Defense. Each lead agency has an agency wage committee made up of two management members, two union members, and a chairperson appointed by the lead agency. The committee advises the lead agency on designing local surveys, interpreting survey findings, and establishing local wage schedules. Finally, the unions as well as management are represented on local wage survey committees that oversee the conduct of the local surveys. Although the president has no power to limit wage rate adjustments under the FWS, Congress has imposed appropriations limitations that have restricted blue-collar wage adjustments to those granted to white-collar employees under the General Schedule.

PAY PRACTICES IN STATE AND LOCAL GOVERNMENTS

State and local governments' payroll costs now amount to more than 50 percent of their expenditures. Research on pay in states and local governments suggests that

- States and local governments pay more for lower paying jobs than the private sector does, but private employers pay more for white-collar jobs, especially at the higher levels of responsibility.
- State and local governments' pay for professional and administrative positions is significantly lower than that offered by private industry, whereas the pattern is mixed for technical, clerical, and blue-collar workers.

Although some studies have indicated that the *average* pay of state and local employees is higher than the *average* annual earnings of private workers, controlling for occupational category produces a different picture. The work forces of state and local governments, like that of the federal government, are increasingly professionalized. Although less than 10 percent of private workers are highly paid professionals, this group makes up more than 30 percent of state and about 40 percent of local government employees. When this difference is taken into account, even though the average wage is much higher in the public sector, the evidence suggests that state pay is comparable with that of the private sector and local governments' pay is somewhat lower. The reasons for state and local success in achieving comparability on the lower levels while falling behind in the white-collar occupations (particularly at the more senior and higher grades) appear to be essentially similar to those operating on the federal level to compress pay scales: the political advantages associated with increasing the pay of large numbers of relatively low-level workers and granting minimal raises to highly graded professional employees (Miller, 1996).

For many states, cities, counties, and school districts, a major factor to be considered during the past 30 years has been collective bargaining. Where collective bargaining takes place on the state and local level, unlike the federal situation, pay and benefits are often negotiated. Initially, the spread of collective bargaining in the public sector during the 1960s substantially improved the pay of workers in some occupations such as police, fire fighters, teachers, and nurses. State and local employers, feeling threatened by the possibility of employee unionization and collective bargaining, often moved unilaterally to upgrade pay as well as other aspects of compensation. There is, nonetheless, no evidence to suggest that collective bargaining has allowed state and local workers to loot the treasury. Actually, after a relatively brief catch-up period during the 1960s, state and local pay raises for most occupations have at best kept pace with inflation. Since the mid-1970s, there has been little if any change in the pay gaps between equivalent public and private sector jobs. Most recently, employee organizations have been forced to concentrate on protecting jobs and fighting proposed cuts in wages and benefits.

Two areas of particular importance on the state and local levels have been pay-for-performance and comparable worth (Nelson & Bridges, 1999). Pay-for-performance is discussed in Chapter 6. Although the comparable worth movement has had little effect on federal pay administration, 20 states and almost 1,000 localities had implemented some form of pay equity adjustment designed to address gender-based pay differentials by the early 1990s (Cook, 1991, pp. 102–104).

THE COMPARABLE WORTH DEBATE

Starting in the 1970s, the issue of pay equity for women began to receive widespread attention. Historically, women have been concentrated in lower-paying public as well as private sector jobs, creating a wide gap between their earnings and those of men (Gibelman, 2003). Since passage of the Equal Pay Act in 1963, it has been illegal in the United States to pay women less than men for the same work. However, the principle of equal-pay-for-equal-work is distinct from the concept of equal pay for work of comparable value and does not address issues related to the value placed on jobs traditionally occupied by women. About 80 percent of women in the workforce are concentrated in 20 of the Labor Department's 427 job categories. Women's groups, with strong support from some unions, legislators, and public officials, maintain that occupational segregation characterizes the labor market, with women shunted into low-paying, dead-end jobs. Because segments of the labor market dominated by women are undervalued, when governments conduct prevailing rate surveys, they simply replicate a systemwide pattern of discrimination against women. Advocates of comparable worth argue, therefore, that public employers should implement a system based on equal-pay-for-work-of-equal-value, an approach they believe will better respond to the traditionally low wages paid for work in occupations dominated by women (Vertz, 1987).

As a way of dealing with gender-based pay disparities, comparable worth is based on the idea that every job has a value or worth to the employer that can be measured. In effect, management agrees in principle when it applies systematic job evaluation procedures because those procedures are designed to determine job worth or value based on considerations such as skills required, effort, responsibility, and working conditions. Comparable worth advocates favor the use of factor-based evaluation systems and are simply saying that sexual bias can and should be removed from the development and implementation of those systems. Their objective is to produce a hierarchy of jobs within an organization that is unbiased by sexual stereotypes or prejudices.

It is useful to consider how sexual bias can be built, perhaps even unintentionally, into a systematic job evaluation system. Consider, for example, the factor/point technique or method. If the job factors selected as the basis for the system are drawn primarily from those more likely to be typical of or found in higher levels in male dominated jobs, then jobs that tend to be held by women will not receive high evaluation scores. Similarly, if selected job factors are defined so that they are more likely to be found in jobs that tend to be held by men, the same problem will occur. Working conditions, for example, may be defined is such a way that they give credit for work performed outside in adverse weather but give no credit for work performed in office environments requiring long periods of time sitting at a computer. Bias can also occur as job factors are weighted and as levels of each factor are defined and weighted. Unless care is taken to consciously remove bias in the design of the job evaluation system, work characteristic of jobs held primarily by women may be undervalued even when the system is applied uniformly across all types of work.

Where job evaluations have been done in the public sector using point/factor systems developed in such a way to minimize sexual bias, they often reveal that jobs predominantly occupied by women have been undervalued and under compensated. Advocates of comparable worth point out that it is imperative that such bias be removed from the evaluation process. Arbitrary and inaccurate job evaluation methods, they argue, result in women being the victims of subjective biases that have infiltrated the evaluation process.

Of course, if women's jobs become more highly valued when a particular jurisdiction applies a sexually neutral evaluation system, the employer will usually face a dilemma in setting salaries or wages because prevailing market rates are not likely to be uninfluenced by sexual biases or stereotypes. What should the public employer do if market rates for selected jobs call for pay that is lower than the unbiased job evaluation system would require? Should market rates be disregarded in such circumstances? Doesn't the public employer have a responsibility to achieve some measure of economy regarding the public payroll? On the other hand, however, isn't there a responsibility also to ensure fairness in the treatment of all public employees? These questions will not be easily dismissed for an employer in such a position. All other things being equal, pay policies based on comparable worth concepts would require at a minimum some compromise between administratively determined pay rates and those that might be based purely on the wage or salary market so that biases that are incorporated into the market are reduced.

Critics of comparable worth counter that although the goal of fairness and pay equity for women is commendable, administratively imposed pay scales can be much more costly than necessary. In practical terms, public employers would be placed in the position of having to substantially raise the pay of many employees, but lowering the pay of others would be impossible for political and labor market supply reasons. There is considerable debate about how much this would cost the taxpayers, but upward pay adjustments throughout the public sector would inevitably be expensive. In addition, the costs to employers associated with job evaluations and pay administration would increase greatly.

From the standpoint of classical economics, a more fundamental and long-term problem would be politically or administratively imposed distortions of the labor market. In other words, comparable worth could force employers to overpay for skills in ample supply and to underpay for scarce and essential human resources. Such economic inefficiencies, critics argue, are not justified by the prospect of eliminating whatever part of the pay gap between men and women is caused by discrimination. Opponents of comparative worth stress their view—a widely accepted one in the United States—that the public money-value of a job cannot in practice be based on the abstract concept of inherent worth, but only on labor prices that clear an open market.

Of course, whether the labor market is actually open is a subject for debate—some say that women are largely forced by social norms into lower-paying occupations whereas others argue that women choose those kinds of jobs for personal or lifestyle reasons. In either case, occupational segregation or concentration along sexual lines remains a fact of contemporary life. If the occupational separation of men and women were to end overnight, the male/female pay gap would be greatly reduced, but, of course, that is not likely to happen. Proponents of comparable worth argue that as long as there are occupational concentrations of men and women, regardless of the reason, pay levels should be determined through an evaluation process that strives to remove sexual bias.

Nevertheless, the theory of comparable worth has not received a warm reception in the courts. In *County of Washington v. Gunther* (1981), the Supreme Court did rule that unequal pay for men and women for work of equal value could be a cause for action under Title VII of the 1964 Civil Rights Act, but the Court did not explicitly endorse the concept of comparable worth. In addition, there has been a long and continuing tradition of allowing employers to defend themselves against wage discrimination charges by showing that they are paying prevailing rates.

A well-known case from the State of Washington is illustrative. Washington had been the first state to recognize sex discrimination and to conduct a study of gender-based pay disparities. In 1974, the state determined that jobs held primarily by women were significantly underpaid, and in 1976, funds were appropriated to implement pay adjustments. However, a newly elected governor blocked this appropriation in 1977, and in 1981, the American Federation of State, County and Municipal Employees (AFSCME) and the Washington Federation of State Employees filed sex discrimination charges with the Equal Employment Opportunity Commission (EEOC). The commission failed to act, and the case was taken to federal district court. In its 1983 decision, the court found intentional discrimination because the state had found that the application of a sexually neutral job evaluation system would require the elimination of a pay gap of about 20 percent between mostly male and mostly female job classifications and the state refused to correct the disparity (*AFSCM, et al. v. Washington et al.*, 1983). The state was ordered to pay thousands of women employees the salaries they were entitled to under the comparable worth plan originally adopted by the state. In a major setback for supporters of comparable worth, a three-judge panel of the Ninth Circuit Court of Appeals reversed the district court in 1985 (*AFSCME v. Washington*, 1985). Anthony Kennedy, who was later appointed to the U.S. Supreme Court, wrote for the unanimous panel.

The appeals court concluded that *intentional discrimination* had not been established, and that "discriminatory intent could not be inferred from statistical evidence, even when joined with the defendant's study showing that the jobs in question were of comparable value." Paying market rates could not be interpreted as intent to discriminate. The court also reasoned that disparate impact (unintentional discrimination) was not demonstrated largely because specific points in the pay determination process that resulted in the pay differential were not identified. Clearly, the appeals court's reasoning presented serious difficulties to those seeking to pursue pay equity or comparable worth through anti discrimination law, but rather than taking this case to the U.S. Supreme Court, the State of Washington eventually settled with the employee unions and a substantial amount of money was allocated for pay raises for individuals in jobs held primarily by women.

In subsequent years, other jurisdictions have made similar adjustments to pay for jobs held mostly by women, and the controversy over comparable worth has been less heated. However, it is unlikely that the comparable worth debate will go away completely any time in the near future. It encompasses key policy issues that divide employers, elective officials, political parties, women's organizations, and even the unions. The political influence of women on all levels of government continues to grow, and the pressure on public employers to close or eliminate the wage gap between men and women may be expected to continue.

Conclusion

Job evaluation is a key target of Civil Service Reform II initiatives because it is at the heart of conventional merit systems. Traditional classification systems are designed and administered by central personnel agencies, and they tend to emphasize the regulatory orientation of Civil Service Reform I, often at the expense of flexibility and responsiveness to management's concerns in areas such as recruitment, selection, work systems design, and pay. Though radical reforms, such as replacing rank-in-job systems with rank-in-person approaches, have not been widely implemented, devolution of job evaluation and classification authority to the agency level, simplification of the classification process, and broadbanding of classification structures are now common features of reform agendas on all levels of government. The trend toward policies that allow public managers the flexibility needed to tailor classification systems and processes to the specific problems and challenges they confront promises to continue.

Although public employees' pay continues in most instances to be closely tied to pay grades determined through job evaluation procedures, past concerns about maintaining internal equity are losing ground to those related to competing successfully in a variety of labor markets. The federal government is in the process of fragmenting into a wide variety of pay plans, many of which are intended to address the needs of individual agencies to attract and retain certain categories of workers, most importantly skilled professionals and occupations that are in high demand. The locality pay reforms of the GS are in response to the federal government's need to adjust its pay to local labor markets across the nation. Although most states and localities have less need for locality adjustments, changes to classification schemes, such as broadbanding, may occur because they are perceived as providing the flexibility needed to attract highly qualified job candidates and to reward outstanding performance because the pay ranges within grades available to management are expanded. Incremental changes to existing pay systems are likely to continue in the near future, but some more drastic options are being discussed. One of these is skill-based pay (SBP), an approach that would pay employees in accordance with the type and extent of their organizationally relevant skills.

According to Shareef (1994), in the SBP format, pay is keyed to one or more measures of skill, including the following:

■ *Depth of skill,* or the individual's expertise in a particular area of specialization, such as a physical science, law, or engineering.

■ *Breadth of skill,* which involves rewarding employees for having knowledge and skills in areas of organizational activity related to their jobs, so that they are more flexible and more able to self-manage.

■ *Vertical skills,* or the ability to self-manage in such areas as "scheduling work, leading group problem-solving meetings, training, consulting, and coordinating other groups." (Shareef, 1994, p. 62)

Although SBP is virtually unknown in the U.S. public sector, research on its use in business organizations suggests that it has had positive effects on workforce flexibility, job satisfaction, and productivity, especially when used in conjunction with gainsharing and total quality management (TQM) (Shareef, 1994, pp. 71–72). Because these results are closely aligned with the goals of current reform efforts in the public sector, SBP, as TQM did several years ago, may attract considerable attention from policy makers in the future (Odden, 2000).

DISCUSSION QUESTIONS

1. Should public employers try to match private sector pay for senior executives on the highest levels of responsibility?

2. Will delegations of authority in the pay and classification areas lead to favoritism and systematic violations of the merit principle by managers?

3. Should public employers be required to negotiate pay rates with employee unions?

4. Would a rank-in-person system work well where you are employed?

5. Should white- and blue-collar pay be based solely on prevailing rates, or should other factors be considered?

6. How do you know if your pay is competitive with what others in similar jobs are getting from other employers in your area?

References

AFSCME et al. v. State of Washington et al. (1983). No.C82–465T, United States District Court for the Western District of Washington.

AFSCME v. Washington (1985). 770F2d. 1401.

Cook, Alice (1991). "Pay Equity: Theory and Implementation," in Carolyn Ban and Norma M. Riccucci (Eds.), *Public Personnel Management: Current Concerns—Future Challenges* (New York: Longman), pp. 100–113.

County of Washington v. Gunther 452 U.S. 161 (1981).

Gibelman, Margaret (2003). "So How Far Have We Come? Pestilent and Persistent Gender Gap in Pay." *Social Work,* Vol. 48, No. 1 (January), pp. 22–32.

Kearney, Richard C. (2003). "The Determinants of State Employee Compensation." *Review of Public Personnel Administration,* Vol. 23, No. 4 (December), pp. 305–322.

Levine, Charles H., and Rosslyn S. Kleeman (1986). *The Quiet Crisis in the Civil Service: The Federal Personnel System at the Crossroads* (Washington, DC: National Academy of Public Administration), December.

Miller, Michael A. (1996). "The Public-Private Pay Debate: What Do the Data Show?" *Monthly Labor Review,* Vol. 119, No. 5, pp. 1–14.

Merrill, Harwood F. (Ed.). (1960). *Classics in Management: Selections from the Historic Literature of Management.* (New York: American Management Association).

National Academy of Public Administration (1991). *Modernizing Federal Classification: An Opportunity for Excellence* (Washington, DC: NAPA), July.

Nelson, Robert L., and William P. Bridges (1999). *Legalizing Gender Inequality: Courts, Markets, and Unequal Pay for Women in America.* (Cambridge, MA: Cambridge University Press).

Nigro, Lloyd G., and Ross Clayton (1984). "An Experiment in Federal Personnel Management: The Naval Laboratories Demonstration Project," in Ronald G. Gilbert (Ed.), *Making and Managing Policy* (New York: Marcel Dekker), pp. 153–172.

Odden, Allan (2000). "New and Better Forms of Teacher Compensation are Possible." *Phi Delta Kappan,* Vol. 81, No. 5, pp. 361–366.

Persson, Leonard N. (1987) *Handbook of Job Evaluation and Job Pricing.* (Madison, CT: Business and Legal Reports, Bureau of Law and Business).

Sayre, Wallace (1991). "The Triumph of Technique Over Purpose," in Frank J. Thompson (Ed.), *Classics in Public Personnel Policy,* 2nd ed. (Pacific Grove, CA: Brooks/Cole), pp. 154–158.

Shafritz, Jay (1973). *Position Classification: A Behavioral Analysis for the Public Sector* (New York: Frederick A. Praeger).

Shareef, Reginald (1994). "Skill-Based Pay in the Public Sector." *Review of Public Personnel Administration,* Vol. 14, No. 3 (Summer), pp. 60–74.

Shoop, Tom (1990). "Wage Wars." *Government Executive* (June), pp. 40–42.

U.S. Department of State (2005). *U.S. Department of State Careers: Foreign Service Officer* (Washington, DC). Accessed http://careers.state.gov/officer/ (November, 2005).

U.S. General Accounting Office (1990). *Federal Pay: Comparisons with the Private Sector by Job and Locality* (Washington, DC), May.

U.S. Merit Systems Protection Board (1991). *The Title 38 Personnel System in the Department of Veterans Affairs: An Alternative Approach* (Washington, DC), April.

U.S. Office of Personnel Management (1981). *A Federal Position Classification System for the 1980s: Report of the Classification Task Force* (Washington, DC).

———. (1997). *The Classifier's Handbook* (Washington, DC: Workforce Compensation and Performance Service, Classification Programs Division), December.

———. (1998). *Navy–"China Lake"* Accessed http://www.opm.gov/demos/demolist.asp (November, 2005).

———. (2005a). *Federal Civilian Workforce Statistics: Pay Structure of the Federal Civil Service as of March 31, 2004* (Washington, DC). Accessed http://www.opm.gov/feddata/html/paystr.htm (May).

———. (2005b). *Demonstration Projects.* Accessed http://www.opm.gov/demos/ (November, 2005).

Van Riper, Paul P. *History of the United States Civil Service* (Evanston, IL: Row, Peterson, 1958).

Vertz, Laura (1987). "Pay Inequalities Between Women and Men in State and Local Government: An Examination of the Political Context of the Comparable Worth Controversy." *Women & Politics,* Vol. 7, No. 2 (Summer), pp. 43–57.

Suggested Readings

Edge, Jerry J., and Jai Ghorpade (1997). *Understanding Skill-Based Pay: An Approach to Designing & Implementing an Effective Program* (Scottsdale, AZ: American Compensation Association).

Houser, Robert (1996). *Pay, Equity, & Discrimination* (Boulder, CO: Westview Press).

Paul, Ellen F. (1988). *Equity and Gender: The Comparable Worth Debate* (New Brunswick, NJ: Transaction).

Risher, Howard W. (1997). *New Strategies for Public Pay: Rethinking Government Compensation Programs* (San Francisco: Jossey-Bass).

Siegel, Gilbert B. (1992). *Public Employee Compensation and its Role in Public Sector Strategic Management* (New York: Quorum Books).

Silvestre, J. J., and F. Eyraud (Eds.). (1995). *Pay Determination in the Public Sector: An International Comparison Between France, Great Britain & Italy* (Washington, DC: International Labour Office).

Sorensen, Elaine (1994). *Comparable Worth: Is It a Worthy Policy?* (Princeton, NJ: Princeton University Press).

Van Riper, Paul P. *History of the United States Civil Service* (Evanston, IL: Row, Peterson, 1958).

Chapter SIX

Performance Appraisal and Pay for Performance

In this chapter, we will be looking at two very closely connected features of personnel policy in the public sector. The first is a renewed interest in creating performance appraisal systems that actively support the performance management efforts of public agencies. The second is an effort to establish "pay-for-performance" systems that have positive effects on the motivation and productivity of public employees. To be credible, pay-for-performance requires that supervisors and employees have confidence in the objectivity and fairness of the performance appraisal process. If performance ratings are going to be major factors in pay decisions, it is important that all concerned believe they are accurate and actually discriminate among levels of performance. Likewise, the pay-related outcomes of these appraisals must be seen to be meaningful, as well as equitable. During the past 20 years, the U.S. public sector has undergone a significant transformation in these areas, a transformation driven by the general shift toward a management-centered approach to personnel administration that is described in Chapter 2.

THE NEW PERFORMANCE APPRAISAL

A striking feature of contemporary thinking about personnel policy is its focus on using employee appraisals as the centerpiece of an organizational *performance management process.* Emphasis is being placed on relating the performance objectives and accomplishments of *individ-*

uals to those of the *organization* and its *programs*. In these terms, the methods used to evaluate and reward employee performance on all levels should be designed to promote the goals and policy objectives of public agencies. In other words, the current emphasis is on the *managerial functions* of performance appraisal systems. The assumption is that greater performance by individual employees will lead to improved organizational performance and that technological issues or characteristics of the organization's environment will facilitate that relationship, or at the very least, will not inhibit it.

The Civil Service Reform Act (CSRA) played a major role in stimulating renewed interest in individualized performance appraisals in the public sector. It should be recalled that the 1978 reform was enacted against a backdrop of intense public criticism of government in general and of bureaucrats in particular. By the mid-1970s, the American electorate was willing to accept the argument being advanced by candidates for office that its taxes were too high and government programs were not meeting expectations because public employees were overpaid and underworked. Removing unproductive public workers or making them improve their performance became a popular public policy goal (and mandatory campaign promise). To improve productivity, it was widely believed that employee performance measurement systems that accurately discriminated among levels of job achievement and made it possible to link employee compensation to performance were badly needed (Daley, 1991).

THE RISE AND FALL OF TRADITIONAL APPRAISAL SYSTEMS

Two factors converged during the 1970s and early 1980s to change state-of-the-art approaches to performance appraisal in government. First, the traditional systems were in disrepute on all levels of government. In technical terms, they simply were not doing what they were supposed to, and few managers took them very seriously. Second, in political terms, the pressures for greater bureaucratic productivity, accountability, and responsiveness created a climate that forced meaningful reforms in a number of areas, including performance appraisals and their uses.

Under conventional merit systems where management's discretion in personnel matters is deliberately limited, appraisals or service ratings are supposed to concentrate on how well an employee is carrying out the tasks associated with a job or position. The supervisor's role is largely to provide answers to trait- and task-related questions derived from job analysis done by personnel specialists. The results are supposed to be used to help make objective decisions regarding personnel matters such as retention, training, pay, and promotion. Technical questions focus on identifying and ranking job elements, and on how to accurately measure a worker's performance along each of these dimensions. In practice, the traditional appraisal process operated in virtual isolation from the planning, program design and implementation, and management control functions of public agencies.

The methods used in many merit systems had their origins in the precepts of scientific management and the aims of Civil Service Reform I. From scientific management came the concepts of job design and analysis, empirical observation, and measurement. Management's role was to design and interrelate jobs in a manner that generated the highest possible levels of technical efficiency. This required a careful empirical analysis of what workers were doing, the identification and combination of tasks into efficient packages or jobs, and measurement of worker performance against key job elements. Followers of the scientific management school firmly believed that appraisals keyed to specific jobs were essential if the workforce was to be managed in an efficient and harmonious manner. For the most part, however, they did not extend their thinking on this matter beyond the "shop" level or systematically consider how appraisals done by first-level supervisors might be linked to the broader concerns of upper management. The civil service reformers, on the other hand, had a different agenda in mind. Based on their experience with spoils, they did not trust managers to objectively administer a personnel system, including performance appraisals. Instead, they favored leaving the design and administration of performance appraisals to specialists housed in nonpartisan civil service commissions.

The idea of rigorously objective performance appraisals formulated by disinterested specialists using scientific methods was particularly attractive because, at least superficially, it meshed nicely with American norms of individualism and egalitarianism. "Science" promised accurate job-related measures free from subjective biases of all kinds. Merit systems were supposed to provide the disinterested and professional environment required to create and administer valid and objective evaluations of the individual's work. Such appraisals, in turn, would guarantee fair and equitable treatment of all workers. Performance, and performance alone, would determine pay and status. These values were very much in line with the merit principles advocated by the reformers, and they were enshrined in civil service laws on all levels of government.

As merit systems were established and expanded on all levels of government, the design and operation of performance appraisal systems came to be dominated by technical specialists working for commissions or their functional equivalents. At their best, the methods used to construct appraisal instruments rather closely followed those recommended by the scientific managers. Line management's role was limited to providing job-related information needed by these specialists as they formulated rating schemes, kept necessary records, and filled in rating forms. In its study of the available research on pay for performance, the National Research Council notes that this "measurement tradition" dominated the field until the late 1970s (Milkovich & Wigdor, 1991). This tradition, based in psychometrics and testing, stresses accurate measurement as a "precondition" for accurate evaluation of performance:

> By and large, researchers in measurement have made the assumption that if the tools and procedures are accurate (e.g., valid and reliable), then the functional goals of organizations using tests or performance appraisals will be met. (Milkovich & Wigdor, 1991, p. 45)

It is difficult to conceive of a genuine merit system without a credible system for appraising individual performance. Nevertheless, although most states and localities have had some kind of rating system on the books for many years, and the federal government has been in the business since the establishment of the old Civil Service Commission, performance appraisals have been a notoriously weak link in the chain of techniques needed to firmly connect merit principles with merit system practices. At least three interrelated kinds of problems plagued efforts to realize the goals of the scientific managers and civil service reformers.

TECHNICAL PROBLEMS

First, for all but the most routine and simple kinds of work, identifying and clearly defining the performance dimensions of civil service positions was not easy. Professional and administrative jobs are often complex and variable. Static and necessarily general position descriptions seldom provided a meaningful picture of what these people were actually doing. Ideally, if we are interested in assessing the performance of an individual, we should identify the work outcomes or products associated with that individual's job and develop measures of those outcomes or products. But the identification of specific work outcomes is often quite difficult. What, for example, are the work outcomes or products that are associated with the job of an administrative secretary? Which of those outcomes should form the basis for performance appraisal, and how can they be accurately measured, especially when their accomplishment may depend in part on the work of others? What standards of performance can reasonably be expected regarding those outcomes? Because these questions are difficult to resolve, appraisal systems often turn to an assessment of individual behaviors rather than tangible work products or outcomes. The assumption is that certain behaviors, such as timeliness in completing tasks or courteous interaction with agency clients, are positively associated with job performance. In addition to behavior-based systems, performance appraisals were also frequently based on assessments of employee traits such as honesty, dependability, or diligence. Trait-based systems were generally easier to develop than behaviorally based systems or those grounded on actual work outcomes, but the link between individual traits and actual productivity may be tenuous.

Even if agreement on performance dimensions can be reached, developing administratively feasible methods for accurately measuring performance on the job is an equally difficult technical problem. The scientific managers had developed their concepts and tested their methods in industrial settings for the most part. Their interest in shop level work had not been extended in any systematic way to supervisory, professional, or administrative jobs. In the end, we typically use simple rating scales with five or more performance categories corresponding to different performance levels specified. Supervisors then check what they see as the performance level corresponding best to the work of an individual employee.

In short, technical problems associated with the appraisal of individual employees are considerable. Furthermore, attempting to solve them are expensive. The development of performance measurement plans and formats based on reasonable performance indicators and standards requires expertise and time. Administering and maintaining these plans is also costly. Predictably, given pressing claims on limited resources, interest in performance appraisals waned throughout the public sector. Funding was minimal, and relatively little staff time was devoted to appraisals. Training programs for supervisors were nonexistent or superficial. In turn, supervisors did not invest much time in the process, and they typically delayed completing evaluation forms until the last minute. Ratings were skewed toward the high end of the scale as supervisors sought to avoid conflict and accusations of being unfair. It was not unusual for more than 95 percent of the ratings to be in the satisfactory or higher categories.

MANAGERIAL PROBLEMS

The second category of problems was managerial. The scant attention paid to performance appraisals by supervisors was not only a reflection of technical problems. It was also a response to the largely peripheral role line management played in their design and use. Investing heavily in these systems did not make much sense. Supervisors were not rewarded for doing so by their bosses, and negative ratings often yielded nothing more positive than stressful interpersonal conflict and time-consuming appeals by resentful workers to suspicious civil service boards. Public managers are asked to effectively and efficiently accomplish objectives established under law and by the policy initiatives of their superiors. From this perspective, performance appraisals are useful only to the extent that they promote managers' efforts to control, guide, and coordinate the actions of subordinates. Did existing performance appraisal systems help managers manage? Overall, the answer was that they did not. At best, they were not very relevant and, therefore, appropriately treated as required formalities or annual rituals. At worst, they erected barriers to effective management by stimulating cynicism and distrust of supervisors, by stripping managers of any meaningful control over incentives such as pay, and most importantly, by greatly constraining supervisors' role in defining performance goals and standards. Under these conditions, veteran managers should not have been expected to take performance appraisals very seriously.

ORGANIZATIONAL PROBLEMS

The third set of problems was organizational. Performance appraisals were not connected to mainline administrative functions such as planning and budgeting. Nor were they used as part of higher administration's efforts to control programmatic activities. Appraisal methods and procedures did little to support administrators' efforts to set goals, to monitor organizational performance, and to allocate human as well as material resources effectively. From the standpoint of those trying to achieve goals on the organizational and program levels, employee performance appraisals, for all practical purposes, were *administratively* irrelevant. Accordingly, like supervisors down the line, higher-level public executives were not inclined to expend their limited resources on efforts to enhance performance appraisals. From an organizational point of view, these were done largely to satisfy on paper the demands of civil service statutes and merit system rules.

A Victory of Forms Over Substance

As might be expected under these conditions, performance appraisals became forms to be filled out, signed-off on, complained about, and forgotten. As indicated earlier, various kinds of plans were used, the most common type being trait rating systems. A graphic rating scale was typically developed where the supervisor marked on a continuum the degree to which a particular factor described the employee. A graphic rating scale allows the supervisor to rate subordinates rapidly by making check marks in the spaces indicated on the form, so it does have the virtue of being easy to administer. Trait rating was widely adopted largely for this reason. Mostly, the factors were personality traits, as described earlier, and their connections to actual job performance could only be assumed. It was not unusual for these rating forms to include some very generally stated items about the quantity and quality of work, but this was usually the extent of inquiry into actual job performance. Traits were seldom clearly defined, and those doing the rating normally were given little or no specific guidance as to how to measure the degree to which a particular trait described an employee. Figure 6.1 is an example of a generic trait rating format; this one was used by a large city during the early 1980s.

Weaknesses commonly associated with the generic trait rating approach include the following:

1. The content of the rating form is not job related or specifically applicable to many positions
2. The format allows so much room for interpretation that ratings often vary widely among supervisors and across organizational units, which tends to undermine the credibility of the ratings workers receive
3. The lack of objective measures of performance creates conditions under which supervisors can exercise their prejudices or, even if they try to be objective, be suspected of biasing their evaluations in favor of some and against others
4. The format encourages a superficial effort by supervisors, since it involves nothing more than checking-off a series of boxes, which can be done in a few minutes

By 1981, the Urban Institute had concluded, "Evidence currently available indicates that systems utilizing supervisor ratings of personal traits and focusing on nonspecific aspects of performance are not valid or effective enough to be worthwhile" (Greiner et al., 1981, p. 227).

Figure 6.1 Example of a Trait-Rating Form

Employee's Name	Employee's Payroll Title	Social Security Number
Bureau Office	Department	Position Number

| Time in Present Classification _____ Years _____ Months | Period of Job Performance Evaluated From: To: | |

Period of Time Evaluator has Supervised Employee: From: To:

Type of Report: ☐ Annual   ☐ First Probationary   ☐ Final Probationary   ☐ Other _____

OUTSTANDING – Almost always does far better than the job requires.
HIGHLY SATISFACTORY – Very often performs noticeably more or better work than is required.
SATISFACTORY – Fully competent employee; does what is required in the position.
MARGINAL – Minimally satisfactory; employee could attempt some improvement.
REQUIRES IMPROVEMENT – Performance unsatisfactory but may improve within a reasonable time.
INSUFFICIENT – Consistent inability or unwillingness to perform satisfactorily.

IF ANY ITEM IS NOT APPLICABLE TO THE PERSON RATED, OMIT THAT ITEM AND NOTE "N/A"

Columns: INSUFFICIENT | REQUIRES IMPROVEMENT | MARGINAL | SATISFACTORY | HIGHLY SATISFACTORY | OUTSTANDING | ... | N/A

ATTENDANCE	–To what extent is employee at work regularly?
PUNCTUALITY	–To what extent does employee report to work on time?
USE OF TIME	–Does employee work steadily, refrain from wasting time?
INITIATIVE	–Does employee take needed action without waiting to be told?
JUDGEMENT	–Are the decisions the employee makes sound decisions?
COOPERATION	–Does employee assist coworkers needing help, avoid quarrels?
REPORTING	–Does employee inform you of work progress, problems that arise?
RELIABILITY	–Does employee complete assignments without excessive supervision?
JOB KNOWLEDGE	–Does employee know what to do and how to do it (without assistance)?
WORK QUANTITY	–How much work does the employee accomplish compared to the amount required?
WORK QUALITY	–Is employee's work usually accurate and complete?

(Evaluate factors below or additional factors IF any apply to the employee's responsibilities)

LEADERSHIP	–Does employee obtain satisfactory performance from subordinates?
PLANNING	–Does employee set appropriate goals, establish priorities, anticipate future needs?
ORGANIZING	–Delegates responsibility and authority effectively; avoids coordination problems?
DIRECTING	–Keeps subordinates informed of work plans, procedures and changes?
FOLLOW-UP	–Ensures that subordinates complete assignments and accurately on time?
FLEXIBILITY	–Does employee change to meet changing requirements of the job?
ACCOUNTABILITY	–Does employee accept full responsibility for all aspects of assignments?

Equal Employment	
Opportunity	-Ensures that affirmitive EEO actions are taken in
	all appropriate aspects of employment?

In the federal government, the situation was very similar. In 1978, while the Carter administration was moving the CSRA through the Congress, the General Accounting Office (GAO) recommended fundamental changes in the performance rating systems being used by federal agencies. It reported that many workers simply were not getting useful feedback about their performance (U.S. General Accounting Office, 1978). Often, performance requirements were nonexistent or so vague as to be useless, and many position descriptions were out-dated. Although the Performance Rating Act of 1950 and agency rules required that they do so, many supervisors had not established performance standards or discussed them with their subordinates. The GAO report also noted that as many as half of all supervisors had *never* received training in the major elements of performance evaluation, and some who had did not think it was very useful.

Federal managers who tried to make the existing system work were frustrated by poorly conceived legislation and restrictive court decisions. The Performance Rating Act of 1950 required summary adjective ratings of overall performance: outstanding, satisfactory, and unsatisfactory. The law provided that outstanding ratings could be given "only when *all* aspects of performance not only exceed normal requirements, but are outstanding and deserve special commenda-tion" (emphasis added). This is a very demanding standard to meet and, from a supervisory point of view, meeting it required a heavy investment in time and effort to document an outstanding rating. Thus, the law encouraged supervisors to give satisfactory ratings to the vast majority of employees who were doing acceptable or *better* work.

For marginal and unproductive employees, the 1950 act pro-vided that a rating of unsatisfactory was grounds for removal from the position in which the performance was unsatisfactory. However, in 1960, a court of claims ruled that the Lloyd-LaFollette Act of 1912 and the Veterans Preference Act of 1944 took precedence. In short, dismissal could not be automatic because the ruling was interpreted to mean that federal workers had *two* statutory appeals rights, the first after receipt of a notice of unsatisfactory performance and the second after initiation of dismissal action by management. Under these con-ditions, federal managers usually by-passed giving unsatisfactory rat-ings and went directly to adverse action proceedings. This strategy saved both time and money, but it meant that virtually all federal employees were rated satisfactory. Between 1954 and 1978, the GAO calculated, 99 percent of all ratings had fallen into this category.

To make matters worse, the Federal Salary Reform Act of 1962 contained a provision eliminating an automatic within-grade pay increase for everybody rated satisfactory or better. Instead, the basis for granting the increases should be an independent determination by the agency head that the employee had met an "acceptable level of competence." The rationale was that supervisors were not critically rating performance because they did not want to deprive employees of within-grade increases or otherwise damage their status. Instead of encouraging and supporting genuine efforts by supervisors to dis-criminate among levels of accomplishment, the 1962 act simply forced agency heads to routinely give certifications of acceptable performance because they were in no position to do otherwise. In general, federal employees were at best ambivalent about the objectivity and utility of pre-CSRA performance appraisals (Ingraham & Ban, 1984, pp. 70–86).

Until the late 1970s, performance appraisal languished as a backwater of public personnel administration. In theory, its importance to merit systems and management effectiveness was recognized. In practice, efforts to define and accurately measure performance experienced minimal success in the public sector, but the idea became firmly entrenched in the professional and research literature, and debate about the relative virtues of a variety of techniques for measuring performance surfaced on a fairly regular basis. Research focused on alternatives to the trait-rating approach such as critical incident methods, behaviorally anchored rating scales, evaluation-by-objectives, and narrative models (Milkovich & Wigdor, 1991, pp. 54–76). However, proposals to overhaul performance appraisal policies and practices in the public sector had relatively little impact until pressures for civil service reform forced the issue. The early 1980s were marked by enthusiastic and optimistic efforts to place appraisals at the center of Civil Service Reform II (Downs & Larkey, 1986, pp. 190–200).

In comments made some 10 years after the enactment of the CSRA, former OPM Director Alan K. Campbell noted that the federal reforms were intended to respond to a personnel establishment that had developed into a "protective negative system primarily designed to prevent patronage, favoritism, and other personnel abuses." He said,

> Attitude surveys of federal managers at that time indicated that they were as disillusioned about how well the system worked as the general public. They did not believe they could manage the system; they believed that the oversight agencies imposed restrictions and regulations that made it impossible for them to be effective. (U.S. General Accounting Office, 1988, p. 12)

Campbell's admonition that performance appraisal systems will not work unless they are "based on a carefully drawn plan for the organization's activities over . . . [its] planning cycle" suggests the outlines of the approach taken to performance appraisals by many U.S. governments during the last 20 years. Emphasis has been placed on the development of appraisal instruments and processes that require supervisors to evaluate employees' performance in terms of specific job responsibilities and organizational objectives. In reformed systems, ratings are visibly connected to a variety of key aspects of human resources management, most importantly pay. In many jurisdictions, administrative control over evaluation formats and procedures has been greatly expanded in response to the argument that effective performance management requires a deregulated and decentralized approach (Thompson & Radin, 1997).

A MANAGEMENT APPROACH TO PERFORMANCE APPRAISAL

Technically, the 1980s were marked by concern "less with questions of validity and reliability than with the workability of the performance appraisal system within the organization, its ability to communicate organizational standards to employees, to reward good performers, and to identify employees who require training and other development activities" (Milkovich & Wigdor, 1991, p. 46). Within the framework of this management tradition, performance appraisals were added to the inventory of resources executives might use to leverage greater bureaucratic responsiveness and accountability. Extensive delegations to departments of authority to design and administer appraisal systems (within broad policy guidelines) came to receive strong support from many personnel specialists as well as line managers. Evaluation methods based on management-by-objectives (MBO) concepts became popular elements of efforts to make agency goals and plans the basis of performance measures used throughout the organization.

Regarding accuracy, attention has shifted from the properties of rating scales to factors affecting the ability of those doing the rating to provide accurate judgments of performance. Employee acceptance and organizational utility are central objectives of the management tradition and, therefore, it stresses the importance of the organizational setting (social, psychological, and technical) within which the appraisal process takes place. Although the influence of the rating technology being used on accuracy is recognized, particular emphasis is placed on "the conditions that encourage raters to use the performance appraisal systems in the way that they were intended to be used" (Milkovich & Wigdor, 1991, p. 47). For example, research evidence supports the idea that the perceived effectiveness of performance appraisal systems is strongly related to employee confidence in their accuracy and fairness (Roberts, 1995, p. 37). Acceptance by supervisors or raters is also critical:

> Rater acceptance is high when raters understand the rationale justifying the system and its goals, are confident in their ability to effectively administer the system, the perceived benefits exceed the costs, the appraisal system does not conflict with other personnel systems . . . ,

and the manager's employees have favorable attitudes toward the system. (Roberts, 1992, p. 22)

By the mid-1990s, the regulatory concerns of the first civil service reform movement had faded into the background, and the executive and managerial uses of performance appraisals had assumed center stage. These uses are now, in one writer's words, "ubiquitous in the public sector" (Fox & Shirkey, 1997, p. 205). One example is the State of Georgia's Performance Management Process (PMP), which is a component of the *GeorgiaGain* project from the mid-1990s. A central element of the project is a performance-based compensation system. The PMP is designed to "set expectations for quality performance and productivity that can be measured, and reward employees for meeting those expectations" (Georgia Merit System, 1997, p. 2).

Under the Georgia PMP, managers and employees are supposed to "share accountability for job performance." They are expected to collaborate on an annual process that "measures actual performance against expectations and rewards on-the-job achievement." According to *Manager's Guide* to the PMP, this interactive process involves four phases: planning, coaching, evaluation, and development.

- In the *planning phase*, the manager "develops an individual Performance Plan, with input from the employee, that clearly defines job responsibilities, performance expectations, and performance measures."

- During the *coaching phase*, the manager "documents employee performance and gives regular feedback and encouragement." The manager is expected to help the employee solve performance problems and to provide formal feedback at least once a year.

- The *evaluation phase* is the point at which the manager and the employee "review the manager's assessment of the employee's overall performance as measured against defined expectations." Two areas of performance are rated, these being job performance and compliance with organizational rules of behavior and attendance.

- The last step in the PMP cycle is the *development phase*, during which the manager and the employee jointly set performance expectations and development goals for the next cycle "that will help improve or enhance the employee's effectiveness at work. The development plan may set specific training objectives or refine/expand the scope of the employee's job" (Georgia Merit System, 1997, p. 3).

Georgia uses its Performance Management Form (PMF) as the centerpiece of its performance planning and evaluation process. The PMF is used to (1) develop a performance plan, (2) record and document the annual performance rating, and (3) "it may also contain the employee's Development Plan." All State of Georgia classified employees must have an individual performance plan, and department heads have the discretion to determine if unclassified employees in their agencies should be included. Normally, performance plans are based on official state job descriptions "to bring as much consistency as possible to the responsibilities (and expectations) assigned to positions in the same job." However, performance plans should describe the responsibilities of someone in a particular position, rather than simply a class or group of positions, and they "can be tailored to fit the *employee* in the position . . ." (Georgia Merit System, 1997, p. 8).

The Georgia PMP was designed to avoid a number of problems that typically combine to seriously undermine the effectiveness of performance appraisal systems. Reviews of appraisals under the CSRA in a number of federal agencies revealed, for example, that

1. For a variety of reasons, employees were not active participants in the development of the performance standards for their jobs.

2. Workers were not informed by their supervisors of the performance standards at the beginning of the appraisal period.

3. Performance standards, if they existed, were not clearly stated in measurable terms, failed to distinguish between levels of accomplishment, and did not clearly define unacceptable performance.

4. Agencies' procedures for linking ratings to personnel actions, such as pay increases, were vague, and employees could not see a direct and logical connection between their ratings and these actions (U.S. General Accounting Office, 1983; U.S. General Accounting Office, 1987).

In its report prepared for OPM, the National Research Council reviewed the available research on performance appraisals in the public and private sectors, and it reached the following conclusions:

■ First, in the applied setting of day-to-day personnel management, heavy investments in measurement precision are not economically viable because they are unlikely to improve the overall quality or usefulness of performance appraisals.

■ Second, the council recommended that performance evaluation policies emphasize "informed managerial judgment and not aspire to the degree of standardization, precision, and empirical support that would be required of, for example, selection tests" (Milkovich & Wigdor, 1991, p. 3).

In the context set by these conclusions, the Council advanced several summary observations concerning the measurement side of appraisals:

■ Job analysis and specification of performance standards are not substitutes for supervisory judgment, but they are important because they may help focus the appraisal process for both the supervisor and the employee.

■ Supervisors are able to form "reasonably reliable estimates of their employees' overall performance levels." However, consistency is not a guarantee of accuracy; systematic error and bias are still possible. It is, for example, possible for supervisors consistently to undervalue the performance of women or members of racial and ethnic minorities.

■ Although there are many rating scale types and formats, they will yield similar results if "the dimensions to be rated are well chosen and the scale anchors are clearly defined." Anchors are more or less specifically described levels of performance displayed on a continuum from, for example, 1 = unacceptable to 5 = exceptional. There was no convincing evidence found to support the proposition that distinguishing between behaviors and traits has much effect on rating outcomes. It seems that supervisors form generalized evaluations which strongly color "memory for and evaluation of actual work behaviors." Likewise, there is little evidence to suggest that rating systems based on highly job-specific dimensions produce results much different from those using "global" or general dimensions. (Milkovich & Wigdor, 1991, p. 144)

All these points imply that the degree to which an appraisal system actually contributes to the performance management process depend largely on the degree to which all concerned are invested in its success through: (1) a commitment to supervisory training and employee development, (2) active and informed participation of supervisors and employees in the setting of standards and developmental goals, (3) use of fair and objective measures of performance, and (4) a visible commitment to procedural fairness in all phases of the rating process (Roberts, 1995; Roberts & Reed, 1996). In these terms, the council's report noted that successful performance appraisal systems in the private sector share certain characteristics:

> [They are] firmly imbedded in the context of management and personnel systems that provide incentives for managers to use performance appraisal ratings as the organization intends. These incentives include managerial flexibility or discretion in rewarding top performers and in dismissing those who continually perform below standard. . . . Managers are themselves assessed on the results of their performance appraisal activities. (Milkovich & Wigdor, 1991, p. 164)

TOTAL QUALITY MANAGEMENT AND PERFORMANCE APPRAISAL

Considerable attention has been devoted to improving and refining performance appraisal techniques and systems that focus on the individual employee. This long-standing approach assumes that the key to improving productivity and quality of services in the public sector is accurately measuring and controlling the performance of each worker. A different approach, *total quality management* (TQM), challenges this assumption. In one writer's words, "most of those using TQM persist in managing performance through individual ratings—a practice antithetical to TQM" (Bowman, 1994, p. 129). TQM has been influential in both the public and private sectors during the past 20 years, so its point of view on performance appraisal should be understood.

TQM approaches the entire organization as a complex set or system of interdependent *processes,* and it asserts that performance problems do not begin with employees, "but from lack of understanding of the work processes" (Bowman, 1994, p. 129). The goals of the TQM approach are to study work processes to identify barriers to quality, to satisfy internal and external customers, and to create an organizational culture that values quality and continuous improvement. The objective of TQM, in other words, is to change organizational systems to improve quality, rather than changing individual workers. Individual performance appraisals, according to their critics, overlook the systemic basis of productivity and quality, and they fuel competition and suspicion, which undermine the cooperation and teamwork needed to sustain a culture of continuous improvement. Supporters of TQM, therefore, recommend that traditional performance appraisals be abandoned and replaced with a concentration on identifying and eliminating systemic sources of variation in the quality of products and services that are *not* under the control of individual employees.

Rather than dropping individual performance appraisals and moving to a group-centered model, the usual response by public employers applying TQM methods has been to try to make traditional performance appraisals work better by increasing employee participation and setting the entire process in a "developmental" frame of reference. This, however, does not move the focus of concern from the individual to the organizational system and its processes. Bowman (1994) identifies several reasons why public managers and employees are reluctant to abandon the traditional systems:

- Managers often use performance appraisals as a way to control their subordinates, and they are reluctant to make changes that would give employees greater discretion and influence over work processes. Organizations using TQM tend to be structurally "flatter" and to have more open communications than traditional bureaucracies, and they give their workers more discretion because "empowerment allows employees to respond to client needs in a timely and customized way" (Berman, 1997, p. 282).

- Managers "may be reluctant not only to embrace radical approaches, but also to abandon those that benefited them during their career. In fact, many find appraisals to be a useful, if technically problematic, ideological tool. When they sign-off on them, their job is done; the responsibility for quality and productivity is returned to where, in their view, it belongs—the subordinate" (Bowman, 1994, pp. 132).

- Employees often are suspicious of management's purposes when changes are proposed, and they tend to prefer evaluation systems that are familiar to those with which they have no experience, even if the familiar system is less than satisfactory.

- For managers and workers alike, traditional performance appraisal systems are hard to abolish because they are so closely connected to many other important personnel functions, such as training, compensation, promotion, and termination. Changing the appraisal process to fit the TQM model would necessarily require making significant and potentially threatening changes to the existing personnel system (Berman, 1997, pp. 283–286; Bowman, 1994, pp. 132–133; Connor, 1997).

Some public employers have made efforts to reform their performance appraisal systems along lines that are more congruent with the central values of TQM by including contributions to team performance and quality of work as evaluation criteria. Overall, however, public employers have not moved away from individual performance appraisals to any significant extent. TQM's reliance on group appraisals and rewards continues to be a widely recognized barrier to its full implementation by government agencies on all levels. As one observer puts it, "Fears that team appraisals will breed free-riding, rating uncertainty, and placing one's financial destiny in the hands of coworkers are real, realistic, and not easily assuaged" (Durant, 1998, p. 465). In practical terms, the American cultural stress on individual effort, achievement, and rewards is unlikely to support anything resembling a complete conversion to TQM's doctrine of evaluating systems, rather than people. However, appropriate combinations of team and individual evaluations should be possible and, in the American setting, necessary.

MULTISOURCE PERFORMANCE APPRAISALS

In addition to the TQM challenge to traditional performance appraisals, there has been considerable interest in the potential advantages of replacing the hierarchical or "top-down" appraisal process with one that obtains feedback from a variety of sources in addition to the supervisor, including subordinates, peers, and customers or clients.

Multisource performance appraisals are designed to overcome the limited perspective inevitably associated with having only one rater: "Since the behaviors a single rater can observe are limited, the result can be an 'unrepresentative sample' of a given employee's or a given manager's performance" (Coggburn, 1998, p. 68). Frequently proposed alternatives or complements to conventional appraisal systems are self-appraisal, peer review, upward feedback from subordinates, and assessment centers. Each of these methods offers some benefits in the areas of reliability, validity, and procedural fairness that may be combined to create a new appraisal model. In this model, performance information comes from several individuals who work or interact with the person being evaluated (deLeon & Ewen, 1997, pp. 25–26).

In brief, under the multisource assessment model, evaluation criteria consisting of core competencies and desired supervisory behaviors are developed by a group of trained employees. Feedback on these criteria is obtained from sources throughout the organization to ensure that they are relevant and fair. Definitions of actual behaviors that would satisfy these standards are then developed. In the next step, the employee being reviewed selects an evaluation team composed of work associates, including his or her supervisor and others in a position to provide accurate feedback on performance. The employee may also provide a self-appraisal. Access to the feedback obtained through this process is limited to the employee and the supervisor, and training is conducted to show employees how to "interpret their performance appraisals and design action plans based upon them" (deLeon & Ewen, 1997, p. 26).

In their study comparing the multisource to the conventional performance appraisal model in a federal agency, deLeon and Ewen found that "employees gave significantly higher approval ratings to the new performance appraisal system on every dimension" (1997, p. 28). These dimensions were fairness, accuracy, usefulness, and understanding. Similarly, Coggburn (1998) reports that subordinate appraisals, if implemented in a manner designed to reassure supervisors about the qualifications and attitudes of subordinates and to provide the training needed by those involved, may be useful in at least two ways. First, they help establish a defensible rationale for personnel actions because the "law regarding performance appraisals and personnel decisions strongly supports the use of more than one rater whenever performance judgments are made to promote, demote, discharge, or determine merit pay" (p. 70). Second, subordinate appraisals may provide valuable feedback that supervisors can use to identify areas where they need to improve their management skills through training or other developmental activities.

PAY-FOR-PERFORMANCE IN THE PUBLIC SERVICE

Pay-for-performance (PFP) is a hallmark of Civil Service Reform II. Virtually all calls for civil service reform and actual reforms have included some form of PFP. An important reason for the popularity of merit pay has been public demands for more bureaucratic accountability and productivity. In James L. Perry's words,

> It [pay-for-performance] is a message from politicians and the public that the governed are in control and things are as they should be. At the same time, it is a way for administrators to communicate that they are responsive to important external constituencies and that they are doing something about perceptions of lagging performance. (Perry, 1991, p. 80)

Using PFP to raise productivity has been a basic element of management thinking in the United States since the late 1800s, and the early scientific managers are well known for their efforts to rationalize pay systems for factory workers along so-called "piece-rate" lines. Their goal was to increase "efficiency" (cost-per-unit-of-output) in the blue-collar workplace. The current emphasis on merit pay in government emerged in a climate of fiscal stress, and it concentrates mostly on motivating and raising the productivity of white-collar workers.

Although some states and localities were experimenting with PFP before passage of the CSRA, Title V of the act was a high-profile break with traditional pay practices in the public sector, which tied wages and salaries to positions and seniority, with pay increases being allocated across-the-board to all satisfactory performers.

> Borrowing from private-sector practices, Title V . . . sought to motivate better performance and to deter poor performance by increasing grade level 13–15 managers' salaries by amounts determined by their rated performance. . . . (Perry, 1991, p. 74)

Since 1978, PFP programs have been adopted by more than 20 states and many local governments (Greiner, 1986; U.S. General Accounting Office, 1990). By the late 1980s, more than 25 percent of major U.S. cities reported that a primary use of performance appraisals was to allocate pay for managerial and nonmanagerial personnel (Ammons & Rodriguez, 1986; England & Parle, 1987).

Pay-for-performance plans come in a variety of forms, including those using one-time bonuses or variable pay, permanent increases to base salary, and group-based bonuses or "gainsharing." Individual bonuses and base-pay increases are by far the most common in the U.S. public sector. In some jurisdictions, only supervisory and managerial personnel are covered, but in others, PFP is restricted to nonmanagerial personnel. In some states and localities, both groups are covered by the same or different systems. In other words, pay-for-performance is a generic term that applies to a wide variety of monetary incentives programs. Their one unifying theme is the goal of establishing clear and reliable linkages between performance ratings and pay and, through the administration of those linkages, to motivate workers and to manage performance.

No matter the form it takes, PFP's widespread popularity is based in large measure on the proposition that it remedies a fundamental flaw in traditional compensation systems by making pay *contingent* on performance, rather than the position grade and seniority of the employee. Logically, it accepts the cognitive model of motivation set forth in the *expectancy theory* discussed in Chapter 3. Expectancy theory suggests that pay can be treated as a management tool because employees value it. Traditional systems of pay administration (membership-based inducements), it is argued, do not give supervisors the kind of discretion and flexibility they need to use pay as an effective motivator (Gabris & Mitchell, 1985).

During the period of initial enthusiasm for PFP, other advantages attributed to it included the following:

1. Improved attractiveness to highly qualified and hard-to-recruit college graduates
2. Increased the probability that superior performers would feel valued and equitably compensated for their efforts
3. Focused management's attention on the importance of accurate performance appraisals using measurable standards and objectives
4. Provided supervisors with an effective means of pressuring poor performers to improve or leave
5. Encouraged supervisors and subordinates to communicate clearly about goals and expectations
6. Enhanced organizations' overall capacity to allocate limited financial resources in an effective manner

Despite these expectations, the public sector's experience with pay-for-performance programs has not been entirely encouraging:

Despite the popularity of pay for performance in the public sector, by the late 1980s and early 1990s, the effectiveness of this compensation strategy was called into question. Research on the topic had generated evidence that pay-for-performance systems, particularly merit pay plans, could often be problematic. Numerous scholars documented difficulties associated with merit pay, including problems connected with performance evaluation, the apparent reluctance of government to adequately fund the systems, and the fact that merit

---

BULLETIN

On CSRA Merit Pay

"A merit pay scheme like the CSRA reform that rewards the relative performance, ambiguously measured, of a fixed proportion of an employment population . . . is apt to have all sorts of undesirable motivational effects that may actually lower individual and organizational performance. Individual expectations are a serious problem. If you reward the top one-third in relative performance, employees who are not selected but nonetheless consider themselves among the top third . . . are apt to be angry and take their anger out on the job. Their response may be to become less efficient . . . particularly if they believe they are already there and that it is only poor measurement, politics, discrimination, and the like that says otherwise."

Source: George Downs and Patrick Larkey, *The Search for Government Efficiency* (New York: Random House, 1986), p. 198.

pay often led to dysfunctional competition among employees. (Kellough & Selden, 1997, p. 6)

The list of possible problems with PFP as a reliable performance management tool is a long one. An over-emphasis on external material rewards such as pay may, for example, undermine intrinsic sources of motivation such as self-esteem and contributions to organizational achievements. Employees' attention and effort may be diverted from organizational goals as they seek to meet personal performance objectives. Merit pay for individuals rather than groups may also promote competition and conflict in situations where interdependencies among jobs require coordination and collaboration. Overall, the experience with PFP in the public sector provides ample reason for caution and careful evaluation. The National Academy of Sciences' recent study of PFP led its authors to conclude that there is no solid empirical evidence that PFP and merit pay programs are effective (Milkovich & Wigdor, 1991).

In its 1991 *Report,* the Pay-For-Performance Labor-Management Committee, established under terms of the Federal Employees Pay Comparability Act, noted the council's findings. It advised OPM, "Government-wide implementation of any new pay-for-performance system for General Schedule employees should be preceded by a period of extensive and comprehensive experimentation involving a variety of programs that are tailored to the contextual conditions of Federal agencies. . . . (PFP Labor-Management Committee, 1991, pp. i–ii). In a similar vein, a committee established to evaluate the federal service's Performance Management and Recognition System (PMRS) determined "that there is virtually no empirical evidence that the PMRS has increased individual or organizational productivity" (PMRS Review Committee, 1991, p. 14).

A CAUTIONARY TALE: THE FEDERAL EXPERIENCE WITH MERIT PAY

The federal merit pay program is by far the most extensively described and evaluated. The national government's experience with PFP is instructive because it highlights several of the problems outlined earlier. The hard lessons learned on the federal level are also of potential value to state and localities seeking better outcomes from their PFP initiatives.

The Merit Pay System (MPS) established under the CSRA is usually seen as the first federal effort to implement PFP but, starting with the recommendations of the first Hoover Commission in 1949, there had been incremental efforts made to strengthen the link between pay and performance. The commission recommended that employees get within-grade increases only when their supervisors certified that they had earned them with satisfactory or better performance. The Classification Act of 1949 established the 10-step pay ranges for each of the General Schedule (GS) grades, and the Performance Rating Act of 1950 required agencies to set up performance appraisal systems with three summary ratings (outstanding, satisfactory, and unsatisfactory), but within-grade step increases were tied to seniority and an outstanding performance rating had *no* monetary consequences.

The first congressional attempt to reward superior performance was the Incentives Awards Act of 1954, which "authorized recognition and cash payments for superior accomplishments, suggestions, inventions, or other personal efforts." The Federal Salary Reform Act of 1962 required that an "acceptable level of competence" standard be used in granting within-grade increases, and it also stressed rewarding exceptional performances with quality step increases (QSIs) to base pay (PMRS Review Committee, 1991, pp. 1–2). By 1977, however, the staff working on the CSRA legislation for President Carter concluded that the linkage between pay and performance was at best weak, with within-grade increases all but automatic and cash awards and QSIs seldom used. The CSRA required that federal agencies set up *real* merit pay plans.

Under the CSRA, GS 13–15 employees covered by merit pay were placed under a "GM" pay plan designation, and the pay range for GM employees' grades was open, which meant that there were no preset rates for steps within the grade. The other major governmentwide feature of the MPS was that half of the GM employees' general comparability adjustment had to be placed in "merit pay pools" that the agencies used to fund merit increases. Funds that agencies would have otherwise used for within-grade increases and QSIs were also diverted to merit pay pools. Based on their performance ratings, GM personnel competed with one another for increases paid out of these pools. GS employees, on the other hand, continued to receive full comparability adjustments as an entitlement. Otherwise, federal agencies were given considerable discretion to develop their own merit pay systems.

The intention of the framers of the CSRA was to make this the first step, to be followed by an extension of merit pay to all federal executive branch personnel if the experience with the GM level proved successful. However, it did not take long for serious problems to develop. In 1981, a decision by the comptroller general resulted in a substantial reduction in the funding for merit pay, and GM employees complained that they were getting smaller pay increases and thus less total pay than their counterparts in the General Schedule. With the funding cuts, unhappiness with the MPS spread rapidly as GM employees received what they saw as meaningless merit increases. By the mid-1980s, the GAO was reporting that support for the MPS was very weak, with about half of the GM group wanting to return to the General Schedule. In its studies, the GAO found that more than 75 percent of the respondents believed that merit pay had not motivated them to be more productive (U.S. General Accounting Office, 1984).

A study of attitudes toward merit pay in five agencies by Pearce and Perry (1983) found that employees were no more motivated under the MPS than they had been under the previous arrangements. Federal managers reported that increased effort was *less* likely to lead to a good performance rating, and they expressed the belief that merit pay did not encourage them to perform their jobs well or contribute to their agencies' effectiveness. Pearce and Perry concluded that the results of the merit pay experiment did not warrant extending coverage to the rest of the GS.

Why did a program intended to motivate better performance fail so badly? First, agency appraisal systems had been put into effect under a very short deadline and without pretesting. As a consequence, many GM employees believed that the performance standards for their positions were not correct and that the ratings they received were inaccurate. Second, a requirement that no more money be spent on merit pay than had been under the previous system (an expenditure-neutral policy) set a restrictive upper limit on the pay increases that could be earned with superior performance ratings. Fixed limits on merit pay pools created conditions under which one employee's gain was another's loss, a win-lose situation that tended to generate small and trivial differences in rewards. For each agency, as the number of superior performers increased, their pay raises decreased. In other words, outstanding performance came to be seen by many as not being "instrumental" to meaningful pay raises.

Third, in response to the these problems, pay pool administrators modified distributions of performance ratings in order to achieve higher payouts for those receiving outstanding ratings, but this undermined confidence in the objectivity and fairness of the MPS. The phenomenon of managed ratings raised the question, "If the ratings are accurate, why should they be manipulated?" Fourth, the MPS was implemented in an atmosphere of hostility toward public employees, an attitude cultivated by the Reagan administration and shared by many in Congress who opposed fully funding the system. Budgetary restraints and rigidities further aggravated employee suspicions about how the MPS was being administered.

In 1984, Congress responded to the MPS's failures by passing legislation abolishing it and replacing it with the PMRS. The PMRS represented a return to more centralized approach to federal pay administration, and many of the MPS's flexibilities were eliminated in order to restore pay equity across agencies and between GS and GM personnel. The PMRS required that GM employees who received performance appraisals of fully successful be given full annual comparability and merit increases of 1 percent (those rated outstanding got 3 percent). Those rated one level below fully successful were guaranteed one-half of the comparability increase, and those rated unsatisfactory received no adjustment. The PMRS also encouraged the use of cash bonuses or performance awards to recognize exceptional performance.

The original legislation contained a five-year sunset provision, and when the Congress evaluated the PMRS in 1989, "they were confronted with major discontent with the current system, but no consensus as to what should replace it." The PMRS was extended for 18 months, with some minor changes, including a requirement that agencies develop a performance improvement plan (PIP) for all employees rated below fully successful. Given the continuing problems with merit pay for managers, an extension of pay-for-performance to the entire federal white-collar workforce was removed from the Comparability Act of 1990, and the Pay-for-Performance Labor-Management Committee was established to study the issue. In early 1991, Congress extended the PMRS through September 30, 1993. One 1991 amendment provided for the establishment of a PMRS Review Committee to review the system and make recommendations to the director of OPM regarding policy for a fair and effective performance management system for federal managers.

The review committee's report concluded that the PMRS had failed to meet three basic standards. First, performance ratings were suspect and not perceived as accurate. Second, there were serious doubts about the extent to which real differences in performance were linked to meaningful payouts. Third, many GM employees saw the system as unfair in its administration as well as outcomes. To address these flaws in the existing system, the committee made some 38 recommendations for improvements. These proposals covered a wide range of topics, including improved performance appraisal processes, expanded system coverage, increased funding of merit increases, and training for GM employees and their supervisors. Overall, the committee expressed support for the *concept* of pay-for-performance, adding that it favored an incremental approach to improving the PMRS, "rather than the creation of an entirely new system." Finally, the committee urged the Congress to allow federal agencies greater "flexibility to expand and adapt pay-for-performance for their particular structure, culture, and objectives" (PMRS Review Committee, 1991, pp. 49–52).

The Pay-for-Performance Labor-Management Committee's report was equally cautious about creating a new merit pay program. Given the existing state of knowledge and research, it concluded that the GS system for measuring and rewarding performance was a "workable pay-for-performance system." Noting that GS employees had to be rated satisfactory to receive within-grade increases and quality step increases were available, the committee urged federal agencies to make better use of the resources available to them:

> What is often lacking in managing the General Schedule system is a commitment to use the flexibilities that are authorized under current regulations governing performance and incentive awards to recognize employee accomplishments. Rather than replacing one base pay adjustment system with another, the Federal Government may be well served by a renewed focus on, and dedication to, improved management of the current General Schedule system. (PFP Labor-Management Committee, 1991, p. ii)

Other committee recommendations included the following:

1. Full and adequate funding of the program so that employees could see pay-outs as meaningful
2. Giving federal agencies "authority to design and administer individual pay-for-performance programs to satisfy their specific needs, objectives, workforce characteristics, and organizational culture"
3. Taking actions designed to assure fairness and to prevent adverse impact "on any class of employees"
4. Creation of mechanisms through which employees would be able to effectively participate "in the design, implementation, and evaluation of pay-for-performance programs"

In 1993, Congress passed the Performance Management and Recognition System *Termination* Act. Employees who had been covered by the merit pay program were returned to the GS pay system. For all practical purposes, this appeared to be a major setback for merit pay, since "the federal service was required to abandon the concept of individualized wage incentives added to base pay" (Kellough & Selden, 1997, p. 6). Subject to OPM policies, federal agencies may now have their own incentives plans, including cash awards and one-time bonuses.

The federal experience, however, does not appear to have deterred state and local employers from implementing merit pay plans. Between 1987 and 1997, the number of states using some form of pay-for-performance grew from 22 to at least 30. In 90 percent of these states, individualized increases to base salary or standard merit pay is the approach being used. In more than half of these states, bonuses are also available to certain categories of workers (Kellough & Selden, 1997). In 1997, for example, the State of Georgia implemented a PFP system for its civil service employees. For Georgia employees who meet, exceed, or far exceed performance standards, annual pay increases (adjustments to base pay) have two components: (1) a market adjustment to increase competitiveness and (2) a variable monetary award amount keyed to the performance rating. Those who receive a rating of "does not meet expectations" receive no increase. In all cases, increases are subject to the availability of state funds.

In their study of states' pay-for-performance systems, Kellough and Selden (1997) found the following:

- The trend toward PFP has continued despite mounting evidence, such as that provided by the federal experience and research studies, that it has not had the desired or expected results in many cases.

- Individual merit pay is the dominant approach, but bonuses and group incentives are also used in some states.

- More than half of the personnel managers responding to the study expressed confidence that their PFP systems had clarified organizational expectations and performance standards. Likewise, more than half believed that PFP had clarified the relationships between performance and monetary rewards.

- Only about a third of the respondents to Kellough and Selden's survey reported that merit pay had increased employee motivation and productivity, and they note that although these are supposed to be the central benefits of PFP, "the relatively small proportions of respondents seeing these outcomes associated with merit pay suggest that this approach to pay-for-performance may not always be a reliable mechanism for enhancing employee motivation and satisfaction" (p. 5).

- Political appointees, in comparison with career civil servants, viewed PFP more favorably. This finding more than likely reflects the symbolic value of PFP in the partisan political arena.

- Personnel managers with private sector backgrounds tended to be more skeptical about PFP's benefits than were those with only public sector experience. Although there is a general assumption that PFP is widely successful in the business world, it has not been without problems. Those with corporate experience also may be more sensitive to the barriers to successful implementation created by the public environment, such as the legal limits on managers' flexibility and discretion in personnel matters (Ingraham, 1993; Kellough & Selden, 1997, p. 10).

- Pay-for-performance systems covering managers *only* were more popular than those including nonmanagerial personnel. Apparently, extending PFP beyond the management ranks creates additional administrative complexities, fuels labor-management conflicts, and raises other problems that make it less attractive to many personnel managers in state governments.

Regarding anticipated benefits, discouraging reports about PFP on the state level were that having a merit pay plan: (1) did not greatly improve recruitment success or turnover rates, (2) did not significantly reduce labor costs, and (3) did not appear to increase political executives' control over career bureaucrats. Negative features of PFP that might be anticipated from previous research on merit pay plans in the federal government and elsewhere did in fact surface on the state level. For example, merit pay was associated with "red tape," increased demands on supervisors' time, and more paperwork. There were also serious concerns and suspicions about objectivity, consistency, and procedural fairness (Kellough & Selden, 1997, pp. 5–6).

About one-third of U.S. local governments had some form of PFP in operation by the mid-1990s, with most reporting that it has been at least somewhat useful. As appears to be the case on the state level, the most significant benefits are related to clarifying goals, expectations, and performance standards and to specifying the relationships between levels of performance and pay outcomes. PFP's effects on motivation, productivity, and job satisfaction, though seen to be somewhat positive by local government personnel managers in one study, were not exceptionally strong (Streib & Nigro, 1993a, 1993b). Problems with PFP in local governments mirror those on the federal and state levels.

Despite the long history of documented problems with pay-for-performance systems, the George W. Bush administration pushed for inclusion of such systems in the new personnel rules established for the

Table 6.1 Top 10 Problems with PFP on the Local Level

1.	Lack of adequate funding
2.	Failure to discriminate among levels of performance
3.	Perceived inequities in performance awards
4.	Conflict between raters and those being evaluated
5.	Lack of employee confidence in performance evaluation techniques
6.	Excessive demands on supervisors' time
7.	Employee suspicion and distrust of management's motives
8.	System failure to meet employee expectations
9.	Lack of supervisory compliance with program requirements
10.	Resistance from unions

Source: Gregory Streib and Lloyd Nigro, "Pay-for-Performance in Local Governments: Use and Effectiveness," in *The Municipal Yearbook: 1993* (Washington, DC: ICMA), pp. 50–56.

Department of Homeland Security and the Defense Department. This development was possible because the personnel rules governing both of those departments were exempted from Title V of the U.S. Code that governs civil service practices for other federal organizations. The ideological and symbolic appeal of pay for performance clearly overwhelmed evidence gathered from empirical observation as far as the Bush administration was concerned.

CONCLUSION

A performance evaluation process that is supported by supervisors and employees is a very important component of any merit system. In practice, the merit principle requires that public employees on all levels be covered by evaluation processes that are valid and have results that may confidently and legitimately be used as the basis for a variety of personnel actions. To the extent that these conditions do not exist, the credibility of the entire system is undermined. Historically, the appraisal systems used by public employers have been technically crude and ineffective as performance management tools. During the past 20 years, the push to create performance appraisal systems that accurately and reliably discriminate among levels of performance has been driven by the popularity of PFP as the centerpiece of virtually all civil service reform initiatives.

The available evidence strongly suggests that individualized merit pay models, though by far the most used, are not realizing the ambitious goals set for them by civil service reformers. Nonetheless, there continues to be strong support for the *concept* of pay-for-performance in government. The continued support for PFP and new ventures, such as Georgia's system, is probably explained by a mix of several factors. First, the traditional approaches to performance evaluation and pay do not conform to the merit principle and they are at odds with the current emphasis on management-centered personnel practices. Second, merit pay has already been adopted by many jurisdictions and "sold" to the public, so giving up on the concept is difficult, both in sunk costs and the credibility of elected executives. Third, it does serve as a symbolic response to public criticism of inefficient bureaucrats and to executives' calls for greater accountability (Kellough & Selden, 1997, pp. 7–8). In all probability, therefore, the public sector will continue to experiment with a variety of approaches to PFP, including bonuses and gainsharing. If TQM becomes more widely used in government, more emphasis may be placed on a *mix* of individual and group performance measures and rewards. It is also likely that multiple-source appraisals will grow in popularity as employers seek ways to enhance participation and communication, to establish employee development as an integral goal of appraisals, and to strengthen confidence in the objectivity and fairness of ratings throughout the organization.

DISCUSSION QUESTIONS

1. Does PFP result in the performance management process relying too heavily on money as a primary motivator?
2. Would you prefer to work for an employer that uses individualized merit pay, or one that relies on group-based rewards?
3. Do U.S. businesses really practice PFP for workers, managers, and executives?
4. Do you believe that supervisors' performance appraisals really can be objective?
5. Do you think multisource appraisals are a good idea? If so, why? If not, why?
6. If you were a supervisor, would you have confidence in your subordinates to provide objective and helpful evaluations of your performance?
7. Do you think one-time bonuses are better than increases to base pay if more effective performance management is the goal?

REFERENCES

Ammons, David N., and Arnold Rodriguez (1986). "Performance Appraisal Practices for Upper Management in City Governments." *Public Administration Review,* Vol. 46, No. 5 (September–October), pp. 460–467.

Berman, Evan (1997). "The Challenge of Total Quality Management," in Carolyn Ban and Norma M. Riccucci (Eds.), *Public Personnel Management: Current Concerns—Future Challenges* (New York: Longman), pp. 281–294.

Bowman, James S. (1994). "At Last an Alternative to Performance Appraisal: Total Quality Management." *Public Administration Review,* Vol. 54, No. 2 (March–April), pp. 129–136.

Coggburn, Jerrell D. (1998). "Subordinate Appraisals of Managers: Lessons From a State Agency." *Review of Public Personnel Administration,* Vol. 18, No. 1 (Winter), pp. 68–79.

Connor, Patrick E. (1997). "Total Quality Management: A Selective Commentary on Its Human Dimensions." *Public Administration Review,* Vol. 57, No. 6 (November–December), pp. 501–509.

Daley, Dennis (1991). "Performance Appraisal in North Carolina Municipalities." *Review of Public Personnel Administration,* Vol. 11, No. 3 (Summer), pp. 32–50.

deLeon, Linda, and Ann J. Ewen (1997). "Multi-Source Performance Appraisals." *Review of Public Personnel Administration,* Vol. 17, No. 1 (Winter), pp. 22–36.

Downs, George W., and Patrick D. Larkey (1986). *The Search for Government Efficiency: From Hubris to Helplessness* (New York: Random House).

Durant, Robert F. (1998). "Total Quality Management," in Stephen E. Condrey (Ed.), *Handbook of Human Resource Management in Government* (San Francisco: Jossey-Bass), pp. 453–473.

England, Robert E., and William M. Parle (1987). "Nonmanagerial Performance Appraisal Practices in Large American Cities." *Public Administration Review,* Vol. 47, No. 6 (November–December), pp. 498–504.

Fox, Charles J., and Kurt A. Shirkey (1997). "Employee Performance Appraisal: The Keystone Made of Clay," in Carolyn Ban and Norma M. Riccucci (Eds.), *Public Personnel Management: Current Concerns—Future Challenges* (New York: Longman), pp. 205–220.

Gabris, Gerald T., and Kenneth Mitchell, (1985). "Merit Based Performance Appraisal and Productivity: Do Employees Perceive the Connection?" *Public Productivity Review,* Vol. 9, No. 4 (Winter), pp. 311–327.

Georgia Merit System (1997). *Manager's Guide: Georgia Performance Management Process* (Atlanta, GA: Training & Organization Development Division).

Greiner, John M. (1986). "Motivational Programs and Productivity Improvement in Times of Limited Resources." *Public Productivity Review,* Vol. 10, No. 39 (Fall), pp. 81–102.

Greiner, J. M., H. P. Hatry, M. P. Koss, A. P. Millar, and J. P. Woodward (1981). *Productivity and Motivation: A Review of State and Local Government Initiatives* (Washington, DC: Urban Institute Press).

Ingraham, Patricia W. (1993). "Pay for Performance in the States." *American Review of Public Administration* Vol. 23, No. 3, pp. 189–200.

Ingraham, Patricia W., and Carolyn Ban (Eds.). (1984). *Legislating Bureaucratic Change: The Civil Service Reform Act of 1978* (Albany: State University of New York Press).

Kellough, J. Edward, and Sally Coleman Selden (1997). "Pay for Performance Systems in State Government." *Review of Public Personnel Administration,* Vol. 17, No. 1 (Winter), pp. 5–21.

Milkovich, George T., and Alexandra Wigdor (1991). *Pay for Performance: Evaluating Performance Appraisal and Merit Pay* (Washington, DC: National Academy Press).

Pay-for-Performance Labor-Management Committee (1991). *Strengthening the Link Between Pay and Performance* (Washington, DC), November.

Pearce, Jone L. and Perry, James L. (1983). "Federal Merit Pay: A Longitudinal Analysis." *Public Administration Review,* Vol. 43, No. 4 (July–August), pp. 315–328.

Performance Management and Recognition System Review Committee (1991). *Advancing Managerial Excellence: A Report on Improving the Performance Management and Recognition System* (Washington, DC), November.

Perry, James L. (1991). "Linking Pay to Performance: The Controversy Continues" in Carolyn Ban and Norma M. Riccucci (Eds.), *Public Personnel Management: Current Concerns—Future Challenges* (New York: Longman), pp. 73–86.

Roberts, Gary E. (1992). "Linkages Between Performance Appraisal System Effectiveness and Rater and Ratee Acceptance." *Review of*

Public Personnel Administration, Vol. 12, No. 3 (May–August), pp. 19–41.

———. (1995). "Developmental Performance Appraisal in Municipal Government: An Antidote for a Deadly Disease?" *Review of Public Personnel Administration,* Vol. 15, No. 3 (Summer), pp. 17–43.

Roberts, Gary E., and Tammy Reed (1996). "Performance Appraisal Participation, Goal Setting and Feedback." *Review of Public Personnel Administration,* Vol. 16, No. 4 (Fall), pp. 29–60.

Streib, Gregory, and Lloyd G. Nigro (1993a). "Pay for Performance in Local Governments: Programmatic Differences and Perceived Utility." *Public Productivity & Management Review,* Vol. 17, No. 2 (Winter), pp. 145–159.

———. (1993b). "Pay-for-Performance in Local Governments: Use and Effectiveness." *The Municipal Yearbook: 1993* (Washington, DC: International City/County Management Association), pp. 50–56.

Thompson, Frank J., and Beryl A. Radin (1997). "Reinventing Management: The Winter and Gore Initiatives," in Carolyn Ban and Norma M. Riccucci (Eds.), *Public Personnel Management: Current Concerns—Future Challenges* (New York: Longman), pp. 3–20.

U.S. General Accounting Office (1978). *Report to the Congress by the Comptroller of the United States: Federal Employee Performance Rating Systems Need Fundamental Changes* (Washington, DC), March.

———. (1983). *Report to the Director, Office of Personnel Management: New Performance Appraisals Beneficial But Refinements Needed* (Washington, DC), September 15.

———. (1984). *Report to the Chairwoman, Subcommittee on Compensation and Employee Benefits, Committee on Post Office and Civil Service, House of Representatives: A 2-Year Appraisal of Merit Pay in Three Agencies* (Washington, DC), March 26.

———. (1987). *Blue Collar Workers: Appraisal Systems Are in Place, But Basic Refinements are Needed* (Washington, DC), June.

———. (1988). *Civil Service Reform: Development of 1978 Civil Service Reform Proposals* (Washington, DC).

———. (1990). *Pay for Performance: State and International Pay-for-Performance* (Washington, DC), October.

Suggested Readings

Borins, Sandford (1998). *Innovating with Integrity: How Local Heroes Are Transforming American Government* (Washington, DC: Georgetown University Press).

Cleveland, Jeanette, and Kevin R. Murphy (1995). *Understanding Performance Appraisal; Social, Organizational, and Goal-Based Perspectives* (Thousand Oaks, CA: Sage).

Gilley, Jerry W. (1998). *Developing Performance Management Systems* (Reading, MA: Addison-Wesley Longman).

Goetsch, David L., and Stanley B. Davis (1996). *Introduction to Total Quality* (Paramus, NJ: Prentice-Hall).

Koehler, Jerry W. (1995). *Total Quality Management in Government* (Delray Beach, FL: Saint Lucie Press).

Milkovich, George T., and Jerry M. Newman (2005). *Compensation.* (Boston: McGraw-Hill).

Shand, David (Ed.). (1996). *Performance Management in Government: Contemporary Illustrations* (Washington, DC: Organization for Economic Cooperation and Development).

Smither, James W. (1998). *Performance Appraisal: The State of the Art in Practice* (San Francisco: Jossey-Bass).

West, Jonathan P. (Ed.). (1995). *Quality Management Today: What Local Governments Need to Know* (Washington, DC: International City/County Management Association).

Chapter SEVEN

Collective Bargaining in the Public Sector

Who should determine the terms and conditions of employment? Should it be the prerogative of management or should labor and management both have a say? The concept of collective bargaining provides one approach to answering to this question. Collective bargaining is a *bilateral* decision-making process in which authorized representatives of management and labor: (1) meet and in good faith negotiate such matters as wages, hours, and working conditions; (2) produce a mutually binding written contract of specified duration; and (3) agree to share responsibility for administering the provisions of that contract. A significant contributor to the social and political turbulence of the 1960s was the rapid spread of unionism and collective bargaining in the public sector (in 1960, about 35 percent of all American workers belonged to unions). Millions of public employees joined labor unions, and many were prepared to be militant in their dealings with employers. During this period, public employee strikes were not uncommon, and employers were often hard-pressed to respond effectively. In many jurisdictions, public employee associations, once satisfied to consult with management and to lobby legislative bodies for improvements in pay and benefits, were transformed almost overnight into aggressive labor organizations with contractual demands that they brought to the bargaining table. Strikes, slowdowns, and political action by organized employees trying to negotiate pay raises, improved benefits, better working conditions, and the right to participate in the making of personnel policies became hallmarks of public sector labor relations.

Arnold M. Zack, a well-known labor arbitrator and mediator, observed that the powerful public sector labor movement of the 1960s had several causes, including the following:

- Although the number of public employees had grown dramatically during the post-war years, their wages and salaries had fallen well below those of their private sector counterparts, many of whom belonged to very strong unions.
- Public employees became generally unhappy with their exclusion from the organizing and bargaining rights afforded private (non-agricultural) workers under the National Labor Relations Act of 1935.
- A new generation of younger and more militant public employees was not content to accept job security in exchange for second-class pay and benefits.
- Private sector unions, experiencing stagnant or even declining memberships, targeted the public sector as an untapped source of new members and revenues.
- State and local government workers interpreted President Kennedy's 1962 executive order granting federal employees limited bargaining rights as a signal to challenge long-standing blanket legal prohibitions on these levels of government.
- The civil rights movement, anti-war protests, and other forms of civil disobedience "convinced militant public employees that protest against 'the establishment' and its laws was fruitful and could be a valued vehicle for bringing about desired change" (Zack, 1972, pp. 101–102).

White-collar workers and professionals who a few years before would have considered union membership and collective bargaining to be things that only blue-collar craft and industrial workers did, eagerly joined unions, many of them affiliated with the American Federation of Labor and Congress of Industrial Organizations (AFL-CIO). Some joined large independents, like the Teamsters. In short order, the rules of the workplace, previously under the more or less benevolent unilateral control of the public employer, became matters to be decided through formal negotiations between management and organized labor in many states and thousands of cities, counties, and school districts.

Across the country, established private sector labor-management practices and concepts invaded the public sector, often to the extreme discomfort of public administrators who saw them as threats to their authority and to the merit principle. Expertise in labor relations had not been needed, and most personnel shops were caught unprepared to help management plan, negotiate, or administer a labor relations program. Early on, employee organizations also suffered from a similar lack of experience and skill. Numerous strikes and other disruptions were the direct result of incompetence and ignorance of the traditions and values underpinning the collective bargaining process. Strikes in public services areas like sanitation and education were powerful and often effective union weapons, even if they were illegal (Zack, 1972, p. 102).

In some states, the unions' efforts to organize public employees and to secure legislation permitting or requiring collective bargaining were beaten back, but their numerous and sometimes startling successes during the 1960s had fundamentally transformed public personnel administration in the United States by the early 1970s. Labor-management relations and collective bargaining were firmly established as objects of public personnel policy, and they became administrative responsibilities as well as areas of technical expertise. On the management side, the need for labor relations training programs in government and for pooling of efforts by governments was soon recognized, and state leagues of municipalities and other existing organizations of public employers became active in this area. New organizations such as the Labor Management Relations Service of the United States Conference of Mayors were established to provide information, training, consulting, and other labor relations services. Labor organizations such as the AFL-CIO also expanded their consulting and training programs to include the public sector.

The strong trend toward unionization and collective bargaining that affected the public sector in many parts of the country between 1962 and 1972 was dramatically slowed by the economic downturn that occurred in 1973. The following decade of widespread fiscal stress in government was marked by an abrupt end to the phenomenal growth and continuous successes of the public employee unions. Although most of the unions did not suffer great losses in membership, their ranks did not expand at anything resembling the previous rate, and they generally were unable to win large salary increases and other major concessions at the bargaining table.

In addition to better prepared management organizations and negotiators, the unions faced growing public hostility to strikes and other job action strategies that had worked so effectively in the past. Opposition to tax increases in any form and for any reason became the norm. Public opinion had turned against the unions to a point that pollster Louis Harris in effect advised politicians to run against the unions. Finding it increasingly difficult to get collective bargaining legislation passed, organized labor sought a federal law requiring *all* states and local governments to establish collective bargaining programs. This strategy collapsed in 1976 when the Supreme Court ruled in *National League of Cities et al. v. Usery* that Congress was not authorized by the commerce clause of the U.S. Constitution to extend provisions of the Fair Labor Standards Act of 1938 to state and local governments. This decision was widely interpreted to mean that the Court would strike down any federal law requiring collective bargaining. The Court's stance, in combination with the lack of political support, ended any realistic expectation that the Congress would act to advance the unions' interests.

The recession ended but was quickly followed by the taxpayer revolt and successful initiatives such as California's Proposition 13, which limited local government tax revenues. In the 1980s, yet another recession and decreasing federal aid to states and localities combined to make life even more difficult for the unions and their members. The 1981 Professional Air Traffic Controllers (PATCO) strike and its disastrous outcome for the union (the strikers were fired and the union decertified) further undermined organized labor's public image, and this encouraged public managers around the country to follow President Reagan's lead by assuming tough stances in their dealings with employee organizations. Public employee unions and their leaders were placed in the position of having to fight hard simply to preserve existing jobs and to prevent severe cuts in pay and benefits. By the end of the 1980s, instead of demanding large pay increases and other improvements, union negotiators were concentrating on keeping pace with inflation, opposing layoffs, resisting contracting out or privatization, and mobilizing opposition to budget cuts affecting their memberships. In the meantime, *private sector* union membership had declined from 20 percent in 1983 to about 12 percent (10.25 million workers) of the U.S. labor force by 1990.

Despite the unions' ongoing difficulties, the survival of collective bargaining in the public sector does not appear to be seriously threatened in any general sense. In fact, for many governments, it has become a routine and accepted way of handling many human resource functions. By 1985, some 40 states had enacted labor relations legislation covering some or all of their workers and more than 20 states now have comprehensive labor relations statutes (AFSCME, 2005).

During any given year, large numbers of public employees are involved in negotiations leading to contracts. About 3 million state and local government employees are covered by collective bargaining agreements. More than 1.1 million federal employees currently are in bargaining units covered by contracts negotiated under provisions of Title VII of the Civil Service Reform Act of 1978 (CSRA).

In 2005, the U.S. Department of Labor described union membership trends in the following terms:

> In 2004, workers in the public sector had a union membership rate more than four times that of private-sector employees. At 36.4 percent, the unionization rate for government workers was down slightly from 37.2 percent a year earlier. . . . Within the public sector, local government workers had the highest union membership rate, 41.3 percent. This group includes several heavily unionized occupations, such as teachers, police officers, and fire fighters. (U.S. Department of Labor, 2005a, p. 1)

TYPES OF PUBLIC EMPLOYEE ORGANIZATIONS

Several kinds of employee organizations are active in the U.S. public sector. Some function at just one level of government, others at two or more. Some are organized along craft lines (for example, electricians) and others by occupation (for example, social workers). Others are analogous to private sector industrial unions, such as the United Auto Workers (UAW) and the United Steelworkers of America (USWA), and include many different kinds of nonsupervisory jobs and skills. There are AFL-CIO affiliated unions such as the American Federation of State, County, and Municipal Employees (AFSCME), and some public employees are in bargaining units represented by the International Brotherhood of Teamsters. There are also independent associations of state and local government employees as well professional associations such as the National Education Association (NEA) that bargain collectively. In combination, the following five types include most public employees covered by negotiated contracts.

Mixed unions have members in government and the private sector. Most of their members work for private businesses, but in recent years, some have substantially increased their memberships from public agencies. *All public or mostly public unions* are those with all or most of their members working for government. Some of these unions are affiliated with the larger labor movement; the others are independent. They do not include police and fire organizations, which form a separate category (see later). *Professional associations* are organizations that draw their memberships from particular professions or occupations such as teachers and nurses. They are not affiliated with national labor organizations like AFSCME. *Independent associations of state and local government employees* have members doing many different kinds of work. They function on a statewide or local basis. Most of these associations were created between 1920 and 1950 to represent the interests of employees in the legislative process and to provide benefits for their memberships, such as low-cost life and health insurance policies. *Police and fire fighter organizations* represent police and fire fighters. Both kinds have been very active in collective bargaining. It should be noted that many public employees covered by negotiated contracts are not members of the unions that negotiated the contracts. Unlike the private sector, negotiated contracts requiring that workers join the union or be dismissed by the employer within a specific period (the union shop) are quite rare in government.

THE MIXED UNIONS

This category includes a wide variety of unions that as a group cross-cut all levels of government in the United States. Those with the strongest representation in state and local government are the Service Employees International Union (SEIU), the International Brotherhood of Teamsters, the Amalgamated Transit Union (ATU), the Communication Workers of America (CWA), and the Laborer's International Union (LIU). Except for the Teamsters, all are AFL-CIO affiliates. In the federal government, the largest organization in this category is the Metal Trades Council, which is made up of several national craft unions.

ALL PUBLIC OR MOSTLY PUBLIC UNIONS

The largest organization of this type is the AFSCME, which currently has about 1.3 million members, most of whom work for state and local governments. It includes workers of all kinds, except teachers. AFSCME started in 1936 as a small union dedicated to advancing the cause of merit in state and local governments. During the mid-1960s, AFSCME changed its orientation under new leadership and aggressively recruited new members, enthusiastically endorsed collective bargaining, and achieved many successes at the bargaining table.

Another large predominantly public union is the American Federation of Teachers (AFT). An AFL-CIO affiliate, the AFT now claims about 1.3 million members, most of whom work for elementary and secondary schools in very large cities. In recent years, AFT has also enrolled many members in colleges and universities where it now represents more faculty and staff than the NEA. The success of the AFT's largest affiliate, the United Federation of Teachers (UFT), in winning the 1961 collective bargaining election in New York City, gave a great nationwide impetus to bargaining in the public schools. The election was the first to be held in a large metropolitan school district, and the UFT succeeded in negotiating a comprehensive contract that was unprecedented in comparison with the then-existing AFT local and NEA affiliate agreements.

Other large mostly public unions may be found in the federal service. With the exception of the postal service employee unions, they all have members in many kinds of positions in a number of federal agencies. Still by far the largest in members and employees represented is the American Federation of Government Employees (AFGE), AFL-CIO, which currently represents almost 600,000 federal employees. The National Federation of Federal Employees (NFFE) is affiliated with the International Association of Machinists and Aerospace Workers–AFL-CIO and represents about 90,000 federal workers. Like the AFGE, NFFE has suffered significant membership loses during the past 20 years. The National Treasury Employees Union (NTEU), another independent union, started in the Internal Revenue Service, expanded to the Treasury Department, and has recently extended its jurisdiction to include workers in other federal agencies. In contrast with the AFGE and NFFE, the NTEU has managed to grow steadily and currently represents about 150,000 workers.

The Postal Reorganization Act of 1970 granted the U.S. Postal Service's workers collective bargaining rights that are far more extensive than those available to other federal employees. Most importantly, they have the right to negotiate compensation. Labor relations in the Postal Service are under the jurisdiction of the National Labor Relations Board, the regulatory body that oversees collective bargaining in the private sector under terms of the National Labor Relations Act. About 700,000 postal workers are covered by negotiated contracts.

The American Postal Workers Union (APWU) and the National Association of Letter Carriers (NALC), both AFL-CIO, each have memberships exceeding 300,000, and together they represent more than 650,000 postal service employees. The APWU was created in 1971 as the result of a merger between the AFL-CIO Postal Clerks, the independent National Postal Union, and three smaller AFL-CIO postal unions. The NALC was established in the late 19th century and was one of the first affiliates of the AFL. The NALC and APWU are very strong unions, both at the bargaining table and in lobbying the Congress.

PROFESSIONAL ASSOCIATIONS

By far the largest organization of this kind is the National Education Association or NEA, which has 2.7 million members. The NEA was established to advance the teaching profession, and to provide a variety of services to its members. It did not see itself as a labor organization. Until the 1960s, its leadership steadfastly rejected the idea that teachers needed to bargain collectively with their employers. However, pressures from the membership and the strong competition from the AFT after its 1961 successes in New York forced the NEA to officially adopt collective bargaining in 1962. It now represents workers on all levels of education, and it is as active in the bargaining arena as the AFT. The NEA has been a major force in organizing and representing the faculties of colleges and universities throughout the United States.

There are over 2.5 million registered nurses in the United States. Many of them are members of the American Nurses Association (ANA). The ANA was the first professional association to adopt collective bargaining. In 1946, it approved an Economic Security Program "committed to the use of collective bargaining as one of the most effective means of assuring nurses' rights to participate in the implementation of standards of nursing employment and practice" (Gideon, 1979). Of the ANA's 54 constituent associations, about half act as collective bargaining agents. The ANA's membership is open to all registered nurses, including those working for public employers on all levels of government.

INDEPENDENT ASSOCIATIONS OF STATE AND LOCAL EMPLOYEES

The state associations were created for a variety of reasons. In some cases, the purpose was to provide unified general representation for government employees. In others, the motive was to support a particular cause or employee benefit. For example, several were organized to promote or protect a merit system whereas others were created to support better retirement systems and insurance benefits. Most of them limit their memberships to state workers, but the number of state associations also admitting local employees has grown recently.

Most of the state associations are federated with the Assembly of Government Employees (AGE), which was established in 1952. The AGE strongly supports merit systems and, like most of its member associations, it did not welcome collective bargaining with open arms. Its membership tended to believe that unions such as AFSCME wanted to completely replace civil service laws and regulations with negotiated agreements. After collective bargaining statutes had been passed in a number of important states, the AGE faced the choice of adapting to the new public policy or of recommending that its members not compete with the unions in collective bargaining elections. AGE leaders chose to accommodate and compete, and many of the state associations have now been engaging in bargaining for some time.

The local associations were formed for basically the same kinds of reasons that motivated state employees. Their total membership has been estimated at about 300,000 nationally. Like their state counterparts, local associations did not originally support collective bargaining, but some now serve as bargaining agents. An increasing number of state and local associations, to build their bargaining power and resources, are affiliating with AFSCME and other AFL-CIO organizations. This pattern is illustrated by the California State Employees Association (CSEA). Established during the early 1930s, the CSEA is now a local of the SEIU that represents about 85,000 workers in 21 bargaining units.

POLICE AND FIRE FIGHTERS

Police officers are members of several different kinds of organizations. A few are members of AFSCME or of one of the mixed unions that admit police (such as the Teamsters and SEIU). There are also many local police associations not affiliated with any national organization.

There are three *national* organizations of police personnel: The Fraternal Order of Police (FOP), the International Union of Police Associations (IUPA), and the National Association of Police Officers (NAPO). The members of FOP, which was established in 1915, are regularly appointed or full-time law enforcement personnel of all ranks who work for the state, local, and federal governments. The FOP does not consider itself a union, but some of its lodges engage in collective bargaining and have taken militant stands. It currently has more than 270,000 members in more than 2,000 lodges. IUPA and NAPO were formed after the dissolution of the International Conference of Police Associations in 1978. The conference's members (state and local police associations) split over the issue of affiliation with the AFL-CIO. One segment formed the IUPA and became a charter member of the AFL-CIO in 1979. By 1997, IUPA had 80,000 members. Those opposed to affiliation created the NAPO as an independent "police only" association.

The International Association of Fire Fighters (IAFF), to which the majority of nation's professional fire fighters belong, currently represents about 267,000 professional fire fighters and paramedics. Most IAFF members are employed by local governments, but there are some in the state, U.S. federal service, and Canadian governments. The IAFF was established shortly after World War I, and it has the longest continuous experience with local-level labor management relations of any of the public employee unions. It has vigorously pursued bargaining agreements in most cities of any size.

ELEMENTS OF A COLLECTIVE BARGAINING SYSTEM

Collective bargaining stands in stark contrast to the traditional merit system because it makes many of the terms of the employment relationship a matter of bilateral negotiations between representatives of two organizations: the public employer and the labor union. Collective bargaining usually takes place within a highly formalized system of laws, rules, and procedures. In the private sector, the National Labor Relations Act of 1935 (NLRA) and its amendments provide the basis for procedures and policies set forth by the National Labor Relations Board (NLRB). Title VII of the Civil Service Reform Act establishes a system of labor relations for the federal service in which the Federal Labor Relations Authority (FLRA) "is responsible for issuing policy decisions and adjudicating labor-management disputes."

In state and local governments, collective bargaining systems are based on statutes or ordinances except in a few cases where they have been set up by executive orders. In New York State, for example, the Public Employees Fair Employment Act (Taylor Law) became effective in 1967. It was the state's first comprehensive labor relations law, and it was among the earliest passed in the nation. Its provisions are typical of those in many other state laws. The Taylor Law

- Gives public employees the right to organize and to be represented by employee organizations of their own choice.
- Requires public employers to negotiate and enter into agreements with public employee organizations regarding terms and conditions of employment.
- Creates impasse resolution processes to deal with collective bargaining disputes.

In some states where it has been approved by the courts, bargaining takes place on a de facto basis. Here, public management has for some reason decided to bargain with union representatives, and the courts have ruled valid the agreements entered into under these arrangements. In Ohio, for example, the state's supreme court ruled in 1975 that public employers did have the power to negotiate and engage in collective bargaining with their employees (Portaro, 1986). Enabling legislation obligating employers to bargain collectively was not passed in Ohio until 1983. In states like Virginia, the courts have decided that public employees may not bargain collectively if enabling legislation does not exist (D'Alba, 1979).

THE LABOR RELATIONS AGENCY

The collective bargaining programs of state and local governments are usually administered by an agency created expressly for that purpose. New York State's Public Employment Relations Board (PERB), Ohio's State Employment Relations Board (SERB), and New York City's Office of Collective Bargaining (OCB) are examples. When collective bargaining is provided for by a local ordinance, the administering agency typically is a board or commission. Members of state boards or commissions are appointed by the governor, in most cases with confirmation of the state senate. On the national level, the three members of the FLRA are appointed by the president with senate confirmation.

BARGAINING AGENTS AND UNITS

Within the traditional framework of collective bargaining, management representatives negotiate with the *exclusive bargaining agent* for a particular *bargaining unit*. All eligible workers within the unit are covered by the negotiated contract, even if they are not members of the union that has won the right to act as the exclusive agent. Although there are variations in procedure, the norm is for exclusive agents to be selected by a majority of those voting in a representation election. The labor relations agency sets the procedures for elections, oversees the process, and certifies the winner. Once certified, the bargaining agent has the exclusive right to represent the unit until such time that it is defeated in another election *or* it is decertified by the labor relations agency because it violated the law governing collective bargaining in its jurisdiction. The FLRA decertified the PATCO, for example, after it called for and orchestrated an illegal strike by controllers. About 20,000 air traffic controllers are now represented by the National Air Traffic Controllers Association (NATCA), which is an AFL-CIO affiliate.

Because they are the "building blocks" of collective bargaining, the size, membership, and number of bargaining units can affect all of the following:

- The efficiency of day-to-day governmental operations
- The quality of the relationship between management and the union
- The quality of the relationships between employee groups within the bargaining unit
- The scope of bargaining and the priorities given to particular issues by management and union negotiators
- The outcomes of representation elections (Hayford, Durkee, & Hickman, 1979)

The criteria and procedures used to establish bargaining units, in other words, are very important to both management and labor. These broad policy issues initially are dealt with on a political level through legislation and executive orders. Historically, one of the principal functions of labor relations agencies has been deciding how actual bargaining units will be constituted when management and labor disagree in their interpretations of the criteria set forth in law or executive orders.

Three different ways of determining bargaining units have been used in the U.S. public sector: (1) case-by-case determinations made by the labor relations agency, (2) specification in the enabling legislation, and (3) determination by the administrative agency through its rule-making procedures.

The case-by-case approach is the most commonly used on the local level, and it is the method used in the federal service. In general terms, the labor relations agency will try to authorize units that group employees so that there is a "community of interest" within each unit based on job classifications, the kind of work or occupation involved, or geographical location. However, these considerations must be balanced against the need for administrative efficiency and an orderly structure of bargaining units.

For public management, the existence of large numbers of fragmented units means that many contracts must be negotiated yearly. Besides increasing the workload, a multiplicity of units improves the unions' chance to "whipsaw" by using a favorable agreement in one unit (for example, police) to press for the same or better terms in another (such as fire). Although management tends to prefer a few large units to a scattering of small ones, neither management nor the unions invariably support larger or smaller units. Each side will develop its strategy in light of the situation it faces. If management is confronted by a powerful union or unions, it may try to divide that power by seeking several small units. Similarly, unions may want larger units if they believe this would increase their bargaining strength.

The case-by-case approach does carry the risk of fragmentation because the administrative agency must deal with requests to establish units as they occur, and it may not be able to wait until units can be rationally constituted. To avoid this problem, the legislatures of a number of states specified units for certain state workers in their legal authorizations. In Hawaii, the legislation requires that there be more than a dozen units, including units for nonsupervisory blue-collar positions, registered nurses, fire fighters, police, and professional and scientific employees. In Massachusetts, the legislature did not specify units, leaving this task to its Labor Relations Commission (MLRC). The commission rejected a case-by-case approach and decided to use its rule-making powers to create a system of broad units based on occupations.

The legislative and rule-making approaches to setting up bargaining units can avoid fragmentation and "greatly reduce the amount of time required to erect a comprehensive unit structure that will not require extensive future alteration" (Hayford, Durkee, & Hickman, 1979). However, a legislature may not be able to develop a successful unit framework, especially if there is intense competition among unions, and management and labor cannot agree on the general outlines of a framework before it acts. "In the absence of such firm policy guidance, the legislative body, which typically lacks expertise in such matters, would probably base its decision on factors (primarily political in nature) other than those normally relied on in unit determination" (p. 95). The rule-making approach does not eliminate political considerations; instead, it shifts the task of dealing with them to the administrative agency.

One bargaining unit determination issue that is unique to the public sector is the status of supervisory personnel. In the private sector, with the exception of a few skilled craft unions, all supervisors are considered to be "management," and they are excluded from bargaining units. This arrangement is firmly imbedded in a larger tradition of drawing a sharp line between management and labor. The NLRA excludes supervisors from bargaining rights, and most employers argue that their supervisors must be a part of the management team. For many public employers, however, the line between supervisors and nonsupervisors is blurred and controversial.

Three questions or issues are involved. First, it may be hard to determine whether a position is *really* supervisory in nature. Merit systems covering entire workforces have not stressed this distinction. The definition of a supervisory position set forth in the collective bargaining statute may be detailed, but there are frequent disagreements about whether the supervision exercised justifies excluding a particular position from a nonsupervisory bargaining unit. In reality, many public employees occupy positions in so-called supervisory classes that actually involve little or no supervisory activity. Because the size of a unit is important to a union's bargaining position, unions will seek to have ambiguous cases classified as nonsupervisory. Management, on the other hand, may try to reduce union strength by convincing the labor relations agency to define these kinds of jobs as supervisory so they can be excluded from the bargaining unit.

Most collective bargaining statutes do not specify which *individual* positions are to be considered supervisory. This determination is left to the administrative agency that decides bargaining units, and some of these agencies will closely examine the actual duties of positions with supervisory titles and exclude only those involving clearly supervisory duties and powers. Nonetheless, disagreement between management, the unions, and the administrative agency about which positions are supervisory is commonplace in the public sector.

The second issue has to do with the desirability of units that contain both supervisors and nonsupervisors. In government, the workforce is predominantly white- rather than blue-collar, and there are numerous levels of supervision. From the beginning, employee associations contained both supervisory and nonsupervisory personnel. Supervisors often were primarily responsible for creating these associations, and it was not unusual for them to hold leadership positions in them. Most of the mixed, predominantly public, and all public employee unions admit lower-level supervisors. Against this is a historical pattern—when collective bargaining programs were established, union leaders resisted legislation prohibiting "mixed" bargaining units. Nevertheless, most state statutes contain such a prohibition and use the definition of supervisors set forth by the National Labor Relations Act.

The reason for the private sector precedent of not mixing supervisors and nonsupervisors is the potential for conflict of interest. In these terms, the groups have opposed, rather than common, interests. Supervisors represent management; the union represents the interests of workers. Bargaining unit are supposed to be composed of persons having a "community of interest," so having them both in the same unit does not make sense. Either the supervisors will permeate the unit with a management point of view, thereby undermining the collective bargaining rights of the workers, or the supervisors will "defect," weakening management's position.

Union leaders who favor mixed units argue that the conflict of interest argument does not hold for the public sector. One of their key points is that supervisors in government do not have the kind of authority and discretion typical of their counterparts in business and industrial settings. Another perspective stresses the idea that in some occupations and services, supervisors and nonsupervisors share a community of interest that outweighs differences between management and labor. Representatives of nurses, teachers, and police and fire services employees have strongly advanced this point of view. In some local governments, almost all levels of supervision in certain departments have been included in the same bargaining unit as nonsupervisory employees. Cases frequently cited are in police and fire departments. When this happens—and it occurs largely because the unions have been politically effective—only a few executives may be left to define and represent management's basic interests.

The third question or issue is whether supervisors should be allowed to form their own units and to bargain collectively with the employer. In the private sector, under the Taft-Hartley amendment to the NLRA, organizations of supervisors do not have bargaining rights. For the most part, government has followed this model, but some states such as New York, Hawaii, and New Jersey do grant bargaining rights to all or some supervisory personnel.

Again, the rationale for not allowing bargaining with units of supervisors is that they are a part of the management team and should represent management's interests in the administration of personnel policies. In other words, if supervisors bargained, it would be very difficult to define managerial roles and responsibilities clearly. Also, if supervisors had bargaining rights, they might see themselves as "labor" and, for example, sympathize with strikes by rank-and-file workers. When strikes or other job actions take place, management often relies on supervisors to perform essential work, and supervisors who have strong feelings of solidarity with organized labor may be unwilling to undermine the workers' position.

For largely practical reasons, many supervisors in both sectors disagree with the idea that consultations with top management is the best way to determine supervisory pay and benefits. It is a fairly common practice for supervisors' compensation to be informally linked to the provisions of negotiated agreements. However, top management is not required to do this, leaving supervisors in a very dependent position. In the public sector, it is not unusual to hear supervisors express the belief that they are disadvantaged in comparison with those who have bargaining rights and the organizational resources needed to pressure management. Many public employers have given inadequate attention to the pay and other needs of their supervisory personnel. Although there may be compelling reasons for not authorizing supervisors' bargaining units, this does not erase an important need to develop alternative organizational mechanisms for representing their interests.

EMPLOYEE RIGHTS

It is the norm for employee rights to be stated in the legal authorization for collective bargaining. The most basic right is to form, join, and participate in employee organizations for the purpose of conferring and bargaining collectively with management. This includes the worker's right to be represented by the majority union in grievances over the terms and conditions of employment. The right of workers *not* to join unions or associations may or may not be stated. If it is, this means that management will not agree to contracts that require those in bargaining units to join the union or to pay dues.

Under such *open shop* arrangements, exclusive bargaining agents are often faced with situations where they are negotiating contracts for units having more nonmembers than members. Having large numbers of "free riders" in units weaken unions' financial positions, and their bargaining power may be affected because they cannot depend on strong, unified, support from those in the unit. Management, for obvious reasons, prefers to negotiate in an open shop environment. The unions, on the other hand, much prefer statutory language that requires employees to join or support unions. If this is the case, it usually means in practice that *union* or *agency* shop agreements may be negotiated.

Under the *union shop*, which is commonplace in the private sectors of states that do not have so-called right-to-work laws, workers must join the union within a specified period after being hired. If they do not, management is obliged to fire them. Union *membership* is not mandatory under an *agency shop*, but the equivalent of the union dues or a "fair share" thereof must be paid for purposes of representation. This payment is in return for services provided by the exclusive bargaining agent, which is required to represent the interests of all persons in the bargaining unit, whether or not they are members of the union. Most states and the federal government require open shops. Where this is not the case (for example, Pennsylvania and Hawaii), unions have succeeded in negotiating union or agency shops for some units.

MANAGEMENT RIGHTS AND SCOPE OF BARGAINING

A key to the relative balance of power between management and the unions is the range of personnel policies and practices that are negotiable. In general, unions prefer a wide range, and management usually seeks to narrow the scope of bargaining. In the private sector, the NLRA defines the scope of bargaining to include wages, hours, and working conditions. The NLRB, in turn, has identified three types of issues: (1) those that are nonnegotiable, (2) mandatory issues that must be negotiated, and (3) those that may be negotiated if management agrees to do so. With regard to mandatory issues, the NLRB and often the courts must decide what the language of the NLRA means in specific circumstances.

In the public sector, overriding laws and court rulings may effectively remove certain issues from the bargaining table; for example, if the enabling state legislation requires the open shop, management and the union are not free to negotiate another arrangement. Employee relations boards and commissions in the public sector are empowered to interpret legislative intent in this area, subject to judicial review. Although they are not bound by its precedents, these agencies have in practice generally followed the NLRB's three-fold classification.

The scope of bargaining in government is generally likely to be narrower than it is in the private sector. Provisions of civil service laws, state education codes, special legislation covering the pay of blue-collar workers, and other statutes (federal, state, and local) make many issues essentially nonnegotiable. Although there are some exceptions, the legal authorizations covering state and local employees typically limit the range of negotiations by providing that subjects already covered by preexisting laws (particularly civil service statutes) may not be negotiated (Williams, 1994). The federal CSRA restricts the scope of bargaining to "conditions of employment," a term the legislation defines as "personnel policies, practices, and matters, whether established by rule, regulation, or otherwise, affecting working conditions, except that such term does not include policies, practices, and matters . . . [that] are specifically provided for by Federal statute." The pay and benefits of federal workers covered by the CSRA are set by law, so they are not negotiable (see Chapter 5).

In addition to limits set by other laws, a "management rights" clause often is included in collective bargaining statutes. It is designed to specify managerial powers that may not be bargained away or shared with labor organizations. Traditionally enumerated "rights" give management control over agency missions, administrative structures, and operating technologies. Other rights include directing the work of employees and to hire, evaluate, promote, assign, and transfer them given agency requirements. The CSRA's language on management rights is typical:

> Nothing in this chapter shall affect the authority of any management official of any agency—(1) to determine the mission, budget, organization, number of employees, and internal security practices of the agency; and (2) in accordance with applicable laws—(A) to hire, assign, direct, layoff, and retain employees in the agency, or to suspend, remove, reduce in grade or pay, or take other disciplinary action against such employees; (B) to assign work, to make determinations with respect to contracting out, and to determine the personnel by which agency operations shall be conducted. . . .

Management rights clauses usually are replicated in contracts, but determining what they mean in specific cases is often a responsibility of the labor relations agency. These interpretations are important because they set the scope of bargaining. Rulings of labor relations agencies and courts concerning which issues are mandatory or permissive vary from state to state. Student-teacher ratios are negotiable in some states, but in others, they are not. In an area of great importance to the unions, contracting out or privatization, there are wide variations.

In their interpretations of management rights, the courts have been "more concerned with preserving those rights that [they] believe management must possess to carry out its public duties and responsibilities under enabling statutes than with providing a safety valve for employees . . . but they do provide some flexibility for employee organizations by making the impact of management actions on wages, hours, and working conditions negotiable" (Gershenfeld & Gershenfeld, 1983, p. 349). In other words, *impact bargaining* expands the arena of mandatory negotiations to include the *affects* of management decisions on those in a bargaining unit. In personnel matters, impact bargaining means that management keeps its power to make program decisions, such as whether or not to carry out a reduction-in-force or to implement a pay-for-performance system. However, because these kinds of actions will almost certainly have an impact on working conditions, management is obliged to negotiate with the union regarding procedural issues and ways of dealing with the consequences for employees. In such negotiations, the union may want management to agree to give laid-off workers first consideration when positions become available. In the federal service, the unions may negotiate aspects of pay-for-performance systems that have an impact on working conditions, with the major exceptions of position classifications and "matters specifically provided for by Federal statute." Of course, management is not compelled to grant union demands regarding impact issues, but it cannot simply say they are nonnegotiable.

UNFAIR LABOR PRACTICES

In their dealings with each other, management and labor are constrained by rules defining unfair labor practices. These rules are designed to prevent "union busting" by management, to make sure that unions do not engage in coercive behavior, and to ensure that both parties negotiate in good faith. Such practices by the *employer* commonly are defined to include the following:

- Interfering, restraining, or coercing employees who are trying to exercise their collective bargaining rights under law. Threatening to fire or transfer workers who participate in union activities is an unfair labor practice.
- Dominating, obstructing, or assisting in the formation, existence, or administration of any employee organization. Employers who try to create "company unions" or to put "their people" into union leadership positions are engaging in an unfair labor practice.
- Encouraging or discouraging membership in any employee organization. Discriminatory personnel practices such as not hiring, promoting, or offering training opportunities to union members are unfair labor practices.
- Discouraging or discriminating against any employee because he or she has joined a union or filed a grievance under the collective bargaining agreement. Actions such as these by management constitute unfair labor practices.
- Refusing to negotiate in good faith, lying or distorting information, deliberately provoking conflict, and other steps taken to undermine negotiations. Behaviors such as these also are unfair labor practices.

Unfair labor practices by *employee organizations* include the following kinds of behaviors:

- Interfering with, restraining, or coercing employees in the exercise of their bargaining rights. For example, one union may try to coerce workers to vote for it as the exclusive bargaining agent.
- Obstructing an employer's efforts to select its labor relations team, including negotiators and representatives in the grievance process. Unions have been known to use political pressure and threats to undermine management's capacity to function effectively.
- Refusing to negotiate in good faith with the employer to provoke an impasse or strike.

A good faith effort by both sides to negotiate, to resolve differences, and to reach an agreement obviously is the foundation of a successful collective bargaining relationship. The parties are entitled to file unfair labor practices charges with the labor relations agency. The agency is authorized to investigate such charges and, if it finds that they are justified, it will order the violator to stop the practice and to take whatever remedial actions are necessary. In the case of dismissals for union activity, management usually will be ordered to reinstate fired employees with back pay. These kinds of orders may be appealed to the courts for a final decision.

Effective labor relations depend largely on each side's fully understanding "the rules of the game." Over the years, labor relations agencies and the courts will issue rulings management and labor are expected to understand and to follow. During the early stages of the expansion of collective bargaining in the public sector, it was not unusual for inexperienced managers and union members to make threatening statements and to behave in ways that provoked charges of unfair labor practices. A derogatory statement about a union and its leadership made in the presence of union members is often enough to bring a complaint against management. Unless management negotiators are aware of which overt acts the labor relations agency considers to be evidence of a lack of good faith bargaining, such as routinely putting off meetings with the union bargaining team or simply refusing to meet with it at all, they run a great risk of being found guilty of an unfair labor practice. The penalties can be substantial. In this, as well as other regards, collective bargaining adds a new dimension to public personnel administration.

Contract Negotiations

In the public sector, most negotiated agreements cover one or two years. This means that both sides are almost constantly preparing to negotiate the next contract in addition to administering the provisions of the one in force. In contrast to the corporate or business environment where it is fairly easy to identify the membership of the "management team" responsible for making preparations, conducting negotiations, and committing the organization to contractual obligations, it is often difficult to say who is "in charge" in government. Thus, when collective bargaining began to spread in government, clearly defining who should have the responsibility for labor relations and the authority to enter into contractual relationships with unions became a difficult issue (Love, 1966, p. 28).

In addition to the intentional dispersal and sharing of power within the formal institutions of government, powerful external interest groups seek influence in the collective bargaining process. Many potentially conflicting roles and points of view make up the management side of the collective bargaining relationship. Although elected executives may recommend or request budgetary appropriations, the legislative body makes those appropriations. Even when legislators delegate to executives the authority to set pay scales, they do not give up their control over fiscal and budgetary matters and they may simply refuse to make needed funds available.

If tax increases will be required to pay for negotiated pay scales, organized interests of many kinds are likely to become very active. Human resource departments, the courts, and other levels of government may be drawn in by contractual provisions concerning issues such as position classifications, appeals processes, and seniority systems. On the union side, important players include national or state labor organizations, factions within the union itself, and community and special interest groups with a stake in the outcome of negotiations. Thus, in addition to the bilateral bargaining that takes place across the table, both sides are conducting a process of multilateral bargaining with constituencies and authorities that must be recognized and accommodated in any negotiated contract.

The fragmentation of authority and power within public employers led to much confusion and lack of coordination on the management side during the early years of collective bargaining. It was not unusual to see city councils reject or attempt to change contracts negotiated in good faith by a management team. Lack of coordination between personnel departments, budget offices, and line managers frequently produced contracts that were inadequately "costed-out" and at cross purposes with efforts to improve productivity. Recognizing this weakness, unions often went around management negotiators and, in effect, tried to negotiate with legislators. On the other side of the coin, union leaders would sometimes find that management was covertly mobilizing legislators, courts, and taxpayer groups in an effort to achieve a dominant position.

One consequence of more than 40 years of unionization and collective bargaining has been that public executives have been expected to take the lead in labor relations, and this has resulted in a significant decline in legislative influence over personnel matters in jurisdictions where collective bargaining is well established. Administratively, the pattern has been for executives to establish a direct line of authority over a unit having responsibility for labor relations.

In state and local governments, the labor relations function often is assigned to the director of personnel or to a separate office of labor relations. In either case, specialists in labor relations will be responsible for the program. Many small jurisdictions use part-time consultants to represent management at the bargaining table. In the federal government, all bargaining takes place on the agency level (the Office of Personnel Management [OPM] serves as a management adviser on labor relations). In most cases, a specialized unit of the personnel office or department handles the federal agency's labor relations program. A few agencies have a completely separate office of labor relations, a model typical of the private sector. When there is one office responsible for labor relations and another for personnel, experience has shown the need for close coordination between the two. Those negotiating agreements must be thoroughly familiar with personnel laws and regulations, and they should be aware of any personnel problems or issues that relate to the agency's dealings with organized employees. Likewise, the personnel department must be in a position to understand and respond to the implications of proposed contractual agreements. When the functions are combined in one office, but they are handled by different staffs, similar coordination is needed. Whatever the structure of responsibilities, those responsible for labor relations should be in constant contact with line officials to ensure that management's needs and perspectives are represented in the negotiating process.

Strikes and Impasse Resolution

At one time, strikes by public employee organizations were probably the single most feared aspect of collective bargaining, at least from management's point of view. Strikes by *private* sector workers are legal, and unions see that right as absolutely essential to maintaining an economic balance of power between management and labor. In contrast, strikes by *public* employees are illegal in most states and the federal government. Two reasons or rationales are advanced for denying the right to strike: (1) Many public services are essential and the public has no comparable alternatives, and (2) strikes by public employees are essentially political weapons that give unions an unfair advantage.

Statutory penalties include dismissal of striking workers, criminal prosecution of union leaders, fines against union treasuries, and decertification of unions calling strikes. Many strikes or work stoppages, nonetheless, have taken place in government, most against local employers and school districts. Although most have been relatively short in duration, some have been protracted, unpleasant, media spectaculars. In many instances, legal penalties could not be enforced and settlements provided for amnesty. In cases where legal penalties have been imposed, such as the PATCO strike in 1981 where more than 10,000 experienced controllers were fired outright and not re-hired, it may take years for the agency to return to normal operation.

Its experience with strikes, though unpleasant, has taught public management that strikes can be survived if contingency plans have been prepared. One measure of confidence on the employer side is legislation in a number of states that permits strikes by *non-essential* workers. Most of these laws were passed in the late 1970s after the period of explosive growth in unionism. The number and duration of work stoppages has declined during the past 20 years. In 1984, for example, there were 62 work stoppages in the public and private sectors involving more than 1,000 workers. By 2004, that number had dropped to 17; 6 involved 5,000 or more workers, and of these only 1 was in the public sector—an AFSCME action against the City of New York that lasted two days (U. S. Department of Labor, 2005b). An overall maturation of the relationship between management and labor has been a contributing factor, along with fiscal stress and public opposition to strikes. In the current environment, there can be no doubt that both sides have many incentives to avoid strikes and job actions such as "slowdowns" and "sickouts."

One feature of legally authorized collective bargaining programs is that they usually set up procedures for resolving bargaining deadlocks or impasses. Where they exist, the labor relations agencies are responsible for seeing to it that these laws are followed and for arranging the services of *mediators, fact-finders,* and *arbitrators* to help resolve impasses. Traditionally, each side shares equally in the costs associated with such third-party interventions.

Mediation usually is the first step. Mediators focus on getting the negotiation process back on track and facilitating communication between the parties. If mediation fails, the next step may be fact-finding. Often, "the facts" are in dispute; for example, a jurisdiction's ability to pay may be in question. Fact-finding is a semi-judicial process in which both sides present their version of the facts with documentation such as cost-of-living data and information on prevailing rates of pay. Expert witnesses are likely to be called in to support each side. The fact finder (or fact-finding panel) studies the evidence and issues a report containing a recommended settlement. If these are not accepted by one or both of the parties, in some states the parties may agree to go to binding arbitration under which an agreement is imposed. In other states, a limited strike is a legal option. In about 20 states, the law requires that police and firefighters submit to binding arbitration if they cannot resolve an impasse at the bargaining table.

In both the fact-finding and arbitration processes, management is required to carefully prepare its case. Personnel departments usually have much of the responsibility for collecting, organizing, and displaying information that supports the employer's position. Although most public sector labor leaders would prefer the strike option, fact-finding and arbitration do compensate somewhat by requiring employers to present a rational justification of the positions they have taken at the bargaining table.

APPROVAL OF AGREEMENTS

Public management seldom has the luxury of being able to finalize a contractual agreement with a union. In many municipalities, agreements must be approved by the local governing body, such as the county board of supervisors or city council. In most school districts, approval by the school board is required before a contract may go into effect. In some state governments, the legislature must ratify the agreement; in most, this is not the case. Agreements take effect in the federal service when they are approved by agency heads. With the exception of public authorities having their own sources of revenue, the legislative body must vote funds to finance contracts and so may exercise a veto power.

On the union side, contracts may be submitted to the membership for a ratification vote, but procedures vary. In the federal service, such votes are not required. Ideally, both agency leadership and the union membership have been kept fully informed about the status of negotiations, have in some manner consulted with their negotiators, and will not be surprised by the content of a proposed contract. Management officials presenting an agreement to those legally empowered to give it final approval should be prepared to fully explain its terms and likely consequences on such matters as budgets and tax rates. Union leaders are responsible for explaining a contract's terms and, if a ratification vote is required, recommending its approval or rejection.

CONTRACT ADMINISTRATION

Once a contract is signed and ratified, the labor relations program enters the contract administration phase. Although negotiations and related impasses attract the most public attention, effective day-to-day administration of agreements is the foundation of a successful labor relations program. Contract administration is a bilateral process in which management and labor share responsibility for implementation of an agreement's provisions. Needless to say, disputes about how to interpret some of those provisions are likely to occur, but the emphasis is (or should be) on building a cooperative relationship.

In a study of the federal labor relations program conducted during the early 1990s, the General Accounting Office (GAO) concluded that a cooperative or joint problem-solving orientation often was sadly lacking (U.S. General Accounting Office, 1991). It also noted, "Labor-management cooperative programs in the private sector reflect the growing view that an 'us versus them' approach is outdated and unworkable." In fact, in the 1990s labor-management cooperation has become an important stated goal of federal personnel policy. In 1993, President Clinton issued Executive Order 12871 calling for a change in federal labor-management relations "so that managers, employees, and employees' elected union representatives serve as partners. . . ." Clinton's Executive Order (E.O.) required federal agencies to set up labor-management partnerships. It established a National Partnership Council to advise the president on labor-management relations, to support and promote labor-management partnerships, and to recommend statutory changes needed to support a cooperative and reform-oriented approach to federal labor relations. Agency heads were required to establish labor-management partnerships by forming committees or councils to support the reform agenda set forth in the National Performance Review (NPR). Agency heads were to

- Involve employees and their union representatives as full partners with management representatives to identify problems and craft solutions to better serve the agency's customers and mission
- Provide training for appropriate agency employees in consensual methods of dispute resolution
- Evaluate progress and improvements in organizational performance resulting from labor-management partnerships

The objectives of E.O. 12871 and the Clinton administration were to replace the traditionally adversarial culture of federal labor relations with one that encouraged mutual respect, partnership, and goal-oriented cooperation (Reeves, 1997). In 2001, however, almost immediately upon assuming office, President George W. Bush issued Executive Order 13203, which revoked the Clinton E.O., dissolved the National Partnership Council, and rescinded all rules, regulations, guidelines, or policies implementing E.O. 12871 (Bush, 2001). Director Kay Coles James of the Office of Personnel Management, in turn, interpreted E.O. 13203 as follows:

> When the President signed Executive Order 13210, there was speculation that it meant the end of labor-management cooperation and communication in the Federal Government. I think that is wrong. He is motivated by his conviction that partnership is not something that should be mandated. . . . But while agencies are no longer *required* to form partnerships with their unions, they are encouraged to establish cooperative labor-management relations. (James, 2002)

In her memorandum to the heads of federal departments and agencies, Director James described OPM's commitment to working with unions, employee associations, and other stakeholders to establish voluntary cooperative labor relations in the federal service. Writing in the wake of the terrorist attacks on September 11, 2001, she stressed the need to build a strong human resource system in the new Department of Homeland Security where workers are not covered by the Federal Labor Relations Act (see Chapter 2). To this date, no systematic review has been conducted of the effect of the Bush administration's policy on the development of cooperative labor relations.

Although federal policy has retreated from mandatory labor-management cooperation efforts, joint labor-management committees

(LMCs) are used on the state and local levels in an effort to achieve successful problem-solving partnerships. LMCs are not a substitute for bargaining, but they provide a mechanism for cooperative efforts to solve a wide variety of problems, like workplace safety, quality control, and communication. Joint LMCs are created by contract to deal with a single issue like health care. There is joint representation on the committee of both labor and management, but the final decision is reserved to management.

Supervisors are considered key figures in the administration of a public personnel program because they have the most direct contact with rank-and-file workers. Perhaps the single most positive impact of collective bargaining on personnel administration has been its focus on the administration of contracts by supervisors. Grievance arbitration clauses are now very common in the public sector (see below), and supervisors are expected to understand a contract's provisions and to be able prevent disputes and resolve conflicts before they result in formal grievances that may undermine cooperation. Although some grievances are unavoidable, many are provoked by supervisory ignorance and a confrontational approach.

For supervisors unused to life under a negotiated contract, the presence of union stewards may come as a somewhat unpleasant shock. Elected by the union membership, stewards are the supervisors' counterparts in the process of contract administration. In this role, they are often more diligent than management and the personnel office in detecting supervisory deficiencies, particularly as they relate to contractual requirements.

Located in the workplace where supervision operates, stewards can have intimate knowledge of work activities and of problems affecting both management and the worker. They are sometimes overzealous and so antagonistic toward management that supervisors may have some cause for considering them "troublemakers," but the capable, conscientious steward is a troubleshooter who can be a valuable problem solver for both the union and management. For supervisors and stewards alike, adequate training in labor relations is crucial to a smoothly functioning collective bargaining relationship.

One very important aspect of contract administration is the process through which disputes about interpretations of a contract and its manner of administration are resolved. Typically, authorizing legislation will require that all contracts contain a mechanism for resolving grievances. The standard mechanism is a negotiated grievance procedure. These procedures are designed to have finality in the sense that disputes that cannot be resolved by the parties are submitted to a third party "neutral" or arbitrator who makes a final and binding decision.

Such finality is essential because neither side can afford to be bogged down in interminable conflicts and ambiguities regarding how to interpret one part or another of the contract. Although one side or the other is likely to be disappointed by the arbitrator's decision, at least it provides an end to the dispute and makes it easier to avoid future misunderstandings.

The definition of a grievance set forth in legislation is very important because it determines what issues employees will be able to grieve under a negotiated process, as opposed to the system established under civil service laws and regulations. The CSRA's language is very broad, and a grievance is defined as "any complaint about employment, or the interpretation and application of the negotiated agreement or any law, rule, or regulation affecting employees' working conditions." Unless the parties agree to exclude them, this means that the negotiated grievance procedure can be used to deal with matters already covered by the statutory appeals process. Not surprisingly, many managers object to broad definitions of grievances because they believe that exposes many of management's decisions on personnel matters to reversals by arbitrators who are not particularly concerned with the day-to-day problems of administering complex organizations and programs.

Conclusion

From a public management standpoint, two concerns about collective bargaining have been its effect on the merit principle and its long-term impact on managerial authority and discretion. Despite early fears about negotiating-away merit and an undermining of public management capacities, collective bargaining appears to have done neither. It has, however, often required public managers to work within legally established bilateral decision-making environments. A good example is the approach to managed competition or contracting out set forth in the State of Hawaii's labor relations law. Hawaii has established an Office of Collective Bargaining and Managed Competition in "the office of the governor to assist the governor in implementation and review of the managed process of public-private competition for particular government services through the managed competition process and negotiations between the State and the exclusive representatives on matters of wages, hours, and other negotiable terms and conditions of employment." The Hawaii Office of Collective Bargaining and Managed Competition

(1) Assists the governor in formulating the State's philosophy for public collective bargaining and for the managed process for public-private competition for government services, including which particular service can be provided more efficiently, effectively, and economically considering all relevant costs; and

(2) Coordinates and negotiates the managed competition process on behalf of the State with exclusive representatives of affected public employees and private contractors. (State of Hawaii, 2005)

In contrast to states where collective bargaining is limited or nonexistent, Hawaii requires a process of negotiation between management and unions representing affected bargaining units when contracting out of state services to the private sector is being considered. Its Office of Collective Bargaining and Managed Competition represents management in this process.

In some ways, collective bargaining may have protected the merit principle and advanced the cause of professional public management. Unions historically have been opposed to patronage systems, and where they have established collective bargaining relationships with public employers, they have negotiated contracts that do more to prevent spoils appointments than have many weakly administered merit systems. In states like California, New York, and Michigan, merit system coverage coexists well with collective bargaining (Douglas, 1992; Elling, 1986). Regarding management's capacity to function effectively, there is at best evidence to support the proposition that collective bargaining has encouraged at least some agencies to use human as well as material resources more efficiently and to develop better supervisory skills. At worst, it seems that provisions of negotiated contracts are no more serious impediments than traditional civil service rules and procedures are.

In most jurisdictions with merit systems and collective bargaining (dual systems), an accommodation of sorts has been reached between the two. Collective bargaining has partly replaced the unilateral civil service system in such areas as compensation and grievances. However, civil service boards and departments have not

BULLETIN

The State of California Supersession Rule

"The following enumerated Government Code Sections and existing rules, regulations, standards, practices and policies which implement the enumerated Government Code Sections are hereby incorporated into this Agreement. However, if any other provision of this Agreement alters or is in conflict with any of the Government Code Sections . . . the Agreement shall be controlling and supersede said Government Code Sections or parts thereof and any rule, regulation, standard, practice, or policy implementing such provisions. The Government Code Sections listed . . . are cited in Section 3517.6 of the Ralph C. Dills Act."

been limited to recruitment and examination functions, as some originally feared would be the outcome if the unions' agenda became reality. They generally retain broad policy authority over promotions, transfers, reductions-in-force, performance standards and evaluation, position classifications, and other aspects of the in-service personnel program. In all or many of these areas, procedures used to implement civil service laws and policies are likely to be governed by contract provisions and, accordingly, the powers of civil service agencies have been meaningfully diminished.

In a number of states such as Wisconsin, the authorizing legislation for state employees requires that negotiated contracts take precedence over civil service rules where conflicts exist (Williams, 1994). Some states, such as California, have arrangements whereby contractual agreements on certain subjects (for example, wages, hours, discipline, and layoffs) have precedence. In others, contracts prevail only on a few topics, such as union security provisions. In most local governments, contracts do not automatically supersede civil service; negotiated terms that conflict with existing law may take effect only if the governing body changes the law.

The most important impact of collective bargaining in the public sector has been a transformation of the relationship between employer and employee. Traditional civil service merit systems are based on the proposition that management's "rules of the workplace" set the terms of the relationship between the employer and the *individual worker.* Under collective bargaining, management is required to negotiate those rules with *another organization,* the labor union or employee association. Beyond bilateral negotiations, these two organizations co-implement and co-administer the rules as they apply to members of bargaining units. For many employees, this means that they may not individually negotiate terms of employment and, if management dealt with them on this level, it would be guilty of an unfair labor practice. For management, it means an extensive sharing of power over and responsibility for the personnel program with the leadership of an employee organization created to serve the interests of the worker. For the human resources units, collective bargaining has done much to clearly identify them as members of the management teams responsible for the design and implementation of labor relations programs that advance the strategic goals and objectives of their agencies.

DISCUSSION QUESTIONS

1. Do management and labor have fundamentally conflicting interests?
2. Should all public employees who are not supervisors or managers be allowed to bargain collectively with their employers?
3. Should all but essential public employees be allowed to strike like their private sector counterparts?
4. Should employees in a bargaining unit be required to pay a representation fee to the union, even if they are not members?
5. Can collective bargaining and the merit principle really coexist in practice?
6. Does unionization and collective bargaining make it hard for managers to motivate workers and to effectively manage performance?
7. Should supervisors be allowed to bargain collectively with public employers?
8. Is privatization or contracting out more often than not a strategy for "breaking" public employee unions?

REFERENCES

AFSCME (2005). "AFSCME Labor Links: Public Sector Collective Bargaining Laws." Accessed http://www.afscme.org/otherlnk/weblnk36.htm (May).

Bush, George W. (2001). *Executive Order—Revocation of Executive Order and Presidential Memorandum Concerning Labor-Management Partnerships,* Washington, DC: The White House. Accessed http://www.whitehouse.gov/news/releases/2001/02/20010221 –1.html (February 17).

D'Alba, Joel A. (1979). "The Nature of the Duty to Bargain in Good Faith," in Public Employment Relations Service, *Portrait of a Process: Collective Negotiations in Public Employment* (Fort Washington, PA: Labor Relations Press).

Douglas, Joel M. (1992). "State Civil Service and Collective Bargaining: Systems in Conflict." *Public Administration Review,* Vol. 52, No. 1 (January–February).

Elling, Richard C. (1986). "Civil Service, Collective Bargaining and Personnel-Related Impediments to Effective State Management: A Comparative Assessment." *Review of Public Personnel Administration,* vol. 6, No. 3 (Summer).

Gershenfeld, Walter J., and Gladys Gershenfeld (1983). "The Scope of Collective Bargaining," in Jack Rabin, Thomas Vocino, Bartley W. Hildreth, and Gerald J. Miller (Eds.), *Handbook of Public Personnel Administration and Labor Relations* (New York: Marcel Dekker).

Gideon, Jacquelyn (1979). "The American Nurses Association: A Professional Model for Collective Bargaining." *Journal of Health and Human Resources Administration,* Vol. 2. No. 1 (August).

Hayford, Stephen L., William A. Durkee, and Charles W. Hickman (1979). "Bargaining Unit Determination Procedures in the Public Sector: A Comparative Evaluation." *Employee Relations Law Journal* (Summer).

James, Kay Coles (2002). "Memorandum for Heads of Departments and Agencies—Labor Management Relations." U.S. Office of Personnel Management, Washington, DC. Accessed http://www.opm.gov/lmr/LMR_memo.asp (June 21).

Love, Douglas (1966). "Proposals for Collective Bargaining in the Public Service of Canada: A Further Commentary," in Gerald C. Somer (Ed.), *Collective Bargaining in the Public Service: Proceedings of the 1966 Annual Spring Meeting, Industrial Relations Association,* Milwaukee, WI, May 6–7.

National League of Cities et al. v. Usery 426 U.S. 833 (1976). Portaro, Ron M. (1986). "Public-Sector Impasse Legislation: Is It Working?" *Employee Relations Law Journal,* Vol. 12, No. 1 (Summer).

Reeves, T. Zane (1997). "Labor-Management Partnerships in the Public Sector," in Carolyn Ban and Norma M. Riccucci (Eds.), *Public Personnel Management: Current Concerns, Future Challenges* (New York: Longman), pp. 173–186.

State of Hawaii (2005). *Hawaii Revised Statutes,* Chapter 89 A-1.

U.S. Department of Labor (2005a). "Union Members Summary." *Bureau of Labor Statistics News,* Washington, DC: U.S. Department of Labor. Accessed http:www.bls.gov/news.release/union2.nr0.htm (May 31).

———. (2005). "Major Work Stoppages in 2004." Bureau of Labor Statistics News, Washington, DC: U.S. Department of Labor. Accessed http://www.bls.gov/cba (April 8).

U.S. General Accounting Office (1991). *Federal Labor Relations: A Program in Need of Reform* (Washington, DC), July.

Williams, Richard C. (1994). "Resolution of the Civil Service—Collective Bargaining Dilemma." *American Review of Public Administration*, Vol. 24, No. 2 (June), pp. 149–160.

Zack, Arnold M. (1972). "Impasses, Strikes, and Resolutions," in Sam Zagoria (Ed.), *Public Workers and Public Unions* (Englewood Cliffs, NJ: Prentice-Hall), pp. 101–121.

SUGGESTED READING

Bender, K. A., and R. F. Elliott (2003) *Decentralised Pay Setting: A Study of the Outcomes of Collective Bargaining Reform in the Civil Service in Australia, Sweden, and the UK.* (Ashgate, England; Burlington, VT: Ashgate).

Brock, Jonathan, and David B. Lipsky (Eds.). (2003). *Going Public: The Role of Labor-Management Relations in Delivering Quality Government Services* (Champaign, IL: Industrial Relations Research Association).

Colosi, Thomas R., and Arthur E. Berkeley (1992). *Collective Bargaining: How It Works & Why: A Manual of Theory & Practice* (New York: American Arbitration Association).

Fernbach, Dan, and Jane R. Henkel (1994). *A Survey of Selected States Regarding Collective Bargaining Laws for State Employees & Experience Under Those Laws* (Upland, CA: DIANE).

Florio, James, and Jerry Abramson (1997). *Working Together for Public Service: Report of the U.S. Secretary of Labor's Task Force on Excellence in State and Local Government Through Labor-Management Cooperation* (Upland, CA: DIANE).

Kearney, Richard C. (Ed.) (1993). "Public Sector Labor Relations: Symposium." *Review of Public Personnel Administration*, Vol. 13, No. 3 (Summer).

Kearney, Richard C., and David G. Carnevale (2001). *Labor Relations in the Public Sector*, 3rd ed. (New York: Marcel Dekker).

Mangum, Garth L. (1992). *Labor Struggle in the Post Office: From Selective Lobbying to Collective Bargaining* (Armonk, NY: M. E. Sharpe).

Najita, Joyce M., and James L. Stern (Eds.). (2001). *Collective Bargaining in the Public Sector: The Experience of Eight States.* (Armonk, NY: M. E. Sharpe).

Rabin, Jack (1994). *Handbook of Public Sector Labor Relations* (New York: Marcel Dekker).

Rhoades, Gary (1998). *Managed Professionals: Unionized Faculty & Restructuring Academic Labor* (Albany: State University of New York Press).

Riccucci, Norma (1990). *Women, Minorities and Unions in the Public Sector* (Westport, CT: Greenwood).

Slater, Joseph E. (2004). *Public Workers: Government Employee Unions, the Law, and the State, 1900–1962.* (Ithaca, NY: ILR Press).

Chapter EIGHT

Public Employees—Rights and Responsibiilities

Although public personnel administration has much in common with its private sector counterpart, especially regarding management techniques associated with such functions as job evaluation, job pricing, and performance appraisal, there are also fundamental differences in practices between the two sectors. Many of those differences are grounded in the political environment of public management. Public personnel practices are open to public scrutiny, and partisan issues and questions of political control are always on the agenda. Other differences, however, stem from the unique legal environment of public personnel management. This chapter will focus on those differences and the ways in which the law makes public personnel management distinct. We will see that many of the most important legal distinctions have their roots in Supreme Court interpretations of the U.S. Constitution. In that regard, we will consider the rights of public employees under the First, Fourth, Fifth, and Fourteenth Amendments and the balance between those rights and employees' responsibilities. Statutory issues will be considered as well, especially laws that have restricted political participation by public workers.

THE CONSTITUTION AND PUBLIC EMPLOYMENT

A hallmark of democracy is that governmental authority is limited. Indeed, many provisions of the U.S. Constitution are specifically designed to restrain the power of government. Several of those restrictions are found in the first ten amendments, known otherwise as the Bill of Rights, which were originally ratified in 1791 to better constrain the federal government. Here we find limitations including constraints on the government's authority to restrict freedom of speech and association (First Amendment), limitations the government's right to conduct searches and seizures (Fourth Amendment), and restrictions the government's power to deny persons life, liberty, or property without due process of law (Fifth Amendment). In addition, the Fourteenth Amendment, ratified in 1868, requires states to provide due process of law, limits state authority to deny any person equal protection of the laws, and has been interpreted to apply other provisions of the Bill of Rights to the states. Numerous other important limitations on government authority are also found in the Constitution and especially in the first 10 amendments, but we highlight the limitations articulated earlier because they each have a direct impact on the daily operation of contemporary public personnel administration. Not only do these constitutional stipulations limit the government's authority to direct the behavior of persons within its jurisdiction in general, but they also restrict the manner in which the government as an employer may direct its employees.

Stated another way, public employees retain important constitutional rights when they enter the public service, and as a result, the actions available to personnel managers in the pubic sector are limited in significant ways. In large part, however, this condition is the product of legal rulings that have emerged since the 1950s. As late as the mid-1950s, the employer-employee relationship in the public sector was dominated by the employer, who was free to impose many conditions on workers that they had to accept to keep their jobs. Historically, the courts had ruled that employees did not have *any* rights in the job that were based on the Constitution. Thus, in fixing the terms of employment, the public employer could and often did deny workers civil and political rights universally enjoyed by those in the private sector. Positions could be offered or denied on nearly any terms the government devised (Rosenbloom & Bailey, 2003, p. 30).

For example, from this point of view, public employees had virtually no rights in termination proceedings. As the Supreme Court reasoned in *Bailey v. Richardson* (1951), "Due process of law is not applicable unless one is being deprived of something to which he has a right." As a consequence, public employees could be dismissed without explanation or any hearing before termination. The classic declaration in 1892 in which Justice Holmes stated for the majority, "The petitioner may have a constitutional right to talk politics, but he has no constitutional right to be a policeman," summarizes this position well (*McAuliffe v. Mayor of New Bedford,* 1892), and significantly, Holmes's point of view held sway for the next 60 years, during which time the scope of judicial review of personnel actions taken by managers was very limited. As one observer wrote in 1955, "from the assertion that there exists no constitutional right *to* public employment, it is also inferred that there can be no constitutional right *in* public employment. The progression is that, since there are no fundamental claims in employment, employment is maintained by the state as a privilege" (Dotson, 1955, p. 87).

Beginning in the 1950s, however, fundamental questions were raised regarding this "doctrine of privilege." If there was no right to public employment, under what circumstances could it legitimately be denied? Could it be denied because an employee favored particular social policies, such as racial integration, or failed to conform to local norms of behavior such as attending church regularly (Rosenbloom & Bailey, 2003, p. 30)? Under the leadership of the Warren Court, the federal judiciary began issuing a series of decisions that ended the "doctrine of privilege" and in its place developed a standard that required a balancing of the interests of public employees, the government, and the public in general. As that new standard began to emerge, administrative scholar David Rosenbloom noted that under the new doctrine, "whenever there is a substantial interest, other than employment by the state, involved in the discharge of a public employee, he can be removed neither on arbitrary grounds nor without a procedure calculated to determine whether legitimate grounds exist" (Rosenbloom, 1971, p. 421). In this manner, the courts narrowed management's discretion by extending certain constitutional protections and guarantees to public employees at all levels of government.

PROCEDURAL DUE PROCESS

For public workers, one of the most important changes was brought about by a series of Supreme Court decisions beginning in the 1970s establishing that they may have property and liberty interests in their jobs that warrant protection under the due process clause of the Fifth and Fourteenth Amendments to the Constitution.

BULLETIN

From *Board of Regents v. Roth* (1972): "The Fourteenth Amendment does not require opportunity for a hearing prior to the nonrenewal of a nontenured state teacher's contract unless he can show that the nonrenewal deprived him of an interest in 'liberty' or that he had a 'property' interest in continued employment, despite the lack of tenure or a formal contract."

As defined by the Court, property interests are established when the government promises that following the successful completion of a probationary period, dismissal will occur for just cause only. With such a promise, public employees have a reasonable expectation of continued employment provided there is a need for the work to be completed and they are performing satisfactorily. Of course, one of the pillars of traditional merit systems in government is relative security of tenure that rests on the idea that government will terminate employees only for just cause. As a result, in traditional merit systems, public employees typically have a property interest in employment and may be removed only when procedural due process is followed. Of course, it is entirely up to the government to make or withhold the kinds of promises that establish a property interest. Recent reforms in the states of Georgia, Florida, and elsewhere have removed such promises from many public employees in an effort to shift their employment to an "at will" basis where termination could proceed for any reason provided it was not specifically prohibited by law.

Liberty interests are triggered when the termination of a public employee is accomplished in such a way that the employee's reputation is damaged and his or her freedom to find future work is limited as a result. This issue can arise whenever the government employer reports negative or otherwise unflattering information regarding an employee's conduct or behavior on the job as a reason for termination. Under such circumstances, which presumably could be common, termination cannot proceed without due process. In addition, it is important to note that the liberty interest will be present even for probationary employees or others, such as at will workers, who have no property interest in their jobs. It is incumbent upon public employers, therefore, to either avoid communicating information that could potentially damage the reputations of terminated employees, or be certain that in all termination proceedings, due process requirements are followed.

In a series of cases including *Board of Regents v. Roth* (1972), *Perry v. Sinderman* (1972), *Arnett v. Kennedy* (1974), and *Bishop v. Wood* (1976), the Court defined the conditions under which property and liberty interests could exist and what standards of due process applied under specific conditions. In an additional case, *Cleveland Board of Education v. Loudermill* (1985), the Supreme Court reiterated that it was up to the government to decide whether or not to establish a property interest for public employees, but that once such an interest was established, procedural due process was necessary and it was the job of the Court to determine what the Constitution required in terms of due process. At a minimum, the Court reasoned, due process would require that an employee be notified of potentially improper work behavior before termination and that he or she be afforded a hearing before termination to provide the employee an opportunity to respond to the allegations made. The purpose of procedural due process is to ensure fairness or justice within the organization regarding dismissal procedures.

FREEDOM OF SPEECH AND EXPRESSION

In the area of freedom of expression, the Court has struggled to carefully balance the interests of public employees and their employers. In *Pickering v. Board of Education* (1968), the Court, ruled that although public employees could not constitutionally be compelled to give up a right "they would otherwise enjoy as citizens to comment on matters of public interest," the state did have an interest as an "employer in regulating the speech of its employees that differ significantly from those it possesses in connection with regulation of the speech of the citizenry in general." In other words, what should be balanced in each case is the interest of public employees as citizens to comment on matters of public concern and that of the public employer in providing services to the public.

Since *Pickering,* the Court has applied this balancing test to a number of cases, often with the minority expressing the opinion that the majority had tilted in the wrong direction. Overall, the Burger and Rehnquist Courts tended to uphold the employer's position more often than the employee's, and they were reluctant to entertain anything but cases involving what they saw to be fundamental (sweeping) constitutional issues. Nonetheless, the Court provided relatively clear guidelines regarding freedom of speech for public employees in *Rankin v. McPherson* in 1987. The case involved a 19-year-old probationary employee (Ardith McPherson) working in the office of a local constable (Rankin) in Texas. Immediately after the assassination attempt on President Ronald Reagan, McPherson was overheard remarking to a colleague, "If they go for him again, I hope they get him" (*Rankin v. McPherson*, 1987, p. 381). When the comment was reported to Constable Rankin, he immediately fired McPherson. The Court ruled that McPherson's First Amendment right to freedom of

> **BULLETIN**
>
> From *Perry v. Sinderman* (1972): "Lack of a contractual or tenure right to employment does not, taken alone, defeat respondent's claim that the nonrenewal of his contract violated his free speech right. . . . Though a subjective 'expectancy' of tenure is not protected by procedural due process, respondent's allegation that the college had a *de facto* tenure policy . . . entitled him to an opportunity of proving the legitimacy of his claim to job tenure. Such proof would obligate the college to afford him a requested hearing. . . ."

speech had been violated, and in doing so, it articulated the manner in which such cases should be reviewed. Specifically, the Court noted that even though McPherson was a probationary employee, she retained substantive constitutional rights. The Court then reasoned that when a public employee's speech is on a matter of public concern (which was true in McPherson's case), and when the speech is not disruptive to the discipline and normal operation of the workplace (which was also true in McPherson's case), it would be constitutionally protected.

FREEDOM OF ASSOCIATION

The right of public employees to associate or refrain from associating with specific organizations is also protected by the First Amendment. For example, public employees have a right not to join a union, but where the law permits collective bargaining, the government employer may designate a union as the exclusive bargaining agent for a designated set of public workers and may require nonunion employees to pay a "fair share" of union dues to support the union's bargaining activities (*Abood v. Detroit Board of Education,* 1977). However, nonunion employees may not be compelled to contribute money to support a union's partisan political activities (*Chicago Teachers Union v. Hudson,* 1986).

It is also well established that public employees may not be required to support or join a particular political party as a condition of employment or to receive beneficial consideration in various employment decisions. Two cases, *Elrod v. Burns* (1976) and *Branti v. Finkel* (1980), involved employees who were dismissed from their jobs when the partisan leadership of their offices changed and they were deemed to be of the "wrong" political party. The Court settled this issue by declaring that dismissal for partisan reasons would only be permissible when the government could show that political party affiliation was essential to performance of the duties associated with the job. Later, in *Rutan v. Republican Party of Illinois* (1990), the Court held that the same standard would apply to other personnel actions beyond termination including promotions, transfers, layoffs, recall after layoffs, and hiring (Daniel, 1992)

THE RIGHT TO PRIVACY

The Fourth Amendment to the U.S. Constitution prohibits government from conducting "unreasonable searches and seizures." In criminal cases, where the government is operating to enforce the law, judicial warrants based on probable cause, or in cases where a warrant is not practical, a reasonable suspicion that criminal activity has occurred are required before searches and seizures (Rosenbloom & Bailey, 2003, p. 35). But what is required when the government as an employer seeks to search public employees or their work surroundings? In 1987, the Supreme Court ruled in *O'Connor v. Ortega* that public employees retain Fourth Amendment rights, especially when the employee has a reasonable expectation of privacy (Rosenbloom & Bailey, 2003, p. 35). Consequently, searches of an employee's office, desk, cabinets, or lockers would be permissible only when there is a reasonable suspicion that the employee has engaged in wrongdoing. Routine or unannounced suspicionless searches of those facilities or items would not be permitted. Searches of an employee's clothes or personnel possessions would also be subject to the same constraint.

In the 1980s, significant attention was focused on this issue as the government increasingly implemented anti-drug programs that required the random compulsory drug testing of public employees. In 1989, in *National Treasury Employees Union v. Von Raab,* the Court upheld a drug-screening program that required urinalysis tests of all Customs Service employees who sought a transfer or promotion to positions having a direct involvement in drug interdiction or requiring the incumbent to carry firearms. The Court reasoned that the government's interest in maintaining a workforce involved in those activities that is free from the influence of illegal drugs out weighed the employees' privacy interest. As a consequence, public employees who work in jobs related to public safety and especially those who may carry firearms may be subjected to drug tests even when there is no individualized suspicion that they have used illegal substances. Other employees, however, who are not in public safety-related positions, may not be constitutionally subjected to drug testing in the absence of reasonable individualized suspicion.

EQUAL PROTECTION OF THE LAWS

Equal protection of the laws is explicitly required by the Constitution's Fourteenth Amendment and, since the Court's ruling in *Bolling v. Sharpe* in 1954, has been found to be implicit in the Fifth Amendment. In practice, equal protection cases arise when government draws distinctions between people. In most instances, the courts will apply one of two standards when reviewing government actions that create such distinctions or classifications. The first standard requires merely that a rational basis exist for the distinctions drawn between individuals. In other words, a rational relationship must be present between the distinctions imposed and a legitimate governmental end. The requirement that public school teachers hold college degrees and state certification would meet that test because there is presumably a rational association between such a requirement and the legitimate governmental objective of ensuring that teachers are relatively competent. Under the rational basis standard, the burden of proof rests with those challenging the governmental classification to show that the challenged government action serves no legitimate purpose or, if there is a legitimate purpose, that the classification is not rationally related to its achievement. This standard is commonly applied in the review of distinctions such as those associated with business regulation or licensing or other forms of economic or social regulation that do not involve issues of race or fundamental rights (Grossman & Wells, 1988).

The second standard of equal protection review requiring a heightened level of scrutiny commonly known as strict scrutiny has usually been applied when government classifications limit fundamental freedoms or rights or force distinctions based on race or national origin. Under the application of strict scrutiny, the burden is on the government to defend the validity of classifications or distinctions it has created by showing that they serve a compelling governmental interest and are narrowly tailored in that there are no alternatives for achieving that interest that are less-restrictive on the interests or rights of parties who may be affected by the classifications. As a result, the laws reviewed under strict scrutiny are typically more vulnerable than are laws subjected merely to the rational basis standard.

When classifications involve sex-based distinctions, a middle ground between the rational basis standard and strict scrutiny is reached. In the language of the Court, sex-based distinctions are "quasi-suspect." In such cases, an intermediate level of review, requiring that classifications be substantially related to important governmental objectives is usually applied.

In recent years, equal protection cases that have been most directly relevant to public personnel administration have involved affirmative action programs that include preferences based on race. Despite the general analytical framework developed for equal protection review, however, the Supreme Court has struggled to determine the appropriate level of review for affirmative action. Preferential affirmative action obviously draws distinctions based on race, and for that reason, some members of the Court have consistently held that such programs must be subjected to strict scrutiny when challenged on constitutional grounds. Other justices, however, argued that the intermediate level of review requiring that such distinctions be substantially related to important (rather than compelling) governmental interests is the appropriate standard because the classifications in affirmative action are essentially benign. By the mid-1990s, however, proponents of strict scrutiny had prevailed, and it was necessary that racial distinctions drawn by governmental affirmative action programs be shown to serve a compelling interest and be narrowly tailored to meet that interest. In the employment context, past discrimination by the government employer involved may provide a sufficiently compelling interest for such a program. Affirmative action strategies that call for the retention of less senior minority employees and the layoff of more senior nonminority employees, or programs that contain preferences for minority groups that are not present in the labor market from which employees are normally drawn, will not, as will be discussed further in Chapter 9, withstand constitutional scrutiny (*Wygant v. Jackson Board of Education,* 1986; *City of Richmond v. J.A. Croson Company,* 1989). More recently, the Court ruled that student body diversity is a sufficiently compelling interest for a preferential affirmative action program for public college or university admissions systems, but it appears unlikely that the Court will find that diversity within the public workforce is an equally compelling government interest. Also, to date, the Court has not ruled at all on the constitutionality of affirmative action preferences for women (see Chapter 9 of this book).

A BALANCE OF RIGHTS AND RESPONSIBILITIES

In all the cases described in this chapter, the Court has worked to balance public employee interests in enjoying constitutional rights with the interest public employers and the public have in the establishment and maintenance of a productive public workforce. During the past 50 years, the Supreme Court has, in seeking that balance, voided or meaningfully limited the power of public employers in several areas of the employment relationship. Public employees may no longer be required to take vague and overly broad loyalty oaths, and their freedom of political association cannot arbitrarily be limited by blanket prohibitions against membership in particular political parties, or any other organization for that matter. Employees typically have due process rights in termination proceedings and are guaranteed freedom from unreasonable searches and seizures. Likewise, public workers can expect equal protection of the laws and any distinctions drawn between them along racial lines will, if challenged in court, be subjected to the most exacting judicial scrutiny. The employer can expect in return loyalty, good faith, and efficient and effective work from the public employee.

POLITICAL ACTIVITIES OF PUBLIC EMPLOYEES

One of the most basic rights of public employers is the right to expect that their employees will conduct themselves in a politically neutral fashion. Statutes establishing merit systems usually require such neutrality from the public workforce, but to strengthen that principle, it has been a long-standing practice in the United States to restrict the political activities of public employees. Prohibited activities typically include running for elective office and actively campaigning for candidates. The intention of federal and state legislation imposing such limitations is to enhance political neutrality of the public workforce by preventing the partisan coercion of public workers. Restrictions on political activity have been regularly challenged in court on grounds that they are unconstitutional, but they have survived judicial scrutiny relatively intact. In effect, the federal courts have ruled that restraints on the political behavior of public employees are permitted to better protect the government's and the public's interest in a politically neutral civil service.

The best-known legislative enactments in this area are the Hatch Acts of 1939 and 1940. The first was passed at least in part because of Congressional fears that President Roosevelt was building an overwhelming political base in the federal bureaucracy by first hiring large numbers of people noncompetitively into the unclassified service and then later extending merit system coverage to their positions and agencies. The 1939 Hatch Act applies to most workers in the federal executive branch, but it does exclude the president and vice president, heads and assistant heads of executive departments, members of the White House staff, and officials who determine national policy and are appointed by the president with Senate confirmation. Principal responsibility for developing and enforcing the rules and regulations needed to implement the Act was assigned to the U.S. Civil Service Commission (CSC) and the Office of Personnel Management (OPM) following the Civil Service Reform Act of 1978.

The Hatch Act coverage was extended in 1940 to state or local employees "whose principal employment is in connection with any activity which is financed in whole or in part by loans or grants made by the United States." Later, in an amendment to the 1974 Federal Campaign Act, state and local workers were permitted to engage in certain partisan political activities (such as soliciting votes in partisan elections and be delegates to party conventions) if state laws did not prohibit them from doing so.

The Hatch Act prohibited the "use of official authority or influence for the purpose of interfering with an election or affecting the result thereof" and, in the case of federal employees, taking "any active part in political management or in political campaigns." For federal employees, the most severe penalty for violation was removal, and the minimum penalty was suspension without pay for 30 days. In the case of state and local workers, if the CSC (and after 1978, OPM) found that a violation had taken place, it decided whether removal was warranted. If the CSC recommended removal but the state or local government employer did not comply, the federal funding agency was required to withhold from the grant or loan an amount equal to two years' pay of the employee concerned.

In *United Public Workers v. Mitchell* (1947) and a companion case, *Oklahoma v United States Civil Service Commission,* the Supreme Court upheld the constitutionality of the Hatch Act and its 1940 amendments covering state and local employees. In 1973, the Court reaffirmed its position in overturning a federal district court ruling that the Act was unconstitutional because it was vague and "capable of sweeping and uneven application." In its six-to-three decision on *United States Civil Service Commission v. National Association of Letter Carriers, AFL-CIO,* the Court found there was nothing "fatally overbroad about the statute." The majority went on to say that the CSC's regulations were "set out in terms that the ordinary person exercising ordinary common sense can sufficiently understand and observe, without sacrifice to the public interest," and were not unconstitutionally vague.

Opponents of the Hatch Act then turned to the Congress in search of a legislative remedy. In 1976, Congress passed a bill to permit federal employees to take part in political campaigns and to seek nomination or election to any office. President Ford vetoed the measure, and subsequent efforts in Congress to pass a similar bill were frustrated until 1993.

In late 1993, President Clinton signed the *Hatch Act Reform Amendments of 1993.* These amendments, effective in 1994, authorized OPM to issue regulations on political activities intended to implement Congress' policy that federal "employees should be encouraged to exercise fully, freely, and without fear of penalty or reprisal, and the extent not expressly prohibited by law, their right to participate or refrain from participating in the political processes of the Nation" (U.S. Office of Personnel Management, 1998). Final rules issued by OPM in early 1998 address two broad categories of federal employees: (1) those residing in certain designated communities or political subdivisions located in Maryland and Virginia and in the immediate vicinity of the District of Columbia, or in other communities where a majority of the registered voters are federal workers; and (2) those living in the District and elsewhere.

For those in the latter category, with certain exceptions, the Reform Amendments allow federal employees to participate in political campaigns and to run for election to *nonpartisan offices,* such as school boards. They are, however, prohibited from becoming candidates for *partisan political office* and from "soliciting, accepting, or receiving political contributions." For those in the former, if OPM determines that "it is in the domestic interest of the employees" to permit them to participate in local elections for *partisan political office,* they may do so by running as *independent candidates.* They are also allowed to "solicit, accept, or receive a political contribution as, or on behalf of, an independent candidate for partisan office. . . ." Other exemptions from the law covering other federal workers include being permitted to solicit and receive uncompensated volunteer services for themselves as, or on behalf of, independent candidates for partisan political offices, and, more generally,

> To take an active part in other political activities associated with elections for local partisan office and in managing the campaigns of candidates for election to local political office . . . but only as an independent candidate or on behalf of, or in opposition to, an independent candidate. (U.S. Office of Personnel Management, 1998, p. 4560)

Federal employees in both categories are not allowed to (1) run as the representative of a political party for partisan office, (2) solicit contributions for partisan candidates, (3) receive political contributions or volunteer services from subordinates, or (4) participate in political activities while on duty, while "wearing a uniform, badge, or insignia that identifies the employing agency," or if "he or she is in any room or building occupied in the discharge of official duties by an individual employed or holding office in the Government of the United States . . ."(U.S. Office of Personnel Management, 1998, p. 4559).

To varying degrees, most state and local governments also restrict their employees' political activities. A few have laws more restrictive than the Hatch Act as amended; for example, they may prohibit voluntary contributions and not allow workers to express their partisan opinions publicly. The pattern on the state level is for most to permit general campaign activities while off-duty. About two-thirds allow their employees to be candidates in partisan elections, but there is no uniformity across the states (Thurber, 1993, pp. 45–46), and the same variability may be found on the local level.

CONCLUSION

Today, public employees enjoy an array of rights that are grounded in constitutional limitations on the exercise of governmental authority. Constitutional limitations of government restriction of freedom of speech or association, for example, means that public employees are often protected from adverse action initiated in response to opinions they have expressed or organizations they have joined or failed to join. Importantly, because the Constitution restricts government action, not the action of private firms, these rights do not normally accrue to employees in private sector unless they are specifically included in contract provisions. In this sense, public employees occupy a somewhat special status among workers in the national labor force. In exchange, government may expect, and indeed may demand, a workforce that is competent, effective, and politically neutral.

DISCUSSION QUESTIONS

1. Does the presence of constitutional rights for public employees help to improve or hinder the quality of the public service?
2. Should public employees be required to take a leave of absence if they want to run for elective office and, if elected, should they be required to resign or retire?

REFERENCES

Abood v. Detroit Board of Education (1977). 431 U.S. 209.
Arnett v. Kennedy (1974). 416 U.S. 134.
Bailey v. Richardson (1951). 341 U.S. 918.
Bishop v. Wood (1976). 426 U.S. 341.
Board of Regents v. Roth (1972). 408 U.S. 564.
Bolling v. Sharpe (1954). 347 U.S. 497.
Branti v. Finkel (1980). 445 U.S. 507.

Chicago Teachers Union v. Hudson (1986). 475 U.S. 292.

City of Richmond v. J.A. Croson Company (1989). 488 U. S. 469.

Cleveland Board of Education v. Loudermill (1985). 470 U.S. 532.

Dotson, Arch (1955). "The Emerging Doctrine of Privilege in Public Employment." *Public Administration Review,* Vol. 15, No. 2 (Spring), pp. 77–88.

Daniel, Christopher (1992). "Constitutionalizing Merit? Practical Implications of Elrod, Branti, and Rutan." *Review of Public Personnel Administration,* Vol. 12, No. 2 (January–April), pp. 26–34.

Elrod v. Burns (1976). 427 U.S. 347.

Grossman, J. B., and R. Wells. (1988) *Constitutional Law and Judicial Policy Making* (New York: Longman).

McAuliffe v. Mayor of New Bedford (1892). 155 Mass. 216, 29 N. E. 517.

National Treasury Employees Union v. Von Raab (1989). 489 U.S. 656.

Oklahoma v. United States Civil Service Commission (1947). 330 U.S. 127.

O'Connor v. Ortega (1987). 480 U.S. 709.

Perry v. Sinderman (1972). 408 U.S. 593.

Pickering v. Board of Education (1968). 391 U.S. 563.

Rankin v. McPherson (1987). 483 U.S. 378.

Rosenbloom, David H. (1971). "Some Political Implications of the Drift Toward a Liberation of Federal Employees." *Public Administration Review,* Vol. 31, No. 4 (July–August), pp. 420–426.

Rosenbloom, David H., and Margo Bailey (2003). "What Every Public Personnel Manager Should Know About the Constitution," in Steven W. Hays and Richard C. Kearney (Eds.), *Public Personnel Administration: Problems and Prospects,* 4th ed. (Upper Saddle River, NJ: Prentice-Hall).

Rutan v. Republican Party of Illinois (1990). 497 U.S. 62.

Thurber, Karl T., Jr. (1993). "Big, little, littler: Synthesizing Hatch Act-based political activity legislation research." *Review of Public Personnel Administration,* Vol. 13, No. 1 (Winter), pp. 38–51.

United States Civil Service Commission v. National Association of Letter Carriers, AFL-CIO (1973). 413 U.S. 548.

United Public Workers v Mitchell (1947). 330 U.S. 75.

U.S. Office of Personnel Management (1998). "Political Activity:
Federal Employees Residing in Designated Localities." *Federal
Register,* Vol. 63, No. 20 (January 30), pp. 4555–4560.

Wygant v. Jackson Board of Education (1986). 476 U.S. 267.

SUGGESTED READING

Deskbook Encyclopedia of Public Employment Law, 15th edition (Malvern,
PA: Center for Education and Employment, 2005).

Rosenbloom, David H., and Rosemary O'Leary. (1997) *Public
Administration and Public Law,* 2nd ed. (New York: Marcel
Dekker).

Chapter NINE

Combating Historical Patterns of Discrimination

$\mathbf{T}$he history of discrimination that has operated historically to prevent women, racial and ethnic minorities, and other persons, including those with disabilities, from achieving all that their talents, skills, and abilities would allow them to achieve, is widely understood. The history of efforts to combat that problem is less well known. The earliest programmatic efforts to counter historical patterns of discrimination began in the United States during the 1940s. Today, those programs have expanded considerably and are an integral part of personnel policy in the public sector. This chapter examines the development and expansion of those efforts within government. We review nondiscrimination law, affirmative action and its implications, efforts to prevent discrimination against the disabled, and the issue of sexual harassment.[1]

Although it has not always the case, most people today would likely agree that elementary notions of justice require that the process by which public jobs are allocated not be closed to selected groups of people because of factors such as race, ethnicity, or sex. The principle of merit, which is the foundation for modern public personnel administration, mandates that job candidates be evaluated on the basis of their relative abilities. It surely follows then, that they should not be screened out or denied promotion solely because of racial or sexual characteristics. It may be argued also that government has a responsi-

---

[1] Some of the material addressed in this chapter is drawn from discussions found in Kellough 2003 and 2006.

bility to provide, through its own employment policies and procedures, a proper example for businesses and nonprofit organizations—that it be a "model employer." As Samuel Krislov noted, if government cannot place its own house in order, we cannot then expect it to effectively counter discrimination among private employers (Krislov, 1967). In addition, an expanding body of research indicates that when the public bureaucracy is representative of the people, especially in characteristics such as race, ethnicity, and sex, the legitimate interests of all groups are more likely to be heard and reflected in policy choices (Meier, 1993; Meier & Stewart, 1992; Selden, 1997; and Selden, Brudney, & Kellough, 1998).

The Earliest Programs to Counter Discrimination in Public Employment

Regardless of the arguments just outlined and despite constitutional guarantees of equal protection of the laws and merit system rules, discriminatory behavior in public employment flourished well into the 20th century. During the administration of President William Howard Taft (1909–1913), for example, white and black employees were segregated from each other in numerous federal offices, and African Americans were systematically excluded from employment opportunities (Rosenbloom 1977). Under President Woodrow Wilson (1913–1921), rest rooms and cafeterias were segregated, and photographs were required to accompany applications for federal employment. The purpose of the photograph was to identify individuals by race so that black applicants could be screened out. As David Rosenbloom put it, "the color of one's skin had become a test of fitness for federal employees" (1977, p. 54).

Through the 1930s, as federal government programs expanded in an effort to put people to work during the Great Depression, and as the government began to increase defense expenditures, African Americans were still systematically excluded from all but the most menial of jobs. In response, early civil rights leaders, led by A. Philip Randolph, planned a mass rally that would bring as many as 100,000 people to Washington, D.C., to protest discrimination by government agencies and defense contractors. Randolph was president of the Brotherhood of Sleeping Car Porters, the first African American union to negotiate and sign a labor contract with a U.S. corporation. The Brotherhood had been formed in 1925, and he led it through a 12-year battle to achieve recognition. This "March on Washington," was scheduled to take place on July 1, 1941, as a dramatic demonstration by African Americans who were demanding an end to government-sanctioned discrimination. It was only in response to this planned mass demonstration that the first tentative steps to end employment discrimination were taken by the federal government (Kellough, 2006).

President Franklin D. Roosevelt (1933–1945) did not want to see a march on the capital by angry African Americans protesting discrimination. He had worked hard to unify Americans to confront the unprecedented economic crisis of the depression and the rise of fascism and German militarism in Europe. He feared that a large protest, designed to call attention to racism within the United States, would divide the country and might even threaten military discipline. There was no guarantee that the march would remain peaceful or that social unrest would not spread across the country. In addition, the success of Roosevelt's policy agenda depended to a considerable extent on the political support of powerful southern Democrats in Congress who violently opposed any efforts by government to benefit or liberate black Americans.

About a week before the march was to take place, and after repeated attempts to have Randolph call off the rally, Roosevelt issued Executive Order 8802 prohibiting employment discrimination and establishing a Fair Employment Practices Committee (FEPC) with authority to investigate charges of discrimination against defense contractors and federal agencies. In response to this historic executive order and the creation of the FEPC, Randolph canceled the march (Garfinkel, 1959).

The FEPC was the first federal entity established to protect African American interests since the brief period of reconstruction following the Civil War (Reed, 1991, p. 15). The order rested on presidential authority to act independently of Congress to set the terms and conditions of executive agency contracts and to regulate the federal personnel system under existing civil service law. There was no chance that substantive anti-discrimination legislation would come from Congress at this time, and consequently, an executive order was the only mechanism available for the creation of an anti-discrimination program of any sort. To avoid the need to ask Congress for funding to support the program, money was drawn from a presidential discretionary fund appropriated for the operation of agencies within the Executive Office of the President.

Thus, the federal government was in effect pushed into responding to the reality of discrimination. Once the program was established, however, investigations of discriminatory practices were held and controversy soon followed. After the conclusion of the Second World War (1945), southern members of Congress were successful in orchestrating the demise of the FEPC, but that action was eventually followed by the issuance of presidential executive orders designed to continue the nondiscrimination policy within federal agencies and among defense contractors. President Harry Truman (1945–1953) issued Executive Order 9980 creating a Fair Employment Board (FEB) within the Civil Service Commission in 1948. The responsibilities of the FEB paralleled those of the earlier FEPC. It could investigate complaints of discrimination arising within federal agencies and could hold hearings and make recommendations. In late 1951, President Truman also sought to strengthen nondiscrimination policy regarding government contracts through the creation by executive order of a Committee on Government Contract Compliance.

In 1953, President Dwight D. Eisenhower (1953–1961) established a new Contract Compliance Committee and strengthened the nondiscrimination clause provided in all government contracts by placing a positive burden on contractors to post notices at work sites acknowledging their agreement to provide employment without discrimination on the basis of race, color, national origin, or religion. Two years later, in 1955, President Eisenhower abolished the FEB and established, again by executive order, a new committee independent of the Civil Service Commission. This organization was known as the President's Committee on Government Employment Policy (PCGEP). It was set up as an "interdepartmental committee" funded by contributions from other executive agencies so that direct appropriations from Congress for its operation were not needed. The PCGEP investigated complaints of discriminatory practices within federal agencies much as the FEPC and the FEB had done, and, like its predecessors, the PCGEP could not compel agencies to change employment decisions even if it found convincing evidence of discrimination. The effectiveness of the program rested to a considerable extent, therefore, on the persuasive abilities of committee members.

THE RISE OF AFFIRMATIVE ACTION

Under the nondiscrimination policies implemented by the Truman and Eisenhower administrations, it did not take long for it to become apparent that a program resting primarily on the investigation of complaints might not be the most effective means of confronting and eliminating discrimination. It was clear to those involved in these programs that the extent of discriminatory behavior was much broader than what was suggested by the number of formal complaints filed. Many individuals who had suffered discrimination were hesitant to register complaints because they feared retaliation or retribution. In response to this situation, staff members from Truman's FEB initiated a very limited and experimental program of "constructive action" to counter discrimination. This program was described by Rosenbloom (1977, p. 64), however, as "ill-defined and ineffective." It consisted of "conferences with fair employment officers and outside organizations, periodic surveys and appraisals, and the adoption of some new recruitment techniques, better training programs, and steps toward further integration" (Rosenbloom 1977, p. 64). Under Eisenhower, this approach was maintained, although it was not a highly visible part of federal policy. It was left to President John F. Kennedy to dramatically increase the government's reliance on these types of efforts.

President Kennedy (1961–1963) significantly reorganized the federal antidiscrimination program. He abolished Eisenhower's contract compliance and federal agency programs through Executive Order 10925, issued on March 6, 1961, and created a single consolidated program to be implemented by a new organization known as the President's Committee on Equal Employment Opportunity (PCEEO). The President's Committee received and investigated complaints of discrimination, as the earlier committees had done, but it also implemented a new policy that called for a significant expansion of the program of constructive action begun under Truman. Kennedy's order referred to that effort as "affirmative action," and it required, among other things, a positive program of recruitment and outreach to the minority community.

In effect, Kennedy's program placed new obligations on federal agencies and contractors. Instead of simply prohibiting employers from engaging in discriminatory behavior, it also directed agencies to take actions to work affirmatively to ensure that those who had historically suffered discrimination were no longer excluded from employment opportunities. Efforts to recruit minorities were undertaken by advertising job opportunities in minority-oriented newspapers and magazines and by visiting historically black colleges and universities. Because minorities in the federal service were found mainly in the lowest level jobs, training for lower-level employees was also emphasized along with the development of career paths that would promote upward mobility. The PCEEO, chaired by Vice President Lyndon B. Johnson, was very aggressive in pursuing this strategy. Under President Kennedy, therefore, federal policy rested on statements prohibiting discrimination, the active investigation of allegations of discriminatory treatment, and early affirmative action grounded firmly on the principle of nondiscrimination.

Shortly after Johnson became president (1963), and with his urging, Congress finally acted to prohibit discrimination by private employers and organizations receiving federal assistance by enacting the Civil Rights Act of 1964. Once that law went into effect, critics argued strenuously that the PCEEO, and its affirmative action program, were no longer needed because the Civil Rights Act had established the Equal Employment Opportunity Commission (EEOC) to implement a policy of nondiscrimination, and contractors subject to PCEEO rules would now fall under the jurisdiction of the EEOC (Graham, 1990).

But the PCEEO also governed the federal civil service (which was not covered initially by the Civil Rights Act of 1964), so to save the federal program and the concept of affirmative action, Johnson, through his 1965 Executive Order 11246, moved authority for the nondiscrimination effort within the federal civil service to the U.S. Civil Service Commission and gave the Department of Labor authority with respect to federal contractors. In 1967, through yet another executive order (E.O. 11375), Johnson added language prohibiting discrimination on the basis of sex to the existing affirmative programs.

Progress in the employment of minority group members remained slow, however. The entire decade of the 1960s was characterized by significant social struggle and national unrest. The civil rights movement had gained momentum under the leadership of Martin Luther King, Jr. Freedom riders were met with violence in the segregated south as they worked to integrate public bus systems in 1961. The long-delayed march on Washington for jobs and racial equality was finally held in 1963. President Kennedy was assassinated later that year. Urban rioting in the largely black ghettos in many metropolitan areas had risen to unprecedented levels. Numerous cities burned in the summers from 1964 to 1968. Martin Luther King, Jr., and Senator Robert F. Kennedy were assassinated in 1968. In the African American community, there was a growing sense of black nationalism and a feeling that simple equality of opportunity was not enough—many believed that equality of results had to be the objective of public policy. Public policies began to shift toward stronger efforts to prevent and to compensate for discrimination in the workplace.

In 1967, the Department of Labor, through its Office of Federal Contract Compliance Programs, began a program in the city of Philadelphia requiring that federal construction contractors establish goals for minority employment as a condition of receiving federal contract dollars (Graham, 1990). The Nixon administration (1969–1974) subsequently strengthened that program, which became known as the "Philadelphia Plan," and eventually required compliance by all major federal contractors. This new approach to affirmative action placed an increased positive burden on employers by forcing them to establish realistic objectives for minority employment and plan for the accomplishment of those objectives. The chairman of the U.S. Civil Service Commission, Robert Hampton, issued a memorandum in May 1971 endorsing this approach and authorizing federal agencies to establish numerical goals and timetables for minority employment (Rosenbloom, 1977, pp. 107–110). Under this policy, numerical goals were established as targets for the representation of women and minorities in an organization. Timetables were dates or time frames within which specified goals were planned to be accomplished. Goals and timetables required no organization to accept individuals who did not possess necessary qualifications, but they did imply that race, ethnicity, and gender would be considered in selection or placement decisions and that qualified minority group members or women could be preferred when they were available.

The policy decision to authorize goals and timetables marked a dramatic shift in the nature of the struggle against discrimination. Embedded preferences for nonminority males were, under specified circumstances, to be replaced with preferences for qualified minorities and women. In that sense, the use of goals and timetables transcended a literal interpretation of nondiscrimination (so-called "color blind" personnel practices). This approach to affirmative action, which eventually came into wide use, was authorized when minority group members or women were significantly underrepresented. Affirmative action in this form spawned substantial political controversy and judicial activity. In fact, so much attention was focused on numerically driven strategies for affirmative action in public employment (and elsewhere) that goals and timetables, and the limited preferences or "quotas" they can imply, became synonymous with affirmative action in the minds of many.

RELATED DEVELOPMENTS IN THE 1960s AND 1970s

During the 1960s and 1970s, several legislative initiatives beyond the 1964 Civil Rights Act were designed to deal with discrimination in housing and voting rights. One of the more important developments for personnel policy was passage of the Age Discrimination in Employment Act (ADEA) in 1967. Congress had considered prohibiting discrimination on the basis of age earlier when it debated and passed Title VII of the Civil Rights Act of 1964, but it was decided that legislative action on that issue should wait until after the

Department of Labor had investigated the problem and issued a report. The ADEA, which was passed three years later, prohibits employment discrimination against persons aged 40 years or older. When it was first enacted, protection was extended only through age 65, but through subsequent amendments, that restriction was eliminated. The law initially covered only private employers, but it was amended in 1974 to cover all state, local, and federal government organizations.

Another major event related to nondiscrimination law and affirmative action was the decision by the U.S. Supreme Court in 1971 in *Griggs v. Duke Power Company*. In that case, the Court unanimously ruled that Title VII of the 1964 Civil Rights Act proscribed not only intentional discrimination but also actions that were "fair in form, but discriminatory in operation." This ruling meant that the actions of an employer could still be in violation of Title VII, even if there was no discriminatory intent, if its employment practices screened out a disproportionate number of minorities or women, and those practices could not be shown to serve a legitimate business necessity. For example, an examination for the screening and selection of employees could be in violation of the law if it eliminated disproportionate numbers of minority applicants and there was no evidence that it was a valid measure of ability to perform on the job.

The concept of unintentional discrimination articulated in the *Griggs* case eventually became known as "disparate impact." This is contrasted with "disparate treatment," which is the term used to describe purposeful or intentional discrimination. In a disparate impact case, according to guidelines originally laid out by the Supreme Court, a minority plaintiff should first carry the burden of demonstrating through the use of appropriate statistics that an employer's practices had resulted in a substantial disparity between minority and nonminority selection or promotion rates. The burden should then shift to the employer to demonstrate that the practices that produced the disparity served a legitimate business purpose such as identifying the most qualified individuals. If the employer was successful in demonstrating that point, then no violation of Title VII would have occurred, unless the plaintiff could demonstrate that there were other, less discriminatory, practices that could serve the same purposes as the challenged practices. If the employer could not meet its burden, however, the practices that led to the disparity were not permitted.

In 1989, the *Griggs*-based definition of the burden of proof in disparate impact cases was overturned by a then more conservative U.S. Supreme Court in its decision in *Wards Cove Packing Company v. Atonio*. Here, the Court ruled that the burden should remain on plaintiffs throughout the process. Plaintiffs would have to show that employers deliberately selected challenged employment practices because of their discriminatory effect. Thus, the very concept of disparate impact was substantially undermined in law. Needless to say, this was not a popular ruling in many quarters, and Congress responded to it and other related rulings from the 1989 term with the Civil Rights Act of 1991, which, among other things, amended Title VII to specifically incorporate the standards associated with disparate impact as originally articulated in *Griggs*.

The implications of *Griggs* and the derived concept of disparate impact have been substantial. Except for the period between *Wards Cove* and passage of the Civil Rights Act of 1991, employers in all sectors have had a strong incentive to engage in employment practices that would ensure their organizations were well integrated. By doing so, they could help shield themselves from charges of discrimination (and potential liability) under disparate impact theory. If there was, in fact, no disparity, then there could be no disparate impact.

The Equal Employment Opportunity Act of 1972 brought all state, local, and federal government entities under coverage of Title VII of the Civil Rights Act of 1964, and thereby brought the incentive for affirmative action grounded in disparate impact theory to the public sector. This legislation gave the EEOC direct responsibility for monitoring state and local employment practices, and it reaffirmed the program covering the federal service implemented earlier by the U.S. Civil Service Commission. Under EEOC guidelines, state and local governments were required to collect and report data on minority and female employment, and by the mid-1970s, goals and timetables were well established as a part of the affirmative action process at these levels of government. A subsequent reorganization order by President Jimmy Carter in 1978 transferred authority for supervision of federal EEOC and affirmative action practices from the Civil Service Commission to the EEOC. Also in 1978, the commission was replaced by the U.S. Office of Personnel Management (OPM) and Merit Systems Protection Board (MSPB) as required by the Civil Service Reform Act (Kellough & Rosenbloom, 1992).

In issuing guidelines for the federal program, the EEOC initially placed great emphasis on numerical goals and timetables in agency affirmative action plans. During the administration of President Ronald Reagan (1981–1989), as the political and legal climate shifted, it backed away from that controversial approach. The EEOC issued regulations in 1987 that permitted but *did not* require agencies to develop numerical goals for minority and female employment in instances when those groups were underrepresented. Since the 1980s, affirmative action in a variety of forms has continued to be socially, politically, and legally controversial. We will focus here on significant developments that have created the complex and challenging environment faced by today's human resources professionals and policy makers.

UNDERSTANDING THE AFFIRMATIVE ACTION CONTROVERSY

The ongoing dispute over affirmative action policies and practices is not surprising, especially when it is understood that affirmative action is designed to have the effect of redistributing opportunity from those who have been historically advantaged to members of groups that have suffered disadvantages rooted in discrimination on the basis of race, ethnicity, gender, or other traits (Edley, 1996; Guenin, 1997). Jobs, the very means by which people earn their livings, are at stake. The outcome is, therefore, extremely important for people on both sides of the issue.

In addition, forms of affirmative action involving the use of preferences are much more likely to generate controversy than are other approaches such as recruitment or outreach. Preferences seem to contradict or undermine equality of opportunity. It is difficult for most to oppose efforts based on the principle of nondiscrimination, such as broader recruitment or upward mobility programs, but numeric goals and timetables are more easily challenged by those who believe a strict interpretation of equal opportunity should prevail. To those opposed to affirmative action, preferences amount to reverse discrimination; numerical goals, often referred to as "quotas," have the effect, it is argued, of discriminating against nonminority males and sometimes nonminority women.

The key question is whether the racial, ethnic, and gender distinctions drawn by affirmative action goals and the accompanying preferences can be justified in broadly accepted terms. Those who see affirmative action as reverse discrimination argue that such distinctions can never be defended. They suggest that hiring and other personnel actions should be based exclusively on individual qualifications or merit. Those who favor affirmative action note that valid and precise measures of qualifications are often beyond our reach. They argue that certain limited advantages for women and minorities should be allowed to make up for past discrimination and to "level the playing field." Usually, this position rests on a concept known as compensatory justice.

Opponents of affirmative action counter that although the compensatory argument may hold for identifiable victims (individuals) of discrimination, it should not be applied to groups because some or most group members may not have suffered discriminatory treatment. Advocates for affirmative action may reply that it is difficult or impossible to determine whether a particular individual has or has not suffered because of discrimination and, furthermore, preferential affirmative action plans are not based solely on remedial or compensatory grounds. They may be defended in more utilitarian terms: They work to integrate society more rapidly, reduce income inequalities, further distributive justice, and promote efficiency by ensuring that the talents of all individuals are used (Taylor, 1991).

A Republican majority elected to Congress in 1994, and conservative gains in state legislatures across the nation, combined to move the issue of preferential affirmative action to a prominent position on the public policy agenda in the mid-1990s. In 1995, for example, the Republican leadership in Congress advocated efforts to eliminate affirmative action (Holmes, 1995). In response, the Clinton administration conducted a complete review of federal affirmative action programs and concluded they should be continued (Stephanopoulos & Edley, 1995). Considerable debate about the issue has also taken place at the state level. A Republican governor of California, Pete Wilson, campaigned vigorously against affirmative action on his way to reelection to a second term in 1994. The following year, the Regents of the University System of California voted to prohibit the consideration of race or gender as a factor in decisions regarding admissions to state universities, and in 1996, California voters approved Proposition 209 amending the state constitution to prohibit the use of preferences based on race, ethnicity, or gender associated with affirmative action by the state and local governments within the state. Two years later, a similar initiative prohibiting racial, ethnic, or gender preferences in state employment, contracting, or higher education appeared on the ballot in the state of Washington and passed with the support of 58 percent of the voters.

The debate over affirmative action should, of course, reflect available information about its effectiveness. If affirmative action is demonstrably ineffective in achieving its stated goals, the position of its proponents is essentially untenable. Has affirmative action been successful? It is difficult to answer this question definitively because so many other factors have operated in the U.S. labor market, but significant increases in the employment of minorities and women in the federal civil service did occur in the years following the initiation of affir-

mative action programs in the 1960s. An analysis of federal employment during the 1970s revealed evidence that agencies using numerical goals and timetables were more successful in recruiting and hiring
minorities than were agencies that did not use this approach
(Kellough, 1989). Numerous other studies also have suggested that
affirmative action has been at least somewhat effective in boosting the
employment of minorities and women (see, for example, Button &
Rienzo, 2003, Goldstein & Smith, 1976; Hyclak & Taylor, 1992;
Leonard, 1984a, 1984b, 1985; and Price, 2002).

THE SUPREME COURT AND PREFERENTIAL AFFIRMATIVE ACTION

Legally, preferential affirmative action arises in three ways. It may be
the result of (1) a court order, (2) a consent decree sanctioned by a
court to settle litigation, or (3) a voluntary decision by an organization. Affirmative action to address discriminatory employment practices required by court order is authorized under certain conditions by
the 1964 Civil Rights Act. Court-ordered preferential affirmative
action has been addressed by the Supreme Court in *Firefighters Local
v. Stotts* (1984) and *United States v. Paradise* (1987). Guidelines for
affirmative action embodied in consent decrees are similar to those for
voluntary affirmative action and are established in *Firefighters v. City
of Cleveland* (1986). Voluntary affirmative action may involve racial or
gender preferences established by an organization at its own discretion
with no obligation arising from litigation (Selig, 1987).

All preferential affirmative action programs voluntarily adopted
by government organizations are limited by the Civil Rights Act of
1964 (as amended) and constitutional guarantees of equal protection
of the laws. Section 703 of Title VII of the 1964 Civil Rights Act
defines as unlawful any employment practice that discriminates against
any individual because of race, color, religion, sex, or national origin.
Thus, race or gender preferences incorporated into affirmative action
by a public employer must be reconciled with Title VII. In addition,
the equal protection clause of the Fourteenth Amendment forbids
states from denying to any person within their jurisdictions the "equal
protection of the laws." Preferences based on race, ethnicity, or sex
established by states and their local subdivisions as part of their affirmative action programs must therefore be reconciled with that equal
protection guarantee. The due process clause of the Fifth Amendment
has been interpreted by the Supreme Court as prohibiting the federal
government from denying equal protection of the laws (*Bolling v.*

Sharpe, 1954); thus preferences found in federal affirmative action programs are also subject to constitutional review.

Title VII limitations on preferential affirmative action have been articulated by the Supreme Court in two important cases. The first was *United Steelworkers of America v. Weber* (1979), where the legality of a plan reserving for African Americans 50 percent of the openings in an in-plant craft training program was at issue. The Supreme Court upheld the plan noting that Title VII, as indicated in section 703(j), does not require preferential treatment to overcome a racial imbalance, but that it also does not preclude voluntary efforts to overcome such an imbalance. Given the legislative history and the articulated purpose of Title VII, the Court held that the prohibition on discrimination should not be read as a prohibition on forms of affirmative action, including preferential plans, that have the objective of countering discrimination directed against racial and ethnic minorities and women. Justice Brennan noted for the majority that if Congress had intended to prohibit all race-conscious affirmative action it easily could have done so "by providing that Title VII would not require or *permit* racially preferential integration efforts" (*Steelworkers v. Weber*, p. 205, emphasis in original).

The second case in which the legality of voluntarily adopted preferential affirmative action was reviewed under Title VII was *Johnson v. Transportation Agency, Santa Clara County, California* (1987). This case specifically addressed a preferential program implemented by a public employer. In effect, the issue was whether the standard decided in *Weber* would apply in a public-sector context involving a sex-based preference. The Transportation Agency of Santa Clara County implemented an affirmative action plan providing that, in making employment decisions within traditionally segregated job classifications where women or minorities were significantly underrepresented, the agency could consider the sex or race of a job candidate along with the individual's qualifications. Significantly, no specific number of positions was set aside for minorities or women, but the eventual objective was to have minorities and women employed in positions roughly in proportion to their representation in the relevant local labor force. In line with that plan, a woman was preferred for a promotion over a man who claimed marginally higher qualifications.

The Supreme Court upheld the agency's affirmative action plan following the precedent it had established in *Weber*. In combination, the *Weber* and *Johnson* decisions provide clear guidance by which the legality of voluntarily adopted affirmative action including racial or sexual preferences can be judged under Title VII. In short, such programs must be designed to address a manifest racial or gender imbalance in traditionally segregated job categories. When considering whether a manifest racial or gender imbalance exists, the employer must consider the proportion of minorities or women in traditionally segregated positions relative to their proportions with the requisite qualifications in the local labor force. In addition, the preferential program must be constructed as a temporary strategy in which race or sex are not the only factors considered in the decision process.

Constitutional constraints on voluntary affirmative action by government organizations evolved through a series of cases from the 1970s to 2003 and have developed in such a way that they have imposed more rigorous limitations than those outlined by the Court in *Weber* and *Johnson*. As a result, the constitutional constraints establish the effective operational limits for governmental affirmative action. The issue is whether preferential affirmative violates the concept of equal protection of the laws found in the Fifth and Fourteenth Amendments. Usually, when considering equal protection cases, the courts apply one of two analytical standards. The first standard requires simply that a rational relationship exist between the distinctions imposed and a legitimate governmental end. Under this standard, individuals challenging governmental policies bear the burden of showing that classifications or distinctions drawn by government between people have no rational foundation. As a result, few laws reviewed under the rationality standard are found in violation of the concept of equal protection (Grossman & Wells, 1988).

A different and much more rigorous standard is applied, however, when government classifications are based on racial differences between people. This standard, known as strict scrutiny, requires that government bear the burden of showing that the distinctions it has drawn serve a compelling governmental interest and are narrowly tailored to meet that interest in that there are no less-intrusive alternatives available. Because preferential affirmative action rests, in part, on distinctions based on race, strict scrutiny is the standard by which those programs are judged when challenged under the constitution. In 1986, in *Wygant v. Jackson Board of Education,* a plurality of the Supreme Court endorsed the principle that strict scrutiny should be the basis for review of racial preferences in affirmative action by state or local government, and later, in 1989, in *City of Richmond v. J.A. Croson Company,* a majority endorsed the application of strict scrutiny to review affirmative action by subnational governments.

Strict scrutiny also became the appropriate level of review for federal government affirmative action programs as the result of the Supreme Court's 1995 ruling in *Adarand v. Peña.* Following that decision, any racial classifications incorporated into voluntary affirmative action programs by state, local, or federal employers must be shown to serve a compelling governmental interest and must be narrowly tailored to meet that interest to achieve constitutional legitimacy. It is not entirely clear what interests will be sufficiently compelling to permit such action, but it appears that one would be the correction of past discrimination by the government employer involved. "Narrowly tailoring" has been interpreted to mean that affirmative action should not impose any undue burden on innocent third parties—that is, the government must use the least intrusive means available to achieve its end. Affirmative action that violates a bona fide seniority system during times of layoffs, for example, will not withstand constitutional scrutiny if it results in a disproportionate number of nonminorities loosing their jobs. Affirmative action in the form of hiring or promotion goals and timetables could presumably be constitutional, in that they are less intrusive than a program that violates seniority rights (see *Wygant*), if they are implemented in response to a history of discrimination by the government employer involved. Of course, there is no way to know this with certainty because such a ruling has yet to be been made.

Although not directly related to public employment, important developments have occurred during the past decade regarding the constitutionality of preferential affirmative action policies for the admission of students to public institutions of higher education. A series of circuit court cases in the 1990s, for example, sent mixed signals on the status of affirmative action in this context. In 1996, the Fifth Circuit Court of Appeals found that preferential admissions policies at the University of Texas Law School were impermissible because student body diversity was not a sufficiently compelling interest to allow those preferences (*Hopwood v. State of Texas*). In 2000, however, the Ninth Circuit in *Smith v. University of Washington* reached the opposite conclusion in a case arising from the University of Washington School of Law. The following year, the Eleventh Circuit rejected such reasoning (*Johnson v. Board of Regents of the University of Georgia*), but in 2002, the Sixth Circuit ruled that diversity was a compelling interest for a state university (*Grutter v. Bollinger*). The U.S. Supreme Court finally addressed this uncertainty in summer 2003 when rulings were issued by that court in *Grutter v. Bollinger* and *Gratz v. Bollinger*. In both cases, the Supreme Court ruled that student body diversity was a sufficiently compelling interest for a state university to allow for a preferential affirmative action policy in the admissions process. The program at issue in the *Grutter* case, which involved the University of Michigan, School of Law, was upheld because the individualized attention given to each application ensured that the program was narrowly tailored. The *Gratz* case involved an undergraduate admissions program that was found unconstitutional because, lacking individualized attention to each application (the affirmative action preference was driven by a mathematical formula), it was not judged to be narrowly tailored.

The Michigan rulings were significant because they made it clear that some approaches to preferential affirmative action in university admissions would withstand constitutional strict scrutiny. Implications of the Michigan cases for affirmative action in employment are unclear, however. On one hand, it might be argued that diversity in the public workforce will assist public organizations in better representing the interests of diverse groups in society, but much of the reasoning by the Court in the Michigan cases focused on the distinctive importance of diversity in the context of higher education.

ADDRESSING DISCRIMINATION AGAINST THE DISABLED

Beginning in the 1970s, the federal government also took action to address the pervasive problem of discrimination against the disabled in all aspects of employment. The first such effort came in the form of the Rehabilitation Act of 1973, which prohibited discrimination against "otherwise qualified handicapped individuals" by any organization receiving federal financial assistance or by federal contractors or agencies. The purpose of the law was to ensure that no qualified individual who also happened to have a disability would be subjected to discrimination under any program or activity supported by federal funds. The focus of the law on all recipients of federal funding meant that essentially all state and local government jurisdictions would be prohibited from discrimination against the disabled. Provisions of the Rehabilitation Act prohibiting discrimination by federal contractors and federal agencies also required "affirmative action" by those organizations, including recruitment, outreach, and training.

In 1990, Congress addressed the problem of discrimination against the disabled for a second time through passage of the Americans with Disabilities Act (ADA). This statute was based on principles established by the Rehabilitation Act of 1973 and the regulations that had been issued to implement it (Kellough, 2000). The ADA is comprehensive in that it extends prohibitions on discrimination against the disabled to private employers without federal contracts, and it applies directly to state and local governments, although affirmative action is not mandated. Federal agencies were not covered by the ADA, however, because it was reasoned that they are sufficiently governed by the Rehabilitation Act and its affirmative action requirements. Needless to say, the ADA has been controversial, especially in its interpretation and implementation. Definitions of disabilities and associated "reasonable accommodations" by employers have been moving targets during the past decade as the EEOC has issued a stream of policy guidance and the federal courts have decided a series of cases (Kellough, 2000; Kellough & Gamble, 1995). In short, employers are prohibited from discriminating against any otherwise qualified disabled person who may, with or without a reasonable accommodation, perform the essential duties of the job.

THE SEXUAL HARASSMENT CHALLENGE

Sexual harassment in the workplace is a form of illegal discrimination that public employers must actively seek to prevent and, if it happens, to address in a manner that punishes the perpetrator and makes whole the victim. Sexual harassment has become a major public issue and concern. During the past decade, for example, a sitting president, Supreme Court nominee, and several members of Congress have been publicly accused of sexually harassing their employees. There is no reason to believe that sexual harassment of women by men in the workplace is something new. It should also be noted that cases of sexual harassment of men by women are not unheard of, and gays may be victimized by both sexes. What has happened in the United States is a reversal of long-standing pattern of tolerance by employers. Sexual harassment is now widely seen to be an unacceptable and costly behavior that public management must address through formal policies that are enforced, disciplinary procedures, training programs, and other ways of eliminating it from the workplace.

The reasons for the spotlight now shining on this previously dark corner of the workplace are not hard to find. First, women are rapidly becoming fully half of the civilian labor force, and they are moving into traditionally "male" job categories, including managerial and professional positions. Thus, in addition to the public attention drawn to sexual harassment by the complaints of a growing number of women who are no longer willing to tolerate it in any form, episodes of blatant harassment by male workers who resent the desegregation of all-male enclaves such the construction trades and police and fire departments have received particular notice. Second, social values and attitudes in this area are changing rapidly. Traditional definitions of "sex roles" and power relations between men and women in society are breaking down, and behaviors once considered at worst "impolite" or "unfortunate" are now simply not acceptable in many settings. Third, in conjunction with shifting social values, the political climate has changed significantly. In response to their growing political influence, women's issues now get far more attention than they did a few years ago, and this reality is reflected in legislation, court rulings, rules promulgated by agencies such as the EEOC, and personnel policies on all levels of government.

SEXUAL HARASSMENT AND THE LAW

Title VII of the Civil Rights Act of 1964 prohibits employment discrimination on the basis of race, color, religion, national origin, *and sex*. The EEOC is responsible for enforcement in this area and it (along with the federal courts) has interpreted Title VII to mean that sexual harassment is a form of sex discrimination. There are other types of sex discrimination, such as refusing to hire or promote qualified women and, of course, paying women less than men for the same kind of work (Lee & Greenlaw, 1996). In other words, sexual harassment is illegal, and violators (including the employer) may be prosecuted and held liable for damages. For the public employer, therefore, sexual harassment charges made by workers or clients are serious legal matters.

What behaviors or practices constitute sexual harassment? The EEOC issued the following guidelines more than 25 years ago:

> Harassment on the basis of sex is a violation of Sec. 703 of Title VII. Unwelcome sexual advances, requests for sexual favors, and other verbal or physical conduct of a sexual nature constitute sexual harassment when (1) submission to such conduct is made either explicitly or implicitly a term or condition of an individual's employment, (2) submission to or rejection of such conduct by an individual is used as the basis for employment decisions affecting such individual or (3) such conduct has the purpose or effect of substantially interfering with an individual's work performance or creating an intimidating, hostile, or offensive working environment. (U.S. Equal Employment Opportunity Commission, 1980)

Items (1) and (2) of the EEOC guidelines are straightforward and evoke little controversy; they prohibit making submission to unwelcome sexual behavior by a superior a condition of employment or using responses to such behavior as grounds for personnel actions (such as firing or denying pay raises to employees who refuse to submit). This is often called *quid-pro-quo* harassment. Most, but not all, federal circuit courts apply the following criteria to determine if a plaintiff has been subjected to *quid-pro-quo* harassment:

- The employee must be a member of a protected class.
- There must be proof that the employee was subjected to unwelcome sexual demands.
- It must be established that the harassment was based on sex.
- It must be shown that the employee was expected to comply in order to avoid a job-related penalty or to receive a job benefit.
- Employer liability under Title VII must be determined; the plaintiff's superior has to have acted as an "agent" of the employer. (Lee & Greenlaw, 1996, pp. 16–17)

Item (3) in the EEOC guidelines relating to the creation of a hostile or offensive environment is far broader in its application, and it does not require that the plaintiff prove that she (or he) was denied a tangible benefit such as a job or promotion. What has to be established is that the defendant's behavior toward the plaintiff created a hostile or offensive working environment. Not surprisingly, most sexual harassment charges in government are based on the hostile environment effect.

The EEOC's inclusion of category (3) violations was a "radical departure from the case law on the subject," but the Supreme Court agreed with it in *Meritor Savings Bank v. Vinson* (1986). This decision provided much-needed guidance for employers, and it established that hostile and abusive work environments are serious matters and that employers should follow the EEOC's guidelines carefully if they expect to prevail in the court (Webster, 1994).

The first point the Court made in *Meritor v. Vinson* was that Title VII is violated if serious and continuing unwelcome sexual behavior creates a "hostile or abusive work environment," even if the plaintiff was not denied any material benefits. In this case, a female bank employee charged her male supervisor with four years of sexual harassment, including fondling, psychologically coerced sexual relations, and rape. After her dismissal for taking "excessive sick leave" in 1978, Vinson brought action against the supervisor and the bank in district court.

In response to Vinson's charges, her supervisor denied allegations of sexual activity and asserted that Vinson's charges were in response to a "business-related dispute." In its defense, the bank claimed that it was unaware of any sexual harassment and, if it had taken place, it was without its consent or approval. The district court ruled against Vinson, stating that if she and her supervisor had "engaged in an intimate or sexual relationship during the time of [her] employment with [the bank] that relationship was a voluntary one having nothing to do with her continued employment or her advancement or promotions at that [bank]."

The court of appeals for the District of Columbia reversed the district court's decision. Previously, the appeals court had ruled that violations of Title VII could be based on either of two kinds of sexual harassment, (1) "harassment that involves the conditioning of concrete employment benefits on sexual favors, and (2) harassment that, while not affecting economic benefits, creates a hostile or offensive working environment." The district court had not considered whether a violation of the second kind had occurred, so the appeals court remanded the case, noting that employers are "absolutely" liable for sexual harassment practiced by their supervisory personnel.

Hearing the case on appeal, the Supreme Court agreed with the court of appeals, stating, "Unwelcome sexual advances that create an offensive or hostile working environment violate Title VII." Regarding the supervisor's and the bank's contention that there was no violation because Vinson had suffered no loss of a tangible benefit, the Court disagreed. Congress, the Court said, intended to "strike at the entire spectrum of disparate treatment of women" in employment. The EEOC guidelines, though not binding on the courts, "do constitute a body of experience and informed judgment to which courts and litigants may properly resort for guidance." Accordingly, the case was sent back to district court for further proceedings consistent with the Supreme Court's opinion.

The second point in *Meritor v. Vinson* focused on employer liability. Meritor Bank had argued that it should not be held liable because it had a written policy against discrimination and Vinson had not used an existing grievance procedure. The Court disagreed with both claims: the policy was vague and did not specifically address sexual harassment, and the grievance procedure discouraged complaints. The Court, however, did not fully resolve the issue of employer liability. Writing for the majority, Chief Justice Rehnquist "noted that while employers are absolutely liable for acts of their supervisors when economic benefits are involved, some limits might be placed on employer liability when hostile work environments were the issue" (Morlacci, 1987–88, pp. 513–515).

Since 1986, the Supreme Court has handed down several important rulings that do much to clarify its position on employer liability. In *Harris v. Forklift Systems, Inc.* (1993), the Court unanimously reasserted the principle it set forth in *Meritor* that Title VII does not require the victim of sexual harassment to show psychological damage before the behavior in question can be considered illegal. The Court stated in its decision that a hostile environment can undermine employees' performance, encourage resignations (constructive discharge), and destroy careers. It noted that it was taking a "middle path" and leaving the determination of whether or not specific instances of offensive conduct were illegal to a case-by-case approach. Although the Court did not specifically describe the behaviors that create an illegal hostile environment, it stated that all relevant factors need to be considered, including answers to the following:

- How often had the conduct in question occurred?
- How serious was the behavior?
- Were physical threats involved or was the behavior limited to verbal statements and comments?
- Did the behavior unreasonably interfere with the victim's job performance?
- Did the victim actually perceive the work environment to be abusive and hostile?

In 1998, the Court issued several anxiously awaited rulings, including *Oncale v. Sundowner Offshore Services Inc., Faragher v. City of Boca Raton,* and *Burlington Industries, Inc. v. Ellerth.* In these rulings, the Court sought to clarify the law regarding: (1) whether a claim of same-sex sexual harassment may be brought under Title VII, (2) what legal standard should be used to determine if employers are liable for sexual harassment by supervisors, and (3) if a claim of *quid-pro-quo* harassment can proceed "without showing that the employee submitted to sexual advances or was harmed for refusing such advances" (Muhl, 1998, p. 61).

In *Oncale,* a unanimous Court ruled that Title VII applies to sexual harassment between members of the same sex. Joseph Oncale charged that while he was working on an oil rig, male coworkers subjected him to sex-related harassment by two supervisors in front of other members of the crew. Although these events were reported to Sundowner's management, no remedial steps were taken. In its decision, the Court stated,

> We see no justification in Title VII's language or our precedents for a categorical rule excluding same-sex harassment claims from the coverage of Title VII. . . Title VII prohibits discriminat[ion] . . . because of . . . sex in the "terms" or "conditions" of employment. Our holding that this includes sexual harassment must extend to sexual harassment of any kind that meets the statutory requirements.

Respondents and their *amici* contend that recognizing liability for same-sex harassment will transform Title VII into a general civility code for the American workplace. But that risk is no greater for same-sex than for opposite sex harassment, and is adequately met by careful attention to the requirements of the statute (*Oncale v. Sundowner Offshore Services Inc.*, 1998)

In *Faragher v. City of Boca Raton*, the issue was employer liability for the harassing behavior of supervisors. Here, the Court ruled that employers are "subject to vicarious—or strict—liability for sexual harassment caused by a supervisor" (Muhl, 1998, p. 61). Beth Ann Faragher, a lifeguard, brought an action against her immediate supervisors and the City, charging that the two supervisors had created a sexually hostile environment at work by repeatedly subjecting her and other female lifeguards to "uninvited and offensive touching," "lewd remarks," and comments that described women in "offensive terms." A district court held the City liable because it concluded that the harassment had created a hostile environment pervasive enough to "support an inference that the City had knowledge or constructive knowledge of it." The district court, therefore, held under traditional *agency* principles, that the supervisors were acting as the City's agents. The Court of Appeals, however, reversed the district court's decision, arguing that constructive knowledge could not be imputed to the city and it could not be held liable for negligence. The Supreme Court, in turn, reversed and remanded, holding that an "employer is vicariously liable for actionable discrimination by a supervisor, but subject to an affirmative defense looking to the reasonableness of the employer's conduct as well as that of the plaintiff victim." In *Meritor*, the Court had indicated that questions of employer liability should be evaluated under principles of agency law, which says that employers can be held liable for the actions of employees if they are within the scope of a supervisor's job-related duties. In *Faragher*, the Court clarified its position by indicating that supervisors are always "assisted in sexual misconduct by the supervisory relationship." Employers, however, are not *automatically* liable whenever a supervisor engages in sexual harassment. The City of Boca Raton was held liable under this standard because: (1) its supervisors created a hostile work environment and they had almost unlimited authority over their subordinates, and (2) the city did not disseminate its sexual harassment policy among beach employees and made no effort to monitor the behavior of supervisors in that setting. Boca Raton, in other words, could not mount an affirmative defense because it had not exercised reasonable care to prevent the supervisors' illegal conduct.

The Court used its reasoning in *Faragher* to decide *Burlington Industries, Inc. v. Ellerth*. In this case, the central issue was whether an employee who does not submit to a supervisor's sexual demands or suffer any material job-related consequences may sue for *quid-pro-quo* sexual harassment. The Court held that employees may be entitled to damages, even if they do not submit to sexual demands by a supervisor and suffer no adverse consequences as a result. Although they are subject to vicarious liability under these conditions, the Court noted that employers may "raise an affirmative defense to liability or damages, subject to proof by a preponderance of the evidence. . . ."

> The defense comprises two necessary elements: (a) that the employer exercised reasonable care to prevent and correct promptly any sexually harassing behavior, and (b) that the plaintiff employee unreasonably failed to take advantage of any preventive or corrective opportunities provided by the employer.
> . . . No affirmative defense is available, however, when the supervisor's harassment culminates in a tangible employment action. (*Burlington Industries, Inc. v. Ellerth*, 1998)

Sexual Harassment Policies

Public employers are legally required to do everything reasonably possible to prevent sexual harassment in the work place. A fundamental part of such an effort is a broadly disseminated written policy statement by management that incorporates the EEOC guidelines, establishes an administrative procedure for initiating and dealing fairly with complaints, and describes clearly the penalties for violations. A member of top management should be ultimately responsible for implementing and monitoring the program. The potential liability of executives,

BULLETIN

From the dissent by Justice Thomas, with whom Justice Scalia joined, to the Court's decision in *Burlington Industries v. Ellerth:*

"When a supervisor inflicts an adverse employment consequence upon an employee who has rebuffed his advances, the supervisor exercises the specific authority granted to him by his company. His acts, therefore are the company's acts and are properly chargeable to it . . . If a supervisor creates a hostile work environment, however, he does not act for the employer. As the Court concedes, a supervisor's creation of a hostile work environment is neither within the scope of his employment, nor part of his apparent authority. Indeed, a hostile work environment is antithetical to the interest of the employer. In such circumstances, an employer should be liable only if it has been negligent. That is, liability should attach only if the employer either knew, or in the exercise of reasonable care should have known, about the hostile work environment and failed to take remedial action."

Explaining that the labels quid-pro-quo and hostile work environment are not controlling for determining employer liability, the Court concluded that Ellerth should have an opportunity to prove on the trial court level that she had a claim that would result in vicarious liability.

supervisors, and others should be explained, including a provision of the Civil Rights Act of 1991 under which victims of sexual harassment may receive up to $300,000 in compensatory and punitive damages.

For purposes of clarity, sexual harassment policies should provide descriptions of unacceptable behaviors. Enforcement procedures should ensure "that swift and proportional remedies will be applied when indicated," and managers and supervisors "must be trained to respond to problems quickly and effectively." It is important that training designed to familiarize all employees with the elements of an agency's sexual harassment policy be required of all employees. Identifying and stopping problems before they become sexual harassment complaints should be a key goal of the policy and related procedures. It is also important to make sure "that the complaint processing system is understood by all trainees and [to] stress that it is constructed to balance the rights of both complainants and respondents" (Spann, 1990, pp. 59–60).

Policies prohibiting sexual harassment are now the norm for public as well as private sector employers. In the federal government, all of the major departments and agencies have policies that are regularly updated. In its 1994 survey, the MSPB found that more than "80 percent of the respondents counted establishing and publicizing sexual harassment policies among the most effective actions an organization can take to reduce or prevent sexual harassment" (U.S. Merit Systems Protection Board, 1995, pp. 40–41). Two-thirds or more of the respondents rated universal training of employees, publicizing penalties and complaint channels, protecting victims from reprisals, training of all managers and supervisors, and enforcement of strong penalties as keys to preventing sexual harassment (p. 41). Although a "sizable minority" of federal employees did not see agency sexual harassment policies as particularly effective, the MSPB concluded that they are "almost as important for what they represent as for what they actually say or do."

> The policies are evidence that agency leaders are on record as intending to deal appropriately with sexual harassment. That stated commitment from the top can be critical in backing up managers and supervisors at levels who are trying to foster a workplace environment in which sexual harassment is not tolerated. (U.S. Merit Systems Protection Board, 1995, p. 41)

By the late 1990s, most states had implemented statewide or agency-level sexual harassment policies, with Michigan's 1979 policy being the first. Although the states have clearly recognized the need to have a policy prohibiting sexual harassment "on the books," as late as 1996 few if any had comprehensive programs that fully met the standards set by the courts (Bowman & Zigmond, 1996). Likewise, most cities with populations over 100,000 have instituted sexual harassment policies, and most of them have some kind of formal training program in place. Typically, the central personnel office or board has responsibility for conducting this training. A 1989 survey of large cities revealed that they were taking "affirmative steps to protect themselves from potential liability suits and damaging publicity" (Kirk-Westerman, Billeaux, & England, 1989, p. 104).

CONCLUSION

Efforts to combat historic patterns of discrimination against minorities, women, and those with disabilities are among the most important policies to be implemented by public personnel managers. These efforts have evolved from simple statements to prohibit discrimination, to programs focused on complaint processing, early affirmative action recruitment and outreach efforts, and finally to programs that include preferences for underrepresented minorities and women and reasonable accommodation requirements for the disabled job applicants and employees. Each step along the way, the antidiscrimination policies and programs have been met with significant political opposition and legal challenges. Today, preferential affirmative action programs are being challenged in the courts and at the ballot box, and it appears that this complex set of issues is far from resolved.

Sexual harassment, a form of discrimination based on sex, is a continuing problem, as are the many barriers confronted by those with physical and mental disabilities. Public employers, by virtue of their unique status under the Constitution, are required, indeed expected, to be model employers in how they operate their personnel systems. This standard requires that they do everything possible to eliminate discriminatory practices of many kinds and to take positive steps to ensure that all citizens enjoy equal protection and opportunity in public employment. All public employers, therefore should

- Consider it their responsibility to determine the extent and seriousness of discrimination of all kinds in their organizations so that they can take appropriate and effective steps in response.
- Make sure that training for workers, managers, and supervisors is available and systematically evaluated to ensure that it is addressing existing problems, meeting legal standards, and

encouraging victims to report discrimination and to make formal complaints without fear of retaliation.

In the final analysis, public employers are obligated to maintain a working environment free of discrimination, including sexual harassment. This duty goes well beyond simply having antidiscrimination policies on the books; it requires employers to take positive steps to prevent discrimination, to identify its causes, and to remedy its effects.

DISCUSSION QUESTIONS

1. In *Grutter and Gratz,* the Supreme Court ruled that diversity within a student body was a sufficiently compelling government interest to permit a preferential affirmative action plan. Could the same argument be made regarding diversity within a public workforce? If so, what would be the central points of that argument? Would you find such an argument compelling? Why? Why not?

2. Does your employer or university have a sexual harassment policy; if so, do you know what it says? Do you think it effectively prevents sexual harassment by supervisors, coworkers, or teachers?

3. Do you agree with the Supreme Court's reasoning about employer liability in *Faragher?* Why or why not?

REFERENCES

Adarand v. Peña (1995). 515 U.S. 200.

Bolling v. Sharpe (1954). 347 U.S. 497.

Bowman, James S., and Christopher J. Zigmond (1996). "Sexual Harassment Policies in State Government: Peering into the Fishbowl of Public Employment." *Spectrum: The Journal of State Government,* Vol. 69, No. 3 (Summer), pp. 24–36.

Burlington Industries, Inc. v. Ellerth (1998). 524 U.S. 742.

Button, James W., and Barbara A. Rienzo (2003). "The Impact of Affirmative Action: Black Employment in Six Southern Cities." *Social Science Quarterly,* Vol. 84, No. 1 (March), pp. 1–14.

City of Richmond v. J.A. Croson Company (1989). 488 U.S. 469.

Edley, Christopher, Jr. (1996). *Not All Black and White: Affirmative Action, Race, and American Values* (New York: Hill and Wang).

Faragher v. City of Boca Raton (1998). 524 U.S. 775.

Firefighters Local v. Stotts (1984). 467 U.S. 561.

Garfinkel, Herbert (1959). *When Negros March: The March on Washington Movement and the Organizational Politics for FEPC,* (Glencoe, IL: Free Press).

Goldstein, M., and R. S. Smith (1976). "The Estimated Impact of the Antidiscrimination Program Aimed at Federal Contractors." *Industrial and Labor Relations Review,* Vol. 29, No. 4, pp. 523–543.

Graham, Hugh Davis (1990). *The Civil Rights Era: Origins and Development of National Policy, 1960–1972* (New York: Oxford University Press).

Gratz v. Bollinger (2003). 539 U.S. 244.

Griggs v. Duke Power Company (1971). 401 U.S. 424.

Grossman, J. B., and R. Wells (1988). *Constitutional Law and Judicial Policy Making* (New York: Longman).

Grutter v. Bollinger (2003). 539 U.S. 306.

Grutter v. Bollinger (2002). 288 F.3d 732.

Guenin, Louis M. (1997). "Affirmative Action in Higher Education as Redistribution," *Public Affairs Quarterly,* Vol. 11, No. 2 (April), pp. 117–140.

Harris v. Forklift Systems, Inc. (1993). 510 U.S. 17.

Holmes, S. A. (1995). "Programs Based on Sex and Race are Under Attack: Dole Seeks Elimination," *New York Times* (March 16), p. 1A.

Hopwood v. State of Texas (1996). 78 F.3d 932.

Hyclak, T., and L. W. Taylor (1992). "Some New Historical Evidence on the Impact of Affirmative Action: Detroit, 1972." *Review of Black Political Economy,* Vol. 21, No. 2, pp. 81–98.

Johnson v. Board of Regents of the University of Georgia (2001). 263 F. 3d 1234.

Johnson v. Transportation Agency, Santa Clara County, California (1987). 480 U.S. 616.

Kellough, J. Edward (1989. *Federal Equal Employment Opportunity Policy and Numerical Goals and Timetables: An Impact Assessment* (New York: Praeger).

————. (1991). "The Supreme Court, Affirmative Action, and Public Management: Where Do We Stand Today?" *American Review of Public Administration,* Vol. 21, No. 3 (September), pp. 255–269.

————. (2000). "The Americans with Disabilities Act: A Note on Personnel Policy Impacts in State Government." *Public Personnel Management,* Vol. 29, No. 2 (Summer), pp. 211–224.

————. (2003). "Equal Employment Opportunity and Affirmative Action in the Public Sector." In Steven W. Hays and Richard C. Kearney, *Public Personnel Administration: Problems and Prospects,* 4th ed. (Upper Saddle River, NJ: Prentice-Hall).

————. (2006). *Understanding Affirmative Action: Politics, Discrimination, and the Search for Justice,* (Washington, DC: Georgetown University Press).

Kellough, J. Edward, and Robert C. Gamble (1995). "The Americans With Disabilities Act: Implications for Public Personnel Management," in Steven W. Hays and Richard C. Kearney (Eds.), *Public Personnel Administration: Problems and Prospects,* 3rd ed. (Englewood Cliffs, New Jersey: Prentice-Hall), pp. 247–257.

Kellough, J. Edward, and David H. Rosenbloom (1992). "Representative Bureaucracy and the EEOC: Did Civil Service reform Make a Difference?" in Patricia W. Ingraham and David H. Rosenbloom (Eds.), *The Promise and Paradox of Civil Service Reform* (Pittsburgh, PA: University of Pittsburgh Press), pp. 245–266.

Kirk-Westerman, Connie, David M. Billeaux, and Robert E. England (1989). "Ending Sexual Harassment at City Hall: Policy Initiatives in Large American Cities." *State and Local Government Review* (Fall), pp. 100–105.

Krislov, Samuel (1967). *The Negro in Federal Employment: The Quest for Equal Opportunity,* (New York: Praeger).

Lee, Robert D., and Paul S. Greenlaw (1996). "The Complexities of Human Behavior: Recent Instances of Alleged Quid Pro Quo Sexual Harassment." *Review of Public Personnel Administration,* Vol. 16, No. 4 (Fall), pp. 15–28.

Leonard, Jonathan S. (1984a). "The Impact of Affirmative Action on Employment." *Journal of Labor Economics,* Vol. 2, No. 4, pp. 439–463

————. (1984b). "Antidiscrimination or Reverse Discrimination: The Impact of Changing Demographics, Title VII, and Affirmative Action on Productivity." *Journal of Human Resources,* Vol. 19, No. 2, pp. 145–174.

————. (1985). "What Promises Are Worth: The Impact of Affirmative Action Goals," *Journal of Human Resources*, Vol. 20, No. 1, pp. 3–20.

Meier, Kenneth J. (1993). "Representative Bureaucracy: A Theoretical and Empirical Exposition," in James L. Perry (Ed.), *Research in Public Administration*, (New Greenwich, CT: JAI Press), pp. 1–35.

Meier, Kenneth J., and Joseph Stewart, Jr. (1992). "The Impact of Representative Bureaucracies: Educational Systems and Public Policies." *American Review of Public Administration*, Vol. 22, No. 3 (September) pp., 157–171.

Meritor Savings Bank v. Vinson (1986). 477 U.S. 57.

Morlacci, Maria (1987–88). "Sexual Harassment Law and the Impact of *Vinson*." *Employee Relations Law Journal*, Vol. 13 (Winter), pp. 501–519.

Muhl, Charles J. (1998). "Sexual Harassment." *Monthly Labor Review*, Vol. 121, No. 7 (July), pp. 61–62.

Oncale v. Sundowner Offshore Services, Inc., et al. (1998) 523 U.S. 75.

Price, Vivian (2002). "Race, Affirmative Action, and Women's Employment in U.S. Highway Construction." *Feminist Economics*, Vol. 8, No. 2 (July), pp. 87–113.

Reed, Merl E. (1991). *Seedtime for the Modern Civil Rights Movement: The President's Committee on Fair Employment Practice, 1941–1946* (Baton Rouge: Louisiana State University Press).

Rosenbloom, David H. (1977). *Federal Equal Employment Opportunity: Politics and Public Personnel Administration* (New York: Praeger).

Selden, Sally Coleman (1997). *The Promise of Representative Bureaucracy: Diversity and Responsiveness in a Government Agency* (Armonk, NY: M. E. Sharpe).

Selden, Sally Coleman, Jeffery L. Brudney, and J. Edward Kellough (1998). "Bureaucracy as a Representative Institution: Toward a Reconciliation of Bureaucratic Government and Democratic Theory." *American Journal of Political Science*, Vol. 42, No. 3 (July), pp. 717–744.

Selig, Joel L. (1987). "Affirmative Action in Employment: The Legacy of a Supreme Court Majority." *Indiana Law Journal*, Vol. 63, pp. 301–368.

Smith v. University of Washington (2000). 233 F. 3d 1188.

Spann, Jeri (1990). "Dealing Effectively with Sexual Harassment: Some Practical Lessons From One City's Experience." *Public Personnel Management*, Vol. 19, No. 1 (Spring), pp. 53–69.

Stephanopoulos, George, and Christopher Edley, Jr. (1995). *Affirmative Action Review: Report to the President* (Washington DC: U.S. Government Printing Office).

Taylor, Bron Raymond (1991). *Affirmative Action at Work: Law, Politics, and Ethics* (Pittsburgh, PA: University of Pittsburgh Press).

United Steelworkers of America v. Weber (1979). 443 U.S. 193.

Wards Cove Packing Company v. Atonio (1989). 490 U.S. 642.

United States v. Paradise (1987). 480 U.S. 149.

U.S. Equal Employment Opportunity Commission (1980). "Discrimination Because of Sex Under Title VII of the Civil Rights Act of 1964: Adoption of Final Interpretive Guidelines." *Federal Register,* Vol. 45 (November), pp. 74676–74677.

U.S. Merit Systems Protection Board (1995). *Sexual Harassment in the Federal Workplace* (Washington, DC: U.S. Government Printing Office).

Webster, George D. (1994). "EEOC's Proposed Guidelines on Harassment." *Association Management,* Vol. 6, No. 5 (May), pp. 142–143.

Wygant v. Jackson Board of Education (1986). 476 U.S. 267.

SUGGESTED READINGS

Kellough, J. Edward (2006) *Understanding Affirmative Action: Politics, Discrimination, and the Search for Justice* (Washington D.C.: Georgetown University Press).

Levy, Anne (1996). *Workplace Sexual Harassment* (Paramus, NJ: Prentice-Hall).

Paludi, Michele A. (1998). *Sexual Harassment, Work, & Education: A Resource Manual for Prevention,* 2nd ed. (Albany: State University of New York Press).

Reese, Laura A. (1998). *Implementing Sexual Harassment Policies: Challenges for the Public Sector* (Thousand Oaks, CA: Sage).

Chapter TEN

Responding to the Changing American Workforce

As we noted in Chapter 1, the characteristics of the civilian labor force (CLF) in the United States have changed greatly during the past 50 years and the pace of these changes continues to accelerate. In many cases, public personnel policies and practices have not been responsive to these changing demographic realities. Human resource specialists are now expected to help public employers implement human capital strategies that respond effectively to this dynamic environment. Here, we will focus on a variety of challenges that public employers will have to address during the early part of the 21st century as the American workforce continues its transformation.

THE CHANGING AMERICAN FAMILY

A very significant change in the CLF is the rapidly growing presence of female workers, many with young children at home. By 2004, 47 percent of all women worked (or were seeking work) within in the U.S. labor force. This rate of workforce participation meant that there were 68.5 million women aged 16 years and older in the CLF. By contrast, in 1971, that number was 31.5 million. The Bureau of Labor Statistics (BLS) anticipates that these trends will continue, "with the female participation rate reaching as high as 66.1 percent and the male participation rate falling as low as 72.9 percent by the year 2005"

(U.S. General Accounting Office, 1992a, p. 23). In addition to contributing to the growing diversity of the American workplace, the movement of women out of the home and traditional roles and into the workplace in many occupations and on many levels presents a whole new set of challenges to the employer.

Primary among these challenges is how to respond to a new set of family-related issues in ways that meet the needs of both employees and employers. For example, the CLF has seen a substantial increase in the number of working mothers over the past 30 years. Less than 20 percent of married women with children under the age of six worked in 1960; by 2004, 62 percent were in the labor market. In 2004, 46 percent of all workers had children under the age of 18 at home. In many families, both parents are full-time workers. Of all workers in the United States with families, about 25 percent are single parents. Personnel policies of public employers regarding benefits, working hours and conditions, and career development opportunities have been very slow to respond to this important change in the workforce.

Public as well as nonprofit and private employers are being forced by necessity to develop human resource policies and practices that are responsive to the needs and aspirations of a workforce that is not dominated by men with wives who are at home taking care of their children. The traditional and to some degree mythical "Ozzie and Harriet" family of the 1950s, in which the husband worked and the wife stayed home to raise the children is now a relatively small segment of American society (Bureau of National Affairs, 1989; U.S. Bureau of the Census, 1992). Overall, of the nation's married couples, in about half, both persons worked (Bureau of Labor Statistics, 2004). Many public employers, however, continue to have personnel policies that assume the workforce of the early 21st century is homogeneous, that traditional families prevail, and that organizational practices and norms based on industrial models represent the only way to structure relationships between employers and employees.

There has also been a dramatic increase in the proportion of highly educated professional women in the CLF. In 1971, only 11 percent of women had four or more years of college compared with more than 37 percent of men. By 2004, 33 percent of both groups had completed four or more years of college. Currently, about 60 percent of U.S. college students are women and many are now graduating from programs in the sciences and professions. Roughly equal percentages of college-educated men and women are now entering professional and managerial occupations. All these trends continue to signal a need for human capital strategies that recognize the rising career aspirations and qualifications of the steadily growing numbers of women in the CLF.

Many working women are the sole source of family income and caregiving. In the words of the Commission on Family and Medical Leave, "Approximately 23 percent of all workers with families have no spouse in the household to share wage-earning or caregiving responsibilities—and women now account for around 80 percent of that group" (Commission on Family and Medical Leave, 1996, p. 5). Children are not the only concern because as many as 15 percent of working adults are giving assistance to an older relative, and another 5 to 10 percent are helping a person under the age of 65 or with a disability (p. 10). Another study conducted in 1997 revealed that more than 40 percent of the U.S. workforce expected to be providing elder care by 2005 (Bond, Galinsky, & Swanberg, 1998, p. 151).

Only during the past 25 years or so has serious consideration been given to questions about the "fit" between public personnel policies such as those governing benefits and working hours and the needs of certain groups of today's workers. It is now better understood that growing numbers of public employees "face the challenge of trying to manage personal responsibilities, such as child care and elder care, from the office or work site" (U.S. General Accounting Office, 1992b, p. 11). It is, in other words, increasingly difficult for many workers to keep family matters isolated from their working lives. For example,

> Throughout the American workforce, the needs of parents and children are acute. Because of economic necessity and a desire to keep their careers afloat, six out of ten American mothers return to work within a year of having children, compared to less than 40 percent two decades ago. . . . (Kiger, 2004, p. 34)

From the employers' standpoint, these kinds of issues have important organizational as well as social and economic implications. Today's workers are more likely to want a balance between their on- and off-the-job responsibilities, and the available research suggests that responsiveness to these concerns can be an important factor in recruitment, retention, and productivity (Friedman, 1991; Seyler, Monroe, & Garand, 1995). The inability of traditional employment practices to deal successfully with the challenges presented by the "new family" has focused attention on a search for new approaches. In practice, there are some signs that public employers are beginning to respond, albeit slowly in some respects. Between 1985 and 1998, the proportion of state and local employees eligible for child care benefits subsidized in some manner by their employers grew from 2 to 23 percent (Bureau of Labor Statistics, 2000). Subsidies may include the following:

- Flexible savings accounts
- In-house or contracted referral services
- Discounts and stipends to support employee child care at offsite centers
- Agency-subsidized onsite child care centers
- Agency-provided emergency backup care
- Afterschool care for older children (Kiger, 2004)

In 2000, some 14 percent of all U.S. workers had direct access to child care resource and referral services. Of state and local workers, 17 percent had such access (U.S. Department of Labor, 2000b).

Social values and demographic trends are largely beyond the direct control of public employers, but personnel policies that reflect and adapt to new realities and exploit new opportunities are certainly possible, and examples may be found in many jurisdictions. These include (1) creative approaches to the content and administration of benefits plans, (2) flexible working arrangements, (3) family leave, and (4) child and elder care programs.

MORE FLEXIBLE AND COST CONSCIOUS EMPLOYEE BENEFIT PLANS

In one writer's words, "The bottom line for human resources is that the solution—and the challenge—is to realize that when it comes to benefits, one size does not fit everyone. . . . Companies must establish . . . programs and policies that all employees can participate in, whether they are married or single, parents or not" (Hammers, 2003, p. 80). For public employers, the costs associated with employee benefits range from 20 to 40 percent of the total compensation package, and "it is necessary to treat benefits with the same strategic pay considerations to which wage and salary decisions are subjected" (Daley, 1998, pp. 5–6; U.S. Chamber of Commerce, 2004). At one time, the benefits received by public employees came in "one-size-fits-all" plans set up by their employers. The components of these plans generally could be expected to include paid time off for certain purposes, health and life insurance, and a retirement or pension plan. However, the contemporary emphasis is on developing flexible combinations of benefits that help public employers to attract and retain needed human resources:

> Creative benefit-packaging includes traditional insurance programs (health, dental, life, vision and disability) and such innovations as flex-time, family-leave options, bonus programs, stock options, office equipment and support, personal access to company-owned technology, general education and training programs, employee assistance programs, child care, food services, transportation, recreation, and domestic partner benefits. (Fredericksen & Soden, 1998, p. 25)

In 1998, the BLS survey of benefits participation rates for state and local public employees revealed the pattern shown in Table 10.1. In the private sector, benefits are often less generous and participation rates are lower. For example, in the U.S. private sector, about 70 percent of workers are eligible for some kind of medical care insurance, but the participation rate is around 53 percent. About 59 percent are eligible for retirement benefits, but the participation rate is around 50 percent. There is also a striking difference between the sectors with regard to the types of retirement systems. Only about 20 percent of private sector workers participate in defined benefit plans whereas some 42 percent are in defined contribution plans (U.S. Department of Labor, 2004).

Rapidly increasing costs and changing employee needs have combined to build strong employer interest in so-called "cafeteria benefit plans" where employees have choices regarding alternative health care and retirement plans, as well as combinations of other optional benefits, such as disability and life insurance, flexible spending accounts, and child care (Moulder & Hall, 1995; Streib, 1996).

In general terms, the combination of a need to address the rapidly rising costs of benefits and to be more responsive to employee needs has driven public employers to consider and, in many cases, implement innovative and more flexible benefits packages (Panepento, 2004; Preston, 2005; Workforce Management, 2003). The steep climb in health care costs to employers has triggered the increasing use of health maintenance organizations (HMOs) and preferred provider organizations (PPOs), both of which are designed to contain and "ultimately to reduce costs, thereby increasing the financial viability of the organization" (Perry & Cayer, 1997, p. 10). There has been a strong trend away from a reliance on traditional fee-for-service or indemnity plans in favor of HMOs and PPOs. Point-of-service (POS) plans are also available to many workers. By 1998, 39 percent of local governments offered HMOs to their workers, and another 35 percent had PPO plans in operation. In 1990, fully 61 percent of localities relied on indemnity plans. By 1998, this figure was down to 25 percent (U.S. Department of Labor, 2000a). For all workers in both the private and public sectors, the percentage having the option of an indemnity plan had dropped to 14 percent by 2003 while 77 percent

Table 10.1 State and Local Government Benefits: Employee Participation Rates in 1998

Paid Time Off	Participation Rate %
Holidays	73
Vacations	67
Personal Leave	38
Funeral Leave	65
Jury Duty Leave	95
Military Leave	76
Family Leave	4*
Sick Leave	96
Insurance	
Long-Term Disability	34
Medical Care	86
Dental Care	60
Life	89
Retirement	
All	98
Defined Benefit	90
Defined Contribution	14

* Paid *family leave* for any reason is rare in both the public and private sectors. In 1998, the average Family Medical Leave Act (FMLA) benefit for state and local workers was about 18 weeks. This is unpaid leave.

had a PPO as one of their choices and 47 percent had an HMO option (Workforce Management, 2003).

Regarding retirement benefits, as the data in Table 10.1 suggest, there has been some movement in the public sector toward making *defined contribution* plans available as alternatives to long-standing *defined benefit* plans. Defined contribution plans typically involve a savings arrangement under which tax-deferred employee contributions are matched in some proportion by the employer. In the private sector, about 20 percent of all employees are eligible for defined benefit plans while 40 percent are eligible for defined contribution plans. Large, heavily unionized, private employers are far more likely to offer a defined benefit option (Workforce Management, 2003).

FLEXIBLE WORK PROGRAMS

Until recently, most public personnel systems had standardized work schedules and job designs for all employees. No effort was made to adjust to the personal and family-related needs of workers. Everybody was on a "9-to-5" type schedule, five days a week. During the past 20 years, however, public as well as private employers have come to recognize that flexible work programs may enhance their capability to recruit, retain, and motivate a high quality workforce (McCurdy, Newman, & Lovrich, 2002). These programs are designed to create a better "fit" between organizational requirements and employees' needs and preferences (Hoyman & Duer, 2004). Specific examples include part-time work and job sharing, alternative schedules, and telecommuting. These and other flexibilities may be highly attractive to potential as well as current employees (Roberts, 2003, pp. 241–242).

A 1998 study of federal agencies and private corporations revealed that flexible scheduling was highly valued by almost 40 percent of the public employees (Fredericksen & Soden, 1998, p. 32). Some public employers, including the federal government, have instituted a variety of flexible work programs, but many states and localities have not implemented family-friendly benefits such as child care, flexible benefit plans, long-term care insurance, wellness programs, flexible workplace policies, and subsidized commuting (Roberts, 2003, p. 242). One area where there has been considerable expansion is flexible or alternative work schedules. By 2004, more than 27 million full-time wage and salary workers in the United States had flexible work schedules. These workers accounted for about 27.5 percent of the American workforce. In 1987, only 15 percent had flexible work schedules. In 2001, more than 34 percent of federal employees were on flexible schedules while 30 percent of state and 14 percent of local workers enjoyed this benefit. According to the Bureau of Labor Statistics, the relatively low percentage of local workers is attributable to the inflexible schedules of public school teachers and staff (Bureau of Labor Statistics, 2005).

Alternative work schedules (AWS) are now found on all levels of government as well as throughout the private sector. The various forms of AWS are modifications of the traditional "9-to-5" five days a week schedule. Two basic forms are widely used. One form, called *flexitime* in the federal government, divides the workday into two kinds of time: core time and flexible time. Under flexitime, the worker must be on the job during core time, but flexible time allows for variations in starting and stopping times. The second form is *compressed time,* which involves an 80-hour biweekly basic work requirement scheduled for less than 10 workdays. Compressed schedules offer a variety of options for workers who want to free up a day or two for personal and family use.

Most evaluations of flexitime are based on private sector studies, but these findings are very likely to apply to government and to nonprofit employers. These studies indicate that flexible scheduling does have positive effects on productivity, morale, absenteeism, and use of overtime (Ezra & Deckman, 1996, p. 175). A study of federal employees showed

- Parents using flexitime were more likely to be satisfied with their child care.
- Parents using flexible schedules "were more likely to be satisfied with their work/family balance than parents who did not." (Ezra & Deckman, 1996, p. 177)

As a trendsetter in the use of AWS, the federal government's experience may offer useful guidance to states and localities. The first flexible work schedules were established by the Bureau of Indian Affairs and the Social Security Administration (SSA) during the early 1970s. Both agencies began their AWS experiments in an effort to deal with "tardiness, lost productivity, low morale, and, in the case of the SSA, an extensive amount of leave without pay (LWOP)." For both, the results were positive. However, AWS programs were not technically legal until 1979 when the *Federal Employee's Flexible and Compressed Work Schedules Act of 1978* became effective.

This legislation created a three-year experimental program intended to evaluate the effects of AWS. The Office of Personnel Management (OPM) had lead responsibility for setting up, managing, and evaluating the program. The Congress required OPM to evaluate the AWS program in six areas: (1) efficiency of government operations, (2) impact on mass transit and traffic, (3) energy consumption, (4) service to the public, (5) opportunities for full- and part-time employment, and (6) responses of individuals and families. Highly favorable results led to passage of the *Federal Employees Flexible and Compressed Work Schedules Act of 1982,* which established AWS as an ongoing program and imposed a three-year "sunset" provision. Subsequently, strongly positive evaluations by OPM, the General Accounting Office (now the Government Accountability Office or GAO), the Congress, and others set the stage for passage of Public

Law 99-196, which made AWS a permanent program in 1985 (U.S. General Accounting Office, 1985).

FLEXIBLE WORK PLACES

Flexible workplace and *flexiplace* are terms describing several forms of paid employment and employer-employee relationships in which the work site is shifted away from the traditional primary office. These include work done at home or at satellite offices and telecommuting, or teleworking, in which sophisticated communication and computer systems are used to carry out work assignments from remote locations.

The idea of designating an employee's home as the official work-site is not new to the public sector. In 1957, the U.S. Comptroller General authorized federal agencies to pay employees for work done at home if the agencies were able to verify and evaluate performance, the work involved could really be done at home, and it made sense from an agency perspective to use the home as a work site. Such arrangements were used informally to handle situations, but no organized federal flexiplace effort existed until 1990 when a pilot program covering 500 federal employees in 13 agencies was launched. The pilot yielded encouraging results, and the GAO stated in 1992 that there were "some early indications that the federal flexiplace initiatives can improve productivity and lower costs." OPM also reported that monthly focus group meetings for participants showed favorable results, and "90% of employees and 70% of supervisors said they consider flexiplace a desirable work arrangement" (U.S. Office of Personnel Management, 1991). By 1997, when the GAO investigated agency policies and views on flexiplace and reported its findings, it noted a significant general growth in the program—from around 4,000 to 9,000 participants (U.S. General Accounting Office, 1997).

Overall, the GAO found that federal agencies saw many benefits, including increased productivity and job satisfaction, decreased need for office space, and lessened environmental impacts (p. 12). Some reasons found for not using telecommuting included isolation, inadequate work space at home, and lack of self-discipline. Agencies felt that "the best flexitime participants are disciplined self-starters who need little supervision" (p. 13). In practice, this means that most telecommuters are professionals. The major source of resistance to telecommuting on the agency level is management opposition, with other barriers being budget constraints, the nature of the work involved, and the need to protect the security of sensitive data.

By 1998, OPM (U.S. Office of Personnel Management, 1998a) was prepared to issue a general rationale for telecommuting for agency use that included the following claims:

- It improves the quality of work life and job performance and productivity by reducing office overcrowding and providing a distraction free environment for reading, thinking, and writing.
- Morale is improved and stress reduced because telecommuting gives employees more options to balance work and family demands.
- It increases customer access to public services by creating more locations where they are available.
- It may allow an agency to continue to provide services when the regular office is closed by disasters or emergencies.
- Telecommuting enhances agencies' ability to recruit and promote diversity by expanding the geographic recruitment pool.
- It extends employment opportunities to those with disabilities and health problems who are able to work at home.
- Traffic congestion, energy consumption, and air pollution can be reduced if significant numbers of workers telecommute.

For these reasons, telecommuting and other flexiplace arrangements such as telecenters may become increasingly popular with public employers on all levels of government.

PART-TIME WORK

These programs respond to the situations of employees who want (or must) spend more time with their families than the normal 40-hour week allows. The BLS defines part-time employment as working less than 35 hours a week.

BULLETIN

Federal Telecenters

"Telecenter sites were selected based on GSA's observation that 16,000 federal employees commuted at least 75 miles each way on congested roads in the Washington, D.C., metropolitan area. In the spring of 1993, GSA began working in partnership with state and local governments in the Washington area, and by December 1994, the Washington area had four telecenters— one each in Hagerstown, Maryland; Charles County, Maryland; Winchester, Virginia; and Fredericksburg, Virginia. These telecenters had a total of 80 workstations, 143 participants, and a 55 percent utilization rate.* Twenty organizations in 10 executive branch departments and agencies used these 4 centers."

* Up to 435 federal employees in 2003.

Source: U.S. General Accounting Office (1997), *Federal Workforce: Agencies' Policies and Views on Flexiplace in the Federal Government* (Washington, DC: GAO/GGD-97–116), p. 24.

The *Federal Employees Part-Time Career Employment Act* was passed in 1978 in an effort to expand part-time opportunities in the federal service. According to the act, "many individuals in our society possess great productive potential which goes unused because they cannot meet the requirements of a standard workweek." Congress determined that making part-time employment available should have a number of benefits, including the following:

- Helping older workers make the transition into retirement
- Opening employment opportunities for persons with disabilities and others who might need a shorter work week
- Making it easier for parents to meet family responsibilities if both have to work
- Supporting students' efforts to finance their education or vocational training by working part-time
- Reducing costly turnover and absenteeism caused by demands on some workers' time that make it difficult to work a full 40-hour week
- Expanding agencies' recruitment pools by adding qualified persons who otherwise could not be attracted to public employment (Public Law 95–437)

Congress acted in 1978 to correct what it saw to be serious weaknesses in the national government's approach to part-time employment. It urged federal agencies to "make a substantial good faith effort to set goals which would represent meaningful progress and to move toward them." In 1986, however, the GAO concluded that not much progress had been made. In 1991, the Merit Systems Protection Board (MSPB) observed that a few agencies like the Department of Veterans Affairs and OPM had established formal programs, but most part-time positions in the federal civil service had probably been created in response to requests from full-time employees, rather than as a part of a planned program or policy (U.S. Merit Systems Protection Board, 1991, pp. 40–42). The MSPB noted at the time that opportunities to expand the number of part-time jobs did exist throughout the federal service and that nothing prevented federal agencies from hiring several part-time employees to fill what were previously full-time positions, and it concluded that the lack of progress was the result of "bureaucratic inertia." Since then, however, some progress has been made. As of 2003, there were over 160,000 part-time and intermittent federal employees, which represented about 6 percent of the civilian workforce (U.S. Office of Personnel Management, 2004).

Job sharing is a form of part-time work where two or more employees share the responsibilities of one full-time position by splitting work days or weeks. In addition to sharing a job on the basis of time, workers may also divide job tasks depending on their skills and expertise. A job's salary and benefits typically are split among the job sharers. Job sharing is a more complicated form of part-time work because it involves using two or more persons to fill one full time slot, so "there must be at least two employees in the same agency and post of duty who are personally and professionally compatible, and who want to share one job" (U.S. Merit Systems Protection Board, 1991, p. 43). For these reasons, job sharing is not widely used in the federal government or elsewhere.

FAMILY LEAVE POLICIES

On the national level, the political debate over family leave rights for American workers has been intense. On two occasions, Congress passed legislation requiring businesses with 50 or more employees to grant them 10 workweeks of unpaid leave during any 24-month period for births, adoptions, and family illnesses. The legislation would also have allowed federal employees up to 18 weeks of unpaid leave for the same reasons. President George H. W. Bush vetoed both bills, arguing that they would undermine productivity and were an unjustified governmental intrusion into the normal operation of the labor market. The introduction to the vetoed *Family and Medical Leave Act of 1989,* clearly defined its rationale:

> H.R. 770 addresses a profound change in the composition of the workforce that has had a dramatic effect on families. Sixty percent of all mothers are currently in the labor force, which is three times what it was thirty years ago. In the great majority of families today, all of the adult members work. The role of the family as primary nurturer and care-giver has been fundamentally affected by a new economic reality. Families are struggling [to] find a way to carry out the traditional role of bearing and caring for children and providing the emotional and physical support to their members during times of greatest need. When families fail to carry out these critical functions, the social costs are enormous. (Family and Medical Leave Act of 1989, p. 2)

The Family and Medical Leave Act (FMLA) was reintroduced and finally signed into law by President Clinton in 1993. This legislation requires all businesses with 50 or more employees and all public agencies (state, local, federal, and educational) to provide up to 12 weeks of *unpaid,* job-protected leave for the following reasons:

- Care of a newborn, newly adopted, or foster child
- Care of a child, spouse, or parent with a serious health condition
- A serious health condition of the employee, including maternity-related disability

Employers must maintain health insurance coverage for workers on leave and place them in the same job or an equivalent when they return. Under the FMLA, employees are covered if they have worked for the employer for one year or a total of at least 1,250 hours (Commission on Family and Medical Leave, 1996, p. 15). In the private sector, the law covers about 11 percent of all work sites or about 60 percent of all workers.

Although they may choose to offer more generous family leave benefits, the FMLA sets a minimum standard that must be followed by virtually all public employers. Roughly 12 million state and local employees are covered, with about 33 percent being eligible for more than the required 12 weeks. Paid family leave is seldom available, but public employers are experimenting with approaches that allow their workers to share or donate annual leave and to use sick leave to care for family members. For example, in 1994, the federal government enacted the *Federal Employees Family Friendly Leave Act,* which allows employees to use up to 13 days of sick leave to care for family members or to arrange for or attend the funeral of a family member. Federal employees may also use sick leave for purposes related to the adoption of a child. In testimony before the House Subcommittee on Compensation and Employee Benefits, Committee on Post Office and Civil Service, a representative of the GAO made the following points in support of this legislation:

> Our work has shown that the practice of giving employees paid time off to care for ill family members is becoming quite common among leader nonfederal employers. In our report comparing federal and nonfederal work/family programs, we found that most of the nonfederal organizations we visited permitted employees to use all or a portion of their paid sick leave to care for family members who are ill. Other approaches to this issue some employers used included providing separate "family emergency" leave allowances and combining vacation and sick time into one account to give employees the flexibility to take time off for any reason. (U.S. General Accounting Office, 1994, p. 3)

Another way of supporting employees is to make *leave sharing programs* available. They are designed to help employees who have used up their paid leave and are faced with the prospect of having to ask for unpaid leave or, even worse, resigning their positions to care for family members. The *Federal Employees Leave Sharing Act of 1988*, as amended, authorizes federal agencies to allow donations of annual leave (paid vacation days) by employees to co-workers who have exhausted their annual leave and face a family medical emergency that requires extended absence from work resulting in loss of income. Under the federal plan, agencies establish leave banks, and employees are allowed to contribute a specified amount of annual leave to the bank every year. Members of the bank with medical emergencies can then withdraw leave from the bank if they use up their own leave (U.S. Office of Personnel Management, 1998b), pp. 1–2). According to the GAO, the leave sharing program is "quite successful and is widely supported by federal agencies and employees alike" (U.S. General Accounting Office, 1994, p. 1).

CHILD CARE PROGRAMS

For single-parent families and those where both parents work, child care is an important issue. Families often have difficulty arranging affordable child care, and those having the most problems are likely to experience frequent work disruptions and high levels of absenteeism (Weisberg & Buckler, 1994, pp. 101–113).

American workers face a chronic shortage of affordable, quality child-care services. Because the availability of affordable child care has a significant impact on workers' productivity, public as well as private employers have a vested interest in doing whatever they can to help meet this need. In addition to the flexible work programs described earlier, public employers have several options to choose from, including: (1) assistance in the form of information

---

BULLETIN

State of Georgia Personnel Board Rule #30

In accordance with the provisions of this rule, an appointing authority may adopt a policy to permit eligible employees to donate or receive leave from other employees of the same department. A leave donation policy shall specify criteria to be utilized in authorizing solicitations for donated leave and designate staff authorized to administer leave donations. Such policy shall be accessible for review by employees. Leave donations shall be from employee to employee and shall be strictly voluntary. The identity of donors shall be confidential and shall not be provided to the recipient or to any other individual unless necessary to administer the donation or required by law.

Source: State Personnel Board, Rule #30, Section 30.100, General Provisions (Atlanta, GA).

about child care resources and referral services; (2) financial assistance for day care, such as vouchers, subsidies, and tax shelters (flexible spending accounts); and, (3) day care facilities on or near the job site.

Child Care Centers for Public Employees

Daycare can be a very expensive proposition, especially for workers on the lower end of the pay scale. Parents may expect to pay several thousand dollars per year or more for each child they have in full-time day care. In general, public employers do not offer their workers direct financial assistance, but some, like the federal government, do subsidize child care by providing space rent-free, negotiating discounts with private providers, and covering initial membership fees and costs associated with joining child care networks.

Since 1985, federal agencies have been authorized to spend public funds for space and services for child care facilities. If the space is available, it will be used for child care services to a group composed of at least 50 percent federal employees, and federal employees will be given priority access. Many civilian agencies have established on-site child care centers on their own or in conjunction with other agencies (U.S. General Accounting Office, 1992a, pp. 85–86). Agency subsidies make costs to parents somewhat lower than those charged by nonfederal child care facilities.

Somewhat different approaches to child care are used by the states of New York and California. In New York, the state provides free space in state buildings and the centers charge sliding fees based on employees' income. In many states and localities, employee organizations and management have negotiated contracts addressing child care for employees. In California, a contract negotiated by the state and employee organizations included the following provisions:

- It shall be State policy to encourage the development of child care services for dependent children.
- The State agrees to establish programs and provide financial assistance, within budgetary constraints, for the development of child care centers.
- The State agrees to establish a State Labor-Management Child Committee, the function of which includes encouraging State employees to form non-profit corporations to provide child care services, to make recommendations to the Department of Personnel Administration about which providers should receive child care funds.

■ The State may provide the use of its facilities for child care centers which may include a rental/lease agreement. (California Department of Personnel Administration, 1998)

Although progress has been made, establishing adequate, safe, and affordable child care facilities for employees will continue to be a major challenge for public employers. Meeting this challenge, of course, will require public policies that make the needed resources available to workers and employers. Employers' attitudes will also need to change in many cases, and it is likely that they will as the connections between "family-friendly" personnel practices and organizational success in the labor market become clearer.

ELDER CARE PROGRAMS

In the United States, the number of persons over age 55 is rapidly increasing. In 1997, about 34 million American were 65 or older and that percentage is expected to more than double by the year 2030.

There are now about 4 million over the age of 84, and this number is projected to grow to 6 million by 2010.

Although most of the elderly are capable of taking care of themselves, a steadily growing group of workers will be providing care for older parents, relatives, or friends. In all likelihood, this group will be composed largely of middle-aged working women (U.S. Department of Labor, 1998). Many public employers, like the federal government, fit the description of those projected to be hit hardest by elder care problems. They already have relatively high proportions of female and middle-aged workers, and the projected trend is for steady increases (West, 1998, pp. 94–96). In other words, for a large part of the public workforce, child care responsibilities will be fol-

BULLETIN

Child Care in France

"In the U.K. as in the U.S., the work-family conflict has been addressed by a combination of partially paid parental leave and the decision of many mothers with young children to work part-time. Public financed child care is virtually non-existent. But France spends more than $40 billion a year on various forms of child care. There, a 10-week paid maternity leave is followed by one of two statutory options: a four-day workweek or a one- to three-year unpaid parental leave, with a guarantee of the same or similar job at the end." Other benefits include: (1) government payments to cover social security contributions for a baby-sitter, (2) payments and tax breaks to help pay for child care, and (3) pre-primary schooling at no cost. "In the U.S., just one-third of eligible children are in preschool programs, and only moms on welfare receive subsidies."

Source: Ann Crittenden (1995). "Work-Family Solutions: Why French Women are Ahead," *Working Women*, Vol. 20, No. 9 (September), p. 12.

lowed or even accompanied by a potentially even longer-term commitment to elder care (Bond, Thompson, Galinsky, & Prottas, 2002, pp. 27–28).

The effects on productivity and turnover are likely to rival those connected with child care problems. In the words of the Commission on Family and Medical Leave (1996):

> To care for elders' many and changing needs, employed primary care givers often put in long hours providing informal care on top of their work hours. They often rearrange their work schedules, work fewer hours than they wish to, or take time off without pay (p. 11).

In addition, other problems found to be associated with caring for elderly relatives are: (1) work interruptions to deal with emergencies and phone calls, (2) increased employee stress that leads to taking time off and resignations, (3) reluctance to relocate or travel, and (4) lowered morale. (Schmidt, 1997, p. 82)

Indifference to the needs of workers providing or contemplating elder care will surely be a competitive disadvantage in the labor market of the future. Public sector responses to elder care needs mostly parallel those of the private sector. Both sectors emphasize educational programs and resources referral networks. The former are designed to help prepare employees for elder care responsibilities, and the latter are intended to assist in finding the services that elderly dependents may require. Overall, about one-third of all private employers offer some elder care benefits. Of these, about 80 percent have resource and referral programs, and about 20 percent make long-term care insurance and counseling available to employees (U.S. Department of Labor, 1998; Walter, 1996).

Other options that may become necessary as the number of working care givers continues to grow include providing on-site elder care centers, subsidizing employee use of elder care centers, and employee assistance programs (EAPs) designed to provide a variety of psychological and "respite" support services. One study of workers in a variety of public service agencies found that they ranked improved leave polices for care of dependent elders as the most

---

BULLETIN

The Benefit of the 1990s

Elder care programs are likely to become increasingly relevant to American workers and their families. A variety of studies show that over 70 percent of care givers are women and almost 65 percent of these are employed outside the home. Care givers spend around $2 billion annually of their own money on food, medicines, and care giver support services. On average, the care giver devotes 18 hours per week to this often stressful and demanding role.

Source: Jo Horne Schmidt, "Who's Taking Care of Mom and Dad?" *Journal of the American Society of CLU &ChFC*, Vol. 51, No. 1 (November, 1997) pp. 82–87.

important benefit an employer could offer. Other benefits that these workers valued were, in order of importance, as follows: (1) home visitors, (2) elder care referral services, (3) adult care facilities, (4) financial assistance, (5) leaves of absence, (6) educational seminars, (7) flexible spending accounts, and (8) job-sharing and part-time work opportunities (Kossek, DeMarr, Blackman, & Kollar, 1993; U.S. Department of Labor, 1998). One interesting innovation is the intergenerational center, where child and elder care facilities and programs are combined. There are more than 200 such centers in operation across the country (Gubernick, 1996).

CONCLUSION

Building family-friendly and flexible workplaces promises to be an ongoing challenge for public as well as private and nonprofit employers, and human resources will be expected to play a major role in an organizationwide effort to meet that challenge (Avery & Zabel, 2001). Establishing workplaces that advance human capital goals rather than creating obstacles starts with eliminating outdated stereotypes and assumptions about the American workforce of today and the future. It also demands a willingness by policy makers and public managers to see flexible benefits, family leave, child and elder care, employee assistance plans, and other practices geared to the changing workforce as rational and prudent *investments* in the organizational capacity needed to achieve and sustain the high levels of performance required of today's governments.

DISCUSSION QUESTIONS

1. What *is* your employer doing to provide a family-friendly work environment?
2. What *should* your employer be doing to be more responsive to the family-related needs of employees?
3. What are the most important benefits employers should offer?
4. Do you agree with the following statement? Making subsidized child and elder care to available to employees is likely to increase job satisfaction and lead to increased productivity. What are the reasons for your answer?
5. Do you believe providing family-friendly benefits, flexible schedules, and child care services creates conditions under

which employees *without children* are treated less generously than those who are eligible because they have children? If so why? If not, why?

REFERENCES

Anonymous (1996). "More Choice, Flexibility Seen in U.S. Benefits Plans." *National Underwriter—Property & Casualty Risk & Benefits Management,* Vol. 100, No. 16 (April 15), p. 29.

Avery, Christine, and Diane Zabel (2001). *The Flexible Workplace: A Sourcebook of Information and Research* (Westport, CT: Quorum Books).

Bond, James T., Ellen Galinsky, and Jennifer E. Swanberg (1998). *The 1997 National Study of the Changing Workforce* (New York: Families and Work Institute).

Bond, James T., Cynthia Thompson, Ellen Galinsky, and David Prottas (2002). *Highlights of the National Study of the Changing Workforce* (New York: Families and Work Institute).

Bureau of Labor Statistics (2000). *Employee Benefits in State and Local Government, 1998.* Accessed http://www.statsbls.gov/ncs/sp/ebb10018.pdf

———. (2005). *Workers on Flexible and Shift Schedules in 2004.* Accessed http://www.bls.gov/news.release/flex.nr0.htm

———. (2004). *Report: Employment Characteristics of Families in 2004.* Accessed http://www.bls.gov/news.release/pdf/famee.pdf

Bureau of National Affairs, Inc. (1989). *101 Key Statistics on Work and Family for the 1990s* (Washington, DC).

California Department of Personnel Administration (1998). State Labor Contract with Bargaining Unit 1, Professional Administrative, Financial and Staff Services (Local 1000 SEIU), Article 20, 1992–1995.

Commission on Family and Medical Leave (1996). *A Workable Balance: Report to Congress on Family and Medical Leave Policies* (Washington, DC: U.S. Department of Labor).

Daley, Dennis M. (1998). "An Overview of Benefits for the Public Sector." *Review of Public Personnel Administration,* Vol. 18, No. 3 (Summer), pp. 3–22.

Ezra, Marni, and Melissa Deckman (1996). "Balancing Work and Family Responsibilities: Flextime and Child Care in the Federal

Government." *Public Administration Review,* Vol. 56, No. 2 (March/April), pp. 174–179.

Family and Medical Leave Act of 1989 (1989). 101st Congress, H.R. 770, April 13.

Fredericksen, Patricia J., and Dennis L. Soden (1998). "Employee Attitudes Toward Benefit Packaging." *Review of Public Personnel Administration,* Vol. 18, No. 3 (Summer), pp. 23–41.

Friedman, Dana E. (1991). *Linking Work-Family Issues to the Bottom Line* (New York: Conference Board).

Gubernick, Lisa (1996). "Granny Care and Kiddie Care." *Forbes,* Vol. 158, No. 15 (December 30), pp. 74–75.

Hammers, Maryann (2003). "'Family-Friendly' Benefits Prompt Non-Parent Backlash." *Workforce Management,* Vol. 82, No. 8, pp. 77–80.

Hoyman, Michele, and Heidi Duer (2004). "A Typology of Workplace Policies: Worker Friendly vs. Family Friendly?" *Review of Public Personnel Administration,* Vol. 24, No. 2, pp. 113–132.

Kiger, Patrick J. (2004). "The Case for Child Care." *Workforce Management,* Vol. 83, No. 4, pp. 34–39.

Kossek, Ellen Ernst, Beverly J. DeMarr, Kirsten Blackman, and Mark Kollar (1993). "Assessing Employees' Emerging Elder Care Needs and Reactions to Dependent Care Benefits." *Public Personnel Management,* Vol. 22, No. 4 (Winter), pp. 617–638.

McCurdy, Arthur H., Meredith A. Newman, and Nicholas P. Lovrich (2002). "Family-Friendly Workplace Policy Adoption in General and Special Purpose Local Governments: Learning from the Washington State Experience." *Review of Public Personnel Administration,* Vol. 22, No. 1, pp. 27–51.

Moulder, Evelina, and Gwen Hall (1995). *Special Data Issue: Employee Benefits in Local Government* (Washington, DC: International City/County Management Association).

Panepento, Peter (2004). "The Escalating Expense of Health Care." *Chronicle of Philanthropy,* Vol. 16, No. 7.

Perry, Ronald W., and N. Joseph Cayer (1997). "Factors Affecting Municipal Satisfaction with Health Care Plans." *Review of Public Personnel Administration,* Vol. 17, No. 2 (Spring), pp. 5–19.

Preston, Mark (2005). "Budget Buster: Cities and Counties can Ill Afford Escalating Health Care Costs." *American City & County,* Vol. 120, No. 5.

Public Law 95–437 (1978). 92 Stat. 1055, October 10.

Roberts, Gary E. (2003). "The Association of Needs Assessment Strategies with the Provision of Family-Friendly Benefits." *Review of Public Personnel Administration*, Vol. 23, No. 3, pp. 241–254.

Schmidt, Jo Horne (1997). "Who's Taking Care of Mom and Dad?" *Journal of the American Society of CLU&ChFC*, Vol. 51, No. 1 (November), pp. 82–87.

Seyler, Dian L. (1995). "Balancing Work and Family: The Role of Employer-Supported Child Care Benefits." *Journal of Family Issues*, Vol. 16. No. 2, pp. 170–194.

Seyler, Dian L., Pamela A. Monroe, and James C. Garland (1995). "Balancing Work and Family: The Role of Employer-Supported Child Care Benefits." *Journal of Family Issues*, Vol. 16, No. 2, pp. 170–193.

Streib, Gregory (1996). "Municipal Health Benefits: A First Step Toward a Useful Knowledge Base." *American Review of Public Administration*, Vol. 26, No. 3 (September), pp. 345–360.

U.S. Bureau of the Census (1992). *Statistical Abstract of the United States; 1992*, 112th ed. (Washington, DC), Table 620.

U.S. Chamber of Commerce (2004). *Employee Benefits Study, 2004* (Washington, DC: U.S. Chamber of Commerce Statistics and Research Center).

U.S. Department of Labor (1998). *Work and Elder Care: Facts for Caregivers and Their Employers* (Washington, DC: Women's Bureau, No. 98-1), May.

————. (2000a). *Employee Benefits in State and Local Governments, 1998* (Washington, DC: Bureau of Labor Statistics), Bulletin 2531, December.

————. (2000b). *Pilot Survey of the Incidence of Child Care Resource and Referral Services in June 2000*, Report 946 (Washington DC: Bureau of Labor Statistics), November.

————. (2004). *National Compensation Survey: Employee Benefits in Private Industry in the United States* (Washington, DC: Bureau of Labor Statistics), March.

U.S. General Accounting Office (1985). *Alternative Work Schedules for Federal Employees* (Washington, DC), July.

————. (1992a). *The Changing Workforce: Demographic Issues Facing the Federal Government* (Washington, DC), March.

————. (1992b). *The Changing Workforce: Comparison of Federal and Nonfederal Work/Family Programs and Approaches* (Washington, DC), April.

———. (1994). *Federal Employment: H.R. 4361, Federal Employees Family Friendly Leave Act,* Statement of Timothy P. Bowling, Associate Director, Federal Human Resource Management Issues, General Government Division (Washington, DC: GAO/T-GGD-94–152), May 18.

———. (1997). *Federal Workforce: Agencies' Policies and Views on Flexitime in the Federal Government* (Washington, DC), July.

U.S. Merit Systems Protection Board (1991). *Balancing Work Responsibilities and Family Needs: The Federal Civil Service Response* (Washington, DC), November.

U.S. Office of Personnel Management (1991). "If It's Wednesday, It Must Be Home." *Federal Staffing Digest,* Vol. 3, No. 3 (December), p. 7.

———. (1998a). Reasons for Telecommuting (Washington, DC). Accessed http://www.opm.gov/wrkfam/telecomm/reasons.htm

———. (1998b). *Family Friendly Leave Policies* (Washington, DC). Accessed http://www.opm.gov/oca/leave/html/fflafact.htm

———. (2004). *Federal Civilian Workforce Statistics: Fact Book* (Washington, DC: U.S. Office of Personnel Management).

Walter, Kate (1996). "Elder Care Obligations Challenge the Next Generation." *HRMagazine,* Vol. 41, No. 7 (July), pp. 98–103.

Weisberg, Anne C., and Carol A. Buckler (1994). *Everything a Working Mother Needs to Know* (New York: Doubleday).

West, Jonathan P. (1998). "Managing an Aging Workforce," in Stephen E. Condrey (Ed.), *Handbook of Human Resource Management in Government* (San Francisco: Jossey-Bass), pp. 93–115.

Workforce Management (2003). "Benefits Costs Reach Crisis Stage." *Workforce Management,* Vol. 82, No. 13, pp. 118–131.

Suggested Readings

Dwyer, Jeffrey W., and Raymond T. Coward (1992). *Gender, Family, and Elder Care* (Thousand Oaks, CA: Sage).

Estess, Patricia S. (1996). *Work Concepts for the Future: Managing Alternative Work Arrangements* (Menlo Park: CA: Crisp)

Kugelmass, Joel (1995). *Telecommuting: A Manager's Guide to Flexible Work Arrangements* (San Francisco: Jossey-Bass).

McCaffery, Robert M. (1993). *Employee Benefits Basics* (Scottsdale, AZ: American Compensation Association).

McDaniel, Charlotte (1994). *Health Care Benefits Problem Solver for Human Resource Professionals and Managers* (New York: Wiley).

Neal, Margaret B., Nancy J. Chapman, Berit Ingersoll-Dayton, and Arthur C. Emlen (1993). *Balancing Work and Caregiving for Children, Adults, and Elders* (Newbury Park, CA: Sage).

Niles, Jack (1998). *Managing Telework: Strategies for Managing the Virtual Workforce* (New York: Wiley).

Reynolds, John D. (1993). *Flexible Benefits Handbook* (Boston: Warren, Gorham & Lamont).

Chapter ELEVEN

Civil Service Reform: A Closer Look

As we have seen in earlier chapters, civil service reform is common at all levels of government in the United States. Indeed, one may argue that it has become something of an American tradition. Public employers across the United States have frequently turned to "civil service reform" when confronted with challenging political and fiscal circumstances. Such reforms have ranged from relatively minor or incremental adjustments to comprehensive, fundamental, changes. Typically, they reflect intellectual and ideological trends in the environment of government and its administrative agencies. Thus, for example, the progressive era sparked a long-term trend away from spoils and its emphasis on partisan loyalties and responsiveness toward the neutral competence norms of traditional merit systems. Those reforms and the more recent ones of the late 20th century were driven by complex and not necessarily congruent values and purposes ranging from the largely partisan to the mostly technical.

The fact the personnel administration is a favorite target of reformers of many sorts suggests that it is far from the boring political and technical irrelevancy that some might have us believe it is. "Bureaucrats" and the systems they work in and administer matter greatly on all levels of society, and they profoundly influence how we are governed. Among other things, it is through the personnel or human resource function that public agencies recruit and select, train and develop, and manage the performance of public workers. Personnel management obviously shapes the public service in many important ways. Public employees on many levels of responsibility exercise the discretion needed to color both the content and execution of government policies. A reality facing human resource practitioners in many countries, including the United States, is that they will be asked to implement fundamental changes and critically important modifications in the design and operation of civil service systems. Schultz (2002) notes, "The constant change in personnel systems in the United States and elsewhere is an indication that they have adapted significantly to changing political environments" (p. 637).

The causes of civil service reform and the contexts within which it takes place are widely varied, but there are at least three kinds of reasons for such initiatives, and in many cases, they are interrelated. The first of these is ideology, or a belief by policy makers that a particular approach to human resources policy and management will lead to better outcomes of all sorts. Typically, the explanation for performance problems in government is that the values underpinning the existing civil service system are contrary to the values embedded in a particular ideology or belief system. Ideologies are action or change oriented and typically offer "a picture of a better . . . life for humans—a goal culture" (Ingersoll, Matthews, & Davison, 2001, p. 5). A simple example would be the idea that privatization and contracting out most if not all public services will yield better results and lower costs than will direct provision by public agencies. This proposition is rooted in a normative preference for the free market economy and the individual liberties associated with it. Another example is the argument that traditional civil service merit systems are inherently inefficient and politically unresponsive because they are based on bureaucratic, regulatory, and command and control norms. This diagnosis is then paired with a set of statutory and management reforms based on the idea that business-like and market-oriented approaches, if implemented, will generate much higher levels of efficiency and responsiveness. For many of today's reformers, "at will" employment and privatization are to be preferred to classified civil services and direct service provision because they conform to free market norms and should generate lower costs and more efficient resource allocations. In one writer's words,

> Remedies rooted in economic and market-based approaches may address needs rooted in normative motives. Interpreting the meaning of a particular reform remedy is a matter of judging the glass half-full. For example, efforts to make working conditions in government and the private sector more similar can be interpreted as equity-based reform or as efficiency-based reform. Similarly, measures to promote human resource development may be rooted in humanistic values or may be grounded in efficiency. Interpretation . . . may be clouded by

differences between rhetoric and symbolic reform and actual implementation. (Wise, 2002, p. 564)

A second set of reasons for civil service reform is political. Here, reforms are designed to re-align or cement the relative power positions of the actors and stakeholders that depend on government bureaucracies for a wide variety of resources. Reforms are vehicles used to establish and advance political interests' ability to influence public policy and the resulting allocations of resources. These capacities include the leverage needed to carry out the agendas of elected executives, legislators, and other policy makers. In other words, civil service reforms serve as vehicles to establish and defend political actors' standing and capacity to influence the authoritative allocation of values. This capacity includes the ability of elected executives and legislators to implement their policy agendas and programs. Structural reorganizations, modifications in the authority and jurisdiction of personnel offices, and changes in hiring and job classification systems, for example, may produce dramatic shifts in the internal political dynamics of agencies and in the balance of power among agencies and branches of government.

In the United States, many state governors like Zell Miller of Georgia and Jeb Bush of Florida have aggressively pushed reforms designed to remove merit system barriers to direct and tight policy control over state agencies and their employees. On the federal level, President George W. Bush insisted that there be provisions in the legislation establishing the Department of Homeland Security exempting its employees from many if not all the collective bargaining rights afforded other federal workers because negotiated arrangements would pose barriers to the flexibility and responsiveness the new agency's management needed to be effective. These three cases are described in detail later in this chapter.

These types of reform initiatives are often sold as a need to enhance executive leadership and accountability for results and, often, to allow the dismissal of the legions of "unresponsive, incompetent, insulated, bureaucrats" who the public is convinced lurk in the shadows of public agencies. The reforms may also serve, in other words, as political symbols designed to convince the public that elected officials are indeed responsive to public opinion and really are working hard to improve government performance.

The third set of reasons for civil service reform is technical. It encompasses a wide range of efforts to design and implement human resource management system changes that executives, managers, and personnel specialists believe will improve performance on one or more levels of government bureaucracy. These reforms involve the implementation of human resources management methods, procedures, and techniques intended to increase the efficiency and effectiveness of the personnel system. Modernizing performance evaluation and compensation systems, streamlining and decentralizing recruitment and selection processes, and broadbanding classification and pay structures are examples. These kinds of reforms, though they may serve as vehicles for the ideological and political agendas of other interests, are the bread and butter of human resource professionals and specialists. Performance management systems, particularly merit pay plans, offer good examples of how technically oriented civil service reforms on all levels of government in the United States and elsewhere are sold to policy makers, interest groups, and the public at large as steps needed to improve performance while rooting out incompetent and unresponsive civil servants.

By the late 1990s, the following key elements of the broad civil service reform agenda in the United States were well established (Kellough & Nigro, 2005; Walters, 2002):

- Structural decentralization and delegation of many human resource functions to line organizations
- Broad grants of discretion to agencies and departments in such areas as recruitment, selection, hiring, and promotions
- Streamlined and simplified job classification and pay systems
- Streamlined reduction-in-force, grievance, and appeals processes
- Performance management systems using a variety of merit pay systems intended to reward individuals
- Lowering labor costs and achieving other efficiencies through contracting-out or privatization
- Moving toward "at will" employment relationships under which public employees do not enjoy the job tenure protections afforded those holding classified positions in traditional merit systems

CIVIL SERVICE REFORM IN U.S. STATE GOVERNMENTS

During the 1990s, as the reinventing government movement swept the nation, it carried with it significant implications for civil service reform in the states (Gore, 1993; Hays & Kearney, 1997; Kearney & Hays, 1998; Kettl, Ingraham, Sanders, & Horner, 1996; National

Commission on State and Local Public Service, 1993; Osborne & Gaebler, 1992; Osborne & Plastrik, 1997). Several states have invested heavily in extensive reforms of their civil service systems during the last 20 years. Others have done very little, and the rest have made significant but far from comprehensive changes (Kellough & Nigro, 2006).

Reform programs have varied greatly from state to state, and so have the reasons for undertaking them (Kellough & Selden, 2003, pp. 171–172). This diversity applies to the degree to which major or sweeping reform has been initiated by state governments and is actually taking place. In two large states, California and New York, for example, very little serious reform has happened. In both states, organized labor and state employee unions have resisted reforms designed to strengthen management's hand. In Georgia and Florida, dramatic reforms have taken place in quite different political settings. In Florida, unlike Georgia where organized labor exerted very little influence, the nature and extent of reform became the centerpiece of a fierce struggle between the governor and his allies and employee unions and their supporters.

Variety also characterizes the aspects of personnel administration that are affected. In some states, such as Arizona and Wisconsin, the focus has been mostly on re-engineering and streamlining human resource technologies such as recruitment and selection, classification and pay, and training and development (Selden, Ingraham, & Jacobson, 2001, p. 606).

In some states, particularly Georgia and Florida, the reform agenda has included a mix of macro-issues such as "at will" employment, privatization or contracting out, deregulation, and decentralization of human resources functions. In the following sections, we focus on the Georgia and Florida experiences. We then turn to a consideration of reform at the federal level in the Department of Homeland Security.

THE STATE OF GEORGIA

In the 1990s, Georgia fully embraced the reform agenda outlined earlier and its elected leadership acted aggressively to implement it. The state's civil service law and public personnel management systems were transformed through two actions. The first undertaking was the implementation of a new performance management system called GeorgiaGain (Georgia Merit System, 1994; Kellough & Nigro, 2002). Initiated in 1995, it included a significant reduction in the number of pay grades, an effort to make entry-level and mid-level salaries more competitive, the establishment of a new performance appraisal system, and a requirement for individualized employee performance plans. New job descriptions that accurately reflected employee responsibilities were also developed.

The centerpiece of GeorgiaGain is a merit pay system. Annual employee pay adjustments are based on individual performance as measured through the new assessment procedure. The state invested heavily in training in the operation of the new system for supervisors and nonsupervisors, but an assessment conducted four years after full implementation found significant disenchantment with GeorgiaGain among employees and managers (Kellough & Nigro, 2002). The state changed the system in 2001, authorizing the payment of one-time bonuses in addition to annual increases and other measures intended to make state compensation more competitive (Georgia Merit System, 2001a; 2001b). The new approach was labeled "PerformancePLUS."

The second important reform of Georgia's civil service system took place in 1996 with enactment of a sweeping reform law by the Georgia legislature. It dramatically changed the structure and legal framework for civil service in Georgia along lines of the reform agenda described earlier (Condrey, 2002; Gossett, 2002; Kuykendall & Facer, 2002; Lasseter, 2002; West, 2002). In general, the goal of this legislation is to create conditions under which (1) bureaucratic responsiveness to executive leadership (the governor and state agency heads) is greatly improved and (2) employee and agency productivity is raised by removing cumbersome merit system procedures and creating an "at-will" employment relationship between the state and its workers. All those hired into state civil service positions following July 1, 1996, or promoted from one position to another after that date were placed in the "unclassified" service, meaning that they have no property interest in their positions and serve at the pleasure of their employers.

The Georgia legislation also significantly decentralized and deregulated public personnel management in state government. State agencies now have wide discretion and flexibility in almost all aspects of human resources management. Agencies are authorized to use streamlined recruiting and hiring processes suited to their specific needs and to employ personnel policies that are intended to support timely and effective responses to executive leadership and policy priorities. The at-will employment relationship allows state agencies to expedite adverse actions and appeals procedures. The decentralization thrust of the Georgia reforms required state agencies to (1) define job classes that are unique to the agency and to set qualifications and pay ranges for these classes, (2) allocate agency positions to job classes,

(3) recruit and screen applicants for jobs, and (4) establish personnel policies needed to assure compliance with employment-related state and federal laws (State of Georgia, 1996, pp. 685–686).

The Georgia reforms, like much of the reinventing government agenda of the 1990s, reflected a marked ideological shift toward market-oriented approaches to the delivery of public services as well as hostility toward the neutral-competence norms associated with traditional merit systems. There was little hard evidence to support the expectation that these reforms would lead to the hiring of more productive employees or to the more efficient operation of state agencies. In fact, the merit pay reform was implemented despite a significant amount of research suggesting that it is a problematic performance management strategy that may contribute more to employee alienation than to positive motivation to work (Kellough & Lu, 1993; Milkovich & Wigdor, 1991; Pearce, 1989; Pearce & Perry, 1983; Perry, 1988–89; and Perry, Petrakis, & Miller, 1989).

The reforms served the political aims of several interests in Georgia. By placing substantially greater personnel authority in the hands of state agencies and their directors, and by removing the property interest in employment, employees were made at least potentially more accountable to executive authority exercised through the agencies and in most instances through the governor's office. The Georgia reforms were explicitly designed to increase political (executive) control over the state bureaucracy. They also served Governor Miller's political agenda in the sense they were evidence of his effort to better manage the state's affairs and to "run the government more like a business." Miller, a Democrat, was able to co-opt the position of his Republican rivals on this issue, and he was narrowly reelected in 1994 despite strong Republican gains in statehouses nationwide.

THE STATE OF FLORIDA

Like its neighboring state, by the end of the 1990s, Florida had turned away from a significant but incremental and largely technical approach to civil service reform in response to an ideologically driven, highly partisan, campaign to demolish traditional civil service and to replace it with a radically different model called Service First. This legislation took effect on July 1, 2001.

Service First offers many of the now-common elements of civil service reform. Like their counterparts in other states and on the national level, these reforms were promoted on the grounds that they would overcome the technical limitations of out-of-date and inadequate civil service (merit) systems and promote the needed high levels of administrative performance. The Florida reforms include the following:

- Decentralization and delegation of many human resource authorities to line agencies of state government
- Broad grants of discretion to agencies in areas such as recruitment, selection, hiring, and promotions
- Broadbanding of job classification and pay systems
- Individual and group performance bonuses
- Streamlined dismissal, grievance, and appeals procedures
- Contracting out of some human resource functions
- Pay for performance or merit pay

The Florida reform removed from civil or classified service and placed in the Selected Exempt Service all supervisory personnel (some 16,000 out of a total of about 120,000 workers at the time of implementation). Those in the Selected Exempt Service now serve at will. They have no property interest in employment and no guarantee of due process in adverse actions. In addition, effective July 1, 2001, the concept of seniority in human resources management and policy was eliminated for all state employees except police, fire, and nurses. In practice, those administering reductions in force and downsizing programs may at their own discretion separate or transfer first those with the most seniority. In the Selected Exempt Service, there is no right to appeal layoffs and reorganizations. Other state employees—those still in the classified service—enjoy procedural protections set in negotiated labor contracts, and they may also appeal adverse actions using a process involving agency heads, the Public Employee Relations Commission (PERC), and a district court of appeals. For the Selected Exempt Service, there is no right to appeal adverse actions.

The ideological and political wellsprings of reform in Florida are clearly reflected in Service First. It embodies a strong preference for a market-oriented or private sector model for personnel management. The interests backing Service First advocated a tightly controlled state government, one that fosters private enterprise and is under the direct control of the governor and the state agency heads he or she appoints. Service First was a major policy victory for a coalition of business and tax-cutting interests working with conservative elected officials led by Governor Jeb Bush. Key actors were the Florida Council of 100, a group composed of influential businesspersons, and Florida Tax Watch, a policy research organization financed by Florida businesses. Governor Bush worked with these groups to publish a report entitled

"Modernizing Florida's Civil Service System: Moving from Protection to Performance" in 2000. In this report, Florida Tax Watch described the state's civil service as not having kept pace with management-centered human resources practices in the private sector. State employees' property and seniority rights were singled out for harsh criticism and described as major causes of inefficiency and resistance of executive leadership in state government.

Initially, Governor Bush pushed reform legislation that would have placed all employees in an at-will status, but this comprehensive coverage was beaten back in the state senate by organized labor (AFSCME). Support for the governor in the previous election appeared to be a factor in the exclusion of two police and one nurses' organization from coverage. On the seniority issue, the governor's coalition emerged with a complete victory. Overall, after a series of court challenges mounted by AFSCME ended with the Florida Supreme Court's ruling that the provisions of Service First were not negotiable, most if not all of the Council of 100's agenda was accomplished.

Of Service First one observer wrote, "The Florida reform efforts have essentially been as effective as the abolitionist approach in Texas and Georgia: Florida now has a civil service system that arguably exists in name only" (Walters, 2002, p. 31). Control over key day-to-day human resources processes of the State of Florida is now largely in the hands of the governor and his agency heads.

THE U.S. DEPARTMENT OF HOMELAND SECURITY

Although federal experiments with comprehensive civil service reform along lines of the 1978 Civil Service Reform Act have for at least the time being ended, other reforms—some very significant—continue on the agency level. One of these took place in the context of the formation of the new U.S. Department of Homeland Security (DHS). The politics of civil service reform were highlighted by the confrontation between the George W. Bush administration and federal employee unions over the president's demand that workers in DHS have limited civil service protections and restricted collective bargaining rights. This political struggle created a deadlock in the U.S. Senate that was not resolved until the Republicans re-established control in the 2002 elections. In political terms, the president's "win" in the contest over personnel policies for the DHS was a major defeat for organized labor and its supporters in the U.S. Congress.

The terrorist attacks of September 11, 2001, had significant impacts on American public policy. Airport baggage screeners were federalized and the Transportation Security Administration (TSA) created, law enforcement and intelligence organizations were given broad new powers, and a number of federal agencies dealing with national security matters were reorganized and placed under central control. The Homeland Security Act of 2002 moved some 22 domestic federal agencies and 170,000 employees with responsibility for national security into the newly established DHS. These agencies included the Coast Guard, the Boarder Patrol, the Customs Service, the Immigration and Naturalization Service, and the Transportation Security Agency.

A major obstacle to final passage of the legislation was President Bush's commitment to a significant reform of the DHS personnel system. His administration sought significant personnel "flexibilities" like those established in Georgia and Florida and limitations on collective bargaining rights enjoyed by employees working in the affected agencies. Democrats, responding to their organized labor constituencies and supporters, united in opposition to these proposals and the DHS legislation stalled until after the midterm election and the shift to Republican control of the Senate. The bill ultimately was passed on November 25, 2002 (U.S. Statutes at Large, 2002).

The Homeland Security Act gave the Bush Administration great discretion regarding personnel reform. It authorized the Secretary for Homeland Security and the Director of the U.S. Office of Personnel Management (OPM) to establish a new personnel system for the new department. The law required that the DHS personnel system be "flexible" and "contemporary." It prohibited modification of certain long-standing federal merit principles associated with hiring, and it required maintenance of the concept of equal pay for equal work, the protection of whistleblowers, and adherence to equal employment opportunity law. DHS employees were guaranteed collective bargaining rights through their labor organizations, but the act specified that right was subject to exclusions permitting the denial of collective bargaining rights for any employees deemed to be involved in matters of intelligence collection, counter intelligence, or investigative work in the war against terrorism. Otherwise, the secretary and the director were given a free hand to reshape DHR human resources policies as long as they did so in collaboration with employees' representatives.

In April 2003, a human resources design team was established, consisting of officials from the new department, the OPM, and 10 representatives from three federal unions representing departmental employees. The team was tasked with developing proposals for the new personnel policies in the six core areas: classification, compensation, adverse actions, appeals, labor relations, and performance management (Clarke, 2003; U.S. Department of Homeland Security and U.S. Office of Personnel Management, 2003; U.S. Government Accountability Office, 2003; Zeller, 2003). Final decisions on the nature of the new system were made and proposed rules and regulations were announced on February 20, 2004 (*Federal Register,* 2004). With the exception of its provisions regarding collective bargaining and the DHS, most of the recommended reforms were in tune with current thinking about civil service reform.

The proposed rules called for establishing a new system for job evaluation and pay administration (*Federal Register,* 2004, pp. 8036–8040). The new structure would be built by grouping jobs into broad occupational categories based on the type of work and skills needed on the job. A new pay system would then be developed with broad salary bands to correspond to work at an entry/developmental level, a full performance level, a senior expert level, and a supervisory level. Individual pay adjustments within each band would consist of market-related adjustments, locality pay supplements, and annual performance-based pay increases. Requirements that supervisors develop specific written performance standards for each employee at the beginning of an annual performance appraisal period are relaxed and managers are authorized to communicate expectations through a variety means, including the use of directives, specific assignments, or other methods as appropriate. In the performance appraisal process, the regulations simply require a minimum of three performance standards including unacceptable, fully acceptable, and above fully acceptable. The results of the individual performance appraisal will be used to determine annual performance-based or merit pay increases in salary. In general terms, these technical reforms were very similar to those implemented in other federal agencies and in states like Georgia and Florida.

Greater management flexibility in labor relations is also set forth in the proposed rules (*Federal Register,* 2004, pp. 8040–8044). The political dimensions of the reform package are clear in this area. For example, oversight of the bargaining process and the adjudication of disputes involving such issues as bargaining unit determination, unfair labor practices, bargaining impasses, and issues of negotiability are to be handled by a Homeland Security Labor Relations Board rather than the independent Federal Labor Relations Authority (FLRA). The Homeland Security Board is to be sensitive to the department's mission and goals while remaining independent and fair. Management retains the right to take any action in all areas of policy and management without advance consultations or notice given to a union. In addition, the secretary of DHS is granted authority to disapprove any collective bargaining provision whenever he or she determines it is contrary to law, regulation, or management rights.

Adverse actions, including removals, suspensions, demotions, and reductions in pay, are also addressed (*Federal Register,* 2004, pp. 8044–8047). Emphasis is placed on giving management enhanced discretionary powers and flexibility. The probationary period for new employees is extended to as many as two years. During this period, which is longer than typically used elsewhere in the federal service, employees will not possess a property interest in their jobs and will be subject to discipline and removal with relative ease. Once the initial probationary service period is completed, employees are subject to adverse action procedures that allow a shorter advance notice period of 15 days and a reduced time of only 5 days during which an employee may respond to charges of misconduct. The secretary of DHS is also given authority to identify offenses that have a "direct and substantial" impact on the department and for which the penalty will be mandatory removal from federal service. In all cases, employees are entitled to a written decision, but the burden of proof on the department is substantially reduced and requires only that it establish a "factual basis for the adverse action and a connection between the action and a legitimate Departmental interest." The factual basis may rest merely on substantial evidence rather than a preponderance of the evidence. Adverse actions may be appealed to the U.S. Merit Systems Protection Board (MSPB), but new standards for MSPB to apply in such cases require that the department's security mission is accommodated, and restrictions are placed on the MSPB's power to alter penalties imposed (*Federal Register* 2004, p. 8046).

Issues of power, authority, and fairness are always in play when civil service reforms such as those related to the DHS are proposed and implemented. In the days immediately following publication of the DHS proposed regulations, Senator Susan Collins of Maine, the Chairwoman of the Senate Governmental Affairs Committee, voiced her concern about the reduced burden of proof on the department in adverse action proceedings and the restrictions placed on the MSPB in the appeals process, but otherwise praised the proposals (Zeller, 2004). In testimony before subcommittees of the Senate Committee on Governmental Affairs and the House Committee on Government Reform, the comptroller general, David M. Walker, was generally supportive of the proposed new personnel system, but called for the identification of "core competencies" as part of the performance appraisal process, urged caution in the specification of mandatory removal offenses, and expressed concern that employees continue to be involved in a "meaningful manner" in departmental affairs despite the reduction in the scope of collective bargaining (U.S. Government Accountability Office, 2004).

In the case of the DHS, civil service and human resource management reforms were driven by a complex and dynamic combination of pressing technical requirements, ideology, and power politics. Reforms were in part framed by a belief by the Bush administration that the private sector model where managers typically have a great deal of discretion is inherently superior to that traditionally used in the public sector. This view is manifest in flexibilities regarding job classification and pay, the limitations placed on collective bargaining, and the streamlined disciplinary procedures. Nonetheless, certain core features of traditional federal civil service were retained. For example, employees are entitled to some form of procedural due process before removal or other adverse action. The right to collective bargaining was not abolished for DHS personnel, although it is significantly limited in its application to many workers. This outcome stands in sharp contrast to what happened in Georgia where all state employees will eventually be serving at will and they have no prospect of collective bargaining rights of any sort.

THE FUTURE OF CIVIL SERVICE REFORM

Strong political or public support for comprehensive and radical reforms, such as those undertaken by Georgia and Florida, has not materialized in most states, although incremental steps have occurred in a number of locations (Hays & Sowa, forthcoming). In part, no tidal wave of radical reform has washed across the states because such reforms have not (or at least cannot show they have) delivered what they promised, and they promised a great deal. Georgia's comprehensive approach was sold as the way to get performance and accountability (Walters, 1997). Credible program evaluation was not a serious consideration in Georgia and elsewhere, so it is not surprising that there is little or no hard evidence about the results achieved by those reforms available to those contemplating reform, comprehensive or otherwise, in their states.

Another reason for skepticism about the prospects of comprehensive reforms is their distinct tendency to punish and demoralize workers. The "bureaucrat bashing" rhetoric of the ideologically and politically driven reformers, the prospect of being "de-privileged" or deprived of their traditional merit system protections, downsized, or privatized, has mobilized active resistance by public employees and their allies. Suspicion and resistance is not limited to those who work for state agencies. Growing awareness among policy makers, public employees and their organizations, and human resource professionals that many of the reforms implemented during the last quarter of the 20th century have not delivered the benefits they promised may very well dampen enthusiasm for civil service reforms involving massive changes in existing systems. Incremental reforms building up from the agency level that do not jettison traditional values of human resource management may be the more typical model (and prescription for something approaching success) during the early decades of the 21st century. Hays and Kearney observed,

> Survey results lend support to the entreaties of . . . reformers who call out for a leaner, more responsive government with particular reference to human resource management. . . . Yet respondents indicate . . . an abiding and even growing attachment to the core values that have guided the field for more than 100 years. As the next decade unfolds, HRM is expected to hold particularly strongly to its traditional values of equity, professionalism, executive leadership, merit, and political responsiveness, while the newer value of efficiency gains further momentum. (2001, p. 594)

Critical scrutiny of the proposition that comprehensive deregulation, privatization, and de-privileging are necessary means to efficiency and responsiveness in state governments is needed (Selden et al., 2001; Thompson, 2002).

By the early 21st century, public personnel managers and policy makers were being asked to solve social problems and meet technical challenges that were simply unimaginable at the start of the 20th Century. Many of the "deregulating and decentralizing" civil service reforms implemented on all levels of government during the previous decade are still in place, but as one observer has noted, concerns about accountability and responsiveness are surfacing as politicians find that they have "far fewer levers available to 'control the civil service' and deregulation and decentralization have reduced their capacity as leaders to exert as much control over policy implementation as they might have had in the past" (Peters, 2001, p. 138).

Nonetheless, the basic challenge of reform has not changed: civil service institutions are still asked to provide public employees who are highly competent and ethical, bureaucracies that are efficient and effective, and civil servants who are responsive to public policies and executive leadership. Elected officials are held accountable in a variety of ways for the performance of the civil service and, therefore, are justifiably interested in reforms that improve performance and responsiveness (Kettl et al., 1996). The ongoing challenge has been and continues to be the "invention" of civil service and human resource management systems that promote responsiveness in its broadest sense, foster the accountability to electorates and other segments of society required of a strong democracy, and support the achievement of desired performance outcomes. Most importantly, in a democracy, these systems must enjoy broad public support and confidence (Hays, 1996).

DISCUSSION QUESTIONS

1. Can the American public be confident of the fairness and integrity of a civil service that uses human resources practices like those typical of the private sector? What are the reasons for your answer?
2. What criteria would you use to evaluate the results of the Georgia and Florida civil service reforms? Why?
3. Civil service reforms in the United States seldom if ever come with any provisions for systematic evaluations of their results or outcomes by impartial observers. Why do you think this is the case?

REFERENCES

Clarke, David (2003). "After the Fall: Unions Cautiously Optimistic About New Personnel Rules." *CQ Homeland Security— Reorganization*. Accessed http://www.cq.com (May 22).

Condrey, Stephen E. (2002). "Reinventing State Civil Service Systems: The Georgia Experience." *Review of Public Personnel Administration 22* (Summer), pp. 114–124.

Federal Register (2004). *Department of Homeland Security Human Resources Management System; Proposed Rule* (February 20), pp. 8030–8071.

Georgia Merit System (1994). "GeorgiaGain: Data Collection on Jobs Begins." *State Personnel News: A Quarterly for and About Georgia State Employees 18* (April), pp. 1, 3.

Georgia Merit System (2001a). *Memorandum: Governor's Recommendations for Salary Increases and Merit System Legislation.* Atlanta, GA: Office of the Commissioner (January 24).

Georgia Merit System (2001b). "State Employees move toward market salaries, bonuses for achievement with PerformancePLUS." *The Georgia Statement 4* (February), p. 1.

Gore, Albert (1993). *Creating a Government that Works Better and Costs Less: Report of the National Performance Review.* Washington DC: Government Printing Office.

Gossett, Charles W. (2002) "Civil Service Reform: The Case of Georgia." *Review of Public Personnel Administration 22* (Summer), pp. 94–113.

Hays, Steven W. (1996). "The 'State of the Discipline' in Public Personnel Administration." *Public Administration Quarterly 20* (Fall), pp. 285–304.

Hays, Steven W., and Richard C. Kearney (1997). "Riding the Crest of a Wave: The National Performance Review and Public Management Reform." *International Journal of Public Administration 20* (January), pp. 11–40.

Hays, Steven W., and Richard C. Kearney (2001). "Anticipated Changes in Human Resource Management: Views from the Field," *Public Administration Review,* Vol. 61, No. 5 (September–October), pp. 585–597.

Hays, Steven W., and Jessica Sowa (forthcoming). "A broader look at the 'accountability' movement: Some grim realities in state civil service systems." *State and Local Government Review.*

Ingersoll, David E., Richard K. Matthews, and Andrew Davison (2001). *The Philosophic Roots of Modern Ideology,* 3rd ed. (Upper Saddle River, NJ: Prentice-Hall).

Kearney, Richard C., and Steven W. Hays (1998). "Reinventing Government, The New Public Management and Civil Service Systems." *Review of Public Personnel Administration,* Vol. 18, No. 4 (Fall), pp. 38–54.

Kellough, J. Edward, and Haoran Lu (1993). "The Paradox of Merit Pay in the Public Sector: Persistence of a Problematic Procedure," *Review of Public Personnel Administration* (Spring), pp. 45–64.

Kellough, J. Edward, and Lloyd G. Nigro (2002). "Pay for Performance in Georgia State Government." *Review of Public Personnel Administration* (Summer), pp. 146–166.

Kellough, J. Edward, and Lloyd G. Nigro (2005). "Radical Civil Service Reform: Ideology, Politics, and Policy," in Stephen E. Condrey (Ed.), *Handbook of Human Resource Management in Government,* 2nd ed. (San Francisco: Jossey-Bass), pp. 58–75.

Kellough, J. Edward, and Lloyd G. Nigro (Eds.) (2006). *Civil Service Reform in the States: Politics and Public Personnel Policy at the Sub-National Level* (Albany: State University of New York Press).

Kellough, J. Edward, and Sally Coleman Selden (2003). "The Reinvention of Public Personnel Administration: An Analysis of the Diffusion of Personnel Management Reforms in the States," *Public Administration Review,* Vol. 63, No. 2 (March–April), pp. 165–175.

Kettl, Donald F., Patricia W. Ingraham, Ronald P. Sanders, and Constance Horner (1996). *Civil Service Reform: Building a Government that Works* (Washington, DC: Brookings Institution Press).

Kuykendall, Christine L., and Rex L. Facer II (2002). "Public Employment in Georgia State Agencies: The Elimination of the Merit System." *Review of Public Personnel Administration 22* (Summer), pp. 133–145.

Lasseter, Reubin W. (2002). "Georgia's Merit System Reform 1996–2001: An Operating Agency's Perspective." *Review of Public Personnel Administration 22* (Summer), pp. 125–132.

Milkovich, G. T., and A. K. Wigdor (Eds.) (1991). *Pay for Performance: Evaluating Performance and Merit Pay.* (Washington DC: National Academy Press).

National Commission on the State and Local Public Service (1993). *Hard Truths/Tough Choices: An Agenda for State and Local Reform* (Albany, NY: Nelson A. Rockefeller Institute of Government).

Nigro, Lloyd G., and J. Edward Kellough (2000). "Civil Service Reform in Georgia: Going to the Edge?" *Review of Public Personnel Administration* (Fall), pp. 41–54.

Osborne, David, and Ted Gaebler (1992). *Reinventing Government: How the Entrepreneurial Spirit Is Transforming the Public Sector.* (Reading, MA: Addison-Wesley).

Osborne, David, and P. Plastrik (1997). *Banishing Bureaucracy.* (Reading, MA: Addison-Wesley).

Pearce, Jone L. (1989) "Rewarding Successful Performance." In James L. Perry (Ed.), *Handbook of Public Administration* (San Francisco, CA: Jossey-Bass), pp. 401–441.

Pearce, Jone L., and James L. Perry (1983)." Federal Merit Pay: A Longitudinal Analysis." *Public Administration Review 43,* pp. 315–325.

Perry, James L. (1988–89). "Making Policy by Trial and Error: Merit Pay in the Federal Service." *Policy Studies Journal 17,* pp. 389–405.

Perry, James L., B. A. Petrakis, and T.K. Miller (1989). "Federal Merit Pay, Round II: An Analysis of the Performance Management and Recognition System." *Public Administration Review 49,* pp. 29–37.

Peters, B. Guy (2001). *The Future of Governing,* 2nd ed., revised (Lawrence: University Press of Kansas).

Schultz, David (2002). "Civil Service Reform," *Public Administration Review,* Vol. 62, No. 5 (September–October), pp. 634–637.

Selden, Sally Coleman, Patricia Wallace Ingraham, and Willow Jacobson (2001). "Human Resource Practices in State Government: Findings from a National Survey," *Public Administration Review,* Vol. 61, No. 5 (September–October), pp. 598–607.

State of Georgia (1996). "Public Officers and Employees' Personnel Administration; Unclassified Service Defined to Include All Positions filled by New Hires; Classified Service Employees to Remain in Classified Service on Certain Conditions." No. 816 (Senate Bill 635). *General Acts and Resolutions,* Vol. 1, pp. 684–691.

Thompson, Frank J. (2002). "Reinvention in the States: Ripple or Tide?" *Public Administration Review,* Vol. 62, No. 3 (May–June), pp. 362–367.

Thompson, Frank J., and Beryl A. Radin (1997). "Reinventing Public Personnel Management: The Winter and Gore Initiatives," in Carolyn Ban and Norma M. Riccucci (Eds.), *Public Personnel Management: Current Concerns, Future Challenges* (White Plains, NY: Longman).

U.S. Department of Homeland Security and U. S. Office of Personnel Management (2003). *Human Resources Management System: Design Team Review of Current Practices* (Washington DC: Department of Homeland Security and Office of Personnel Management).

U.S. Government Accountability Office (2003). *DHS Personnel System Design Effort Provides for Collaboration and Employee* (September). (Washington DC: Government Printing Office).

U.S. Government Accountability Office (2004). *Preliminary Observations on Proposed DHS Human Capital Regulations* (February 25). (Washington DC: Government Printing Office).

U.S. Statutes at Large (2002). *Public Law 107–296,* Vol. 116, pp. 2135–2321.

Walters, Jonathan (1997). "Who Needs Civil Service?" *Governing,* Vol. 10, No. 11, pp. 17–21.

Walters, Jonathan (2002). "Life After Civil Service Reform: The Texas, Georgia, and Florida Experience." *IBM Endowment for The Business of Government: Human Capital Series* (October).

West, Jonathan P. (2002). "Georgia on the Mind of Radical Civil Service Reformers." *Review of Public Personnel Administration 22* (Summer), pp. 79–93.

Wise, Lois Recascino (2002). "Public Management Reform: Competing Drivers of Change," *Public Administration Review,* Vol. 62, No. 5 (September–October), pp. 555–567.

Zeller, Shawn (2003). "OPM Releases Suggestions for Homeland Security Personnel System." *Govexec.com.* Accessed http://www.govexec.com/news (October 6).

Zeller, Shawn (2004). "Lawmaker Questions Proposed Changes to DHS Appeals Process." *Govexec.com.* Accessed http://www .govexec.com/news (February 23).

Chapter TWELVE

The Future of Public Personnel

The 1990s were years of significant change for public personnel on all levels of government in the United States. Civil service reform, re-invention, re-engineering, privatization, and related ideas became popular agendas with public managers as well as elected officials. The diagnoses and recommendations of the Winter and Volcker Commissions, and the National Performance Review (NPR), have had a major impact on policy makers' thinking about the central tasks of human resource offices and, very significantly, about how to evaluate their performance. Public personnel—human resources management—enters the 21st century stressing policies and practices keyed to management's needs, organizational performance, and responsiveness to the policy agendas and programs of elected officials. Attracting, developing, and retaining the people and skills public agencies need to sustain effectiveness and efficiency are and will continue to be critically important, but methods used to meet these challenges are changing at an accelerating pace.

CIVIL SERVICE REFORM

Interest in and support for the civil service reforms discussed in preceding chapters does not appear to be waning. The era of building personnel systems on merit principles designed primarily to regulate and restrict public managers' discretion seems now to be over. The reduction of bureaucratic structures and procedures, the decentralization of authority and accountability, the contracting-out or privatization of public services, and support management are dominant values driving state-of-the-art thinking about how to design and run public personnel systems of the future. Criteria used to judge the effectiveness of personnel systems will stress agency performance and program outcomes, rather than adherence to civil service rules and procedures.

In 1998, Richard Kearney and Steven Hays noted, "Efforts to debureaucratize and decentralize, privatize, and managerialize public management have had a marked impact on public management, and they show no sign of abating in the foreseeable future" (1998, p. 44). In a similar vein, Selden, Ingraham, and Jacobson reported that the 1998 Government Performance Project survey of state governments revealed continuing movement toward replacing traditional systems with more flexible and varied approaches to recruitment, classification, and that compensation (2001, p. 606). They anticipated

- Decentralization and streamlining trends will continue
- State personnel systems will need to align human resource management with strategic planning functions of state governments
- Human resource management will become "more interwoven into the fabric of agency operations and thus less isolated from managers" (Selden et al., 2001, p. 606)

Hays and Kearney, reflecting on the results of their survey of members of the International City Management Association, also concluded that pressures for civil service reform had not abated:

> Public personnel administration remains in a state of flux and turbulence. Change has become a constant in the practice of HRM as reform proceeds apace across virtually every conceivable front. (Hays & Kearney, 2001, p. 595)

WORKFORCE PLANNING AND HUMAN RESOURCE DEVELOPMENT

Although many of the human resources management tasks assigned to personnel or HR departments will not change, the ways in which they are carried out will be changed by new technologies and organizational arrangements that require enhanced as well as new skills. A growing proportion of government jobs will require highly trained and extensively educated professionals who must *continuously* upgrade their abilities to keep pace with the intellectual and technical demands of their positions. In 2005, the Government Performance Project reported its survey of state governments had revealed the following:

> There is a personnel tornado on the horizon: In more than half the states one in five employees will be retiring over the next five years. . . . Clearly, there needs to be planning for the future or else the future will be bleak for anyone who relies on state services. (Barrett & Greene, 2005, p. 27)

Public employers have a long history of failing to engage in future-oriented workforce planning and failing to make sustained investments in the training and development of their workforces. Often, they have been reluctant to spend the money needed to provide anything but the most basic training, and training and development budgets traditionally are among the first to be cut or eliminated during periods of fiscal stress (Barrett & Greene, 2005, p. 27–28).

Strategic planning and human capital development programs designed to identify and meet anticipated human resource needs have been rare and often precarious initiatives in the public sector. Historically, traditional merit systems' emphasis on positions rather than careers has encouraged a static view of the "fit" between organizational needs and workforce qualifications. The assumption was that those hired would have the skills, knowledge, and abilities needed to perform a specific job. The pace of change, however, is such that position descriptions, qualifications, and classification plans are seldom current, and they are even less likely to be coordinated with agencies' shifting mandates, technological developments, and the shifting patterns of supply and demand in the labor market.

Position-based systems, to make matters worse, make formal career planning and development systems very difficult to establish because they do not assume that employees will be continuously moving through a *predictable* series of different and increasingly more complex and challenging roles. Under these conditions, there is little incentive for employers to build the training and development infrastructures needed to support *careers involving a series of different jobs and responsibilities,* as opposed to *positions.* Public employees have not been encouraged to think in terms of anticipating and acquiring the knowledge, skills, abilities, and experience that they will need in the future. Individual's efforts in this regard are seldom supported because employers commonly require that any training they pay for be directly related to a job, not a career plan (U.S. Office of Personnel Management, 2005). Training and development programs, to the extent they exist, are focused often on what employees need to perform well in their current positions.

In all likelihood, public employers increasingly will be forced to deal with the reality that sustained investments in workforce planning, training, and human resource development are needed and, in the long run, will be cost-effective. The fiscal and political costs associated with not making such investments and then having to address problems in a crisis mode could be very high. A trend that is likely to accelerate over the next decade as public personnel becomes much less regulatory in perspective and moves away from position-dominated merit systems is a shift toward a human resources development (HRD) perspective (American Society for Training and Development, 1990, p. 3). HRD encompasses at least three areas of human capital planning and development:

- *Training and Development,* which involves identifying and helping to develop in a planned manner "the key competencies that enable individuals to perform current or future jobs" (p. 4). Training and development concentrates on people in organizational roles or jobs, and it uses a variety of methods, including on- and off-site training, on-the-job-training or OJT, supervisory coaching, and other ways of encouraging learning by individuals.

- *Organization Development,* which concentrates on building effective and productive social-psychological relationships within and between work groups in organizations. Organization development uses a variety of process-oriented interventions on the individual and group levels with the goal of improving the overall performances of organizations.

- *Career Development,* which seeks to coordinate individual career planning and organizational career management processes to "achieve an optimal match of individual and organizational needs" (p. 4).

Increasingly, the narrow term "training program" is being replaced with the much broader "human resource development program." In the federal government, such programs may be authorized to carry out a wide variety of training and development activities, including the following:

- Orienting new employees to the federal government, their agencies, their jobs, and conditions of employment.
- Providing the guidance new employees need to achieve satisfactory performance during their probationary period.
- Providing the skills and knowledge employees need to improve job performance.

- Equipping selected employees with the skills and knowledge they will need to handle increased responsibility as a part of the agency's overall strategic plan for meeting future staffing requirements.

- Providing or arranging continuing technical and professional training to prevent knowledge and skills obsolescence.

- Developing the managerial workforce's competencies on the supervisory, middle-management, and executive levels in such areas as interpersonal skills, communication, leadership, financial management, and program evaluation.

- Providing education and training leading to academic degrees if necessary to attract and retain workers with critical skills in occupations where shortages and highly competitive markets are expected.

- Assisting in career transition, training, and re-training of employees who have been displaced by downsizing and restructuring.

Federal agencies are required by law to have processes for identifying their performance improvement needs, and they must have human resource development programs designed to meet these needs in efficient and effective ways. These processes include the following elements:

- Setting performance goals and determining the gaps, if any, between these goals and actual performance.

- Identifying the reasons for performance gaps and deciding if specific training and development initiatives should close or eliminate them.

- Regularly collecting and analyzing information about organizational training needs and using these data to guide decisions about investments in human resources development.

- Involving management and employees on all levels in planning and implementing HRD activities, and integrating training plans and programs with other human resource management functions.

Overall, there is little reason to doubt that workforce planning and human resource development will become increasingly important for public employers on all levels of government. Although workforce planning (see Chapter 3) is still far from commonplace, pressures for effective and efficient delivery of public services are likely to force a recognition among many public employers that "strategic adaptations

in HRM operations . . . emphasizing new skill and knowledge requirements for present and future employees and adopting more aggressive
training and education strategies" will be necessary (Hays & Kearney,
2001, p. 595).

THE EMPLOYMENT RELATIONSHIP

Public employers will continue to experience fiscal and political pressures to move away from the idea that government should be a
"model employer." Efficiency, cost-savings, and flexibility may be
expected to drive the choices made by public policy makers, and this
trend has encouraged human resources strategies that stress investing
limited resources (pay, benefits, technology, career development
opportunities) in *essential* or *mission-critical* positions and workers. As
the costs (pay, benefits, working facilities, and the HR system itself)
associated with attracting, motivating, and retaining highly educated
and skilled personnel who are needed to achieve and sustain necessary
levels of organizational performance escalate, controlling and lowering
labor costs in other areas has become a prime objective for public as
well as private employers. Two major ways of trying to achieve this
objective are privatization or contracting-out and extensive use of
temporary or part-time workers. Both strategies will be widely used,
especially contracting-out.

   Privatization comes in a variety of forms, including transferring
previously public functions to the private sector, voucher systems and
tax expenditure subsidies instead of direct governmental provision of
services, and contracting out of services traditionally performed by
public employees. In all its forms, privatization seeks to use competitive markets to allocate resources efficiently and to control costs. In
general terms, advocates of privatization argue that bureaucracy and
bureaucrats are inherently inefficient because they are effectively insulated from the disciplining forces of a competitive marketplace.

   The affects of privatization on public employees have been
widely debated, but evidence suggests that privatization initiatives,
particularly moves to contract-out public services, are likely to have
three kinds of consequences. First, public employee unions will be
placed on the defensive as they seek to defend themselves against
charges that collective bargaining is an essentially political process that
results in artificially high labor costs. Private contractors often are able
to keep labor costs down because they do not deal with unionized
workers. Second, to the extent that privatized arrangements are
implemented, public employees stand to lose their jobs. Even if their

functions have not been privatized, many public employees now work under the threat that they will lose their jobs to contractors if costs are not lowered and program performance levels raised. An organizational climate driven by fear of privatization is likely to have strongly negative consequences for worker morale and commitment. Third, privatization inevitably raises serious questions about how to ensure fair and equitable treatment of the combinations of public and private employees who are now performing once exclusively governmental functions, such as operating prison systems. Current enthusiasm for organizational flexibility, results-oriented management, and market mechanisms threaten to undermine long-standing rights and protections enjoyed by public employees under merit systems. Those working for private contractors also are placed in legal and political environments that expose them to new challenges, such as exposure to civil liability for violating the constitutional rights of citizens (Cooper & Newland, 1997).

A related trend is the increasing use of temporary (contingent) and part-time employees by public as well as private employers. Governments on all levels also may enter into service contracts with private firms that use large numbers of contingent and part-time workers (Bureau of Labor Statistics, 2005a). Contingent workers are those who have no explicit or implicit employment contracts. These include temporary workers—who numbered about 1.2 million in 2005—that are employees supplied to clients by temporary help firms. Although the client supervises the temporary worker, he or she is on the payroll of the temporary services supply firm. In addition to temporary workers, there are about 10 million independent contractors, and 2.5 million on-call workers in the U.S. labor market (Bureau of Labor Statistics, 2005a).

In comparison with full-time, permanent, employees, part-time and contingent workers tend to receive fewer and less generous benefits. Often, contractors' ability to provide services at lower costs than public agencies can be explained at least in part by their not having to spend a great deal on employee benefits. Health insurance is provided by only about half of all temporary service firms, and paid holidays and vacations are provided by about three-quarters of those organizations (Bureau of Labor Statistics, 2005b). However,

> Few temporary workers actually receive these benefits, either because they fail to meet the minimum qualification requirements or, as in the case of insurance plans, they elect not to participate. In firms employing most of the temporary workers, less than one-half of the workers—often less than one-tenth—qualified for holiday and vacation benefits. Similarly, most firms reported that less than 10 percent of

their temporary workers participated in a company-sponsored health insurance program. These insurance plans typically require the employee to pay part or all of the cost of coverage. (Bureau of Labor Statistics, 1999, p. 3)

To the degree that government contracting-out brings more private sector part-time workers into the labor force engaged in delivering public services, pressures to reduce the benefits of part-timers employed by public agencies may build. Another result may be a steady decline in the number of part-time workers in civil service on all levels as governments seek to exploit the advantages of lower labor costs.

The issues confronting public employers in this area of human resources policy are difficult. Should they follow the lead of the private sector and concentrate on developing competitive pay, benefits, and working conditions for a "core" of highly skilled and essential workers, or do they have an obligation to serve as "model employers" by offering a set of relatively expensive benefits to all of their employees? Is it part of government's role as an employer to set a positive example for the rest of the society in areas such as equal opportunity, pay equity, employee rights and legal protections, meaningful jobs for the disabled, and benefits? How important should these values be in comparison with organizational efficiency, program cost effectiveness, and management flexibility as choices are made about how to provide or arrange public services? In one very important sense, the more things change, the more they stay the same: Public personnel administration will continue to be an arena within which competing values and interests vigorously compete, and the outcomes of these clashes will have profoundly important consequences for American society.

DISCUSSION QUESTIONS

1. Will the merit principle survive as civil service reform progresses? Should it?
2. Should public employers pay for training and education that is not directly related to the requirements of the position or job held by the employee?
3. Are there other major trends related to public personnel/human resources that you believe will be important during the early part of the 21st century?

REFERENCES

American Society for Training and Development (1990). *An Introduction to Human Resource Development Careers,* 3rd ed. (Alexandria, VA: American Society for Training and Development), September.

Barrett, Katherine, and Richard Greene ((2005). "Grading the States: A Management Report Card." *Governing: Special Issue* (February), pp. 24–95.

Bureau of Labor Statistics (1999). "Employee Benefits Survey: Table 3. Percent of Employees Participating in Selected Employee Benefits Programs, Various Employment Groups, 1995–1997." Accessed http://stats.bls.gov/news.release/ebs3.t03.htm (May 5, 1999).

———. (2005a). "Contingent and Alternative Employment Relationships, September 2005." *News,* USDL 05-1433 (Washington, DC: U.S. Department of Labor), July 27, 2005.

———. (2005b). "National Compensation Survey: Employee Benefits in Private Industry in the United States–March 2005," (Washington, DC: U.S. Department of Labor), August.

Cooper, Philip J., and Newland, Chester A. (Eds.). (1997). *Handbook of Public Law and Administration* (San Francisco: Jossey-Bass).

Governing (1999). "Grading the States: A 50-State Report Card on Government Performance." *Governing,* Vol. 12, No. 5 (February).

Hays, Steven W., and Richard C. Kearney (2001). "Anticipated Changes in Human Resource Management: Views from the Field." *Public Administration Review,* Vol. 61, No. 5 (September-October), pp. 585–597.

Kearney, Robert C., and Hays, Steven W. (1998). "Reinventing Government, The New Public Management and Civil Service Systems in International Perspective." *Review of Public Personnel Administration,* Vol. 18, No. 4 (Fall), pp. 38–54.

Selden, Sally Coleman, Patricia Wallace Ingraham, and Willow Jacobson (2001). "Human Resource Practices in State Government: Findings from a National Survey." *Public Administration Review* (September–October), pp. 598–607.

U.S. Office of Personnel Management (2005). *Training and Development Fact Sheets with Questions and Answers.* Accessed http://www.opm.gov/hrd/lead/policy/fea-00.asp (December 4, 2005).

Index